An Introduction to

Student–Involved
Assessment FOR Learning

Seventh Edition

An Introduction to
Student–Involved
Assessment FOR Learning

Jan Chappuis

Rick Stiggins

 Pearson

330 Hudson Street, NY NY 10013

Vice President and Publisher: Kevin M. Davis
Editorial Assistant: Anne McAlpine
Executive Field Marketing Manager: Krista Clark
Senior Product Marketing Manager: Christopher Barry
Program Manager: Janelle Rogers
Project Manager: Pamela D. Bennett
Procurement Specialist: Carol Melville

Cover Photo: Getty Images/Hero Images
Media Project Manager: Lauren Carlson
Full-Service Project Management: Katrina Ostler, Cenveo Publisher Services
Composition: Cenveo Publisher Services
Printer/Binder: RR Donnelley/Crawfordsville
Cover Printer: RR Donnelley/Crawfordsville
Text Font: Sabon LT Pro 55 Roman 10/12

Library of Congress Cataloging-in-Publication Data
Names: Chappuis, Jan. | Stiggins, Richard J.
Title: An introduction to student-involved assessment for learning / Jan Chappuis, Rick Stiggins.
Description: Seventh edition. | Hoboken : Pearson, 2017.
Identifiers: LCCN 2016028552 | ISBN 9780134450261
Subjects: LCSH: Educational tests and measurements--United States. | Examinations--United States.
Classification: LCC LB3051 .S8536 2017 | DDC 371.26--dc23
LC record available at https://lccn.loc.gov/2016028552

23 2022

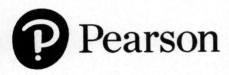

Print:
ISBN 10:   0-13-445026-4
ISBN 13: 978-0-13-445026-1

eText:
ISBN 10:   0-13-355144-X
ISBN 13: 978-0-13-355144-0

MyEducationLab with Enhanced eText:
ISBN 10:   0-13-343651-9
ISBN 13: 978-0-13-343651-8

This book is dedicated to aspiring teachers everywhere. May you use assessment as the gift to teaching and learning it can be.

BRIEF CONTENTS

CONTENTS

PREFACE

Very few people choose teaching as a profession because they can't wait to assess. We would venture to say that most people don't regard assessment as integral to learning and even fewer still regard assessment as "the fun part." Yet when we do it right and use it well, assessment can be a gift we give our students. It becomes a mirror we hold up to show them how far they have come. When we understand assessment's power to nurture learning and not just measure it, we use it not to punish or reward, but to guide students along a path to self-direction as learners.

This may not have been your experience with assessment as a student. We have written the seventh edition of *An Introduction to Student-Involved Assessment FOR Learning* to prepare you to begin your teaching career on Day 1 understanding how to make sure your assessments are accurate. Assessment is, in part, the process of gathering information to inform instructional decisions. Those decisions, when made well, drive student learning success. Effective instructional decision-making requires accurate assessment. Beyond that, we want you to be prepared to use assessment processes and information to help students increase their achievement. Classroom assessment is far more than merely a source of evidence for grading. When we understand how it can contribute to student confidence and motivation by meeting students' information needs, classroom assessment can become a very strong contributor to student success.

We intend this text to function as a long-term companion guide, first as your preservice preparation for classroom assessment and then as your primary resource throughout your teaching career. Only with practice over time can you develop the level of personal understanding needed to make these concepts and procedures part of your teaching routine. To learn what is needed to begin your career with competence, we offer the following suggestions:

1. You are going to spend a great deal of your professional time directly involved in assessment-related activities. If you merely study this book with the purpose of committing key ideas to short-term memory for a course grade, you will finish being neither confident with nor competent in your assessment practices. We urge you to take this learning task very seriously, striving to master the lessons that follow for the sake of the well-being of your students. Each chapter is structured around a set of learning targets. Those learning targets, taken together, define what it means to be competent at classroom assessment. Some of the end-of-chapter activities are designed to offer you practice with those learning targets. We urge you to complete them even if they are not assigned.

2. Throughout the content and structure of the text we have modeled the partnership that must exist between you and your students. We want the work you do in conjunction with this book to keep you in touch with, and therefore feeling in control of, your own growing professional competence in assessment.

Specifically, several of the end-of-chapter activities provide opportunities for reflection on what you are learning, how it compares to your past experiences as a student, and how it applies to your current learning. We urge you to select one or more of these activities to complete, again, even if they are not assigned.

3. You will learn more, faster, and with deeper understanding if you collaborate with others who are engaged in the same learning. The research literature on adult learning and professional development supports this contention. For this reason, consider forming small teams within your class. Meet between classes to discuss key concepts, work through unfamiliar parts, compare your responses to the practice exercises, complete end-of-chapter activities together, and/or discuss the social and cultural issues raised. This collaborative learning time is very important to solidifying your understanding.

The vision of excellence in assessment presented here arises from decades of research, our own experiences as teachers, and interactions with hundreds of other practicing teachers who have worked to make assessment serve learning. Our mission is to help you begin to develop the know-how and practical skills you need to be confident in and comfortable with the assessment practices you adopt as a teacher. And our hope is that you will find joy in refining your assessment proficiencies throughout a long and rewarding career.

■ New to This Edition

Much has changed in education policies and practices since the first edition of *An Introduction to Student-Involved Assessment FOR Learning* was published in 1994, but the principles of sound classroom assessment have remained the same. Updates to the editions over the years have mirrored the changes while remaining deeply rooted in those principles. In this seventh edition, we have made a number of significant revisions to better equip you, as new teachers, to do assessment right and use it well beginning on your first day. Major content changes include the following:

1. More detailed explanations of formative assessment practices, including offering effective feedback and preparing students to self-assess and set goals for next steps
2. More examples of how to involve students in the assessment process day to day
3. Updated explanations of the types of content standards in use today
4. Step-by-step guidance on assessment planning and development
5. More guidance on how to design performance tasks and rubrics and how to audit them for quality
6. A deeper treatment of questioning strategies designed to promote deeper thinking
7. A more robust explanation of how to track both formative and summative information

8. Specific instruction on how to derive accurate grades for use in a standards-based reporting system
9. Updated explanation of standardized testing

Changes to text features include the following:

1. Each chapter begins with a set of clearly stated learning targets and ends with a series of activities designed to help you master those learning targets. Some activities are designed to deepen your understanding of the chapter content, some are set up to give you practice with concepts taught, and some are designed to elicit reflection on key ideas. Many are structured so that you can complete them collaboratively if you wish, which has the potential to increase their learning value. In addition, each chapter's activities include one designed to prepare you to answer an interview question based on the chapter content.
2. Anecdotes, called "From the Classroom," are woven throughout the chapters. Written by practicing teachers who have worked with our materials to implement sound assessment practices in their classrooms, the anecdotes describe how specific assessment practices have improved their teaching as well as their students' attitudes and approach to learning.
3. Also woven throughout the chapters are video clips of elementary, middle school, and high school teachers and students engaged in formative assessment practices and discussing their impact on learning.

■ New Digital Features in the MyEducationLab with Enhanced eText

The most visible change in the seventh edition (and certainly one of the most significant changes) is the expansion of the digital learning and assessment resources embedded in the eText. They are designed to bring you more directly into the world of K-12 classrooms and to help you see the very real impact that high-quality assessment practices can have on learners.

The online resources in the MyEducationLab with Enhanced eText include:

Video Examples. Throughout the eText, embedded videos provide illustrations of sound assessment practices in action. See pages 27 and 34 for some examples.

Self-Checks and Application Exercises. Throughout the chapters you will find MyEducationLab: Self-check exercises. The self-checks include practice items designed to help you develop mastery of the content for each chapter learning outcome as well as quiz items to help you assess your level of mastery of chapter learning outcomes. These exercises are made up of self-grading multiple-choice items that not only provide feedback on whether questions are answered correctly or incorrectly, but also provide rationales for answers. In addition, the self-checks include application exercises, which challenge you to apply chapter content to authentic classroom assessment contexts. See pages 22 and 30 for some examples.

■ Acknowledgments

We are indebted to a host of capable professionals who have shepherded this latest edition from revision outline to final printing: Kevin M. Davis, Director of Education at Pearson Education, our editor and developer for many years; Pamela D. Bennett, Project Manager, who oversaw production of the text from copyediting through paging; Katrina Ostler, Project Manager, who provided day-to-day (and sometimes hourly) guidance through production and copyediting; Janelle Rogers, Program Manager, who cheerfully managed the schedule, budget, timeline, and permissions; Anne McAlpine, Editorial Assistant; and Lauren Carlson, Project Manager of Media Development and Production. We so appreciate your skill at working as a team to make all of the pieces come together.

Thank you also to the educators who reviewed the sixth edition and offered insightful comments about its strengths and suggestions for changes and additions to the seventh edition: Leigh Ausband, University of North Carolina–Charlotte; Christopher DeLuca, University of South Florida; Catherine Hogg, Rutgers University–Newark; Xyanthe Neider, Washington State University; and Kathleen Svoboda Ed.D., Eastern Michigan University.

And finally, our deepest gratitude goes to all of the teachers and administrators who have shared their insights, challenges, and solutions with us throughout the last twenty-five years. You have been our best teachers.

Jan Chappuis
Rick Stiggins
Portland, Oregon
July 2016

ABOUT THE AUTHORS

Jan Chappuis, educator and author, joined Rick Stiggins at the Assessment Training Institute in Portland, Oregon in 2001. Prior to that she had been an elementary and secondary teacher as well as a curriculum developer in English/Language Arts, Mathematics, Social Studies, and World Languages.

For the past twenty years Chappuis has written books and developed workshops focused on classroom assessment literacy, presenting both nationally and internationally. She is recognized as a national thought leader in the area of formative assessment for her work in translating research into practical classroom applications. Chappuis is author of *Seven Strategies of Assessment for Learning*, 2e (2015) and *Learning Team Facilitator Handbook* (2007). She is co-author of *Classroom Assessment for Student Learning: Doing It Right—Using It Well*, 2e (2012), *Creating and Recognizing Quality Rubrics* (2006), and *Understanding School Assessment—A Parent and Community Guide to Helping Students Learn* (2002).

Rick Stiggins, B.S., M.A., Ph.D., founded the Assessment Training Institute in Portland, Oregon, in 1992 to provide professional development for educators facing the challenges of day-to-day classroom assessment. In 2009, the Institute joined the Pearson Education team to extend its professional development services around the world.

Dr. Stiggins received his bachelor's degree in psychology from the State University of New York at Plattsburgh, master's degree in industrial psychology from Springfield (MA) College, and doctoral degree in education measurement from Michigan State University. Dr. Stiggins began his assessment work on the faculty of Michigan State before becoming a member of the faculty of educational foundations at the University of Minnesota, Minneapolis. In addition, he has served as director of test development for the ACT, Iowa City, Iowa; as a visiting scholar at Stanford University; as a Libra Scholar, University of Southern Maine; as director of the Centers for Classroom Assessment and Performance Assessment at the Northwest Regional Educational Laboratory, Portland, Oregon; and as a member of the faculty of Lewis and Clark College, Portland.

Classroom Assessment for Student Success

Chapter 1 Learning Targets

As a result of your study of Chapter 1, you will be able to do the following:

1. Know how classroom assessment fits into the big picture of your job as a teacher
2. Become familiar with the guiding principles for accuracy and effective use that underpin sound classroom assessment practice
3. Understand relationships among student motivation, success at learning, and assessment

"I wish we'd learned this in preservice." We have heard this comment and its companion question, "Why didn't they teach us this in college?" regularly over the past 20 years when giving presentations on classroom assessment to teachers and administrators around the country. Many of the practicing educators we work with throughout the nation believe they were inadequately prepared to assess student learning—with good reason. The lack of focus on classroom assessment in most teacher preparation programs has been repeatedly documented over several decades (Stiggins & Conklin, 1992; Popham, 2009; Andrade, 2013). When available, preservice classes addressing assessment have often focused on psychometric principles and related formal, technical, and statistical topics (McMillan, 2013). To be sure, these matters of assessment quality are important. But what has been missing is consideration of the use of assessment as an instructional tool. Many students planning to become teachers have not had the opportunity to learn about assessment in the classroom in the context of day-to-day teaching and student learning needs.

As a result, many practicing educators have learned what they know about classroom assessment through replicating what they themselves experienced as students, through discussions with colleagues, from the teacher's edition of textbooks, and through trial and error. Unfortunately, many of the most common assessment practices passed on through generations of teachers do not meet standards of quality

figure 1.1 ■ Definition of Classroom Assessment Literacy

Assessment Literacy:

The knowledge and skill to measure and report student achievement accurately and to use the assessment process and its results to improve learning.

for ensuring accuracy of information and are not grounded in research on learning or motivation. The content of this book is drawn from the field of educational measurement, shaped by decades of experience in translating psychometric principles into practical classroom applications, and by current research into the connections between assessment and learning. The goal of this book is to create a generation of educators who are *assessment literate*; that is, who are able to measure and report student achievement accurately and to use the assessment process and its results to improve learning (Figure 1.1). Becoming assessment literate requires a foundation of knowledge coupled with experience in applying that knowledge in everyday teaching and learning environments. Therefore, our mission as authors is to prepare you to do two things:

1. To use sound assessment practices thoughtfully beginning on your first day of teaching
2. To be committed to increasing your assessment expertise throughout your education career

■ The Teacher's Classroom Assessment Responsibilities

Assessment is, in part, the process of gathering evidence of student learning to inform instructional decisions. This process can be done well or poorly. To maximize student learning we all must be able to do it well. That means we must do the following:

- Gather *accurate evidence* of student achievement—the quality and impact of our instructional decisions depend on it.
- Interpret assessment results of all types to *communicate clearly* about student achievement.
- Integrate the classroom assessment process and its results into daily instruction in ways that *benefit students'* learning; that is, in ways that enhance both their motivation to learn and their achievement.

Figure 1.2 lists the specific competencies that underlie each of these responsibilities.

figure 1.2 ■ Classroom Assessment Competencies

1. *Clear Purpose* Assessment processes and results serve clear and appropriate purposes.	**a.** Identify the key users of classroom assessment information and know what their information needs are. **b.** Understand formative and summative assessment uses and know when to use each.
2. *Clear Targets* Assessments reflect clear student learning targets.	**a.** Know how to identify the five kinds of learning targets. **b.** Know how to turn broad statements of content standards into classroom-level learning targets. **c.** Begin instructional planning with clear learning targets. **d.** Translate learning targets into student-friendly language.
3. *Sound Design* Learning targets are translated into assessments that yield accurate results.	**a.** Design assessments to serve intended formative and summative purposes. **b.** Select assessment methods to match intended learning targets. **c.** Understand and apply principles of sampling learning appropriately. **d.** Write and/or select assessment items, tasks, scoring guides, and rubrics that meet standards of quality. **e.** Know and avoid sources of bias that distort results.
4. *Effective Communication* Assessment results function to increase student achievement. Results are managed well, combined appropriately, and communicated effectively.	**a.** Use assessment information to plan instruction. **b.** Offer effective feedback to students during learning. **c.** Record formative and summative assessment information accurately. **d.** Combine and summarize information appropriately to accurately reflect current level of student learning.
5. *Student Involvement* Students are active participants in the assessment process.	**a.** Identify students as important users of assessment information. **b.** Share learning targets and standards of quality with students. **c.** Design assessments so students can self-assess and set goals on the basis of results. **d.** Involve students in tracking, reflecting on, and sharing their own learning progress.

Gathering Accurate Information about Student Learning

Two requirements for assessment accuracy are *validity* and *reliability*. These two constructs can help us identify and avoid problems that will compromise the accuracy of our evidence of student learning.

Validity   One way to think about the quality of an assessment is in terms of the fidelity of the results it produces. Just as we want our high-definition television to produce a high-quality representation of the real thing, so do we want assessments to provide a high-fidelity representation of the desired learning. In the assessment realm, this is referred to as the *validity* of the test. All assessment results (scores, for example) provide outward indications of an inner state. To understand the concept of validity, imagine you weigh yourself at home and your bathroom scale reads 140 pounds; then you drive immediately to a doctor's appointment and the doctor's scale reads 147 pounds. One (or both) of these scales is not providing an accurate representation of your weight. Within the classroom, the entity we intend to measure is *achievement,* and an assessment's results are said to be valid if they accurately represent the level of student achievement on a predetermined set of learning targets. Let's say the intent of an assessment is to measure mastery of a body of knowledge related to the immune system. For the results to be valid, the assessment must provide a representative sample of the information about the immune system that was to be mastered. Otherwise, the score will not be an accurate read of what a student has actually learned.

A second validity consideration is the extent to which the results can be used successfully to accomplish the intended purpose of the assessment. A valid assessment is said to serve the purpose for which it is intended. For instance, a diagnostic test should help the user identify specific student strengths and needs. If it can't provide that level of detail, even though the score may accurately reflect learning, it is not a valid assessment for that purpose. We always seek to develop and use assessments that fit the context at hand—that are valid for a specific purpose or set of purposes.

Reliability   An assessment's ability to give consistent results is known as its *reliability.* Using the bathroom scale example again, if when you step on it the first time it reads 142 and then you step on it again and it reads 145, you are not getting consistent results. If your scale's results were reliable, you could step on and off repeatedly and it would produce the same number each time. Similarly, an educational assessment is said to be reliable if it reflects the same level of learning (i.e., a consistent score) each time we administer it. Additionally, as learning grows and improves, a reliable assessment will reflect those improvements with changing results. Over the course of this book, we will identify factors other than students' actual level of achievement that influence test scores—bad test items, test anxiety, distractions during testing, teacher scoring and grading practices, and the like. When this happens, the score is distorted by factors extraneous to achievement level and is said to have provided unreliable results.

Supporting Student Learning

Our model of assessment quality is not complete without consideration of how well both assessment processes and instruments contribute to increased achievement. In the past both large-scale and classroom assessments have served the purpose of identifying and weeding out unable and unwilling learners (many of whom drop out of school) and ranking those who remain to graduate from the highest to lowest achiever. However, after decades of a sort-and-select assessment system, our society has come to understand that it is unfair and inadequate. In light of accelerating change in technology, growing international interconnectedness, and the increasing challenge of securing living-wage employment, all students now more than ever must succeed in school.

Assessment processes and instruments have the opportunity to do far more than serve as the basis of grading and ranking students. They can accurately diagnose student needs, track and enhance student growth toward standards, motivate students to persist at learning, and teach them to self-assess and set goals for next steps. What types of assessments we use, what we do with the results, what we communicate to students and to their parents, and when we communicate all factor in to supporting student learning. This brings us back to our second validity consideration: Are the assessment processes and instruments we use capable of supporting learning in these ways? Are they valid for these uses?

MyEdLab **Self-Check 1.1**

MyEdLab **Application Exercise 1.1** The teacher's classroom assessment responsibilities

---

■ Keys to Assessment Quality

Considerations of validity, reliability, and the extent to which assessment instruments and practices contribute to learning come together in a set of guiding principles (Figure 1.3, which we refer to as *Keys to Quality Assessment*). The four keys to quality represent the foundation on which we will build the framework for understanding how to assess well in the classroom.

Key 1: Start with a Clear Purpose

Anyone designing or selecting an assessment must begin with a clear sense of purpose: Who will use the information? What decisions will the results be used to inform? At the classroom level, assessment information is used summatively, to *report* learning, as when test scores are combined to create a final grade. It is also used formatively, to *support* learning, as when diagnostic assessment information leads to further instruction. However, classroom-level assessment is part of a larger system that exists within schools and districts to meet the information needs of a variety of different users. Beyond the classroom, certain types of assessments are used for

figure 1.3 ■ Keys to Quality Assessment

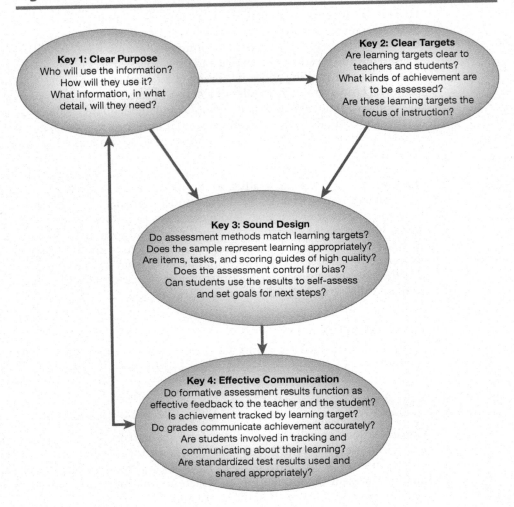

accountability purposes as well as for program evaluation and improvement across a school district. And at the district and state levels, assessment information is used to identify areas of need, to allocate resources, to provide accountability information, and to shape policy decisions. These different assessment users bring different information needs to the table. For this reason, the starting place for the creation of a quality assessment for use in any particular context must be a clear sense of the information needs of the decision makers to be served. Without a sense of what kind of information will help them and, therefore, what kind of assessment must be conducted, the results will likely lead to poorly informed decisions that run counter to teacher effectiveness and to increasing student achievement. Chapter 2 describes the key users of classroom assessment information and their information needs. It also explains the impact formative assessment practices can have on learning and what strategies we can put in place to maximize that impact.

Key 2: Establish Clear and Appropriate Learning Targets

Learning targets are statements of what we want students to know and be able to do. The written curriculum in each subject takes the form of an ordered progression of learning expectations across grade levels. These statements of expected learning are sometimes called *content standards*, *learning outcomes*, or *achievement expectations*. We will use the term *learning targets* throughout the text to refer to these learning expectations, for the sake of clarity and consistency.

Assessment validity requires that we begin with clearly defined statements of the learning our students will be responsible for achieving prior to creating or selecting assessments of that learning. There are many different kinds of learning targets within our educational system, from mastering content knowledge to complex problem solving, from performing a flute recital to speaking Spanish to constructing an effective argument. All are important. One of the precursors to accurate assessment at the classroom level is to be masters ourselves of the learning targets we are responsible for teaching. Only then can we ensure that our assessments accurately represent that learning. Chapter 3 explains the five categories of learning targets, how to determine if our learning targets are clearly defined, how to deconstruct complex content standards, and how to make learning targets clear to students.

Key 3: Create High-Quality Assessments That Yield Dependable Information

High-quality assessments of all types attend to four design standards. They must do all of the following if they are to support valid and reliable inferences about student learning:

1. Rely on an assessment method capable of reflecting the target. Assessment methods are not interchangeable. Certain methods will yield accurate information only for certain learning target types.
2. Sample student achievement appropriately. How much information to gather is dependent on the type of learning target to be assessed and the purpose for assessing it.
3. Include only high-quality items, tasks, and scoring procedures.
4. Eliminate or minimize distortion of results due to bias. Regardless of how carefully an assessment is planned, things can still go wrong, causing the results to be inaccurate.

All assessments must meet these accuracy requirements. Chapter 4 describes four assessment methods, when to choose each, and how to plan an assessment with each of these four standards in mind. Chapters 5 through 8 expand on these standards for each individual assessment method: selected response (Chapter 5), written response (Chapter 6), performance assessment (Chapter 7), and personal communication (Chapter 8).

Key 4: Communicate Results Effectively

Mention the idea of communicating assessment results and the first thoughts that come to mind are of test scores and grades. When the purpose of the communication is summative, that is, to report the level of student achievement for accountability purposes, scores and grades can work. Assessment-literate teachers know how to combine results from a variety of sources to derive a fair and defensible end-of-term grade.

When the purpose of the communication is formative, that is, to support learning, then summaries such as grades, scores, or ratings will not do the job. In those cases, teachers and students need access to diagnostic information that helps them understand what the students have done well, what they still need to work on, and what their next steps might be. In other words, numbers and grades are not the only—or in formative contexts even the best—way to communicate about achievement.

Effective communication of assessment results is in part driven by the purpose for the assessment. Assessment-literate teachers balance their use of assessment results to offer feedback during learning with use of results to report level of achievement at the conclusion of learning. And beyond the classroom assessment context, they are able to interpret, use, and communicate about standardized test results appropriately. Chapters 9, 10, 11, and 12 address the different aspects of effective communication related to classroom assessment, from recordkeeping and grading to portfolios, and conferences. Appendix B addresses the interpretation and use of standardized test results.

■ An Overarching Principle: Student Involvement

A strong belief underpinning this book is that the greatest potential value of classroom assessment to increase achievement comes when we open up the process during learning and welcome students in as full partners. Within each of these four guiding principles—clear purpose, clear target, sound design, and effective communication—we can involve students in assessment from the beginning and all the way through the learning. We start in Key 1 by acknowledging that students are central decision makers in the educational system—if they decide not to try, no other decision maker's actions will cause learning. We can and should plan our assessment practices and instruments to meet students' information needs as well as ours and the system's needs. We continue in Key 2 by making the learning targets clear to students at the outset of instruction so they know how to focus their effort. In Key 3 we design or select assessments that are capable of providing the basis for student self-assessment. And in Key 4 we make time in the instructional cycle to allow students to track, reflect on, and share their growth in achievement to keep them in touch with their learning progress.

A Classroom Example of Student-Involved Assessment

At a district school board meeting toward the end of the school year, a high school English department faculty presented the results of their evaluation of the writing instruction program they had implemented over the past year. As the first step in presenting program evaluation results, Ms. Weathersby, the department chair, distributed a sample of student work to the board members, asking them to read and evaluate the writing. They were critical in their commentary. As the members registered their opinions, a faculty member recorded them on chart paper. The list included *repetitiveness, problems with organization, run-on sentences*, and *lack of connection among ideas*. Next, Ms. Weathersby distributed another sample of student work, asking the board members to read and evaluate it. They commented on how much better the second sample was and offered specific comments such as *words and phrases that make meaning clear, strong sentence structure*, and *interesting introduction*. At this point, Ms. Weathersby revealed that the two samples they had just evaluated, one of relatively poor quality and one of outstanding quality, were written by the same student, the first at the beginning of the year and the second toward the end of the year. She explained that this is typical of the growth the English teachers had seen in student writing over the course of the year. The rest of the English faculty joined the presentation and shared graphs charting the growth of student competence on each of six dimensions of writing over time. They too offered "before" and "after" samples of student papers.

The board members were interested in knowing more about the new program, and Ms. Weathersby explained it briefly. In preparation for implementation, the faculty had attended an institute the previous summer on integrating writing assessment with instruction, with a specific focus on teaching students to use rubrics to improve their writing. They began the year by introducing the content of the rubrics to students and then having students use the rubrics to evaluate samples of writing representing a range of quality. This helped students understand the differences between good and poor-quality writing. The teachers used the rubrics to diagnose specific needs and taught focused lessons to help students improve on one aspect of quality at a time. They used the language of the rubrics in their feedback comments, taught students to offer peer feedback in writing groups, and provided time for students to self-assess prior to revising their work.

Then Ms. Weathersby informed the board that Emily, the student whose writing they had evaluated, was present in the audience and invited her to come forward. Emily highlighted the practices that helped move her from a struggling writer to a competent one. "To begin with, Ms. Weathersby taught us to do what you just did. We analyzed other people's writing. We looked at good writing and not-so-good writing—passages from books, newspaper articles, and other students' writing. Pretty soon we could look at our own writing that same way. We kept our writing in a portfolio so we could keep working on it and see that we were getting better. She was the first teacher to tell me that it was okay not to be very good at something at first and that my goal was to get a little better each time. She didn't want us to give up on ourselves. If we kept improving over time we could learn to write well. I wish every teacher would do that. She would say, 'There's no shortage of success around here. You learn to write well, you get an A. My goal is to have everyone learn to write well.'" As the presentation concluded, it was clear to all in attendance that this application of student-involved classroom assessment had contributed to significant learning.

The Keys to Success   What conditions were in place in Ms. Weathersby's classroom for Emily and her classmates to have experienced such success?

- First, the assessment purpose was crystal clear—to help students assess the quality of their own writing and to fix it where it needed work.
- Second, Ms. Weathersby introduced a well-defined vision of the learning target that identified key attributes of effective writing and was designed to help students understand different levels of quality so she could engage them in the study with her of writing samples representing various levels of quality.
- Third, this vision of high-quality writing (represented by the writing rubrics she used) was aligned to the district writing content standards and was designed to be used for the intended purpose.
- Fourth, students were engaged regularly in giving and receiving feedback during learning to guide their next steps.
- Last, students assessed their own strengths and weaknesses repeatedly over time and intentionally tracked their own improvement.

In a nutshell, the keys to success in Ms. Weathersby's class were *clear purpose*, *clear targets*, *sound design*, *effective communication*, and a heavy dose of *student involvement*.

MyEdLab **Self-Check 1.2**
MyEdLab **Application Exercise 1.2**   The keys to quality to assessment in your personal classroom experiences

---

■ Understanding Motivation to Learn

It would be so much easier to teach if all students decided to put forth the effort needed to succeed. Many studies (Ames, 1992; Black & Wiliam, 1998a; Butler, 1988; Halvorson, 2012; Hattie & Timperley, 2007; Schunk, 1996) have found that students' willingness to persist at a task is influenced by their *goal orientation*. This is a term researchers use to define different ideas students have about why they are doing their work in school. A goal orientation can be thought of as how a student answers the question, "What is the aim of my work?" or "Why am I doing this assignment?"

To illustrate the concept of goal orientation, let's say you ask a student what she learned today in school. It's possible she will draw a blank. She may tell you what she did—"We worked on a math problem about camping," or "We watched our teacher cook stuff in Science and then we got to eat it"—but she may not be able to tell you why. This student's attention is focused not on what she is supposed to be learning but on what she is supposed to be doing. She may not even know the goal in math class is to learn to use the problem-solving strategy "draw a picture" to solve a problem or that the intended learning behind the teacher's cooking was for students to draw inferences about the differences between a physical change and a chemical change.

Goal orientations typically fall into one of three categories (Figure 1.4) (Ames, 1992; Black & Wiliam, 1998a; Halvorson, 2012):

1. A learning orientation, where the student's goal is to get better
2. An ego-involved orientation, where the student's goal is to prove ability or hide a perceived lack of ability
3. A task-completion orientation, where the student's goal is to get it done and get a grade

Learning Orientation

Students who adopt a learning goal approach focus their effort on improving their work and getting better. Their goal is to find out what they don't know and master it. Students with this orientation believe that success means improving their level of competence and that their job in school is to develop new skills and master the intended learning. Their goals focus on continuous improvement; they are motivated by a desire to become competent and by evidence of increasing mastery. They tend to seek help more frequently in developing competence and explain help avoidance in terms of attempting independent mastery (Ames, 1992, p. 262; Halvorson, 2012, pp. 43–52). "What does 'done well' look like?" is a guiding question of students with a learning orientation.

figure 1.4 ▪ Three Common Goal Orientations

What is the aim of my work?

1. Learning Orientation: "To get better"
2. Ego Orientation: "To prove ability" or "To hide perceived lack of ability"
3. Task Completion Orientation: "To get it done and get a grade"

Ego-Involved Orientation

Students who adopt an ego-involved goal approach to school focus their effort on protecting their sense of self-worth. Their goal is to attain public recognition of having done better than others or having performed at a superior level. Students with this orientation often believe successful achievement is a function of ability, not a result of effort. Their sense of self-worth is tied to their capacity to demonstrate high ability by doing better than others or achieving success with little effort. Their goals focus on being judged as smart or being seen as competent in relation to others. They are motivated by judgments indicating superior performance. Students with ego-involving goals are working with a focus primarily on maintaining positive self-esteem by either demonstrating that they have high ability or masking their perceived low ability. They tend to avoid seeking help and in research studies have explained this behavior in terms of hiding their lack of ability (Ames, 1992, pp. 262–263; Halvorson, 2012, pp. 43–52). "What do I need to do to outperform others?" or "How do I avoid being seen as stupid?" are guiding questions of students with an ego-involved orientation.

Task-Completion Orientation

Students who adopt a task-completion approach to school focus their effort on assignment completion. They believe it is their job to finish the task—to get it done—and to get the points. Students with this orientation believe that points and grades, rather than learning and mastery, are the aim of their work (Schunk, 1996; Black & Wiliam, 1998a). "When is it due?" or "How much is this worth?" are guiding questions of students with a task-completion orientation. See Figure 1.5 for a comparison of the impact each of these three goal orientations can have on motivation and learning.

Goal Orientations and College and Career Readiness

Within each of these three orientations, we see that students are motivated to accomplish different goals and in only one orientation do the goals focus on learning. Let's now compare the goal orientations to the characteristics of college- and career-ready students described by the Common Core State Standards (NGSS, 2010a). Students who are college- and career-ready are:

- Self-directed learners who know how to assess their own learning needs
- Inclined to seek out and use resources to assist them in learning

They exhibit willingness to try and persistence in the face of difficulty. Only when students adopt a learning orientation are they able to commit to and sustain the effort-based strategies characteristic of college- and career-ready students.

figure 1.5 ■ Impact of Goal Orientations on Motivation and Learning

	Learning Orientation	Ego Orientation	Task-Completion Orientation
Belief about effort	Effort will lead to success: "I can do this if I keep trying."	Succeeding with little effort proves ability. "I'm smart." Trying hard when it doesn't lead to success proves lack of ability: "I'm not smart enough."	Will expend as much effort as needed to get work turned in or earn points/get grades
Direction of effort	To develop new skills, try to understand their own work, improve their level of competence, and achieve a sense of mastery relative to their own past level	To exceed the performance of others or hide perceived lack of ability: "If I can't be the best, it's not worth it."	To complete an activity or assignment: "Get it done."
Response when faced with difficulty	Leans in: Increases level of involvement and sustains commitment to effort-based strategies to produce quality work	Backs off: highest value is achieving success with little effort, which leads to unwillingness to try effort-based strategies	Works for points and grades rather than understanding; looks for ways to get points/higher grade
Response to perceived failure	"Failure tolerance": belief that failure can be overcome by a change in strategy	Anxiety and poor performance ("I don't know what I'm doing, so I lack ability"); quits, cheats, or chooses easier work	Looks for ways to get more points/higher grade
Help avoidance	Explains help avoidance in terms of wanting to figure it out alone: "Let me see if I can do it by myself first."	Explains help avoidance in terms of wanting to hide perceived lack of ability: "If I need help that means I'm not as smart as I want people to think I am."	Will accept help if it means more points/higher grade Doesn't resist help: it matters less who does the work as long as it's turned in
Attitude toward school	Motivation to learn and a willingness to engage in the process of learning Development of an intrinsic valuing of learning	Appearing to already know is safer than revealing learning needs Resistant to risk-taking required to learn	Learning is a by-product rather than a goal External rewards-driven motivation

Goal Orientations and the Connection to Assessment

It is clear that students who adopt a learning orientation have a far greater chance of succeeding at school. The good news is that goal orientations are a response to a set of conditions: students can hold one orientation in one classroom and another in a different one. We can think of them as *modes* that students shift into and out of. We create the conditions for shifting into learning mode through the assessment practices that we establish in our classrooms. For example, if we ourselves do not have clear learning targets, or if we don't share them with students, many of them will conclude that it is their ultimate job to do the work with the goal of completing the assignment and getting a grade, a task-completion mode. What they are learning, and how well they are learning it, will not be part of their thinking. Or, if we rely solely on grading to provide feedback to students, those who do not do well at first will be at risk of concluding they are not "good" at the subject and moving into an ego-protecting mode. For an example of how assessment practices can help students shift into learning mode, read seventh-grade teacher Janna Smith's explanation in Figure 1.6.

Assessment's power to increase achievement relies in part on its ability to increase motivation not through a carrot-and-stick, reward-and-punish mechanism, but rather through developing in students an understanding that learning is the goal of schooling and fostering a commitment to effort-based strategies to attain that goal. In Chapter 2, we will explore how formative assessment practices can help us accomplish this goal.

MyEdLab **Self-Check 1.3**

MyEdLab **Application Exercise 1.3** Student motivation and goals in classroom assessment

---

figure 1.6 ■ From the Classroom: Janna Smith

I used to think of assessment as an "ending" to a learning event. When preparing to teach a unit, my planning primarily consisted of looking at the objectives and crafting activities that would engage all students. The word *assessment* was a noun that referred only to a task generally used at the end to determine a grade. The things students were asked to do as part of an endpoint assessment task may—or may not—have been aligned to the key objectives. Items on an end-of-unit test were usually selected response or short-answer/essay, but for the most part that was just for variety's sake.

Now *assessment* is not a singular noun referring to an individual test or task, but refers to an ongoing process that is interwoven with instruction. The process no longer happens only at the end; in fact, it begins with pre-assessment. With my current group of 7th-grade mathematics students, I introduce a grid at the onset of each unit. The grid lists the learning targets for that unit, with space for students to record their analysis of the results of their pre-assessment, target by target.

Additional boxes are included for each target, where students list sources of evidence from daily work, quizzes, etc. Throughout the unit, we periodically pause for students to select which of the learning targets their evidence indicates they are doing well with and on which they need more support. I use their self-assessments along with my own records of their performance to determine mini-lessons, small-group instruction topics, and areas where we might move more quickly.

When I was first introduced to the principles of assessment *for* learning, I was a district-level administrator. My role consisted of providing professional development and supporting principals and teachers in implementing quality classroom assessment practices. I believed it could work and spoke passionately about how to integrate these strategies into instruction. I modeled lessons to demonstrate how learning targets could be turned into student-friendly language. I even taught a graduate-level course on classroom assessment in a school district, but I had never actually used assessment *for* learning in my own classroom! When I finally had that opportunity, I was determined to "walk my talk" with a group of 7th graders who have struggled with mathematics. I wanted to see my own "Inside the Black Box" (Black & Wiliam, 1998b) with my students, hoping it would result in increased achievement and motivation.

Making assessment *for* learning come to life in my own classroom has renewed my zeal for teaching. I am more focused on essential learning targets, and my students always know what we are learning, how they are doing, and what we can work on together to close any gaps. They have become fantastic self-assessors, using their "evidence files" to determine their own strengths and challenges. Most importantly, they are becoming more confident problem solvers who no longer avoid and complain about math. By going back to the classroom, I now know firsthand that using these strategies can have a significant positive impact on student learning.

Source: Reprinted with permission from Janna Smith, Classroom Teacher, Far Hills Country Day School, Far Hills, NJ, January 2011.

■ Summary: The Importance of Sound Assessment

Quality classroom assessment produces accurate information that is used effectively to both report and support student learning. An assessment-literate teacher is able to do the following:

- ■ Identify the information needs of those instructional decision makers who will use classroom assessment results.
- ■ Establish clear learning targets as the basis of instruction and assessment.
- ■ Select assessment methods that are capable of reflecting student mastery of the learning target(s) accurately.
- ■ Select or design and build high-quality assessments that lead to confident conclusions about level of student achievement.
- ■ Communicate assessment results in a timely and understandable manner to intended user(s) for both formative and summative purposes.
- ■ Involve students in the assessment process to develop their capabilities as self-directed learners.

■ Suggested Activities

End-of-chapter activities are intended to help you master the chapter's learning targets. They are designed to deepen your understanding of the chapter content, provide opportunities for personal reflection on ideas presented, and serve as a basis for discussion among peers. You may wish to do all of them or select those that you believe will be most useful to your learning. Each activity is correlated to one or more chapter learning targets to help with your selection.

Chapter 1 Learning Targets

As a result of your study of Chapter 1, you will be able to do the following:

1. Know how classroom assessment fits into the big picture of your job as a teacher
2. Become familiar with the guiding principles for accuracy and effective use that underpin sound classroom assessment practice
3. Understand relationships among student motivation, success at learning, and assessment

Chapter 1 Activities

Activity 1.1   Keeping a Reflective Journal (All chapter learning targets)

Activity 1.2   Comparing Your Prior Thoughts to Information in the Text (Learning Target 1)

Activity 1.3   Connecting Your Experiences to the Keys to Assessment Quality (Learning Target 2)

Activity 1.4   Reflecting on Your Experiences with Student-Involved Assessment (Learning Targets 2 and 3)

Activity 1.5   Evaluating Classroom Assessment Scenarios (Learning Target 3)

Activity 1.6   Thinking More about Student Goal Orientations (Learning Target 3)

Activity 1.7   Reflecting on Your Learning from Chapter 1 (All chapter learning targets)

Activity 1.8   Setting Up a Growth Portfolio (All chapter learning targets)

Activity 1.1: Keeping a Reflective Journal

Keep a record of your thoughts, questions, and insights as you read Chapter 1.

Activity 1.2: Comparing Your Prior Thoughts to Information in the Text

After reading the section "The Teacher's Classroom Assessment Responsibilities," write a short reflection explaining how the three responsibilities described match your own prior understanding of what a teacher's assessment responsibilities are. How does what you've read compare to what you thought before taking this class?

Activity 1.3: Connecting Your Experiences to the Keys to Assessment Quality

Think of an assessment experience from your personal educational past that was a good experience for you. What made it a productive experience? What emotional and learning impact did it have for you?

Now think of one that was a negative experience for you. What made it a counterproductive experience? What emotional and learning impact did it have for you?

What was a significant difference between the two experiences? How does that difference relate to the Keys to Quality Assessment (including the principle of student involvement) described in this chapter?

Activity 1.4: Reflecting on Your Experiences with Student-Involved Assessment

During your K–12 schooling experience, did your teachers engage you in activities that are described in this chapter as student-involved? If so, what did they do? What impact did the experience have on you? If they did not, where in your schooling might your involvement in assessment have helped you?

Activity 1.5: Evaluating Classroom Assessment Scenarios

Read the following classroom assessment scenarios and decide if each is likely to increase or decrease student motivation to learn. Give a reason related to Chapter 1 content for each of your decisions.

- Mr. Green is having his students score each other's quizzes and then call out the scores so he can enter them in his gradebook. He feels this practice motivates students to learn from mistakes and provides students with immediate feedback. It also saves him time.
- Students in Ms. Brown's science class are examining a range of anonymous samples of lab notes to decide which are great examples and which are poor examples. They will then make a list of what good science notes should look like.
- Jeremy's teacher tells him that because his grades on practice quizzes and chapter tests have been so low, no matter how well he does from now on, the highest grade he can possibly receive is a D.

Activity 1.6: Thinking More about Student Goal Orientations

After reading the section "Understanding Motivation to Learn," respond to the following questions:

1. What else might students be focused on as the goal of their schoolwork *other than learning*?
2. How might that other focus *inhibit* success at learning?
3. What are key factors in *developing* a learning focus in students?

Activity 1.7: Reflecting on Your Learning from Chapter 1

Review the Chapter 1 learning targets and select one that struck you as most significant. Write a short reflection that captures your current understanding. If you are working with a group, discuss what you have written.

Activity 1.8: Setting Up a Growth Portfolio

We encourage you to collect evidence of your progress throughout the course of this study and recommend that you assemble the evidence in a growth portfolio—a collection of work selected to show growth over time—focused on your developing classroom assessment literacy.

You may not want to include evidence of everything you have learned—you may want to narrow your focus somewhat. Each chapter begins with a list of learning targets for that chapter. If one or more of those learning targets is an area of focused growth for you, you may wish to complete the corresponding chapter activity or activities and use them as portfolio entries, along with anything else you develop along the way.

Many people find it helpful to keep a record of their thoughts and questions as they read each chapter and try the activities, both for their own learning and to prepare for class discussions. The first activity for each chapter is to create a reflective journal entry that documents your thoughts, questions, and activities. If you choose to do this activity, it can also become part of your growth portfolio.

Why We Assess

Chapter 2 Learning Targets

As a result of your study of Chapter 2, you will be able to do the following:

1. Define the meaning of the terms *formative assessment* and *summative assessment*
2. Understand the positive impact of formative assessment on student achievement
3. Understand how formative assessment and summative assessment fit into a balanced assessment system
4. Understand research-based strategies for implementing formative assessment practices in the classroom

---

In Chapter 1, we established that we can assess for two different reasons: to *support* learning or to *report on the sufficiency* of the learning. Traditionally schools have placed far greater emphasis on the latter purpose: assessing to evaluate and report on how much students have learned. There is still the belief today among many teachers and most students that the primary purpose of classroom assessment is to generate a grade. While grades are important, they are not the only or even the most powerful purpose for assessing if we wish to maximize school quality.

Being an effective teacher requires that we understand both of the ways assessment can be used, when to employ each, and how to ensure that our assessment practices serve student well-being. Assessment-literate educators know how to use assessment to meet the information needs of all important instructional decision makers including students, parents, instructional leaders, and policy makers. Figure 2.1 highlights the key to assessment quality we address in Chapter 2: *Clear Purpose*. In this chapter we will explore the range of assessment purposes (users and uses), both inside and outside of the classroom, with an emphasis on understanding how to use assessment to enhance achievement, not merely measure it.

Our first step in becoming assessment literate is to understand the range of possible users and uses of assessment information.

figure 2.1 ■ Keys to Quality Assessment

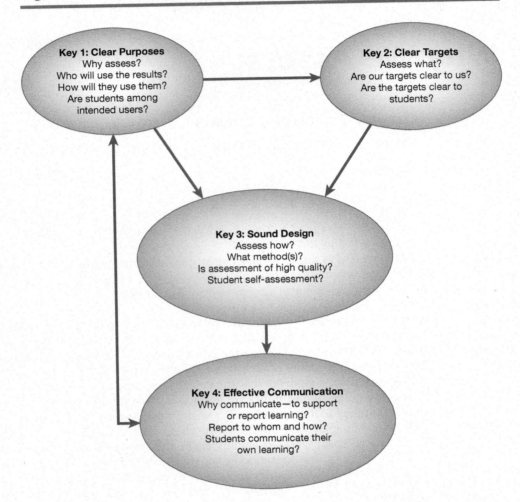

■ Formative and Summative Purposes for Assessment

Assessments provide evidence of learning. What we do with the evidence, as you remember from Chapter 1, can be thought of as falling into one of two categories, which we have labeled as *supporting* learning and *reporting* on the amount learned. The supporting function is also known as *formative assessment* and the reporting function is known as *summative assessment* (Figure 2.2). We define *formative assessment* as a collection of formal and informal processes teachers and students use to

figure 2.2 ■ Formative and Summative Assessment

Formative Assessment
Formal and informal processes teachers and students use to gather evidence for the purpose of informing next steps in learning.

Summative Assessment
Assessments that provide evidence of student achievement for the purpose of making a judgment about student competence or program effectiveness.

Source: Chappuis, Jan, *Seven Strategies Of Assessment For Learning*, 2nd Ed., ©2015. Reprinted and Electronically reproduced by permission of Pearson Education, Inc., New York, New York.

gather evidence for the purpose of informing next steps in learning. Formative assessment practices occur during the learning, while students are practicing and improving, and before student achievement levels are measured for a report card grade. Research conducted around the world over the past three decades has revealed formative assessment applications that have given rise to profound achievement gains. For this reason, interest in this purpose has intensified in American schools in recent years.

We define *summative assessment* as the process of gathering information to be used to make a judgment about level of competence or achievement. Summative assessment results are generally used to evaluate rather than improve learning. Summative assessments are conducted after the learning has occurred as a way to communicate to

> What we do with assessment information determines whether the event is formative or summative.

students and others about how much they have learned. In the classroom, this information is usually translated into a grade that is used to help determine students' final grade for the report card.

MyEdLab **Self-Check 2.1**

High-Impact Formative Assessment Practices

In 1998, British researchers Paul Black and Dylan Wiliam published a review of research on formative assessment practices which triggered a growing awareness of the importance of formative assessment. Their research review (1998a) examined an international array of studies that represented a range of subject areas, involved students from kindergarten level to college level, and were conducted in countries throughout the world. In their analysis of these studies, they noted achievement gains associated with formative applications that were among the largest found for any instructional intervention. Their reporting of these results put formative assessment center stage in the school improvement literature. For this reason and not surprisingly, the adjective *formative* has been attached to a plethora of assessment products and practices. But calling a product or practice *formative* does not make it so. For Black and Wiliam and for many other experts in the field, formative isn't a characteristic of the assessment itself; it is a reflection of how the assessment information is used. Formative assessment is a collection of practices with a common feature: each leads to some action that improves learning. Black and Wiliam (1998b) concluded that the following practices had the highest impact on student growth:

- Use of evidence gathered during classroom work and from homework to determine the current state of student understanding, with action taken to improve learning and correct misunderstandings
- Provision of feedback during the learning, with guidance on how to improve
- Development of student self-assessment and peer-feedback skills

Let's look at each of these three categories in a bit more detail. In the first category, the teacher is examining information, interpreting it, and acting on it. Practices that help teachers obtain, interpret, and act on student information help them answer questions critical to good instruction (Chappuis, 2015, pp. 8–9):

- Who is and is not understanding the lesson?
- What adjustments should I make to instruction?
- What are each student's strengths and needs?
- What misconceptions do I need to address?
- How should I group students for instruction?
- What differentiation do I need to prepare?
- Are students ready for feedback? If so, what feedback should I give?

In the second category of high-impact practices, the teacher is examining the information, interpreting it, and sharing it with students, but the students must also examine their work, interpret what the teacher has shared, and finally act on it. So, in this instance, both teacher and student are active users of assessment information. In the third category, the student is examining the work, interpreting the results, and acting on them. Australian researcher D. Royce Sadler (1989) concludes that formative assessment's greatest potential derives from teaching students to monitor the quality of their own work during production:

> The indispensable conditions for improvement are that the student *comes to hold a concept of quality roughly similar to that held by the teacher, is able to monitor continuously the quality of what is being produced* during the act of production itself, *and has a repertoire of alternative moves or strategies from which to draw at any given point* (p. 121, emphasis in original).

It is not the *giving* of feedback that causes achievement gains—it is the *acting* on it that causes gains. No action, no gains.

The power of formative assessment lies in its ability to guide both teacher and student actions, to keep learning on a successful track, and to maintain student belief that success is within reach.

MyEdLab **Self-Check 2.2**

MyEdLab **Application Exercise 2.1** Formative assessment practices and student achievement

■ How Formative and Summative Assessment Fits into a Balanced Assessment System

So, how do we balance formative and summative assessment to meet the needs of all stakeholders? The answer turns on understanding how information needs of decision makers differ across contexts of assessment use. Some users face the need to make instructional decisions continuously, day to day in the classroom. Others use assessment results far less frequently—sometimes only once a year. We balance our assessment systems when we build them to meet the information needs (serve the purposes) of all of these different users.

Let's examine classroom-level uses of formative and summative assessment information first and describe a balanced classroom approach. Then we will review the district-level and state-level uses of formative and summative assessment information and describe the elements of a balanced assessment system. Figure 2.3 summarizes the three levels of assessment, the purposes they serve, the stakeholders who use the information generated, and the uses they make of it.

figure 2.3 ■ Elements of a Balanced Assessment System

Level of Assessment	What Is the Assessment Purpose?	Who Will Use the Information?	How Will It Be Used?
Classroom assessment	To measure level of student achievement on learning targets taught	Teachers	Summative: To determine grades for reporting purposes
		Individual teachers, teacher teams	Formative: To revise teaching plans for next year/semester
			Formative: To plan further instruction; to differentiate instruction
	To diagnose student strengths and areas needing further work	Teachers, students	Formative: To provide feedback to students
		Students	Formative: To self-assess and to set goals for next steps
District benchmark, interim, or common assessments	To measure level of student achievement toward content standards	District and school leadership, teacher teams	Summative: To evaluate program effectiveness
			Formative: To identify standards in need of more effective programs
	To identify students and/or portions of the curriculum needing additional/ different instruction	District and school leadership, teacher teams, individual teachers	Formative: To plan interventions for groups or individuals

figure 2.3 ■ Elements of a Balanced Assessment System (*Continued*)

Level of Assessment	What Is the Assessment Purpose?	Who Will Use the Information?	How Will It Be Used?
Annual testing	To measure level of student achievement on preset content standards	District and school leadership, teacher teams, individual teachers	Summative: To evaluate achievement level of each student and summarize across students
		District and school leadership, teacher teams	Summative: To determine program effectiveness
			Formative: To identify program or curriculum needs
	To identify percentage of students meeting state content standards	State leadership, district and school leadership	Summative: To evaluate schools and districts
			Summative: To issue sanctions and rewards
		State leadership, district and school leadership, teacher teams	Formative: To develop programs or interventions for groups or individuals

Balancing Formative and Summative Assessment in the Classroom

Let us say for argument's sake that the only answer we have to the question "who will use assessment information?" is "the teacher" and the only answer we have to the question "How will they use it?" is "to assign a grade." In this scenario basically we are only addressing a summative purpose for assessment. We will plan instruction, deliver it, give students an assignment, and then grade the results.

In fact, the preservice education many of us veteran teachers experienced focused primarily on this application of assessment. Consequently, we began teaching with a repertoire of four steps: plan, instruct, assign, and grade (Figure 2.4). First, we planned what we would do and what our students would do. Then, we prepared the materials and resources. Next, we did what we planned, and they did what we planned. Last, we graded what they did. However, learning and teaching turned out to be far messier than we had been prepared for. Somewhere between "we taught it" and "they learned it," the straight shot downstream to achievement sprung surprisingly into an array of diverging tributaries. Over the course of our first years of teaching, we discovered there are a thousand ways for learners to "not get" a lesson.

The belief underpinning our teacher preparation seemed to be that learning trots right along after good instruction, a sort of stimulus-response system, in which instruction alone will create learning. However, when students have continued learning needs after instruction, it is not necessarily an indication that something went wrong. Learning is an unpredictable process; instructional correctives are part of the normal flow of attaining mastery in any field.

figure 2.4 ■ Summative Assessment Model of Teaching

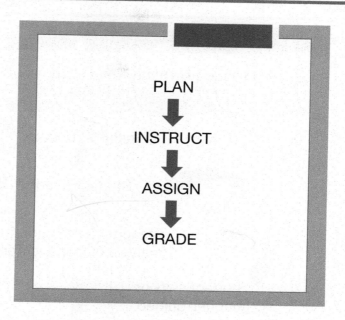

When we teach along a straight path of "plan, instruct, assign, and grade," we don't weave in the time or mechanisms needed to respond to students' instructional needs. Yet *whether* learning occurs is directly influenced by the steps we and our students take *after* instruction. Do we reteach and relearn or move on? This is where formative assessment practices can be so helpful—they provide the ongoing "back and forth" between *instruct* and *assess* that allows us to respond to what student work shows us they know and do not yet know, before we assign a grade and move on.

John Hattie (2009) calls this the zone of "what happens next" and describes it as a *feedback loop*. In this conception of learning, formative and summative assessments each play a role, but they are in balance (Figure 2.5). The feedback loop begins with a "knowledge-eliciting activity"—what students do in response to instruction. Teachers examine student responses—the "assessment." Then teachers and students take action based on what students' responses reveal. The next step may be to offer feedback to the student, but it may not be. Feedback isn't always the best teaching tool: identification of the student's learning need determines whether feedback is the appropriate next step or whether further instruction is called for (Wiliam, 2013).

This feedback loop was missing from the beginning instruction of most of us veteran teachers. We planned for instructing, but not for learning. When our students did something in response to instruction, we were not prepared to "loop back" and help them move further along the continuum of learning, either by giving feedback to focus their revisions or by reteaching the parts not yet learned.

When formative and summative assessment purposes are in balance in the classroom, we use formative assessment first to seek evidence of what students do

figure 2.5 ■ Balanced Formative and Summative Assessment Model of Teaching

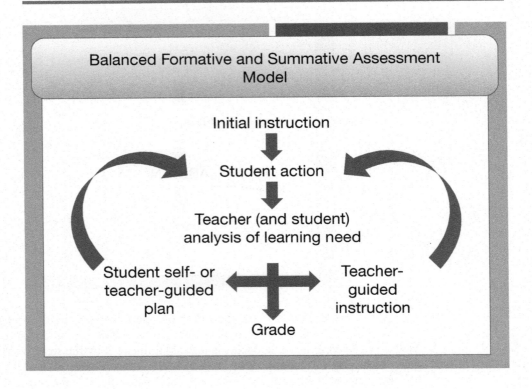

not "get." We make sure our assessment processes and instruments have sufficient instructional traction to identify specific learning needs for each student throughout a unit or teaching cycle. And we plan time in our teaching cycle to respond to each student's learning needs so we can move all students forward to the point of mastery. Assessing for a grade is what we do last, after the practice events, feedback, and revision opportunities have caused increases in learning. Summative assessment is quite important—we must know how to create fair and defensible grades that represent achievement accurately. However, summative assessment can and often does happen too soon in the teaching cycle: when everything that students do is worth points that count toward a grade, everything is summative, thus introducing accountability for having learned before sufficient opportunity to accomplish it.

Wiliam (2013, p. 205), citing Crooks' research, reports the following effects of students' experiencing a steady diet of summative assessment:

■ Reduction in intrinsic motivation
■ Increase in text anxiety

- Increased ability attributions (attributing success or failure to innate intelligence or lack of it), which undermines effort
- Lowered self-efficacy in struggling students

> With summative assessment, we welcome having learned. With formative assessment, we welcome the learning journey.

MyEdLab

Video Example 2.1

Using Assessment Results to Guide Learning

On the other hand, if we make space for students to "grow" their learning before points and grades are assigned, we can help students understand that "not knowing" is not a problem, it's a place on a continuum that all successful learners pass through. Making space for learning and emphasizing learning as the goal also helps students drop a *task-completion* orientation –"I'm doing this because it's worth points"—and develop a *learning* orientation—"I'm doing this because it's worth learning." Watch Video Example 2.1 to hear teachers and students describe the impact of using assessment results to shape action.

So the first step in the development or selection of any assessment is to determine its purpose. Why are you doing it? Who will use the results and what will those results help you (them) accomplish? Figure 2.6 is a form you can use to work through the planning decisions of this first step.

figure 2.6 ▪ Assessment Development Step 1: Clear Purpose

Name of Assessment:

Who will use the information?
- Teacher
- Student
- Other

How will the information be used?
- To plan instruction
- To differentiate instruction
- To offer feedback to students
- To use for student self-assessment and goal setting
- To measure level of achievement for an end-of-term grade
- Other

What types of information will be needed?
- Formative
- Summative

If formative, does it meet the following conditions?
- The instrument or event provides information of sufficient detail to pinpoint specific problems, such as misunderstandings, so that teachers (and students, if appropriate) can make good decisions about what actions to take.
- The results are available in time to take action with the students who generated them.

Balanced Assessment throughout the School System

One of the challenges school districts face is in crafting a multilevel, balanced assessment system to ensure that the information needs of all instructional decision makers are met. Because the teacher's role is to engage in sound assessment practices in the classroom (as just discussed previously), the classroom level of Figure 2.3 will be the focus of most of our attention in the chapters that follow. In addition, however, you may be involved in the development of local benchmark, interim, or common assessments and the content of this book will prepare you to do that as well. It will also be important to understand the purposes for the other assessments your students will be taking (as represented by the district and state levels in Figure 2.3) and the appropriate use of the resulting information.

Formative and Summative Uses of District Benchmark, Interim, and Common Assessments   It is increasingly common for teacher teams, schools, and districts to adopt or develop and administer assessments periodically throughout the school year to track student progress in mastering pre-established achievement standards. These assessments can be purchased from a test publisher, developed in-district, or provided by the state or other entity. These tests can be used formatively to answer questions such as the following:

- Are there particular standards that our students struggle to master?
- How can we improve our instruction on those standards right now?
- What patterns of student success emerge, and what patterns of difficulty can be identified?
- Can we identify individual students or groups of students who are struggling?
- What assistance can be provided right now to help these students before the annual accountability test?

We see the following patterns emerge from district-level uses summarized in Figure 2.3:

- The decisions to be made often focus on the instructional program or on groups of students in the classroom.
- Because such decisions are made periodically, the assessment need only be periodic.
- The results are most helpful when they can show how each student is doing in mastering *each* standard. Assessments that sample many standards and blend results into a single overall score will not help due to their low resolution results, that is, their lack of sufficient instructional detail.
- At this level, reliance is placed on using assessment results from instruments or procedures held constant across classrooms, sometimes termed *common* assessments. In other words, some standardization is required if sound information and good programmatic decisions are to result.

figure 2.7 ■ Comparing Classroom and Interim Levels of Formative Assessment Use

	Classroom Level	Interim Level
Achievement focus	Student progress toward each standard	Student mastery of each standard
Student focus	Results provide achievement info for each individual student separately	Results are aggregated across students to summarize group results
Frequency of assessment	Continuous	Periodic
Results inform	Student and teacher	Teachers and school leaders
Key instructional decision	What comes next in the learning?	How can instruction be improved?
Consistency of assessment	Can be unique to an individual student	Typically standardized across students (same test for all)

Interim assessments also can serve two kinds of summative purposes. One takes the form of program evaluation in which the purpose of data gathering is to test the level of success of the program under school or district scrutiny. For example, is this program of instruction effective and worth continuing (or purchasing), or should it be abandoned or replaced? A second summative application of an interim assessment occurs when a school or district decides to gather evidence of student mastery of individual standards one or a few at a time periodically throughout the year rather than testing all relevant standards at once at the end of the year. In this case, each such summative assessment would need to provide compelling evidence of student mastery of its particular standard(s).

Comparing Classroom and Interim Formative Uses   Both classroom and interim assessments are important, because they can inform decisions that, if made well, can influence student learning while instruction is still taking place. But it is important that you understand that they are different, and that they accomplish different things. Figure 2.7 highlights the differences.

Annual Testing

The final level of assessment serves teachers and principals, curriculum directors and other district-level administrators, state-level leaders and policy makers, and community members by providing evidence of achievement annually on standardized tests. These can take the form of districtwide, statewide, national, or even international examinations. Based on the assessment results received, users make comparisons to similar districts or states to identify those in need of help, allocate resources to overcome weaknesses, set procedural policies that guide instructional practices, identify groups of students at risk, and use results to evaluate the impact of commercial instructional programs. And so, once again at this level, we can identify formative and summative uses.

We can make the following generalizations about annual testing on the basis of the information in Figure 2.3:

- On the summative side, they ask: Who attained mastery of each standard? Did enough students achieve mastery? What can be inferred about overall school effectiveness?
- On the formative side, the key question is the same as with interim assessments: Which standards do students consistently struggle to master? Where do we need to improve our programs long term? Can we identify students or groups of students in need of additional instruction/assistance?
- As with the interim level, data are summarized across students to fulfill program improvement and accountability needs.
- As with the interim level, periodic assessment will suffice—typically once a year.
- At this level too, assessment procedures must be standardized across contexts and over time—the decisions to be made require it.

A note of caution regarding this level of assessment is warranted here. Because of the large numbers of students tested in annual districtwide or statewide testing programs, the costs of test development, administration, scoring, and reporting are high. For this reason, this level of assessment has traditionally relied on the most economical of testing formats: multiple-choice tests. When we are limited to only that assessment format, we severely restrict the kinds of achievement targets that can be assessed to mastery of content knowledge and simple patterns of reasoning. More complex learning targets such as multistage reasoning and academic behaviors, which require different assessment methods, typically have been left out. We will illustrate this problem in greater detail in later chapters. But for now, suffice it to say, total reliance on the selected response testing format to yield only gross test scores annually has caused their results to be representative of achievement on only a portion of the content standards in any given subject and those results are of extremely limited use for day-to-day instructional decision-making in the classroom.

MyEdLab **Self-Check 2.3**

MyEdLab **Application Exercise 2.2** Formative assessment and summative assessment in a balanced assessment system

■ Assessment for Learning in the Classroom

In recent years, a special type of formative assessment has emerged that places a high priority on meeting students' information needs, as well as those of teachers. This type of formative assessment plays out while students are learning and so is known as *assessment for learning*. Its purpose is to support student growth by using the assessment process to keep them in touch with the development of their own academic capabilities as they learn. The effect of this ongoing feedback system is to keep students believing that ultimate success is within reach if they keep trying. The confidence-building and motivational effects of this way of assessing can be profoundly positive. The learning gains associated with consistent reliance on assessment for learning strategies have turned it into one of our most important purposes for assessment.

Those strategies serve the purpose of supporting learning by connecting assessment very tightly to students, their learning targets, and their mastery of those standards. We teach the strategies in a framework of seven strategies that apply high-impact formative assessment practices across disciplines, content standards, and grade levels. (Think back to Black and Wiliam's three categories of high-impact practices [1998b]: use of evidence gathered during instruction to determine next steps; provision of feedback during the learning with guidance on how to improve; and development of student self-assessment and peer-feedback skills.) The seven strategies are organized by three questions, "Where am I going?", "Where am I now?", and "How can I close the gap?" derived from the three conditions Sadler (1989) contends are necessary for students to improve:

- They know what high-quality work looks like ("Where am I going?")
- They are able to objectively compare their work to the standard ("Where am I now?")
- They have a store of tactics to make work better based on their observations ("How can I close the gap?")

The seven strategies, some of which are teacher actions and some of which are student actions, reflect practices that have always been a part of good teaching (see Figure 2.8). What may be new is their strategic use, focusing on ways both we and

figure 2.8 ■ Seven Strategies of Assessment for Learning

Where Am I Going?
Strategy 1: Provide students with a clear and understandable vision of the learning target.
Strategy 2: Use examples and models of strong and weak work.

Where Am I Now?
Strategy 3: Offer regular descriptive feedback during the learning.
Strategy 4: Teach students to self-assess and set goals for next steps.

How Can I Close the Gap?
Strategy 5: Use evidence of student learning needs to determine next steps in teaching.
Strategy 6: Design focused instruction, followed by practice with feedback.
Strategy 7: Provide students opportunites to track, reflect on, and share their learning progress.

Source: Chappuis, Jan, *Seven Strategies Of Assessment For Learning*, 2nd Ed., ©2015. Reprinted and Electronically reproduced by permission of Pearson Education, Inc., New York, New York.

our students can use assessment intentionally and in collaborative ways to support learning. The strategies are described briefly here; specific applications will be explained in more detail at the end of each chapter.

Where Am I Going?

Strategy 1: Provide a Clear and Understandable Vision of the Learning Target.   The opening step in this use of assessment to support learning is to give students a vision of the learning destination. We share with our students the learning targets, objectives, or goals either at the outset of instruction or before they begin an independent practice activity during instruction. It is important to check to make sure students understand what learning target is at the heart of the lesson by asking, "Why are we doing this activity? What are we going to be learning?" Strategy 1 helps students develop a learning goal orientation and direct their effort to important features of the task. It also prepares students to think more deeply and accurately about what constitutes quality.

Strategy 2: Use Examples and Models of Strong and Weak Work.   To help students sort through and come to see what is and isn't quality work we can share strong and weak models from anonymous student work, examples from life beyond school, and from our own work. We ask students to analyze these samples for quality and then justify their judgments. When we engage students in analyzing examples or models, they develop a vision of what the knowledge, understanding, skill, product, or performance looks like when it's executed well. Engaging with Strategy 2 provides the following benefits:

- It helps students develop a more refined vision of the differences between high- and low-quality work—a vision that is more closely aligned to that of the teacher.
- It helps students become better able to produce work at higher levels of quality on the first try if they have engaged in Strategy 2.
- It prepares students to understand and act on feedback.
- It helps prepare students to self-assess.
- It helps prepare students to offer effective peer feedback.

Where Am I Now?

Strategy 3: Offer Regular Descriptive Feedback during the Learning.   When students' work demonstrates at least partial mastery of the learning target, they are ready to receive feedback. Effective feedback identifies strengths and areas for improvement with respect to the specific learning target(s) they are trying to achieve in a given assignment. It helps students answer the question, "Where am I now?" with respect to "Where do I need to be?" and it points the way to "How can I close the gap?" With those insights in mind, we can offer feedback, instead of grades, on work that is for practice and give students opportunities to act on it and improve before being held accountable for mastery. Giving students time to practice after offering feedback allows them to grow with guidance. Also, providing this kind of feedback models the kind of thinking you want students to engage in when they self-assess and identify next steps. Additionally, research literature reveals strong learning gains attributable to peer feedback (c.f., White & Frederiksen, 1998). To offer each other useful feedback, students must understand the intended learning targets, objectives, or goals (Strategy 1); be clear about how to distinguish levels of quality (Strategy 2); and have practiced with protocols for offering feedback in a controlled situation (Strategy 3).

Strategy 4: Teach Students to Self-Assess and Set Goals for Next Steps.   With this strategy, we transfer the ownership of learning to the student. In essence, when we teach students to self-assess and set goals, we teach them to generate their own feedback. To be accurate self-assessors, students need a clear vision of the intended learning (Strategy 1), practice with identifying strengths and weaknesses in a variety of examples (Strategy 2), and exposure to feedback that models "self-assessment" thinking: "What have I done well? Where do I need to continue working?" (Strategy 3). This strategy is a proven contributor to increased learning and a necessary part of becoming a self-regulated learner. It is *not* what we do only if we have the time or if we have the "right" students, for example, those who can already do it. Monitoring and regulating their own learning can be taught to all kinds of students, including those with mild to moderate learning disabilities (Andrade, 2010). While assessment for learning strategies work well for all students, struggling students have the most to gain from learning how to do this kind of thinking.

How Can I Close the Gap?

Strategy 5: Use Evidence of Student Learning Needs to Determine Next Steps in Teaching.   With this strategy, we build a feedback loop into the teaching cycle, checking for understanding and continuing instruction guided by information about what students have and have not yet mastered. After having delivered a lesson and after students have done something in response, we use what they have done to determine further learning needs. Do their responses reveal incomplete understanding, flawed reasoning, or misconceptions? Are they ready to receive feedback? Strategy 5 includes a repertoire of approaches to diagnose the type of student learning needs in preparation for addressing them.

Strategy 6: Design Focused Instruction, Followed by Practice with Feedback. This strategy scaffolds learning by narrowing the focus of a lesson to address specific misconceptions or problems identified in Strategy 5. If you are working on a learning target having more than one aspect of quality, it is critically important to build competence one block at a time by addressing one component at a time. After delivering instruction targeted to an area of need, let students practice and get better before reassessing. Give them opportunities to revise their work, product, or performance, based on feedback focused just on that area of need prior to the graded event. This narrows the volume of feedback students, especially struggling learners, need to attend to at a given time and raises their chances of success in doing so. It is a time-saver for you and more instructionally powerful for students.

Strategy 7: Provide Opportunities for Students to Track, Reflect on, and Share Their Learning Progress. Any activity that requires students to reflect on what they are learning and to share their progress reinforces the learning and helps them develop insights into themselves as learners. These kinds of activities give students the opportunity to notice their own strengths, to see how far they have come, and to feel in control of the conditions of their success. By reflecting on their learning, they deepen their understanding and remember it longer. By sharing their progress, students develop a deeper commitment to making progress.

The Seven Strategies as a Progression

These seven strategies are not a recipe to be followed step by step, although they do build on one another. Strategy 4 (engaging students in self-assessment and goal setting) and Strategy 7 (tracking, reflecting on, and sharing learning progress) are "destinations," Strategies 1 through 3 (making the target clear, using a range of examples, and providing feedback) are "enablers," and Strategies 5 and 6 (identifying learning needs and offering targeted instruction with sufficient time to practice) are "floaters." The destination strategies are where we want students to arrive as a result of being learners in our classrooms. These essential learnings can be developed starting as early as prekindergarten. The enabler strategies, especially Strategies 1 and 2, generally have been undervalued, and yet without them—without a clear picture of where we are going—it is hard to determine where we are now and even harder to identify actions to close the gap. Imagine attempting to get from Point A to Point B using a GPS system that only gives your current location, which is akin to what grades do. Strategies 1 and 2 equip the GPS system with information it needs to communicate next steps. The floater strategies 5 and 6 can happen any time and often employ the use of the preceding strategies as part of the lessons. Taken together, these formative assessment strategies represent actions that will strengthen students' sense of self-efficacy (their belief that effort will lead to improvement), their motivation to try, and ultimately, their achievement.

MyEdLab
Video Example 2.2
Developing a Learning Culture in the Classroom

Watch Video Example 2.2 to hear a teacher and students discussing the classroom learning environment created by the use of the formative assessment practices embedded in the seven strategies and the impact it has had on their achievement. For an example of how a teacher uses student self-assessment to help gauge level of understanding, read sixth-grade teacher Kristen Gillespie's explanation in Figure 2.9. For an example of how they use strong and weak examples, read the explanation provided by fourth-grade teachers Jessica Barylski, Audrey Eckert, and Robyn Eidam in Figure 2.10.

figure 2.9 ■ From the Classroom: Kristen Gillespie

I used to . . .

At the end of a class I would ask if there were any questions. I left it up to the individual to raise his or her hand to signal the level of understanding and ask questions.

Now I . . .

Each student is assigned a sticky note with his or her name on it. When prompted, students move their names to one of three boards. One board states that the child is on track and feels comfortable with the information from class. The second board signals to me that the child still has some questions and needs more practice. The third board lets me know that the child needs individual attention to understand the material. Students are asked to move their sticky notes approximately 3–5 times per week.

Why I changed. . .

I noticed that it was simply easier and less embarrassing for the student to not raise his or her hand when asked if anyone needed clarification. I realized that each student had to take more responsibility for his or her own learning. Student self-evaluation is priceless, not only to the student but also the teacher. I wanted to create an environment where students practiced self-monitoring and made deliberate decisions about their comprehension levels.

What I notice as a result . . .

The students look forward to moving their sticky notes. Those on the first board feel satisfied and proud of themselves. On the other hand, the students on the other two boards get the extra help they need, ultimately leading to a feeling of success.

Over the course of the school year, students realize that placing their sticky notes in the accurate location has rewards. My students are able to self-assess and get additional help thereby avoiding a poor test grade.

Source: Reproduced with permission from Kristen Gillespie, 6th-grade Mathematics, Reading, and English Teacher, Olmsted Falls City Schools.

figure 2.10 ■ From the Classroom: Jessica Barylski, Audrey Eckert, and Robyn Eidam

We used to . . .

When concluding a writing lesson, we used to have students conduct a peer review of their work with a partner. We would provide them with checklists and tell them to use these checklists, assuming that they would know what to do. While students were giving each other feedback, we would monitor their conversations. We noticed that students simply read their writing pieces to each other and gave very few suggestions to improve their writing because they believed that was what peer review was.

Now we . . .

We have begun providing strong and weak examples in many of our lessons. To introduce peer review now, we list the criteria for quality peer feedback. Then we show the students a videotape of ourselves modeling weak and strong examples of peer feedback. Including this component adds a visual model to help the students engage. As students watch the clips, they are looking for the criteria that will help them identify the strong example. After thoroughly discussing each video clip, the students apply the peer feedback criteria to their own writing pieces.

Why we changed . . .

Peer feedback was often an area of difficulty for students due to its higher level of thinking. Students never really understood how to participate in the peer review process beyond reading the paragraph and we, as teachers, knew we needed to find a better way to teach them. When we began using formative assessment practices in our classrooms, we became more aware of how using strong and weak examples can impact student learning.

What we notice as a result . . .

First and foremost, the skills the students acquired from this activity were above and beyond our expectations. The students were engaged and focused throughout not only the videos but also during their peer feedback conferences. It was more meaningful for them to see their teachers engaged in a video that was outside of their normal routine. They took ownership of their peer review process, they followed the peer feedback model and criteria, and they took their time and allowed for corrections. They used constructive criticism and their conversations were more meaningful than in the past. We saw growth and improvement in our students' final writing pieces as well.

Source: Reprinted with permission from Jessica Barylski, 4th-grade Language Arts Team teacher, Olmsted Falls Intermediate School.; Reprinted with permission from Audrey Eckert, 4th-grade Language Arts Team teacher, Olmsted Falls Intermediate School.; Reprinted with permission from Robyn Eidam, 4th-grade Language Arts Team teacher, Olmsted Falls Intermediate School.

MyEdLab **Self-Check 2.4**

MyEdLab **Application Exercise 2.3** Research-based strategies for implementing formative assessment practices

■ Summary: Assessment for Many Purposes

For any assessment to work well, it must be developed with a clear purpose in mind: What decision(s) will it inform, who will be making the decision(s), and what kind of information and in what form is likely to be helpful? Therefore, the starting place for the creation and use of any assessment are these two questions: Why am I assessing? How will the results be used?

One level of assessment use is the classroom. Teachers and students use assessment information as a feedback loop to determine learning successes and needs during the learning. Teachers also use assessment information to evaluate level of mastery on content standards after learning is supposed to have occurred. Both teachers and students need a steady flow of assessment information to guide next steps. Teachers also need to collect summative assessment evidence over the course of a grading period in order to complete report cards.

Another level of assessment use focuses attention on student achievement on an interim basis, typically across classrooms, and sometimes schools. Teacher teams, principals, and curriculum personnel may use these periodic assessments to gather information on which standards are and are not being mastered by individual students and groups of students, and which curricular and instructional programs are working and which need adjustment.

Finally, there is the annual district or policy level of assessment use where school, district, and state leaders use assessment to evaluate which students, schools, and districts are performing effectively by helping students meet standards. This is the high-stakes accountability level of the annual standardized achievement tests typically administered statewide or districtwide.

When a school district's assessment system provides needed information to all assessment users and all three of these levels—classroom, interim, and annual—and all relevant purposes are being served, we think of that system as being balanced. Classroom teachers have always been and always will be key players in the balancing of these systems.

One unique contribution teachers can make to the balance of local assessment systems—a contribution that can be made by no one else—is to incorporate assessment practices into daily instruction that meet students' decision-making needs. In this way the seven strategies of assessment for learning introduced in this chapter offer a sequence of research-based practices that link *assessment* and *learning*. They meet both teachers' and students' information needs in ways that maximize both motivation and achievement by involving students from the start in their own learning.

While all levels of use are important because they provide valuable information, in this book we will center mostly on the classroom, where the classroom teacher is responsible for ensuring the accuracy of the evidence gathered and for the effective use of that information both formatively and summatively.

■ Suggested Activities

End-of-chapter activities are intended to help you master the chapter's learning targets. They are designed to deepen your understanding of the chapter content, provide opportunities for personal reflection on ideas presented, and serve as a basis for discussion among peers. You may wish to do all of them or select those that you believe will be most useful to your learning. Each activity is correlated to one or more chapter learning targets to help with your selection.

Chapter 2 Learning Targets

As a result of your study of Chapter 2, you will be able to do the following:

1. Define the meaning of the terms *formative assessment* and *summative assessment*
2. Understand the positive impact of formative assessment on student achievement
3. Understand how formative assessment and summative assessment fit into a balanced assessment system
4. Understand research-based strategies for implementing formative assessment practices in the classroom

Chapter 2 Activities

Activity 2.1   Keeping a Reflective Journal (All chapter learning targets)

Activity 2.2   Auditing One of Your Courses for Balanced Assessment (Learning Targets 1 and 3)

Activity 2.3   Summarizing the Seven Strategies of Assessment for Learning (Learning Targets 2 and 4)

Activity 2.4   Comparing Your Experiences with Information from the Chapter (All chapter learning targets)

Activity 2.5   Answering an Interview Question (All chapter learning targets)

Activity 2.6   Reflecting on Your Learning from Chapter 2 (All chapter learning targets)

Activity 2.7   Adding to Your Growth Portfolio (All chapter learning targets)

Activity 2.1: Keeping a Reflective Journal

Keep a record of your thoughts, questions, and insights as you read Chapter 2.

Activity 2.2: Auditing One of Your Courses for Balanced Assessment

In this activity, you will use assignments and assessments you have completed for a course you are taking now or have recently taken.

1. List the assignments and assessments you have completed for the course.
2. For each, identify whether it was formative in nature or summative in nature. Provide a brief explanation of why it was formative or summative. (Hint: If it was figured into the end-of-course grade, it was summative.)
3. Make note of your answers to the following questions:
   - What is the ratio of formative to summative use of assessment results for this course?
   - After having read Chapter 2, what do you think the ideal ratio for this course should be?
   - Why?
   - What, if any, changes to the ratio would you recommend?
4. Write a short summary of your findings and your thoughts about the ratio. Include a description of suggested changes and rationale for them. If you do not think changes are needed, explain why. If appropriate, share your summary with the instructor of the course you have analyzed.

Activity 2.3: Summarizing the Seven Strategies of Assessment for Learning

Write a brief explanation of each of the seven strategies. Explain one benefit the strategy will provide to students and/or teachers. Describe one problem its absence might cause.

Activity 2.4: Comparing Your Experiences with Information from the Chapter

Read one of the "From the Classroom" entries in Chapter 2 and compare it to your experience as a student.

How is it similar?

What differences do you notice?

What conclusions about the benefits of formative assessment might you draw?

Activity 2.5: Answering an Interview Question

Imagine that you are about to interview for a teaching position. The interview team (often a combination of administrators and teachers) is interested in understanding your level of classroom assessment literacy. Review Chapter 2's learning targets and think about what concepts and procedures were most significant to you from the chapter. Then think about what type of question an interview team might ask related to this significant learning. Write the question and draft a short response—one that you could give in one to two minutes orally.

Activity 2.6: Reflecting on Your Learning from Chapter 2

Review the Chapter 2 learning targets and select one that struck you as most significant from this chapter. Write a short reflection that captures your current understanding. If you are working with a group, discuss what you have written.

Activity 2.7: Adding to Your Growth Portfolio

Any of the activities from this chapter can be used as entries for your own growth portfolio. Select activities you have completed or artifacts you have created that will illustrate your mastery of Chapter 2 learning targets:

1. Define the meaning of the terms *formative assessment* and *summative assessment*
2. Understand the positive impact of formative assessment on student achievement
3. Understand how formative assessment and summative assessment fit into a balanced assessment system
4. Understand research-based strategies for implementing formative assessment practices in the classroom

What We Assess: Clear Learning Targets

Chapter 3 Learning Targets

As a result of your study of Chapter 3, you will be able to do the following:

1. Explain the necessity of clear targets to assessment quality
2. Classify learning targets by type
3. Deconstruct learning targets as needed
4. Select from options for sharing learning targets with students

In Chapter 2, we established that valid classroom assessments arise from and serve clear purposes. So in every context, we must know why we are assessing—that is, who will use the assessment and how will they use it. Different users need different information in different forms at different times to do their jobs. Every assessment must be valid for its intended purpose; that is, it must be designed so that its results can be used for that purpose.

In this chapter, we move on to the second key to excellence in classroom assessment: *Clear Targets* (Figure 3.1). It is entirely possible to create an assignment, have students complete it, score it, and derive a grade without a clear understanding of the intended learning. What learning have they practiced? What learning is at the heart of their work? The score and the grade are meaningless if we can't attach a learning goal to the level of achievement: a "B" for what?

As we discussed in Chapter 2, assessments that appropriately represent the intended learning are said to have *content validity*; that is, a student's score supports valid inferences about the student's mastery of the material taught and tested. If we have difficulty articulating our achievement targets, it is unlikely we will be able to create lessons to help students master them or develop exercises and scoring procedures that assess them. In addition, only when the type of target is clear can we select an assessment method capable of reflecting the learning accurately. Further, we will find it difficult to share with our students a clear picture of what they are to learn if we ourselves don't begin with a clear picture. Valid, reliable, and fair assessments arise from and accurately reflect clear and appropriate achievement targets. In preparation for teaching and assessing we must ask, "What do I expect my students to learn?"

figure 3.1 ■ Keys to Quality Assessment

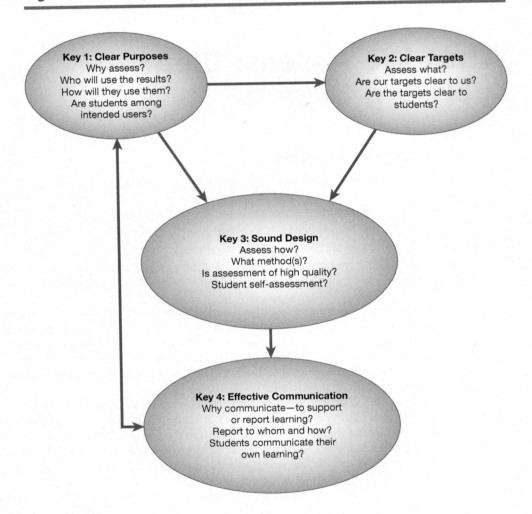

■ Defining Learning Targets

Learning targets define academic success—they state what we want students to know and be able to do. Visualize a target with its concentric circles and a bull's-eye in the middle. The bull's-eye describes the highest level of performance students can achieve: a high-quality piece of writing, the most fluent oral reading, the strongest level of performance on a math problem-solving exercise. This center circle represents the

figure 3.2 ■ Writing a Good Introduction

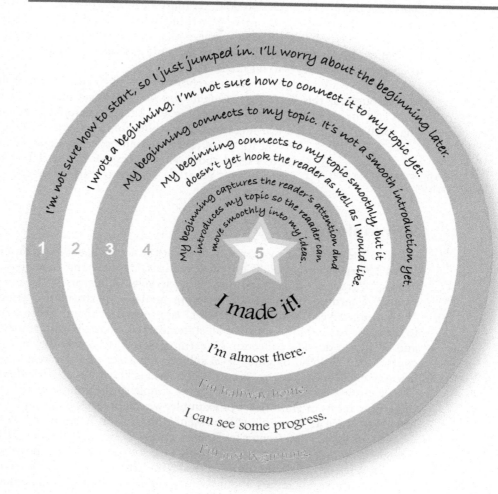

I'm not sure how to start, so I just jumped in. I'll worry about the beginning later.

I wrote a beginning. I'm not sure how to connect it to my topic yet.

My beginning connects to my topic. It's not a smooth introduction yet.

My beginning connects to my topic smoothly but it doesn't yet hook the reader as well as I would like.

My beginning captures the reader's attention and introduces my topic so the reader can move smoothly into my ideas.

1 2 3 4 5

I made it!

I'm almost there.

I'm halfway home.

I can see some progress.

I'm just beginning.

ultimate learning target—the level students are aiming to hit. Beginning at the outermost edge, each ring defines a level of performance closer to proficiency; as students improve, they progress from the outer rings toward the bull's-eye. Figure 3.2 shows an example of this concept applied to one aspect of high-quality writing: writing a good introduction.

Our mission as teachers in standards-driven schools is to help all of our students "get there." To reach that goal, we must know exactly where "there" is. What are the attributes of a good piece of writing? How does this level of performance differ from performance of lesser quality—that is, from the outer rings of the target? In Chapter 1, we saw that Ms. Weathersby and her students knew what was needed to progress to mastery—to hit the bull's-eye.

We have adopted the target metaphor to allow us to point out now and repeatedly throughout this book that *students can hit any target that they see and that holds still for them.* But if they are guessing at what success looks like, in effect putting forth effort to hit a learning target while blindfolded, success will be a random event for them. There should never be a question in the student's mind about what success looks like. The only question should be, "What do I need to learn to achieve success in those terms?"

> Students can hit any target they can see that holds still for them.

Terminology

Districts and states use a variety of labels for the achievement expectations we have called "learning targets." "Content standards," "goals and objectives," "benchmarks," "grade-level expectations," "grade-level indicators," "learning progressions," "learning outcomes," "learning goals," "performance expectations," "lesson objectives," and "competencies" are several of them. These terms all refer to the same basic thing—they are all statements of what we want students to know and be able to do. The collection of learning targets (whatever they are called) for a course (e.g., Biology) or grade-level subject (e.g., second-grade reading) written as learning expectations at the unit or lesson level is known as a *curriculum*.

Learning targets can range from the simple to the complex, a feature we can think of in terms of *grain size*. For example, we might think of a simpler lesson-level learning target as a *pebble* ("Represent addition on a number line," National Governors Association Center for Best Practices, CCSS Mathematics, 2010b, p. 48), a moderately complex unit-level learning target as a *rock* ("Use measures of center and measures of variability for numerical data from random samples to draw informal comparative inferences about two populations," National Governors Association Center for Best Practices, CCSS Mathematics, 2010b, p. 50), and a challengingly complex yearlong learning target as a *boulder* ("Reason abstractly and quantitatively," National Governors Association Center for Best Practices, CCSS Mathematics, 2010b, p. 47). We know that it is virtually never the case that students immediately master standards at the rock or boulder size. Rather, over time, students progress through ascending levels of proficiency to a place where they are ready to demonstrate that they have met each of these increasingly complex learning targets. Lesson-level learning

> Lesson-level learning targets are the scaffolding on which students climb to achieve mastery of complex content standards.

targets can be thought of as the scaffolding on which they climb during the process of becoming competent, and they are the focus of day-to-day classroom instruction and assessment. One of your proficiencies as a teacher will be to understand how to unpack, or deconstruct, more complex learning targets into lesson-level targets. We will go into more detail about the deconstructing process later in this chapter.

Where Learning Targets Come From

Districts and states develop curriculum guides on the basis of content standards that have been created by national organizations and consortia and adopted by the state (or approved by the district, in the case of no state-approved adoption). At this level, content standards are usually written as end-of-course standards for the purpose of guiding state- or district-level curriculum development. States and districts use these content standards to create the unit- or lesson-level learning targets that comprise the curriculum.

Content Standards Developed by National Organizations and Consortia

Each subject area has one or more professional organizations linked to it; these organizations develop content standards either separately or collaboratively. Examples of professional organizations active in the United States include the International Reading Association, the National Council of Teachers of English, the National Council of Teachers of Mathematics, the National Academy of Sciences, the American Association for the Advancement of Science, the National Science Teachers Association, the National Council for the Social Studies, the Center for Civic Education, the Geography Education National Implementation Project, the International Society for Technology Education, the National Association for Sport and Physical Education, the American Alliance for Theatre and Education, the Arts Education Partnership, the National Arts and Education Network, the National Association for Music Education, and the American Council on the Teaching of Foreign Language. This list is not exhaustive; you can type a subject area and the word "education" into any search engine and find one or more organizations dedicated to supporting education in that field. We offer this list here to give you a sense of the different groups at work behind developing curriculum in a given area of study. Next we will look briefly at the various organizations that have come together to create content standards in four subject areas: English Language Arts, Mathematics, Science, and Social Studies.

Common Core State Standards for English Language Arts and Mathematics

Content standards known as the Common Core State Standards (CCSS) have been developed in the areas of mathematics and English language arts (reading, writing, speaking, and listening) by representatives of participating states, practicing teachers, content experts, researchers, national organizations, and community groups under the leadership of the National Governors Association Center for Best Practices and the Council of Chief State School Officers. Published in 2010, the CCSS are designed to establish clear, consistent guidelines for what every student should know and be able to do in mathematics and English language arts from kindergarten through twelfth grade to be prepared for today's entry-level careers, freshman-level college courses, and workforce training programs. Additionally, the Common Core State Standards include College and Career-Readiness Standards and Standards for Literacy in History/Social Studies, Science, and Technical Subjects. At this writing, the Common Core State Standards have been adopted by 43 states, the District of Columbia, four territories, and the Department of Defense Education Activity (schools for military dependents).

Next Generation Science Standards   In science, content standards known as the Next Generation Science Standards (NGSS) have been created by a consortium of 26 states, under the leadership of the National Research Council, the National Science Teachers Association, the American Association for the Advancement of Science, and Achieve, Inc., with support from the Carnegie Corporation of New York. Published in 2013, the NGSS represent rigorous, internationally benchmarked science standards developed through collaboration between states and other stakeholders in science, science education, higher education, business, and industry. They also were developed to prepare students well for college and careers.

College, Career, and Civic Life (C3) Framework for Social Studies State Standards   In 2010, the National Council for the Social Studies published the National Curriculum Standards for Social Studies. A year later, a collaborative of over 20 states and 15 social studies content organizations joined together to create the C3 Framework for Social Studies State Standards to guide states in upgrading their social studies standards and to help local districts and schools strengthen their social studies programs. The C3 Framework includes standards for civics, economics, geography, and history. Its three objectives are (a) to enhance rigor; (b) to build critical thinking, problem-solving, and participatory skills; and (c) to ensure inclusion of the Common Core State Standards for English Language Arts and Literacy in History/Social Studies.

MyEdLab **Self-Check 3.1**
MyEdLab **Application Exercise 3.1**   Clearly-defined learning targets in assessment

---

■ Categories of Learning Targets

When content standards have been formatted to function as a curriculum, they take the form of unit- or lesson-level learning targets. These targets represent different kinds of learning. Some call for learning at the knowledge level, some call for the use of knowledge to reason or solve problems, some call for the performance of a physical skill, and some call for the creation of a product that meets standards of quality.

figure 3.3 ■ Categories of Learning Targets

Knowledge Targets
Knowledge targets represent the factual information, procedural knowledge, and conceptual understandings that underpin each discipline.

Reasoning Targets
Reasoning targets specify thought processes students are to learn to do well within a range of subjects.

Performance Skill Targets
Performance skill targets are those where a demonstration or physical skill-based performance is at the heart of the learning.

Product Targets
Product targets describe learning in terms of artifacts where creation of a product is the focus of the learning target. With product targets, the specifications for quality of the product itself are the focus of teaching and assessment.

Disposition Targets
Disposition targets refer to attitudes, motivations, and interests that affect students' approaches to learning. They represent important *affective* goals we hold for students as a byproduct of their educational experience.

Source: Chappuis, Jan; Stiggins, Rick J.; Chappuis, Steve; Arter, Judith A., *Classroom Assessment for Student learning: Doing it Right—Using it Well*, 2nd Ed., ©2012. Reprinted and Electronically reproduced by permission of Pearson Education, Inc., New York, New York.

In addition we have aspirational goals for students, which can be thought of as motivational predispositions (attitudes, values, etc.). These five categories of learning target types (Figure 3.3) were first proposed by Stiggins and Conklin (1992) after an extensive study of the various kinds of learning expectations reflected in classroom instruction and assessments:

■ Knowledge-level learning targets represent factual subject matter content, procedural knowledge of how to execute a series of steps, and conceptual understanding where the intent is to be able to explain a concept.

■ Reasoning-level learning targets define thought processes students are to learn to execute—the ability to use knowledge and conceptual understanding to figure things out and to solve problems, as in scientific inquiry, math problem solving, and comprehension of subject matter text.

■ Performance skill–level targets require the development of physical skills, such as playing a musical instrument, reading aloud fluently, conversing in a second language, or using psychomotor skills.

■ Product-level targets call for the creation of tangible products, such as research papers, models of geometric figures, and works of art.

■ Disposition-level targets specify the development of the attitudes, interests, and motivational intentions that support learning success.

Clear learning targets guide instruction, assignments, and assessment. As you will see, these categories become useful in thinking about classroom assessment because they permit us to think about how they relate to one another in understandable and useful ways and they point the way to how to assess them. Classifying targets according to type prior to instruction offers three significant benefits:

1. Help with knowing how to structure the lesson
2. Help with deconstructing (or "unpacking") a content standard to determine which activities and assignments will lead most effectively to mastery of the target
3. Guidance in selecting the assessment methods that will yield the most accurate achievement data

Classifying learning targets takes some practice, but with time it will become a primary filter to determine both your approach to instruction and the assessment method you will use. We offer the following in-depth explanations of each target type to assist you as you develop this expertise.

Knowledge-Level Targets

Mastery of prerequisite knowledge is essential to success with other levels of achievement; part of our jobs as teachers is to be sure our students learn important content that underpins successful performance in our subject area. Knowledge-level targets fall into one of three subcategories: factual information, procedural knowledge, and conceptual understanding.

Factual Information   When we were in school, we were asked to learn certain facts and information "by heart": what happened in 1066, the authors of the Declaration of Independence, the presidents of the United States, what the symbol "Au" refers to on the periodic table of elements, vocabulary words, and multiplication facts. These are "recall" statements and they are a part of the *Knowledge* category; that is, they specify memorization of factual information. These types of knowledge targets range from the simple, for example, "Know the formula for area of a circle" to the complex, for example, "Acquire and use accurate grade-appropriate general academic and domain-specific words and phrases" (National Governors Association Center for Best Practices, CCSS English Language Arts, 2010a, p. 53).

Beyond knowing information outright, another way of knowing is via reference—knowing where to find needed information. Of all of the information students need, what will we ask them to memorize, and what will we teach them to find? Will they need to memorize the entire list of prepositions (*above, aboard, about...*), the complete table of periodic elements, or the capitals of the 50 U.S. states? Perhaps or perhaps not depending on the context. But preparation to teach knowledge-level targets includes reflecting on which targets students will need to know outright and which targets it makes more sense for students to consult a reference to retrieve.

Procedural Knowledge   Some knowledge-level learning targets call for procedural knowledge: knowing how to execute a protocol or carry out a series of steps. For example, "Apply the distributive property to the expression $3(2 + x)$ to produce the equivalent expression $6 + 3x$" (National Governors Association Center for Best Practices, CCSS Mathematics, 2010b, p. 44). Procedural knowledge involves memorization of the protocol—how to execute each step and the order in which the steps are to be carried out.

Conceptual Understanding The world around us is full of things we know but don't understand. For instance, we may be able to identify a bridge as a suspension bridge, but we may not know how its structure supports weight sufficiently to keep it from falling into the water. When we can explain how a suspension bridge remains intact despite a heavy load, we have knowledge at the conceptual understanding level. Similarly, when we can define the word *watershed* and explain what not to do in a watershed environment and why, we are demonstrating conceptual understanding. If the learning target calls for conceptual understanding, students must learn more than a definition: surely the learning target "Understand that a function is a rule that assigns to each input exactly one output" (National Governors Association Center for Best Practices, CCSS Mathematics, 2010b, p. 55) is not mastered by reciting "A function is a rule that assigns to each input exactly one output." A conceptual understanding target at the knowledge level means that students can explain the concept. We would not call this "low-level" knowledge; conceptual understanding is essential for reasoning effectively in any discipline.

Relationship to Other Targets Content knowledge forms the foundation of all other forms of academic competence. We cannot speak a foreign language unless we know the vocabulary—vocabulary knowledge isn't sufficient, but it is essential. We cannot solve science problems unless we bring science knowledge to the table or find algebra solutions without conceptual understanding in that domain. We suggest that it is time to retire the term *higher-order thinking* because it implies that "lower-order thinking," traditionally defined as mastery of content knowledge, is less important. If "less important" means we don't expect students to master important content knowledge and conceptual understandings, we deny our students access to the platform they need to engage in productive reasoning using that knowledge. Without a foundation of relevant knowledge in any context, problem solutions remain beyond reach. For this reason, you will find no further reference to higher- or lower-order thinking in this book. Rather, we will honor the acquisition of useful knowledge and the ability to use it to reason, solve problems, perform skillfully, and create high-quality products all as valuable components of a rigorous education.

> Content knowledge provides the foundation of other forms of academic competence.

Examples of knowledge-level learning targets can be found in Figure 3.4.

Reasoning-Level Targets

Reasoning learning targets specify thought processes students are to learn to apply effectively within a range of subjects, for example, solve problems, make inferences, draw conclusions, and form and justify judgments. Mastering content knowledge is

figure 3.4 ■ For Example: Knowledge Targets

Subject	Learning Target
English Language Arts	1. Use an apostrophe to form contractions and frequently occurring possessives. 2. Explain the function of verbals (gerunds, participles, infinitives) in general and their function in particular sentences.
Mathematics	3. Recognize area as an attribute of plane figures and understand concepts of area measurement. 4. Understand that statistics can be used to gain information by examining a sample of the population.
Science	5. (Understand that) plants depend on water and light to grow. 6. Define a variety of cell structures.
Social Studies	7. Explain what governments are and some of their functions. 8. Explain the powers and limits of the three branches of government.
Health/Physical Education	9. Describe how each food group contributes to a healthy body. 10. Describe barriers to physical activities and strategies to overcome them.
The Arts	11. Identify and write notes on a treble clef. 12. Identify and describe elements of design in a work of art.

Sources:
1: Grade 2 *CCSSI Language Standards*, p. 13
2: Grade 8 *CCSSI Language Standards*, p. 52
3: Grade 3 *CCSSI Mathematics Standards*, p. 25
4: Grade 7 *Mathematics CCSS*, p. 51
5: Grade 2 *NGSS*, p. 18
7: Grades K–2 *C-3 Framework*, p. 32
8: Grades 6–8 *C-3 Framework*, p. 32 Reprinted with permission from National Academy of Sciences.
9: Grade 2 *Washington State Health and Fitness Standards*, p. 4
https://www.k12.wa.us/HealthFitness/Standards.aspx
10: High school *Washington State Health and Fitness Standards*, p.6
https://www.k12.wa.us/HealthFitness/Standards.aspx
11 and 12: North Thurston Public Schools K–12 Arts Curriculum

not the sole aim of education today. Students must also develop the ability to apply knowledge in authentic contexts—those contexts that transfer to the workplace and to life beyond school.

Each subject-area curriculum includes reasoning processes such as *predict, infer, hypothesize, estimate, classify, compare, summarize, draw conclusions, analyze, evaluate,* and *justify.* The collection of reasoning processes found in the various academic disciplines can be classified into one of six overall patterns: inference, analysis, comparison, classification, evaluation, and synthesis (Figure 3.5). These six patterns encompass those reasoning proficiencies most commonly found in various taxonomies and content standards as well as in the application of academic disciplines in life beyond school.

figure 3.5 ■ Common Patterns of Reasoning

Inference: Making a reasonable guess based on information or clues

Analysis: Examining the components or structure of something

Comparison: Describing similarities and differences between two or more items

Classification: Sorting things into categories based on certain characteristics

Evaluation: Expressing and defending an opinion, a point of view, a judgment, or a decision

Synthesis: Combining discrete elements to create something new

---

Source: Chappuis, Jan; Stiggins, Rick J.; Chappuis, Steve; Arter, Judith A., *Classroom Assessment for Student learning: Doing it Right—Using it Well*, 2nd Ed., ©2012. Reprinted and Electronically reproduced by permission of Pearson Education, Inc., New York, New York.

Inference   An *inference* is a reasonable guess or conclusion based on information. Inferences can take one of two forms: *inductive* or *deductive*. When we make an inductive inference, we use evidence or facts to infer a general rule or principle. Sound inductive reasoning requires that we select relevant evidence or facts, interpret them accurately, and then draw careful conclusions based on them. Examples of inductive inference include the following:

- Identifying the main idea
- Predicting
- Making analogies
- Generalizing
- Hypothesizing

A deductive inference also involves drawing a conclusion based on information. We can engage in deductive reasoning in two ways. The first is to begin with a general rule or principle and then infer a specific conclusion or solution. To do this well, we apply the general rule to a specific case and draw a plausible conclusion about that specific case.

General rule: *All people get mad sometimes.*

Specific case: *Mom (a person)*

Conclusion: *Mom gets mad sometimes.*

A second way to make a deductive inference is to begin with a set of premises that we know to be true and then infer a specific conclusion or solution.

Premise 1: *Boston is east of Chicago.*

Premise 2: *Chicago is east of Salt Lake City.*

Conclusion: *Boston is east of Salt Lake City.*

Analysis   When we *reason analytically*, we examine the components or structure of something. We undertake analysis to understand something more deeply, to see how it works, to provide an interpretation of it, or to evaluate it. Analysis often requires that we investigate how the components relate to each other or how they come together to form a whole. For students to be successful, they must be able to identify the parts of something and then have practice at describing the relationships among the parts or between the parts and the whole. Examples of analytical thinking include the following:

- Analyzing a controversial decision, identifying arguments for and against a particular action
- Conducting an experiment to analyze a compound to determine its component chemicals
- Determining the meaning of unknown words by breaking them into prefixes, suffixes, and root words

Comparison   Describing similarities and differences between two or more items is at the heart of *comparative reasoning*. In this definition, comparative reasoning encompasses both *compare*—to find similarities—and *contrast*—to find differences. Venn diagrams and T-charts are two common graphic organizers used to help students understand the structure of comparative reasoning.

In the simplest form of comparison, students can say how two things are alike or different. In its more complex form, students first select appropriate items to compare, then select salient features to base their comparison on, and, last, perform the actual comparison (Marzano, Pickering, & McTighe, 1993).

The act of contrasting can also take the form of *juxtaposition*, whereby we place two significantly different things, such as objects, emotions, thoughts, melodies, colors, textures, arguments, or people, side by side to define each in sharp relief or to cause the differences between them to stand out distinctly. *Contrast*, used in this sense, is a device we manipulate for effect in areas such as writing, music, art, and drama.

Classification   *Classification* can be thought of as sorting things into categories based on certain characteristics. In its simpler form, classification consists of sorting objects into predetermined, carefully defined categories. To sort well at this basic level, students need practice at identifying and observing the pertinent characteristics that will help them determine in which category the object belongs.

A more complex classification exercise requires students to select or create the categories and then do the sorting. The game "Twenty Questions" is an exercise in creating categories. The first question might be, "Is it an animal?" to classify the object by general type. The next question could be, "Is it bigger than a bread box?" to classify the object according to size. The third question might be, "Does it live around here?" to narrow possibilities according to habitat. The trick in Twenty Questions, as in all classification challenges, is to identify relevant categories.

Evaluation   *Evaluative reasoning* involves expressing and justifying an opinion, a point of view, a judgment, or a decision. It can be thought of as having three facets—an assertion, the criteria the assertion is based on, and evidence that supports the assertion. Students are generally able to make an assertion or judgment, but often do not follow up with the criteria on which the judgment was based or with the evidence they used. Instead, they express an opinion and do not follow up with a credible justification. This can't be considered sound evaluative thinking until students are able to identify the criteria for making their assertion or judgment and are able to provide evidence that aligns with the criteria.

Content-specific examples of "assertion, criteria, and evidence" include the following:

- In mathematics problem solving, students select a strategy by first examining the options and judging the usefulness of each in the context of the problem and, second, by evaluating how well the strategy they selected is working as they use it.
- In science, students evaluate the validity of their conclusions based on what they know about experimental design.
- In social studies, students evaluate the quality of the arguments a politician makes against a set of criteria for accuracy and relevance.
- In English, students assess the credibility and accuracy of information gathered from multiple sources.

Synthesis   *Synthesis* is the process of combining discrete elements to create something new. Cookies are an example of synthesis because the end product is something more than a collection of parts. When we combine eggs, milk, sugar, flour, salt, and vanilla, we get something new—cookie dough—which some people bake before eating. Creating a tower out of blocks would not qualify as synthesis under this definition. Synthesizing involves selecting relevant ingredients to combine and then assembling them in such a way as to create a new whole.

Writing a report is an act of synthesis; we want students to create something new (e.g., in their own words or with their own thoughts) from separate ingredients. To do this they must locate and understand various chunks of relevant information, sort through them, think about how they fit together, and then assemble and present them in a way that does not simply copy the original sources. Although the assembly process differs according to the context, what all synthesis activities have in common is that they result in something more than the original ingredients.

Examples of reasoning-level learning targets can be found in Figure 3.6.

About Bloom's Taxonomy   Finally, we want to distinguish between reasoning generally conceptualized in current professional literature and another conceptualization about which you may hear a great deal: Bloom's Taxonomy (Bloom, Englehard, Furst, Hill, & Krathwohl, 1956). Bloom's Taxonomy has been a dominant conceptualization of reasoning proficiency for decades, so it is important that you understand how it differs from our categorization of reasoning learning targets. That original framework includes the following levels of objectives: knowledge, comprehension, application, analysis, evaluation, and synthesis. As you can see, they are closely linked with those described previously with four important differences.

figure 3.6 ■ For Example: Reasoning Targets

Subject	Learning Target
English Language Arts	1. Identify basic similarities in and differences between two texts on the same topic. 2. Delineate and evaluate the argument and specific claims in a text, assessing whether the reasoning is valid and the evidence is relevant and sufficient.
Mathematics	3. Compare two two-digit numbers based on meanings of the tens and ones digits. 4. Prove theorems about triangles.
Science	5. Analyze data from tests of two objects designed to solve the same problem to compare the strengths and weaknesses of how each performed. 6. Analyze a major global challenge to specify qualitative and quantitative criteria and constraints for solutions that account for societal needs and wants.
Social Studies	7. Evaluate a source by distinguishing between fact and opinion. 8. Evaluate the credibility of a source by examining how experts value the source.
Health/Physical Education	9. Analyze a food journal for missing nutrients. 10. Compare and contrast personal progress in relationship to national physical fitness standards.
The Arts	11. Compare purposes of chosen musical examples. 12. Evaluate quality of own work to refine it.

Sources:
1: Grade 1 *CCSSI Reading Standards*, p. 13
2: Grades 9–10 *CCSSI Reading Standards*, p. 40
3: Grade 1 *CCSSI Mathematics Standards*, p. 16
4: HS *CCSSI Mathematics Standards*, p. 77
5: Grades K–2 *NGSS*, p. 23
6: HS *NGSS*, p. 129
7: Grades K–2 *C-3 Framework*, p. 54
8: Grades 9–12 *C-3 Framework*, p. 54
9: Grade 4 *Washington State Health and Fitness Standards*, p. 4
https://www.k12.wa.us/HealthFitness/Standards.aspx
10. HS *Washington State Health and Fitness Standards*, p. 2
https://www.k12.wa.us/HealthFitness/Standards.aspx
11 and 12: North Thurston Public Schools K–12 Arts Curriculum

First, the levels in Bloom's Taxonomy are structured to ascend from the lowest order to the highest level of complexity with each level carrying greater mental challenge. However, each level described can vary profoundly in cognitive demand from simple to very challenging. Thus, it is possible to conceive of an advanced analytical problem that far outreaches a simple evaluation in cognitive demand. We do not disagree with the assertion that various levels can be more cognitively challenging, just with the assertion that all exercises at a certain level fit into a hierarchy established by the levels. This hierarchical presentation has also led to the labeling of knowledge as involving only "low-level" cognition, and yet not all knowledge targets involve a simple act of memorization and even those that do should not be dismissed as unimportant because they are "low level."

Second, Bloom's Taxonomy separates knowledge and comprehension. In our view, this differentiation is impractical: comprehension equals understanding, which we view as a knowledge-level learning target. Knowledge without understanding cannot feed productively into reasoning in any academic context. The taxonomy defines *comprehension* as ways to demonstrate understanding, for example, organizing, comparing, translating, and interpreting. We suggest that comprehension as a level per se is a bit of a catchall and prefer to call out the underlying verbs as falling into either the knowledge/understanding category or into their own categories such as comparison and inference.

Third, the taxonomy includes *application* as a unique level of reasoning. Every reasoning context requires that the user apply knowledge to that cognitive challenge and apply the appropriate reasoning proficiencies to arrive at a defensible solution. Thus, we believe that application is only conducted in conjunction with one or more patterns of reasoning.

Fourth, Bloom's Taxonomy does not include *inference* as a category. So many of our current content standards are heavily infused with types of inferences—determine main idea, hypothesize, predict, generalize, and so forth—that we believe it is more practical to make *inference* a separate category, both for ensuring that it is taught well and for help with assessing it.

Relationships among Patterns of Reasoning   In line with current thought, we have not indicated a hierarchy of difficulty or importance among these reasoning categories. However, some patterns of reasoning depend on others to be carried out effectively. For example, before evaluating an issue, you might need to analyze it to identify the main problem, describe the different points of view on the issue, discover the assumptions that underlie various positions, and determine the information needed to inform a position on the issue; you might also need to compare positions to identify the most salient features of disagreement and agreement.

Also, the patterns are not completely separate from each other. For example, classifying and comparing are presented by some authors (e.g., Klauer & Phye, 2008) as types of inductive or deductive inferences because they involve either looking at the objects to be compared to detect commonalities (induction) or using the categories to identify examples (deduction). We present the six categories of inference, comparison, classification, evaluation, and synthesis as separate patterns here because they are commonly referred to separately in content standards documents and they can be taught and assessed separately as well as in combination.

Patterns of reasoning are not completely separate from one another.

Relationship to Other Targets   It is important that we understand that there is no such thing as "content-free" thinking. An auto mechanic can diagnose the reason for a car problem in large part because he knows and understands the systems that make a car run. An attorney can help with legal problems because she knows or can look up relevant law and judicial precedent. Accountants prepare taxes correctly because they know proper procedures. A physician can help someone get well because she knows the human body and understands medical remedies. All reasoning arises from a foundation of knowledge; if the knowledge isn't there, there will be no problem solving.

Performance Skill Targets

Performance skill targets are those having a real-time demonstration or physical performance at the heart of the content standard. By this definition, the performance skill category is a narrow one. Subject areas such as fine arts, music, physical education, performing arts, and world languages have many performance skill targets in their curricula. Other subjects may have few or none. Examples of performance skill targets include "Read aloud with fluency," "Make observations and/or measurements to produce data," "Dribble the ball to keep it away from an opponent," and "Converse in the target language in a host family scenario."

Examples of performance skill–level learning targets can be found in Figure 3.7.

Relationship to Other Targets   To perform skillfully, students must possess fundamental knowledge combined with reasoning proficiency. For example, to perform CPR effectively, students must have knowledge of the steps to take and the ability to analyze a situation to determine what steps to take. However, you don't want the people staffing an aide car to possess only those sets of competencies. You also want them to have the skill required to execute the steps effectively.

As with the CPR example, performance skill targets represent an end in and of themselves. But they also often function as a building block for product-development capabilities. For example, students cannot produce a quality piece of writing (a product target) unless they have the physical skills to get their thoughts from their head onto paper—handwriting, keyboarding, or dictation proficiency (performance skills).

In this category of learning targets, the student's learning objective is to integrate knowledge and reasoning proficiencies with skillful performance. This is precisely why performance skill targets often require more sophisticated assessments. Success in mastering product-level learning targets—the next kind of target—often (but not always) has as a prerequisite the ability to perform some kind of skill.

Product-Level Targets

Product-level targets are just that: the content standard itself specifies the creation of a product. Product targets range from the simple to the complex. Examples include the following:

- Create tables, graphs, scatter plots, and box plots to display data effectively (mathematics)
- Create a personal wellness plan (health)
- Create a scripted scene based on improvised work (theater arts)

figure 3.7 ■ For Example: Performance Skill Targets

Subject	Learning Target
English Language Arts	1. Create engaging audio recordings of stories or poems that demonstrate fluid reading at an understandable pace. 2. Present claims and findings, sequencing ideas logically and using pertinent descriptions, facts, and details to accentuate main ideas or themes; use appropriate eye contact, adequate volume, and clear pronunciation.
Mathematics	3. Measure the length of an object by selecting and using appropriate tools such as rulers, yardsticks, meter sticks, and measuring tapes. 4. Measure angles in whole-number degrees using a protractor.
Science	5. Measure properties of objects using balances and thermometers. 6. Use laboratory equipment safely.
Social Studies	7. Use appropriate protocols to greet people from other countries. 8. Participate in civic discussions.
Health/Physical Education	9. Maintain balance while walking on a line or a balance beam. 10. Demonstrate trapping, dribbling, and passing to a partner in a modified soccer game.
The Arts	11. Perform songs using appropriate expression to reflect music. 12. Integrate voice into character development.

Sources:
1: Grade 3 *CCSSI Speaking and Listening Standards*, p. 24
2: Grade 6 *CCSSI Speaking and Listening Standards*, p. 49
3: Grade 2 *CCSSI Mathematics Standards*, p. 20
4: Grade 4 *CCSSI Mathematics Standards*, p. 32
9: Grade 1 *Washington State Health and Fitness Standards*, p. 1
https://www.k12.wa.us/HealthFitness/Standards.aspx
10. Grade 8 *Washington State Health and Fitness Standards*, p. 1
https://www.k12.wa.us/HealthFitness/Standards.aspx
11 and 12: North Thurston Public Schools K–12 Arts Curriculum

- Develop a model to describe a phenomenon (science)
- Produce clear and coherent writing (English language arts)

In all cases, student success lies in creating products that possess certain key attributes when completed. Instruction focuses on the attributes the product must have to be judged of high quality. The instruction and assessment challenge is to be able to define clearly and understandably communicate what those attributes are.

Examples of product-level learning targets can be found in Figure 3.8.

Relationship to Other Targets Once again, successful product creation arises from mastery of prerequisite knowledge and application of prerequisite reasoning and skill strategies. In addition, students may need to perform certain predefined

figure 3.8 ■ For Example: Product Targets

Subject	Learning Target
English Language Arts	1. Write informative/explanatory texts in which they name a topic, supply some facts about it, and provide some sense of closure. 2. Produce clear and coherent writing in which the development, organization, and style are appropriate to task, purpose, and audience.
Mathematics	3. Draw a picture graph and a bar graph to represent a data set with up to four categories. 4. Construct and interpret two-way frequency tables of data when two categories are associated with each object being classified.
Science	5. Report observations of simple investigations using drawings and simple sentences. 6. Create a simplified model of a complex system.
Social Studies	7. Create a time line to show personal events in a sequential manner. 8. Create a map of new world regions based on cultural and environmental factors.
Health/Physical Education	9. Develop a home fire escape plan. 10. Develop a personal health-related fitness plan.
The Arts	11. Create drawings demonstrating one- and two-point perspectives. 12. Create a scripted scene based on improvised work.

Sources:
1: Grade 1 *CCSSI Reading Standards*, p. 13
2: Grades 9–10 *CCSSI Reading Standards,* p. 40
3: Grade 1 *CCSSI Mathematics Standards*, p. 16
4: HS *CCSSI Mathematics Standards*, p. 77
5: Grades K–1 *Washington State Science Learning Standards*, p. 25
https://www.k12.wa.us/Science/Standards.aspx
6: Grade 9 *Washington State Science Learning Standards*, p. 82
https://www.k12.wa.us/Science/Standards.aspx
7: Grade 1 *Washington State Social Studies Learning Standards*, p. 20
https://www.k12.wa.us/SocialStudies/EALRs-GLEs.aspx
8: Grade 12 *Washington State Social Studies Learning Standards*, p. 112
https://www.k12.wa.us/SocialStudies/EALRs-GLEs.aspx
11 and 12: North Thurston Public Schools K–12 Arts Curriculum

steps to create the desired product. Prerequisite achievement underpins the creation of quality products, but evidence of ultimate success resides in the product itself: To what extent does it meet standards of quality for the given product?

Disposition Targets—the Affective Domain

This final category of targets that we have for our students includes those characteristics that go beyond academic achievement into the areas of affective and personal feeling states, such as attitudes, sense of academic self-confidence, interests, and motivation. For example, many teachers have a goal that students will develop positive academic self-concepts or positive attitudes toward school subjects ("I like math"), predisposing them to enjoy learning. Without question, we want our students to develop strong interests, as well as a strong sense of internal control over their own academic well-being.

We can define each disposition in terms of three elements: focus, direction, and intensity. Each disposition has a focus—we develop and carry within us attitudes, interests, and motivations that focus on certain things. Those dispositions can be positive or negative in direction and vary in intensity from strong to weak feelings. When we assess a disposition, for example, *attitude toward writing*, we are interested in information about both the direction and level of intensity of the attitude. We might offer a series of statements such as "I like writing," "I am good at writing," and "I like to write in my spare time," which students would rate on a continuum of "strongly agree," "somewhat agree," "neither agree nor disagree," "somewhat disagree," and "strongly disagree." In this example, we have the focus—attitude toward writing, the direction—positive or negative, and the intensity—strong, somewhat, or neutral.

The remainder of our discussion of classroom assessment will center on achievement expectations—knowledge, reasoning, performance skills, and products—rather than student affect. However, additional information about the definition and measurement of these kinds of student characteristics is presented in Appendix A.

Examples of disposition-level learning targets can be found in Figure 3.9.

figure 3.9 ■ For Example: Disposition Targets

Subject	Learning Target
English Language Arts	1. Enjoy writing. 2. See self as capable of succeeding at reading with sufficient effort.
Mathematics	3. See mathematics as important to learn. 4. Look forward to math class.
Science	5. Curious about how things work. 6. Want to conduct experiments at home.
Social Studies	7. Inclined to probe the validity of own and others' positions on issues. 8. Explore topics further outside of class.
Health/Physical Education	9. Seek out opportunities to engage in physical activities. 10. Choose to avoid drug and alcohol use.
The Arts	11. Value practice as necessary to improvement and enjoyable in its own right. 12. Want to participate in community theater.

Relationship to Other Targets   Dispositions very often result from success or lack of success in academic performance. In that sense, they accompany each learning target a student engages with. Students bring dispositions to the table preceding the first attempt, change them during the course of practice (or not), and perhaps change them again (or not) at the conclusion of instruction. Students also bring dispositions to the assessment experience; they are in play both during and after the event. We can structure both instruction and assessment so that they contribute to the development of productive dispositions in students.

Classifying Targets by Type

When classifying a learning target by type, it is important to read the whole learning target rather than simply relying on the verb in the learning statement. Most often, the verb will signify the type, but there are times when the verb will mislead you. For example, if the target begins with "explain" and is followed by a statement of something beyond the knowledge level, then it most likely is not a knowledge-level target. Figure 3.10 gives some examples of verbs typically associated with different types of targets.

Identifying Knowledge Targets   Learning targets requiring recall of information often begin with verbs such as *know*, *explain*, *list*, *name*, *identify*, and *recall*. However, consider these two examples: "Know how healthy practices enhance the ability

figure 3.10 ■ Classifying Learning Targets: Key Words

Target Type	Key Words
Knowledge/ Understanding	Explain, understand, describe, identify, tell, name, list, identify, define, label, match, choose, recall, recognize, select
Reasoning	*Inference*: Determine main idea, draw conclusions, generalize, hypothesize, interpret, predict, state implications
	Analysis: Examine parts or components, determine ingredients, dissect, identify logical sequence, order, take apart
	Comparison: Distinguish between, identify similarities and differences, juxtapose
	Classification: Categorize, determine, give examples, group, sort
	Evaluation: Appraise, assess, critique, debate, defend, dispute, evaluate, judge, justify, prove, support opinion
	Synthesis: Adapt, blend, combine into, create, formulate, modify
Performance Skills	Observe, focus attention, listen, perform, do, question, conduct, work, read, speak, assemble, operate, use, demonstrate, measure, investigate, model, collect, dramatize, explore
Products	Design, produce, create, develop, make, write, draw, represent, display, model, construct

to dance" and "Know folk dances from various cultures" (Kendall & Marzano, 1997, p. 387 and p. 386). While the intent of the first may be knowledge of the connection between healthy practices and success at dance, the second may include the expectation that students can perform a variety of folk dances. In this case, it is really a performance skill target, even though it begins with the word *know*.

Targets specifying procedural knowledge usually refer to an algorithm or other process involving a set of steps. Sometimes a target may look like procedural knowledge but in fact is a reasoning target. For example, the target "Know how to broaden or narrow inquiry when appropriate" begins with the phrase "Know how to," which may be a clue to procedural knowledge but in this case is not. Rather, determining whether a topic is too narrow or too broad requires reasoning, and if the target's intent is that students be able to broaden or narrow a topic, that is also reasoning.

When conceptual understanding is called for, the target usually includes the verb *understand*. However, the verb *understand* can also signify a reasoning target. Is the intent that students explain something, such as the differences between a food chain and a food web? If so, it's a knowledge target at the conceptual understanding level. (To reiterate, labeling a target as knowledge doesn't make it a "lower-order" or simple target—in order to explain a concept clearly, you have to know it well.)

Identifying Reasoning Targets   While reasoning targets can most often be identified by the verbs they contain, some reasoning targets do not include a reasoning verb. For example, the learning target "Draw examples of quadrilaterals that do and do not belong to any of the subcategories" may look like a product target because it begins with the word *draw*. The intent of this target, however, is to have students draw quadrilaterals in order to classify them. You might even consider this a knowledge target if you interpreted it to be a test of their understanding of types of quadrilaterals. Another example is "Given a set of data or a word problem, create an equation or inequality to solve the problem." The verb *create* may lead you to think of this as a product target, but the focus is students' ability to solve problems using equations and inequalities, a reasoning target.

When the verb *understand* signifies a reasoning target, then it calls for something more than conceptual understanding and it will be accompanied by information about what level of understanding will be demonstrated. The information will (or should) include one or more patterns of reasoning, and teaching to this target will include instruction on how to carry out the pattern or patterns of reasoning specified.

Sometimes a reasoning target in the curriculum guide becomes a knowledge target in practice. For example, "Compare and contrast main characters in a novel" is a reasoning target as written. However, if the teacher compares and contrasts the main characters in the novel and then tests students' ability to replicate her reasoning with the same characters, it is not the students' ability to compare and contrast that is being tested; it is their recall of what the teacher shared. It may have started out as a reasoning target but it was tested as a knowledge target. To assess a reasoning proficiency, we must provide students with a novel (new) application of the pattern of reasoning they have been practicing. The key to making the determination here lies in asking, "Who is doing the reasoning?" Are students doing more than remembering the answers the teacher previously provided?

Identifying Performance Skill Targets   The performance skills category can be confusing. You will hear phrases such as "problem-solving skills," "reading skills," and "thinking skills." While there is nothing inherently wrong about calling these cognitive exercises *skills*, the ultimate goal of those listed is some form of thinking. If you were to take them apart, you would find a combination of knowledge and reasoning. The term *performance skill targets* identifies a small set of content standards that holds an *outwardly visible or audible performance* at the heart of the intended learning. The differentiation between cognitive "skills" and performance skills becomes an important distinction in both teaching and assessing the learning, which we will address more fully in Chapter 4.

Additionally, when the target in question is a measurement skill, the line between procedural knowledge and performance skill becomes blurry. Measurement skills requiring manual dexterity and fine motor control, such as those often encountered in mathematics and science, are largely procedural knowledge—knowing how to use the tool correctly, as in the case of measuring an angle with a protractor. But because they also require the physical act of carrying out the measuring protocol, we classify them as performance skill targets.

Identifying Product Targets   Classifying a target as a product target can be challenging, too. We are quite used to asking students to create products to demonstrate learning, but the content standard to be assessed may not have any relation to the product-development capabilities required by the assignment. For example, when a student makes a diorama (a three-dimensional scene inside a shoebox turned on its side) as a reading assignment, what is the intended learning target? Perhaps it has to do with identifying literary elements. If so, the diorama should be assessed for the extent to which the student demonstrated understanding of the literary elements specified rather than characteristics of the diorama itself; even though the student has created a product, the learning targets to be assessed do not have to do with the ability to create a scene that conveys meaning. If the content standard is truly a product target, the statement will call for the product.

In English language arts, the content standards calling for the creation of different types of writing are considered by definition to be product targets. In other instances where students are asked to produce writing, the content standard may not require a written product, in which case it is not a product target. When we confuse the activity with the target, we cause problems for ourselves and our students in instruction and in assessment. The ability to distinguish between the task—the activity the students will engage in—and the learning target—what they are to master by doing the assignment—is crucial to classifying targets and to creating an accurate assessment. The key question in classifying targets is "What is the intended learning?" not "How will students demonstrate the learning?" The choice of demonstration comes after the classification itself, and we discuss that choice in depth in Chapter 4.

Identifying Disposition Targets   Dispositions are not often found in the written curriculum. "I look forward to coming to school each day" is a disposition we hope students develop as a result of being in our classes, but it doesn't show up in the list of content we are to teach. An exception comes from the Common Core State Standards for Mathematics, which includes productive dispositions in the Standards for Mathematics, defined as "habitual inclination to see mathematics as sensible, useful, and worthwhile, coupled with a belief in diligence and one's own efficacy" (National Governors Association Center for Best Practices, CCSS Mathematics, 2010b, p. 6).

Dispositions can more often be found in overarching goals of school and in mission statements. We typically do not hold students accountable for achieving certain dispositions in the same way that we hold them accountable for mastering the other types of learning targets, but that doesn't mean they are not important or that we would never inquire about them. Understanding students' dispositions can give us insights that help us work more effectively with students as individuals and in groups. If, for example, we found that a majority of students in our class clearly indicated a dislike for reading, that information might cause us to review how we are teaching reading.

MyEdLab **Self-Check 3.2**

MyEdLab **Application Exercise 3.2** Classifying learning targets by type

---

■ Deconstructing Complex Content Standards

As discussed earlier in this chapter, learning targets can range from the simple to the complex. When you begin teaching, you will most likely receive a curriculum guide that lists the expected learning for your subject(s) by grade level. If these statements of expected learning have not been *deconstructed*, or *unpacked*, into lesson-level learning targets, that is something you will need to do prior to beginning instruction. We recommend that this work be done in collaboration with colleagues as opposed to alone, but practicing with the process individually will prepare you to participate with a team charged with this task.

> Deconstructing a content standard is the process of analyzing it to determine which underlying learning targets will be needed for mastery.

Once you have identified a content standard that needs deconstructing prior to instruction, follow these three steps (Figure 3.11).

Step 1. Classify the Content Standard According to Target Type.

figure 3.11 ■ The Process for Deconstructing a Content Standard

Step 1.   Classify the content standard according to target type.

Step 2.   Identify underlying or prerequisite knowledge, reasoning, and/or performance skill targets.

Step 3.   Check the results for alignment and reasonableness.

Using the information about target types, determine if the content standard is ultimately a knowledge, reasoning, performance skill, or product target. If the content standard includes more than one learning target as written, separate the learning targets and classify each according to type. See Figure 3.12 for examples of the work at Step 1.

Step 2. Identify Underlying or Prerequisite Knowledge, Reasoning, and/or Performance Skill Targets.

If the ultimate target type is knowledge, and if there are underpinning targets, they will all be at the knowledge level. If the ultimate target type is reasoning, it will have knowledge underpinnings but no performance skill or product prerequisites. If the content standard calls for a performance skill, it will have knowledge underpinnings. It will usually have reasoning prerequisites as well. It will not have product targets as prerequisites. If the content standard is a product target, it will have underpinning knowledge and reasoning targets. It may or may not require performance skill targets as prerequisites. See Figure 3.13 for an example of work at Step 2.

Step 3. Check the Results for Alignment and Reasonableness.

First, review your work to ensure all of the targets listed are truly necessary to mastery of the ultimate content standard. Check for reasonableness by paying attention to the number of enabling learning targets you have listed. Have you

figure 3.12 ■ For Example: Step 1 of the Deconstructing Process

Content Standard:			
Determine the meaning of words and phrases as they are used in a text, including figurative and connotative meanings; analyze the impact of a specific word choice on meaning or tone.			
Knowledge ___	**Reasoning** _X_	**Performance Skill** ___	**Product** ___

figure 3.13 ■ For Example: Step 2 of the Deconstructing Process

Content Standard:
Determine the meaning of words and phrases as they are used in a text, including figurative and connotative meanings; analyze the impact of a specific word choice on meaning or tone.

Knowledge ___   Reasoning X   Performance Skill ___   Product ___

Knowledge Target(s)	Reasoning Target(s)	Performance Skill Targets	Product Targets
■ Understand what *figurative language* means ■ Identify figurative words and phrases in a passage ■ Understand what *connotative language* means ■ Identify connotative words and phrases in a passage ■ Understand what *tone* means	■ Infer the meaning of figurative words and phrases in a passage ■ Infer the meaning of connotative words and phrases in a passage ■ Determine the impact of word choice on meaning in a passage ■ Identify the tone of a passage ■ Determine the impact of word choice on tone of a passage	*none*	*none*

taken the prerequisites back several grade levels? Make sure you have not listed more learning targets than necessary for students *at your level* to master the ultimate standard. In a well-thought-out curriculum, the deconstructing work at the prior level or grade will address prerequisites students should have before coming into your level or grade.

The State of Kentucky used this protocol to deconstruct the English Language Arts and Mathematics Common Core State Standards (see Figure 3.14). In Figure 3.15, sixth-grade teacher Jessica Cynkar explains how deconstructing content standards helped her to plan instruction.

MyEdLab **Self-Check 3.3**

MyEdLab **Application Exercise 3.3** Deconstructing learning targets as needed

figure 3.14 ■ For Example: Kentucky's Deconstructing Standards Flowchart

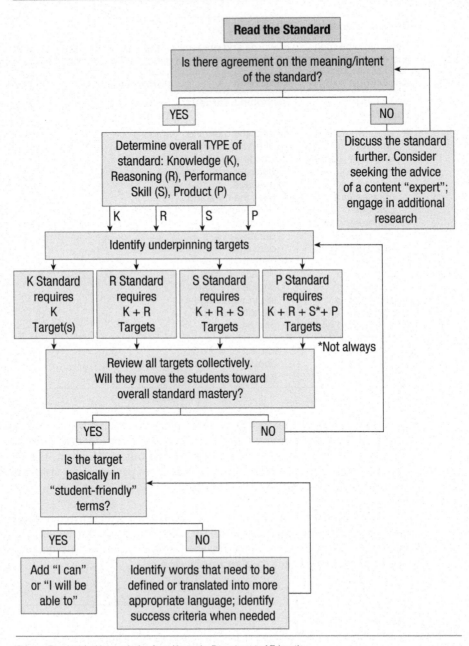

Source: Reprinted with permission from Kentucky Department of Education.

figure 3.15 ■ From the Classroom: Jessica Cynkar

What we did . . .

One of the most important things that we did to expand our formative assessment practices was to deconstruct the state standards and indicators. Our 6th-grade English department requested two professional development days to create common definitions and understandings of the content standards and indicators. We felt that we needed to be on the same page as to "what" we were teaching, but how we got there was up to us as professionals.

We wanted the focus of this time to be very intentional and specific, so we set norms at the beginning. We wanted to make sure that we stuck to one topic at a time and the time wasn't about sharing, "This is what I do in my classroom"; that it was more about what we need to teach and how we get there. During this time we reviewed several sources of information: standards and indicators at our grade level (6th), standards and indicators for 5th and 7th grades, standardized testing information, and a variety of classroom resources. Together we deconstructed the indicators into their underpinning learning targets. We created common definitions and "I can" statements, added resources, and developed assessment questions. We also began to note lessons and ideas we each had for teaching each target.

How we benefited . . .

These tips have been invaluable when I've started to plan a unit or concept to teach. They have become a bag of tricks to reference, especially when students need additional support or a way to stretch their learning. Another benefit is that it has become very clear what lessons are not working or do not fit the content we need to teach.

Source: Reprinted with permission from Jessica Cynkar, 6th-grade Language Arts Teacher, Olentangy Local School District, Lewis Center, OH, 2011.

■ Communicating Learning Targets to Students

As you recall from Chapter 1, one of the conditions necessary for students to adopt a learning orientation to their work is that teachers have a clear vision of the intended learning and share that vision with students at the outset of instruction. So, once learning targets are clear to us, it is time to work on how we will make them clear to students. Many schools now require that learning targets be posted on the wall. While that is not a bad idea, it does not bear much relationship to the underlying need that students *be aware of the learning associated with the activities they are asked to complete.* For that, they need more active engagement with the targets.

Targets on the wall are not targets in the head.

There are three basic options for developing awareness of the intended learning, each suited to the type of target you are teaching (see Figure 3.16).

figure 3.16 ■ Options for Sharing Learning Targets with Students

1. Share the target "as is."
2. Convert terms of the target to student-friendly language.
3. Share a student-friendly version of a rubric.

1. For straightforward knowledge targets and a few reasoning targets, share the target "as is."
2. For more complex knowledge targets and most reasoning targets, convert the language into student-friendly terms.
3. For many reasoning targets and all performance skill and product targets, find or develop a rubric that defines levels of quality; then convert that rubric to student-friendly language.

1. Share the Target "As Is"

Lots of knowledge targets (see, for example, Figure 3.4) and some reasoning targets can be shared in their original form. Figure 3.17 shows an example of learning targets printed on the assignment. Alternatively you can have students write the

figure 3.17 ■ Example Targets Printed on the Assignment

Name _____   Date _____

I can comprehend what I read by reflecting on important information.

I can summarize main ideas in a text.

Title _____

What do you think is the most important thing you learned from reading this book?

_____

_____

_____

Tell why you think it is important.

_____

_____

_____

Summarize what this book about. (Squish up the main ideas or most important points about the topic.)

_____

_____

_____

Source: Reprinted with permission from Amy Meyer, Third-grade Teacher, Worthington City Schools: Worthington OH. Unpublished Classroom Materials.

figure 3.18 ■ For Example Content Standards ⟶ Learning Targets ⟶ Statements for Students

---

Content Standard: Explain that some structures in the modern eukaryotic cell developed from early prokaryotes, such as mitochondria, and in plants, chloroplasts

Learning Targets: The wording of this standard implies knowledge/ understanding. In fact, reading the standard effectively teaches it to you. I expect my students to explain a little more about how those structures developed. This standard requires an understanding of the vocabulary terms *prokaryote* and *eukaryote* primarily, with *mitochondria* and *chloroplasts* being secondary vocabulary terms (you don't actually need to know what a chloroplast or mitochondrion is to learn the standard). Students should be able to describe the pieces of evidence that lead scientists to the conclusion that the standard is true.

Student-Friendly Targets:

- I can define *prokaryote* and *eukaryote* and give examples of each.
- I can describe where mitochondria and chloroplasts come from.
- I can describe the evidence that explains where mitochondria and chloroplasts come from.

Content Standard: Explain the role of cell membranes as a highly selective barrier (diffusion, osmosis, and active transport)

Learning Targets: If you were to limit the scope of this standard to only what is written, students would simply have to describe that cell membranes are selective—that is, they let some things in and out but not others. I expect my students to do a lot more with this standard. They should be able to distinguish between types of membrane transport and describe what would happen in a variety of scenarios. As written, the content standard is knowledge/ understanding, but it lends itself well to reasoning learning targets.

Student-Friendly Targets:

- I can define *osmosis*, *diffusion*, and *active transport*.
- I can predict what will happen when cells are placed in a variety of solutions.
- I can determine if a process is *osmosis*, *diffusion*, or *active transport* based on how materials are moving into or out of a cell.

Source: Reprinted with permission from Andy Hamilton, West Ottawa Public Schools: Holland, MI. Unpublished Classroom Materials.

learning target in their paper's heading. Figure 3.18 shows an example of biology content standards deconstructed into lesson-level learning targets and then phrased as "I can" statements.

2. Convert the Terms in the Target to Student-Friendly Language

This strategy is especially well suited to reasoning targets. Consider the target "Summarizes text." When some student summaries are longer than the passage to be summarized, that indicates a basic misconception about the nature of *summarize*.

Defining the word *summarize* as "to make a brief statement about the main ideas, important facts, or major events" helps students by providing a clear vision of the task at hand. They need to know that *summarize* has two working parts: *brief* and *main*. In actuality, most students are pretty good at *brief*—it's *main* they generally need to understand to be successful. Note in Figure 3.17 that third-grade teacher Amy Meyer has included a student-friendly definition of *summarize* next to the writing prompt in the assignment.

This transformation to a student-friendly version is quite straightforward:

1. Identify the word or words in the learning target that would benefit from clarification.
2. Define the word or words. You may want to refer to a dictionary, the text-book, your content standards, or other reference specific to the subject.
3. Convert the definition into language students will understand, if it's not there yet. Include the original terms in the first part of the definition. (For instance, you want students to come to know that "give a brief statement of the main ideas" means "summarize.") You may wish to use a frame similar to one of the following:

   ■ "I am learning to _____. This means I am learning to _____."
   ■ "We are learning to _____. This means we are learning to _____."
   ■ "I can _____. This means I can _____."
   ■ "We can _____. This means we can _____."

4. Try the definition out with some students and adjust as needed to ensure understanding.
5. Let students try this process with a pattern of reasoning you think they could successfully define (via reference) and paraphrase. Make sure the definition they ultimately use is congruent with your vision of the target.

See Figure 3.19 for examples of patterns translated into student-friendly terms. In Figure 3.20, middle school science teacher Elizabeth Schoo describes how she uses student-friendly learning targets.

3. Share a Student-Friendly Version of a Rubric with Students

Reasoning, performance skill, and product targets are most often assessed with a rubric. A *rubric* is a type of scoring guide that lists the criteria for a strong response, product, or performance and describes each criterion at three or more levels of quality, ranging from strong to weak. So for reasoning, performance skill, and product targets, the rubric provides the vision of quality that clarifies the meaning of the target.

figure 3.19 ■ For Example: Student-Friendly Definitions of Reasoning Learning Targets

Inferring

I can infer. This means I can make a reasonable guess based on information.

Generalizing

I can generalize. This means I can compare pieces of evidence to see what they have in common. Then I can make an umbrella statement that is true for them and is also true for a broader array of instances.

Predicting

I can predict. This means I can use what I already know (or evidence) to guess at what will happen next.

Identifying Cause and Effect

I can identify causes and effects. This means I can describe relationships between events by answering two questions: "What happened?" and "Why did it happen?"

Drawing Conclusions

I can draw conclusions. This means I can begin with a general ("umbrella") idea or statement and identify specific situations in which it is true.

Comparing

I can compare and contrast. This means that I can tell how things are alike and how they are different.

Evaluating

I can make evaluations. This means I can identify criteria upon which to make a judgment, apply it to a specific situation, and express an opinion based on the criteria. I can also justify my opinion by using the criteria.

Summarizing

I can summarize. This means I can make a short statement of the big ideas or main message of what I read (hear, view, observe).

Determining Main Idea and Supporting Details

I can determine main ideas and identify supporting details. This means I can find important ideas in the text and point out which facts or information help to make (or contribute to) that main idea.

Source: Chappuis, Jan; Stiggins, Rick J.; Chappuis, Steve; Arter, Judith A., *Classroom Assessment for Student learning: Doing it Right–Using it Well*, 2nd Ed., ©2012. Reprinted and Electronically reproduced by permission of Pearson Education, Inc., New York, New York.

figure 3.20 ■ From the Classroom: Elizabeth Schoo

I used to . . .

I used to teach my physical science class by following district objectives derived from state standards. These objectives were easy for me to understand and my lessons were based on these, but nowhere in my teaching was I telling my students what the goal for their learning of that day was to be. I just assumed it was obvious.

Now I . . .

Now my classroom units and lessons are all based on student-friendly "I can" statements. I have provided these statements to my students in numerous ways. In our science binders at the beginning of each chapter, I provide a sheet stating the chapter's new "I can" statements as well as any previous "I can" statements that will be reinforced. Our science team has developed a pre-assessment for the students to determine what level of knowledge they would rank themselves as having concerning the "I can" targets. Students rerank their level of knowledge at the end of the chapter and use the information to help them structure their studying for the final assessment.

To be even more student friendly, I have started to include the chapter "I can" statements on each set of notes, reinforcement worksheets, labs, quizzes, etc. that I give my students. When assessing my students at the end of a chapter, my review guide consists of revisiting these statements. I have taught my students to structure their studying based on how well they can answer the "I can" statement.

Why I changed . . .

I always told my students that there was no secret to what I was going to be teaching that day, but in reflection, by not writing student-friendly chapter targets and using them with my students, I was, in fact, keeping them in the dark.

What I notice as a result . . .

By providing my students with easy-to-understand targets for the day's lesson, they are able to focus their learning and understand the outcome for that day; they aren't left guessing what they were supposed to have learned. When surveyed to see if they liked this new format, most students responded that their study time was now more productive. They knew what to study—their time was spent more wisely on studying the statements that they lacked detail in answering rather than reviewing haphazardly everything from the chapter.

My assessments are more accurate now because I create questions that match the "I can" statements. In turn, my students see more success. The secret is out and the light is on! Simply put, changing to writing student-friendly targets and providing them with those targets has allowed me to create a classroom environment that invites students to create ownership of their learning.

Source: Reprinted with permission from Elizabeth Schoo, 8th-grade Science Teacher, Community Unit School District 95, Lake Zurich, IL, 2011.

Examples of learning targets assessed with a rubric include the following:

- Evaluate the strengths and weaknesses of candidates in terms of the qualifications required for a particular leadership role.
- Plan and conduct a simple scientific investigation.
- Develop a personal health-related fitness plan.
- Write opinion pieces on topics or texts, supporting a point of view with reasons and information.

It is not necessary that these types of targets be turned into student-friendly language. Rather, what is important is that the rubric you use accurately describes features of quality with respect to the learning target and that it is written so that students can understand it well enough to use it during the learning. We will address the characteristics of a high-quality rubric and how to convert one to student-friendly language in Chapter 7.

When to Share the Target and How to Check for Understanding

The point in the lesson at which you share the target can vary. It may be the first thing you share or, as in the case of many science lessons, understanding of the intended learning may evolve over one or more lessons. For example, the knowledge-level target "Understand that plants depend on water and light to grow" (NGSS Lead States, 2013, Grade 2, p. 18) is intended to be discovered by students through investigation. Sharing the target at the outset would ruin the experience and the learning. In such instances, it is important that students know the learning target before you ask them to engage in independent practice with it.

MyEdLab
Video Example 3.1
Making Targets Clear to Students: Kindergarten

It is a good idea to check periodically to see if students know what the intended learning of an activity is. You can walk around the room and ask individuals why we are doing the activity. If they can't identify some learning purpose, you may want to clarify it for them. Many teachers use a technique involving "exit slips," where students write a short note as their ticket out the door at the end of a lesson. Students write down what they think they were to learn in the lesson (Harlen, 2007) or answer the prompt "Why we did _____ (activity) today."

You can also begin the lesson by phrasing the learning target as a question that students should be able to answer at the end of the lesson ("How do you find the lowest common denominator for a pair of fractions?"). Have students write their response to the question at the conclusion of the lesson (Wiliam & Lee, 2001). This also provides you with information about what further instruction may be needed. See Figure 3.21 for an explanation of how seventh-grade teacher Jeff Overbay uses student-friendly targets to organize his instruction and assessment.

MyEdLab
Video Example 3.2
Making Targets Clear to Students: Grade 4

Watch Video Example 3.1 to see how kindergarten teacher Emily Roberts makes the learning target "I can recognize compound words" clear to students. Watch Video Example 3.2 to hear fourth-grade

figure 3.21 ■ From the Classroom: Jeff Overbay

I used to . . .

Over the years I had developed a routine for teaching a new unit. All assessments would be CD-Rom generated. Students would use the textbook to define vocabulary at the end of a chapter. All activities would be a topical match for the content being taught. These activities came from the textbook materials or those I had gathered over the years of teaching. I would use the state standards and the textbook to create objectives for a unit. The textbook was what I used to drive my teaching.

Now I . . .

I have developed a new procedure for teaching a new unit. State standards are deconstructed first. Assessments are now both formative and summative. The pre-assessment is 10 to 12 questions in the agree–disagree format. The vocabulary and activities are congruent with the deconstructed standards. Students are given a self-assessment guide that consists of student-friendly learning targets. This guide is also generated from the deconstructed standards. These work together to help students be more involved in both the learning and assessment processes.

   The daily classroom procedure has also changed. At the beginning of class I place a guiding question on the board. This question is based on one of the student-friendly learning targets. Under this question I put an "I can" statement. This is something that the students must master that day or in the next few days. When appropriate I give an exit-slip question to measure mastery of a concept. Quizzes are given as the unit progresses. Finally, the summative assessment is given after the content has been taught.

Why I changed . . .

There are many reasons for changing my methods of teaching. First, there never was congruency from the beginning to the end of a unit. Even though I had objectives, there was never a true relationship between what was being taught and the state standards. The pre-assessment also needed to be changed. The information gathered is now useful in driving instruction. Next is that the vocabulary is now the critical vocabulary. Students are not wasting time looking up definitions. Finally, the assessment process needed to be changed. The self-assessment of learning targets is a valuable way of getting the students involved in their own learning process. Guiding questions and "I can" statements help the students stay focused from day to day. The quizzes match the targets so students know if they are succeeding as they go instead of waiting until the end of a unit. The summative assessment is now an accurate measurement of student achievement.

What I notice as a result . . .

This new format is helpful to both the students and myself. I now have a well-designed congruent "roadmap" to follow and the students have a better understanding of where they are going and how they are going to get there. As a result I have seen an increase in student achievement in the classroom and on the state assessment.

Source: Reprinted with permission from Jeff Overbay, 7th-/8th-grade Science Teacher, Bell County School District, Pineville, KY, 2011.

teacher Crystal Thayer explain the importance of clear targets and how she teaches vocabulary of a learning target to her students.

MyEdLab **Self-Check 3.4**
MyEdLab **Application Exercise 3.4** Sharing learning targets with students

■ Summary: Clear Targets Are Essential for Sound Assessment

In this chapter we have argued that the quality of any assessment rests on the clarity of the assessor's understanding of the achievement target(s) to be assessed. Content-valid assessments arise directly from clear and appropriate targets. Therefore, the second step in design or effective use of any particular assessment is to answer the question, "What achievement do I need to assess?"

We have identified four kinds of interrelated types of achievement expectations, plus *affect*, as useful in thinking about and planning for instruction and assessment:

- Mastering content knowledge (including understanding)
- Using that knowledge to reason and solve problems
- Demonstrating certain kinds of performance skills
- Creating certain kinds of products
- Developing certain dispositions

We will make this clarity the second criterion by which to judge classroom assessment quality. High-quality assessments arise from defined and clearly articulated learning targets. Poor-quality achievement targets (1) are missing, (2) are too broad or vague to guide assessment development, (3) fail to link to important academic standards, or (4) fail to accurately reflect the content of the field of study.

We have also argued that each teacher has a responsibility to students to be clear and accurate in representing the learning targets they will be responsible for mastering. As soon as you enter your first classroom, a bunch of students will show up needing to master content, to reason proficiently, to develop performance skills, and to create quality products. Additionally, they will benefit if you have structured your classroom environment to nurture productive dispositions. They will count on you to know how to teach what they need to learn, to guide them as they practice, and to assess them accurately, both formatively and summatively. One of the most important steps you can take to becoming a good teacher is to be clear about the learning at the heart of your lessons.

■ Chapter 3 Suggested Activities

End-of-chapter activities are intended to help you master the chapter's learning targets. They are designed to deepen your understanding of the chapter content, provide opportunities for personal reflection on ideas presented, and serve as a basis for discussion among peers. You may wish to do all of them or select those that you believe will be most useful to your learning. Each activity is correlated to one or more chapter learning targets to help with your selection.

Chapter 3 Learning Targets

As a result of your study of Chapter 3, you will be able to do the following:

1. Explain the necessity of clear targets to assessment quality
2. Classify learning targets by type
3. Deconstruct learning targets as needed
4. Select from options for sharing learning targets with students

Chapter 3 Activities

Activity 3.1   Keeping a Reflective Journal (All chapter learning targets)

Activity 3.2   Describing the Relationship between Clear Targets and Assessment Quality (Learning Target 1)

Activity 3.3   Classifying Targets by Type (Learning Target 2)

Activity 3.4   Deconstructing a Content Standard (Learning Target 3)

Activity 3.5   Sharing Learning Targets with Students (Learning Target 4)

Activity 3.6   Comparing Your Experiences with Information from the Chapter (All chapter learning targets)

Activity 3.7   Answering an Interview Question (All chapter learning targets)

Activity 3.8   Reflecting on Your Learning from Chapter 3 (All chapter learning targets)

Activity 3.9   Adding to Your Growth Portfolio (All chapter learning targets)

Activity 3.1: Keeping a Reflective Journal

Keep a record of your thoughts, questions, and insights as you read Chapter 3.

Activity 3.2: Understanding the Relationship of Clear Targets to Assessment Quality

Write a short essay in which you describe four or more reasons for beginning assessment planning with a list of clearly defined learning targets. Also describe two to three assessment problems attributable to unclear or absent learning targets.

Activity 3.3: Classify Targets by Type

Select a short unit you are preparing to teach, consisting of at least four learning targets. (Alternatively you can select a portion of content standards from a curriculum guide.)

- List the learning targets that will be the focus of the unit.
- Classify each as Knowledge (K), Reasoning (R), Performance Skill (S), or Product (P).
- If you are unable to classify some targets as written, mark them with a question mark (?) and write a short explanation of what you might need to do to clarify the target type.
- Discuss your classifications with a partner or group.

Activity 3.4: Deconstructing a Content Standard

Select a complex content standard from a subject and level you are preparing to teach. Verify that the content standard is sufficiently complex to warrant deconstructing. Identify its ultimate target type and then deconstruct it into its underpinning learning targets. Use the following questions as a guide.

1. What knowledge will students need to have to be successful?
2. What patterns of reasoning, if any, will students need to master to be successful?
3. What performance skills, if any, will students need to master to be successful?
4. What products, if any, will they need to learn to create to be successful?

Activity 3.5: Sharing Learning Targets with Students

List each learning target for a unit you are preparing to teach. Decide the following for each:

- Will I share it "as is?" If so, why?
- Will I rewrite it in student-friendly language? If so, create a student-friendly learning target.

■ Will I define it with a student-friendly rubric? If so, why?

Share your work with a partner or your group.

Activity 3.6: Comparing Your Experiences with Information from the Chapter

Select one "From the Classroom" entry from Chapter 3 and compare it to your experience as a student.

■ How is it similar?
■ What differences do you notice?
■ What conclusions about the benefits of clear targets might you draw?

Activity 3.7: Answering an Interview Question

Imagine that you are about to interview for a teaching position. The interview team (often a combination of administrators and teachers) is interested in understanding your level of classroom assessment literacy. Review Chapter 3's learning targets and think about what concepts and procedures were most significant to you from the chapter. Then think about what type of question an interview team might ask related to this significant learning. Write the question and draft a short response—one that you could give in one to two minutes orally.

Activity 3.8: Reflecting on Your Learning from Chapter 3

Review the Chapter 3 learning targets and select one that struck you as most significant from this chapter. Write a short reflection that captures your current understanding. If you are working with a group, discuss what you have written.

Activity 3.9: Adding to Your Growth Portfolio

Any of the activities from this chapter can be used as portfolio entries. Select any activity you have completed or artifact you have created that will demonstrate your mastery of the Chapter 3 learning targets:

1. Explain the necessity of clear targets to assessment quality
2. Classify learning targets by type
3. Deconstruct learning targets as needed
4. Select from options for sharing learning targets with students

Designing Quality Classroom Assessments

Chapter 4 Learning Targets

As a result of your study of Chapter 4 you will be able to do the following:

1. Select the appropriate method(s) to assess specific learning targets
2. Follow the steps in the assessment planning process and create an assessment blueprint
3. Use an assessment blueprint with students as assessment for learning

Perhaps the first thing that comes to mind when you hear the phrase "assessment quality" is the properties of the test items or tasks and scoring guides. Yet, as we have seen in the two previous chapters, before we concern ourselves with what's on the assessment itself, we need to establish the purpose for the assessment and then clarify and categorize the learning targets. Only when that work is done can we begin the task of designing the assessment instrument or event that fits into its intended context. In this chapter, we focus on Key 3: Sound Design (see Figure 4.1). In the first part of the chapter we will review the four assessment methods available and then discuss when to use each. In the second part we will introduce the assessment development process we recommend regardless of method used, examine important considerations for sampling student performance, learn how to create a test blueprint, and address matters of fairness by describing factors that can bias results.

This chapter provides an overview of keys to effective assessment design and, in doing so, sets the stage for the four chapters that follow, each of which applies the design principles to one of the four specific assessment methods available for use in the classroom.

figure 4.1 ■ Keys to Quality Assessment

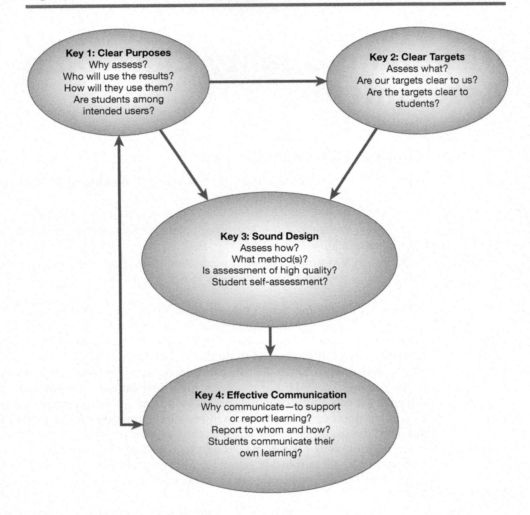

■ The Assessment Options

The four assessment methods are not interchangeable. To ensure accurate results, the overriding criterion for selection of method is consideration of the type of learning target to be assessed.

Throughout your experience as a student, you have encountered thousands of different assessments and, while the variations are endless, all of those assessments fall into one of four basic categories: (1) selected response, (2) written response, (3) performance assessment, and (4) personal communication (see Figure 4.2). Each method presents unique development challenges and provides its own form of evidence of student learning. Each is a legitimate option but only when

figure 4.2 ■ Assessment Options

Selected Response
■ Multiple-choice items
■ True/false items
■ Matching items
■ Fill-in-the-blank items

Written Response
■ Short-answer items
■ Extended response items

Performance Assessment
■ Assessment based on observation of a performance or product and a judgment of level of quality

Personal Communication
■ Instructional questions
■ Interviews
■ Conferences
■ Oral examinations
■ Student journals and logs

---

its use is closely matched with the kind of learning target to be assessed and with the intended use of the information.

Selected Response Assessment

With selected response assessment students are asked a series of questions, each of which is accompanied by a range of alternative responses. The task is to select either the correct or the best answer from among the options. The measure of achievement is the number or proportion of questions answered correctly. Format options within this category include the following:

■ Multiple-choice items
■ True/false items
■ Matching exercises
■ Fill-in-the-blank items

Fill-in-the-blank items are included here because they require a very brief response selected from within a respondent's knowledge base or reasoning that is judged to be either right or wrong.

Chapter 5 will provide you with the details you need to develop and use selected response assessments.

Written Response Assessment

For this method, students are asked to write an answer in response to a *prompt*—a question or task. Written response assessments can be thought of as falling into one

figure 4.3 ■ For Example: Written Response Items

Short-Answer Items
■ Explain the relationship between the pitch of a sound and the length of the vibrating object.
■ Name four ways that rhombuses, rectangles, and squares are alike.
■ What is the main idea of this story? Give two details from the story that helped you decide what the main idea is.

Extended Response Items
■ Describe why we need to know about the carbon cycle and how it works.
■ Evaluate two solutions to a mathematics problem. Determine which is better and explain your reasons.

of two categories: short answer and extended response (Figure 4.3). Short-answer items call for a brief response having a limited range of possible right answers. Extended response items require a response that is at least several sentences in length. They generally are more open-ended than short-answer items; they usually have a larger number of possible correct answers or a range of acceptable responses. Responses are judged by comparing them to a scoring guide, which takes the form either of a list of points assigned to desired information or of a scoring rubric describing a progression of levels of quality for the intended answer.

Details on how to develop and use written response items and scoring procedures are provided for you in Chapter 6.

Performance Assessment

With performance assessment, we ask students to complete a task and then we evaluate their work for quality using a scoring rubric that describes different levels of quality. Even though we call this method *performance assessment*, it can be used to judge both real-time performances (demonstrations) and products students create (artifacts). In the case of demonstrations, students carry out a specified activity while being observed by an evaluator, who judges the level of achievement demonstrated with a rubric. Examples of demonstrations (reflecting *performance skill* targets) include the following:

■ Speaking a foreign language fluently
■ Reading aloud with fluency
■ Performing a physical movement routine
■ Carrying out the steps required to analyze soil samples by titration

In the case of artifacts, students create a tangible product. Here it is not so much the process of creating that counts (although that may be evaluated, too) but rather the characteristics of the creation itself. Examples of artifacts (reflecting *product* targets) include the following:

■ A research paper
■ A work of art
■ A graphic representation of data

Chapter 7 will fill in details about how to develop and use performance assessment tasks and scoring rubrics.

Personal Communication

One of the most common ways teachers gather information about student learning is by talking with them. While this does not seem to be assessment in the same sense as a multiple-choice test or a performance assessment, clearly a well-crafted question eliciting an immediate response from students can provide clues regarding student level of understanding and misconceptions. In that way, personal communication serves well as a formative assessment tool, helping teachers diagnose student or class instructional needs on the spot.

This form of classroom assessment includes questions posed and answered during instruction, class discussions, interviews, conferences, and oral examinations. For instance, a math teacher might have a student "think out loud" to talk through her approach to solving a math problem. Depending on the context, the teacher might respond with feedback to support learning (a formative use) or with a judgment about the sufficiency of learning (a summative use). Given appropriate questioning strategies, personal communication is a flexible, on-demand means of assessment that we can bring into play literally at a moment's notice. Selected response items can be posed orally, written response exercises can be posed orally, and some performance assessment tasks can be demonstrated orally in either a formative or a summative assessment context. When we do so, the assessment method is considered to be personal communication.

Further insights about the development and use of personal communication forms of assessment will be provided in Chapter 8.

A final note on assessment methods: Sometimes you may hear "portfolio assessment" referred to as an assessment method. While portfolios can be a powerful aid to learning, they are a vehicle for teachers and students to use to track, reflect on, and communicate about achievement. Portfolios often contain pieces of evaluated work, each representing a learning target or portion of one. Each piece will be evaluated according to the type of learning target it represents, so there may be multiple assessment methods used within one portfolio. The portfolio itself is the repository of evidence; it is not the method by which the evidence is assessed. (See Chapter 10 for an in-depth discussion of portfolios.)

■ Selecting an Appropriate Assessment Method

As you prepare to assess student learning, it is helpful to maintain a balanced perspective regarding the use of these assessment options. Keep in mind that none of these methods is inherently superior to the others: different methods work well (or not so well) with different types of achievement targets. At various times in education in the United States one method or another has emerged as the popular option. For decades it was the traditional multiple-choice (selected response) test, often economically machine scored with an optical marks reader or via computer online for ease of reporting. Then, with the intention of making assessment a more "authentic" experience, the focus shifted to performance assessment. However, neither ease of scoring or "authenticity" (the degree to which the assessment matches an application from life beyond school) is an acceptable basis upon which to select the appropriate assessment method. Recently we have experienced a more justifiable approach to expanding the repertoire of assessment methods used. The increased focus on content standards designed to prepare students for college and career opportunities has dictated more complex learning in all subjects, which has necessitated greater reliance on a more expansive range of written response and performance assessment options.

Our goal in assessment design is to use the most powerful assessment option available. Power is maximized by using a method capable of accurately reflecting the target in question and by selecting the method that generates results with greatest efficiency. Accuracy should be nonnegotiable for every assessment: we always want the highest-resolution picture of achievement we can get. This requires beginning with the proper method. Efficiency is a secondary consideration: we also want maximum information for minimum cost. That means, for example, that we want to use the smallest possible sample of student performance that can lead us to a confident conclusion and we want the method that is the least time-consuming and easiest to score.

Note that three of the four assessment methods described here call for students to develop original responses. Some require written responses, others call for demonstration of complex performance skills, and still others entail the creation of products. These take more time to administer and certainly more time to score than, say, a true/false test. So given this fact, you might ask, why not just use this most efficient option—selected response—all the time? The reason is that selected response assessment formats cannot accurately reflect all of the kinds of achievement we expect of our students. The challenge, given a choice of methods, is first to pick the viable candidates (those methods capable of reflecting the target accurately) and then to select the most efficient method for your context—the one providing the most accurate evidence per unit of time.

Unfortunately, over past decades the great efficiency (low cost) of multiple-choice test development, scoring, and reporting has caused many to limit their achievement expectations of students to those that can be reflected using this format. This has had the effect of severely restricting the range of valued outcomes of schools. Luckily, the impact of this trend has been uncovered and important complex targets have been reintroduced into the curriculum.

> An assessment's power comes from its ability to provide accurate information as efficiently as possible.

Because matching the assessment method to the learning target is so crucial to the creation of a quality assessment, let's start our exploration of good design there. We have established the need to assess four kinds of achievement (knowledge, reasoning, skills, and products) and that we have four assessment methods at our disposal to do so (selected response, written response, performance assessment, and personal

figure 4.4 ■ Target-Method Match Activity

Target Type	Assessment Method			
	1. Selected Response	2. Written Response	3. Performance Assessment	4. Personal Communication
Knowledge				
Reasoning				
Performance Skill				
Product				

communication). Figure 4.4 crosses these sets of four to create a table, each cell of which connects a kind of achievement with an assessment method. As it turns out, some cells capture strong matches where we can count on the method to work well for that target, while other cells result in matches that make no sense and cannot work well. Your assessment literacy begins by learning where the strong and weak matches reside.

As the first step in your learning process, we want you to begin by simply relying on your common sense to see if you can figure out where the strong and weak matches are. Then we will share our sense of the good and bad matches.

1. Begin with the "Knowledge" row and decide which assessment methods can work for that kind of target. Refer to Figure 3.4 in Chapter 3 to review examples of knowledge targets. Mark each cell in the "Knowledge" row using the following key:

   Strong: The method can provide accurate evidence for all kinds of *knowledge* targets.

   Good: The method can provide accurate evidence for many to most kinds of *knowledge* targets. There are some exceptions.

   Partial: The method can provide accurate evidence for some kinds of *knowledge* targets, with cautions.

   Poor: The method cannot provide accurate evidence for any kinds of *knowledge* targets.

2. After completing the "Knowledge" row, move down to the "Reasoning" row and mark each cell following the same procedure. Refer to Figure 3.6 in Chapter 3 to review examples of reasoning targets. Use the key from Step 1, substituting *reasoning* for *knowledge*.

3. Follow the same procedure for the "Performance Skill" row. Refer to Figure 3.7 in Chapter 3 to review examples of performance skill targets. Use the key from Step 1, substituting *performance skill* for *knowledge*.

4. Follow the same procedure for the "Product" row. Refer to Figure 3.8 in Chapter 3 to review examples of product targets. Use the key from Step 1, substituting *product* for *knowledge*.

When you have completed the chart in Figure 4.4, continue reading in the text to compare your evaluations with ours.

Assessing Knowledge Targets Accurately

Knowledge targets represent the factual information, procedural knowledge, and conceptual understandings that underpin all other learning targets in each discipline. Among the methods, there are two strong matches, one good match, and one partial match. *As you read through the following explanations of the matches for the "Knowledge" row, please circle on the chart the cells containing choices you made that differ from the answers here.*

1. Knowledge Targets × Selected Response Assessment: *Good Match* We can use selected response assessment to measure student mastery of discrete elements of knowledge such as important history facts, spelling words, foreign language vocabulary, and parts of a cell. However, this method is not always an accurate measure of knowledge targets calling for conceptual understanding, such as "Describe how each food group contributes to a healthy body" or "Describe elements of design in a work of art." For that reason, it is a good match rather than a strong match: some types of knowledge targets are not captured well by selected response methodology.

These tests are efficient in that we can administer large numbers of multiple-choice or true/false test items per unit of testing time, permitting us to sample widely and draw relatively confident generalizations from the content sampled. Just remember, this option only works well when students bring to the table a sufficiently well-developed reading proficiency to be able to understand what each question is asking. So use it cautiously in primary grades and with struggling readers.

2. Knowledge Targets × Written Response Assessment: *Strong Match* When the domain of knowledge is defined, not as elements in isolation, but rather as important relationships among elements or understanding of larger concepts—in other words, where the knowledge to be mastered is organized in complex relationships—we can test student mastery by having them respond to a prompt calling for a written explanation. We might, for example, ask students to describe causes of westward migration in U.S. history or differences among igneous, metamorphic, and sedimentary rocks.

In this case, we sample with fewer exercises than with multiple-choice tests because each written response can provide more evidence of mastery of deeper levels of knowledge and understanding. Besides, students need to spend more time composing their response than merely selecting their response. And, remember, with this format students must also possess sufficient writing proficiency to demonstrate their knowledge and understanding with this method. At the primary level, before students are writing sentences, a substitute for written response is often a task involving creating a drawing with labels. Older primary students might know and understand the material but be unable to write well enough to communicate it in this manner, so we should be prepared to use another assessment method when this is the case.

3. Knowledge Targets × Performance Assessment: *Partial Match*   You may have predicted that the match between performance assessment (observation and professional judgment) and content knowledge would be stronger. In some instances it can be a good choice, but in most contexts, it is problematic.

It is a good match with primary students and with older students who cannot read or write. To assess their mastery of knowledge targets, we can observe them engaged in a task, such as pointing to the letter *d* when shown a picture of a dog to test their recognition of initial consonant sounds.

In all other instances, it is a good match only when the student performs well. A performance assessment calls for the use of knowledge in some context—either in a demonstration, such as an oral presentation, or in the creation of a product, such as a brochure or editorial. If a student is successful at the task (and if the task requires the knowledge we are intending to test), then we can conclude that the student has mastered the underpinning knowledge target(s). However, if the student doesn't perform well, it is difficult to say that the problem was lack of knowledge. Success at a performance task always requires more than knowledge. It also requires some reasoning; that is, the performer must figure out how to use the requisite knowledge to carry out the task. A lack of success cannot be attributed to a lack of knowledge.

For example, to complete a successful engine repair, mechanics must know how engines work and use that knowledge to figure out what's going wrong. When presented with a malfunctioning engine in the context of a mechanic's certification test, if candidates succeed in producing a smoothly running engine, we can infer that they did, in fact, know what they needed to know to succeed. But what if they fail? Is that failure attributable to a lack of requisite knowledge? We just don't know. If may be due to failed reasoning proficiency—they may not have identified the right cause of the problem. Or it may be due to misuse of the tools needed to complete the repair—a performance assessment problem. This confounding is present whenever a performer fails a performance assessment.

Here is the point: If all we want to find out is if a student is a master of some important knowledge, why would we elect to go through all of this? We have three better choices than performance assessment that don't confound success with reasoning proficiency: selected response, written response, and personal communication. To assess mastery of knowledge, we need only ask if our students know. Notice also that, in the example of a mechanic's failure or any performance assessment failure, if we wanted to find out why the student failed, we would need to turn immediately to one of these other methods to try to ferret out the true cause. As a teacher in any context, if we wanted to plan instruction to promote the future success of the struggling learner, we would need to find the true cause in order to plan the teaching and learning remedy.

4. Knowledge Targets × Personal Communication: *Strong Match*   The final option for assessing mastery of knowledge is direct personal communication with students, for example, by asking questions and evaluating answers. This is a strong match across all grade levels, especially with limited amounts of knowledge to be mastered, few students to be assessed, and in contexts in which we need not store records of performance for long periods of time.

However, this is a time- and labor-intensive assessment method; if our domain of knowledge to assess is large, we are faced with the need to ask a large number of questions to cover it well. That doesn't fit the resource realities in most classrooms. Further, if the number of students to be assessed is large, this option may not allow enough time to sample each student's learning well. And, if we must store records of performance over an extended period of time, written records will be needed for each student over a broad sample of questions. This, too, eats up a lot of time.

Assessment via personal communication works well in those situations when teachers are checking student mastery of content in order to make immediate adjustments during instruction. Further, with some students in some contexts, it is the only method that will yield accurate information. For various reasons, some students just cannot or will not participate in the other forms of assessment, such as those who experience debilitating evaluation anxiety, have difficulty reading English, or have learning disabilities.

Assessing Reasoning Targets Accurately

Reasoning targets specify ways we want students to learn to use their knowledge to solve problems. In the previous chapter, we described five patterns of reasoning: inference, analysis, comparison, classification, evaluation, and synthesis. All four available methods of assessment represent acceptable options here: two are good matches and two are strong matches. *As you read through the following explanations of the matches for the "Reasoning" row, please circle on your trial run chart the cells containing choices you made that differ from the answers that follow.*

1. Reasoning Targets × Selected Response: *Good Match*   This answer may also surprise you. Many mistakenly believe that selected response assessment can tap only discrete elements or bits of knowledge (e.g., recall). While it is a good choice for that type of knowledge, this method can also serve us well with patterns of reasoning when sound reasoning results in a correct or best answer. For example, selected response items can determine whether students can make inferences, compare elements of a text, and make generalizations in reading as shown in the following examples of questions from a reading test:

- *Make inferences*—Which sentence tells an idea you can infer from this passage? (Offer options, only one of which is correct.)
- *Summarize information*—Which sentence best summarizes what the passage is about? (Offer options, only one of which is correct.)
- *Compare information*—Which sentence tells how the two types of meat-eating plants are alike? (Offer statements of similarity, only one of which is correct.)
- *Make generalizations*—Which statement can you support after reading the passage? (Offer response options, only one of which is supported by the text.)

One benefit of using multiple-choice items for these types of reasoning proficiencies is that we can craft plausible wrong answers that respondents might select when the knowledge they rely on is incorrect or their reasoning is flawed. In a formative context, test items built in this way can help teachers diagnose and correct common flaws in students' reasoning.

But understand also that there are limits to the role of selected response in the reasoning domain. For example, evaluative reasoning—the ability to express and defend a judgment, opinion, or point of view—cannot be tested using multiple-choice or true/false items because this kind of reasoning requires at least a presentation of the defense for the judgment made or position taken. In this case, it is the strength of the defense that is evaluated. Similarly, synthesis does not lend itself to being measured through selected response items either. Answers are not merely right or wrong—they vary in quality. Still further, when complex reasoning problems involve several steps or the problem solution requires application of several different patterns of reasoning, the assessor must turn to the more complex assessment methods. When straightforward patterns of reasoning such as inference, analysis, comparison, and classification are being assessed, selected response can be a good choice.

2. Reasoning Targets × Written Response Assessment: *Strong Match*   Written response assessment is an excellent way to assess student reasoning and problem solving. Student writing provides an ideal window into their thinking. Teachers can create challenging exercises that ask students to analyze, compare, draw complex inferences, evaluate, or use some combination of these proficiencies, explaining their reasoning in writing.

Of course, the key to evaluating the quality of student responses to such tasks is for the assessor to understand the pattern of reasoning required and be able to verify its presence in student writing. This calls for exercises that ask students to reason through an issue or solve a problem, not just regurgitate something that they learned earlier. And these exercises must be accompanied by clear and appropriate scoring criteria that reflect sound reasoning, not just content mastery. The rubrics for the reasoning patterns provided in Chapter 6 can be helpful in formulating those scoring guides.

3. Reasoning Targets × Performance Assessment: *Good Match* We can watch students in the act of problem solving in a science lab, for example, and evaluate their proficiency. To the extent that they carry out proper procedures or find solutions when stymied, they reveal their ability to carry out a pattern of reasoning. When we watch students work with math manipulatives to demonstrate a problem solution or figure out how to use a computer software program to accomplish something that they haven't done before, we may be able to see their reasoning unfolding in their actions.

However, again, evaluating reasoning proficiency on the basis of the quality of student performances or products does have some risks. If the performance is weak or the product is weak, did the student fail to perform because of a lack of basic knowledge, failure to reason productively, lack of skills required by the demonstration, or insufficient expertise at completing the product? We must be sure that the task given to students does not ask for skills or product-development capabilities beyond their experience if we are to get an accurate read of their reasoning proficiencies. For example, it would be acceptable to ask students to create a poster to demonstrate their ability to compare and contrast two objects or concepts, but it would be problematic to ask them to create a commercial that compares and contrasts those two objects. In the latter case, there are just too many factors that could lead to a poor performance that don't relate to students' ability to compare and contrast, which is the learning target to be assessed.

4. Reasoning Targets × Personal Communication: *Strong Match* One of the strongest matches between target and assessment method is the use of personal communication to evaluate student reasoning. Its power resides in the fact that teachers can do any or all of the following:

- Ask questions that probe the clarity, accuracy, relevance, depth, and breadth of reasoning.
- Have students ask each other questions and listen for evidence of sound reasoning.
- Have students reason out loud, describing their thinking as they confront a problem.
- Have students recount their reasoning processes.
- Simply listen intentionally during class discussions for evidence of sound reasoning.

Just talking informally with students can also reveal much about student learning when we know what we're looking for. However, with this method, it will take more time to carry out the assessment and to keep records of results. Once again, quality scoring rubrics will be the key to unbiased assessment. The rubrics provided in Chapter 6 will be helpful in developing those scoring criteria.

Assessing Mastery of Performance Skills Accurately

Performance skill targets are those where a demonstration or physical skill-based performance is at the heart of the learning. *As you read through the following explanations of the matches for the "Performance Skill" row, please circle on the chart the cells containing choices you made that differ from the answers here.*

1. Performance Skill Targets × Selected Response Assessment: *Partial Match*   This answer may surprise you. It surprised us, too. For a long time we had this rated as a poor match because how could a multiple-choice or matching item measure a skill, such as *Performs CPR effectively*? But upon closer examination, we found a few measurement skills that are routinely assessed with multiple-choice or fill-in-the-blank items. When the learning target calls for measuring with tools, there is a degree of physical dexterity involved, so these are classified as performance skill targets and we can and do evaluate them with selected response items. For example, we can present a drawing of an angle, ask students to use a protractor to determine its measure, and then to either choose the correct measure from a list of options or write their answer in the space provided.

This is a very partial match, however. Beyond those limited cases, selected response is a poor match for performance skill targets. We can check for prerequisite knowledge, but we cannot use a multiple-choice test to determine whether students can actually play their instruments in band class.

2. Performance Skill Targets × Written Response Assessment: *Poor Match*   Assessing a student's ability to converse in Chinese using a written response makes no sense. Few of us would think of doing that. We cannot evaluate this kind of oral communication proficiency or any other behavioral manifestation of competence using written communication.

3. Performance Skill Targets × Performance Assessment: *Strong Match*   When our assessment goal is to find out if students can demonstrate performance skills, such as play a role in a dramatic performance, play a musical instrument, effectively give a formal speech, or maintain balance while walking on a beam, then there is only one way to assess. We must observe them while they are demonstrating the desired skills and make judgments as to their quality. This calls for performance assessment.

4. Performance Skill Targets × Personal Communication: *Partial Match*   Finally, personal communication represents an excellent means of skills assessment when the skills in question have to do with oral communication proficiency, such as speaking a foreign language. In these instances, personal communication *is* the focus of the performance assessment. When the skill target is *not* related to oral proficiency, however, personal communication cannot provide accurate information about level of mastery.

Assessing Product Targets Accurately

Product targets describe learning in terms of artifacts where creation of a product is the goal of the learning target. Only one assessment method is suited to products. The others are poor matches. *As you read through the following explanations of the matches for the "Product" row, please circle on the chart the cells containing choices you made that differ from the answers here.*

1. Product Targets × Selected Response Assessment: *Poor Match*   We can only use selected response to determine if students possess some types of prerequisite knowledge, but that does not equate to proficiency in creating the product itself. This method will not give accurate information about mastery of any kind of product target.

2. Product Targets × Written Response Assessment: *Poor Match*   The same is true for written response assessment of product targets. If you rated this method more highly, chances are you were thinking of the written report or essay as written response assessment. Remember, by definition written response is a short or extended answer to a question or prompt and by definition we limit it to assessing knowledge and reasoning targets.

3. Product Targets × Performance Assessment: *Strong Match*   If our assessment goal is to determine whether students can create a certain kind of achievement-related product such that it meets certain standards of quality, there is no other way to assess than to have them actually create one and evaluate it using those standards. In fact, performance assessment represents the only means of direct assessment. The best measure of the ability to create a quality ceramic pot is the quality of the finished pot. The best measure of the ability to write an informative text is the quality of the writing itself.

4. Product Targets × Personal Communication: *Poor Match*   Personal communication is a poor match for assessing product targets. We can only use it to determine if students have the prerequisite knowledge required to successfully create the artifact.

Figure 4.5 provides a summary of the range of matches between target types and assessment methods. Figure 4.6 gives some examples of learning targets, their classification, and their possible assessment choices.

figure 4.5 ■ Matching Learning Targets to Assessment Methods

	Selected Response	Written Response	Performance Assessment	Personal Communication
Knowledge	**Good** Can assess isolated elements of knowledge and some relationships among them	**Strong** Can assess elements of knowledge and relationships among them	**Partial** Can assess elements of knowledge and relationships among them in certain contexts	**Strong** Can assess elements of knowledge and relationships among them
Reasoning	**Good** Can assess many but not all reasoning targets	**Strong** Can assess all reasoning targets	**Good** Can assess reasoning targets in the context of certain tasks in certain contexts	**Strong** Can assess all reasoning targets
Performance Skill	**Partial** Good match for some measurement skill targets; not a good match otherwise	**Poor** Cannot assess skill level; can only assess prerequisite knowledge and reasoning	**Strong** Can observe and assess skills as they are being performed	**Partial** Strong match for some oral communication proficiencies; not a good match otherwise
Product	**Poor** Cannot assess the quality of a product; can only assess prerequisite knowledge and reasoning	**Poor** Cannot assess the quality of a product; can only assess prerequisite knowledge and reasoning	**Strong** Can directly assess the attributes of quality of products	**Poor** Cannot assess the quality of a product; can only assess prerequisite knowledge and reasoning

Source: Chappuis, Jan; Stiggins, Rick J.; Chappuis, Steve; Arter, Judith A., *Classroom Assessment for Student learning: Doing it Right—Using it Well*, 2nd Ed., ©2012. Reprinted and Electronically reproduced by permission of Pearson Education, Inc., New York, New York.

figure 4.6 ■ For Example Target × Method Matches

Learning Target	Target Type	Assessment Method(s)
Distinguish between situations that can be modeled with linear functions and with exponential functions. (CCSS Mathematics, 2010, p. 70)	Knowledge	Selected Response, Written Response, Personal Communication
Know the remainder theorem for polynomial division.	Knowledge	Selected Response, Written Response, Personal Communication
Use ratio and rate reasoning to solve real-world and mathematical problems. (CCSS Mathematics, 2010, p. 42)	Reasoning	Selected Response, Written Response, Performance Assessment, Personal Communication
Given a two-digit number, mentally find 10 more or 10 less than the number without having to count; explain reasoning used. (CCSS Mathematics, 2010, p. 16)	Reasoning	Personal Communication
Make strategic use of digital media in presentations to enhance understanding of findings, reasoning, and evidence and to add interest. (CCSS ELA, 2012, p. 50)	Performance Skill	Performance Assessment
Tell a story or recount an experience with appropriate facts and relevant descriptive details, speaking audibly in coherent sentences. (CCSS ELA, 2010, p. 23)	Performance Skill	Performance Assessment, Personal Communication
Draw geometric shapes with given conditions. Focus on constructing triangles from three measures of angles or sides, noticing when the conditions determine a unique triangle, more than one triangle, or no triangle. (CCSS Mathematics, 2010, p. 50)	Product	Performance Assessment
Write informative/explanatory texts to examine and convey complex ideas and information clearly and accurately through effective selection, organization, and analysis of content. (CCSS ELA, 2010, p. 45)	Product	Performance Assessment

Source: Common Core State Standards (CCSS) found in National Governors Association Center for Best Practices (2010a, 2010b)

MyEdLab **Self-Check 4.1**

MyEdLab **Application Exercise 4.1** Selecting the assessment method for the learning target type

■ The Assessment Development Cycle

All assessments, regardless of the method chosen, need to go through the same thoughtful development process to ensure quality. That process is comprised of three stages: planning, development, and use (Figure 4.7). In this section we will describe the planning stage. Then we will address the development stage and use stage in more depth in each of the four "methods" chapters that follow.

figure 4.7 ■ The Assessment Development Cycle

Planning Stage
1. Determine the intended users and uses of the assessment information.
2. Identify and classify the learning targets to be assessed.
3. Select the appropriate assessment method or methods.
4. Determine the appropriate sample size.

Development Stage
5. Develop or select items, tasks, and scoring procedures.
6. Critique the overall assessment for quality.

Use Stage
7. Conduct and score the assessment, making note of difficulties.
8. Revise as needed for future use.

The Assessment Planning Stage

The planning stage includes four steps: (1) determine the assessment purpose, (2) specify the intended learning targets, (3) select the appropriate assessment method(s), and (4) determine appropriate sample frame. So far in Chapters 2 through 4, we have introduced the first three steps. Now we want you to see them in action. Then we'll address the matter of sampling.

Step 1: Determining the Assessment Purpose   Our first planning decision is the application of Key 1: Clear Purpose. This establishes the assessment *context*. Who will use the results of this assessment? How will the results be used—to inform what decisions? As you recall from Chapter 2, the use may be formative—to guide further teacher and student actions—or it may be summative—to report level of achievement. Figure 4.8 offers a form you can use to guide your decisions at this first planning step. See Figure 4.9 for high school science teacher Amy James's explanation of the benefits of planning multiple formative assessment events into instruction prior to giving the summative assessment.

Step 2: Specifying the Intended Learning Targets   Our second planning decision is the application of Key 2: Clear Targets. This establishes the assessment *focus*. What learning targets do you want to gather information about? At this step, simply

figure 4.8 ■ Step 1: Determining Assessment Purpose

Who will use the information?	
■ Teacher ■ Student ■ Other: _____	
How will the information be used?	
Summatively To measure level of achievement for inclusion in an end-of-term grade Other summative/accountability use:	**Formatively** To diagnose instructional needs To offer feedback to students For student self-assessment and goal setting Other formative use:

list the learning targets you will be teaching, along with their classification (knowledge, reasoning, performance skill, or product), as explained in Chapter 3. Deconstruct any complex content standards into lesson-level learning targets as needed prior to listing them if the focus of the assessment will be on the lesson-level targets.

figure 4.9 ■ From the Classroom: Amy James

I used to . . .

When I began teaching, I would teach a concept over one to two weeks assuming that my students were "getting it" along the way and then would quiz students over that concept. The quiz did very little to inform my instruction, but instead rewarded those students who "got it" and punished those who didn't. Then we moved on and any misunderstandings only accumulated over the course of the unit. At the end of the unit, I was faced with trying to remediate several students over large amounts of material, while other students were ready to move on to the next unit.

Now I . . .

Now I am probing constantly for understanding with both formal and informal styles of formative assessment. I give both verbal and written feedback, as opposed to simply grades, so that both the student and I know what they understand and where they are struggling. I have broken units of study into manageable chunks, or specific learning targets, and assess students in a progressive manner on each learning target. Remediation occurs immediately, allowing students to revisit learning targets that they struggle with. This allows for easy differentiation and grouping, focusing on what each individual student needs help with and allowing those students who have reached understanding to delve deeper into the concepts.

figure 4.9 ■ From the Classroom: Amy James (*Continued*)

Why I changed . . .
I felt as though I wasn't meeting the needs for all of my students, and there just wasn't enough of "me" to go around.

What I notice as a result . . .
I have found that by structuring instruction and assessment in this way, students take more ownership of their learning. Grades become less punitive and intimidating and instead are more of a gauge of the learning progression. Students who often struggle can more easily see their successes and can manage areas that they need to focus their attention on, which raises their confidence. I find that the classroom environment is more positive and focused. Students help each other and work together. I am more able to confer with individual students and groups, meeting more students' needs. And as a whole, I feel that I am more intentionally working to ensure that *all* students reach proficiency for each learning target in each unit. And isn't that the goal for every teacher?!

Source: Reprinted with permission from Amy James, High School Science Teacher, Oldham School District, Crestwood, KY, 2011.

Figure 4.10 shows an example of one teacher's decisions at this second planning step. See Figure 4.11 for second-grade teacher Christine Heilman's explanation of the benefits of clearly specifying the intended learning targets in advance of instruction.

figure 4.10 ■ For Example: Step 2: Specifying the Intended Learning Targets

Learning Targets for a Middle School Quiz on Chemical Changes

Learning Target	Target Type
1. Understand the difference between a physical change and a chemical change.	Knowledge
2. Know that substances can be classified according to their reactive properties.	Knowledge
3. Classify substances according to their reactive properties.	Reasoning
4. Infer real-life applications based on a substance's chemical reaction.	Reasoning

Step 3: Selecting the Appropriate Assessment Method(s)   At this third planning step we apply what we have learned about matching assessment methods to learning target types, which is one component of Key 3: Sound Design. This step is fairly straightforward: once the assessment's learning targets are identified and classified, we select the assessment type or types that we will use to measure them by following the guidelines explained in this chapter and summarized in Figure 4.5.

figure 4.11 ■ From the Classroom: Christine Heilman

I used to . . .

I used to be unclear on what I was supposed to teach, what kids were supposed to learn, and what I should do with students who didn't demonstrate understanding. I carefully planned what I was teaching, but didn't pay much attention to what students were learning. I used textbook assessments and recorded percentages in my grade book, but did no reteaching. Tests were for grading purposes. There was no structure for collaboration or discussion of results. I taught what I thought was important and then "hoped" students would perform well on standardized tests.

Now I . . .

I now have essential learnings planned out for each content area. I focus instruction on student-friendly learning targets that are clearly posted. I write assessments based on state benchmarks with five to eight questions per learning target. I assess student understanding to fine-tune my instruction for the whole class and for individual students. I plan reteaching, interventions, and enrichment as necessary to ensure all students demonstrate understanding of learning targets. I include student reflection pieces, rubrics for student feedback, and error analysis opportunities. Student homework is aligned to learning targets. I send an essential learnings update to parents each month filled with suggestions for how they can follow up at home.

Our team now plans six-week instructional goals, action steps, and instructional strategies that support each goal. We use a variety of written response assessments, checklists, multiple-choice assessments, and student reflections to gather information about student understanding of targets. We share our goals and instructional plans with our resource support teachers so we are all working together to support goals. At the end of each six-week goal, our team comes together to share data. We display our data graphically, analyze student performance on each target, and make plans for intervention. We discuss instructional strategies that worked well in our individual class-rooms so we all have an opportunity to learn from one another.

As a team, we are now very clear in what we are teaching, what we expect students to learn, and how they will demonstrate their learning. We use data to make plans for intervention and ensure remediation opportunities for those who need it. "Hope" is no longer our strategy for test preparation. We have data throughout the year that helps us measure progress on learning targets on an ongoing basis.

Source: Reprinted with permission from Christine Heilman, 2nd-grade Classroom Teacher.

Step 4: Determining the Appropriate Sample Size   In general terms, *to sample* means to select a small portion of something to evaluate it. Is the soup warm enough or the food in need of salt? We sample, taste, infer, and act accordingly. So it is with assessment and student achievement. When we sample, we gather a subset from a population that is so large that examining the whole of it is impracticable or impossible. In our assessment context, we sample *achievement* because, realistically, any assessment can include only a subset of all the questions or tasks we could pose to determine mastery of a given learning target were time unlimited.

We sample achievement to infer the degree to which a student has mastered a given learning target.

Time is never unlimited, so we include only a portion of the possibilities and then use performance on the sample to infer or generalize how much of the material to be learned each student has mastered.

Our sampling challenge in the classroom is to assemble enough evidence to draw a confident conclusion about students' level of achievement without wasting time gathering more than we need. Sample size is in large part determined by teacher judgment. The five major factors to consider are the following:

1. The assessment purpose
2. The nature of the learning target
3. The importance of the learning target to later learning
4. The assessment method
5. The students themselves

Sampling Consideration 1. The Assessment Purpose   With respect to the instructional decision to be made based on assessment results, the more important the decision is, the more certain you must be about achievement status and, in general, the larger (more dependable) should be your sample. So, for example, when designing an assessment to be used formatively to guide immediate instructional decisions, you might be willing to work with a limited sample size. If you misdiagnose, it is relatively easy to correct in the moment. However, if you are assessing to determine an end-of-term grade, the sample size should be sufficiently large to provide a high degree of confidence in the resulting decision because it will be more difficult to reverse the decision later if the assessment proves inaccurate.

Sampling Consideration 2. The Nature of the Learning Target   The broader the scope of the learning target or the greater its complexity, the larger the sample required to cover it thoroughly. For example, measuring students' mastery of using commas in a series correctly will require fewer pieces of evidence than will measuring students' mastery of the use of subject and object pronouns. This sampling challenge is simplified to a certain extent by adopting clear learning targets that identify and thus limit the scope of what students are responsible for learning. In the past, teachers have had to sample broad, vaguely defined domains of achievement such as a semester's worth of world history. When the curriculum is defined in terms of a more focused set of achievement targets, the sampling challenge becomes more manageable.

> When our curriculum is defined in terms of a focused set of achievement targets, the sampling challenge becomes manageable.

Sampling Consideration 3. The Importance of the Learning Target to Later Learning   The more important the learning target is as the foundation of later learning, the more confident you want to be about student mastery, which will require a larger sample of evidence. For example, mastering use of commas in a series is not foundational to mastering other learning targets related to English language conventions, while knowing how to solve quadratic equations with one variable is foundational to other algebra learning targets.

Sampling Consideration 4. The Assessment Method   The more information provided by one assessment item, exercise, or task, the fewer items may be needed to cover the domain of the content standard. For example, a multiple-choice test item typically provides one specific piece of evidence. Its focus and coverage are narrow. So typically we use several of them to cover the range of content to be assessed. A written response or performance task, on the other hand, tends to provide more evidence and thus samples broader targets in students' responses. So we typically need fewer of them. Each assessment method brings with it specific rules of evidence for sampling within these considerations. We will address those in more detail in Chapters 5–8.

Sampling Consideration 5. The Students Themselves   The level of individual student achievement comes into play more on the formative side than the summative side, that is, during the learning. The key variable is where any given student is on the continuum of mastery. If initial evidence shows that a student has clearly mastered or clearly *not* mastered the learning target, you can stop there. For example, if you ask a couple of questions and a particular student gets them all right or all wrong, then a trend is clear. However, if the student gets some right and some wrong, it may be necessary to keep asking until the trend becomes apparent. Here is the guideline for thoughtful application: you have probably gathered enough evidence if, based on that evidence, you can guess with a degree of certainty how that student would do if you offered one more chance.

In summary, in high-stakes decision contexts, with broader and more complex learning targets, and when employing selected response methodology, you will want to think about gathering relatively richer samples of evidence. But while the learning is underway in the classroom with lesson-level targets or when relying on assessment methods that yield more information per item, smaller samples may suffice.

Combining the Planning Decisions into an Assessment Blueprint

An assessment blueprint is simply a record of the decisions you have made in assessment planning Steps 2, 3, and 4, with consideration for the decisions made in Step 1. It is used when more than one learning target will be assessed. (If you are only assessing achievement of one learning target, you can dispense with the blueprint.) Here's how it works:

1. List the learning targets that will be the focus of instruction, being clear about the classification of each. If you are planning an assessment that is completely comprised of one method, use Figure 4.12 as your template. If you are planning an assessment that includes multiple methods, use Figure 4.13 as your template.
2. Determine the sample frame by deciding how many items or exercises you will need for each learning target to be assessed. In a formative context, there may

figure 4.12 ■ For Example: Assessment Blueprint (Single Assessment Method)

Grade 5 Reading Selected Response Quiz

Content Standard: Know and apply grade-level phonics and word analysis skills in decoding words.

a. Use combined knowledge of all letter-sound correspondences, syllabication patterns, and morphology (e.g., roots and affixes) to read accurately unfamiliar multisyllabic words in context and out of context (National Governors Association Center for Best Practices, 2010a, CCSS ELA, p. 17).

Learning Targets	Problems	# of Points
Identify syllabication patterns	1–3	3
Identify root words	4–8	5
Explain meanings of prefixes and suffixes	9–14	6
Define words with Latin roots	15–20	6

be only one target as you help students ascend toward success in small steps. The sample must be large enough to support an inference about student mastery of that one target. When the assessment is to cover more than one achievement target, again, you will need to determine how many you will need to support inferences about student mastery of each.

If the context demands a summative assessment, such as a final exam in high school, and it must cover various learning targets, some of which are more important

figure 4.13 ■ For Example: Assessment Blueprints (Multiple Assessment Methods)

Middle School Quiz on Chemical Changes

Learning Target	Target Type	Method	# of Points
1. Understand the difference between a physical change and a chemical change.	Knowledge	Selected Response	3
2. Know that substances can be classified according to their reactive properties.	Knowledge	Selected Response	2
3. Classify substances according to their reactive properties.	Reasoning	Written Response	4
4. Infer real-life applications based on a substance's chemical reaction.	Reasoning	Written Response	4

(Continued)

figure 4.13 ■ For Example: Assessment Blueprints (Multiple Assessment Methods) (*Continued*)

Grade 2 Quiz on Place Value

Learning Target	Target Type	Method	# of Points
1. Understand that the three digits of a three-digit number represent amounts of hundreds, tens, and ones.	Knowledge	Selected Response	3
2. Read numbers to 1,000.	Knowledge	Performance Assessment	2
3. Write numbers to 1,000.	Knowledge	Selected Response	4
4. Order numbers through three digits.	Knowledge	Selected Response	4
5. Compare numbers through three digits.	Reasoning	Written Response	2

than others, those priority targets should command more items. This will have the effect of weighting the priority targets more heavily in the final score (Figure 4.14).

Whether you will be creating an assessment or selecting one from published materials, doing so without having a blueprint can result in lack of congruence between instruction and assessment, which is a *validity* issue. If you yourself have ever taken a test that didn't seem to measure what the teacher taught, you know what this feels like from the student's point of view. The results simply are not an accurate representation of what you learned. Read middle school science teacher Ken Mattingly's explanation of how he has used the steps in the planning stage of assessment development to improve his teaching (Figure 4.15).

figure 4.14 ■ For Example: Secondary Social Studies Assessment Blueprint

Secondary Social Studies Quiz on Structures of Governments

Content	Knowledge	Comparison
1. Characteristics of different systems of government	9	5
2. Structure of U.S. government	4	5
3. Rights and responsibilities of citizens in different systems of government	7	5

figure 4.15 ■ From the Classroom: Ken Mattingly

I used to . . .

I always believed I was a good teacher. My instructional activities engaged the students, confronting their preconceptions and misconceptions. Everything focused on the big idea of the unit and getting students to mastery of the standards.

Students were periodically assessed throughout the unit to determine how they were doing. I used the results to make adjustments in my teaching and hopefully fill in any gaps that appeared in student understanding. At the end of the unit students took an assessment that contained a mix of essay and multiple-choice questions.

The end-of-unit assessment was designed to address the big ideas of the unit. The multiple-choice questions had answers that attended to student misconceptions and identified specific problems. The essay questions were written to determine the depth of student understanding of key points. After taking the assessment, students received feedback on their performance in the form of a percentage grade.

Now I . . .

I begin my instructional design process long before I start a unit. I take the standards for the unit and deconstruct them into the knowledge, reasoning, skill, and product targets that make up each standard. I then decide how I will assess each target *during* the unit and at the *end* of the unit. A test plan for the end-of-unit assessment is created, paying attention to match the target to the correct assessment method and determining the proper question sample size.

With my targets developed and unit assessment determined, I now turn my attention to selecting instructional strategies that will enable my students to reach the targets. Whereas before I would pick activities that tied in to the big idea, I now select those that attend to a specific target or group of targets. Any activity, lesson, or strategy that doesn't move students toward mastery of a target is weeded out of my instructional plans.

Throughout the unit, students receive feedback on their performance on targets along with a discussion of how they can close the gap to mastery. Then on the unit assessment student performance is broken out by target so that students can see how they did on each individual target. This diagnosis allows for continued, focused work on gaining target mastery.

Why I changed . . .

I changed because it didn't make sense not to. Years of getting roughly the same results from group after group of students left me searching for a way to do things differently. After being exposed to assessment *for* learning practices and comprehending the classroom responsibility shift that would occur with its implementation, I slowly began to incorporate it into my teaching.

What I notice as a result . . .

Everything in my classroom now is more transparent than before. Students no longer have to guess about what they are supposed to learn. I am clearer on my instructional goals, and my students and their parents know what they are expected to learn and do. Involving students as partners in their learning, through feedback and self-analysis, encourages them to continue to try and improve. Student accountability and subject interest has improved, as has overall performance.

Source: Reprinted with permission from Ken Mattingly, 7th-grade Science Teacher, Rockcastle County School District, Mt. Vernon, KY, 2011.

MyEdLab **Self-Check 4.2**
MyEdLab **Application Exercise 4.2** Creating and evaluating an assessment blueprint

The Assessment Development Stage

Step 5 is to develop or select items, tasks, and scoring procedures. Once we select an assessment method and plan how to sample, we need to use our method of choice in a manner that will ensure an accurate portrait of achievement. This means we must build it out of high-quality items or tasks, paying attention to development guidelines specific to each method. We will explore these in the following four chapters.

Step 6 is to review and critique the overall assessment before using it. Regardless of how carefully we plan, things can still go wrong that result in inaccurate measures of achievement. These are known as sources of bias and distortion. Part of becoming assessment literate is recognizing those potential sources of bias and knowing what to do to prevent them while developing, administering, or scoring assessments. Figure 4.16 provides a list of fairness and bias issues that are applicable to all

figure 4.16 ■ Potential Sources of Bias and Distortion Common to All Assessment Methods

Barriers that can occur within the student
■ Language barriers
■ Emotional upset
■ Poor health
■ Physical handicap
■ Peer pressure to mislead assessor
■ Lack of motivation at time of assessment
■ Lack of testwiseness (understanding how to take tests)
■ Lack of personal confidence leading to evaluation anxiety

Barriers that can occur within the assessment context
■ Insufficient time allotted
■ Noise distractions
■ Poor lighting
■ Discomfort
■ Lack of rapport with assessor
■ Cultural insensitivity in assessor or assessment
■ Lack of proper equipment

Barriers that arise from the assessment itself
■ Directions lacking or vague
■ Poorly worded questions
■ Misleading layout
■ Poor reproduction of test questions
■ Missing information

Source: Chappuis, Jan; Stiggins, Rick J.; Chappuis, Steve; Arter, Judith A., *Classroom Assessment for Student learning: Doing it Right–Using it Well*, 2nd Ed., ©2012. Reprinted and Electronically reproduced by permission of Pearson Education, Inc., New York, New York.

assessment methods. We will explain the method-specific sources of bias to avoid as we describe how to develop each type of assessment in the following four chapters.

The Assessment Use and Refinement Stage

Step 7 is to conduct and score the assessment, making note of difficulties encountered. Step 8 is to revise the assessment as needed, based on observations you made while conducting and scoring the assessment.

■ Formative Assessment Ideas for Use with Assessment Blueprints

MyEdLab
Video Example 4.1
Making Targets Clear to Students: AP Calculus

The blueprint you create for any assessment can become the foundation of assessment for learning and student-involvement activities. With information provided by the blueprint, you can do any of the following:

- Group students for further instruction based on their results on individual learning targets.
- Distribute the blueprint with students at the beginning of instruction to build a clear vision of the learning they will be responsible for attaining.
- Ask students to determine where on the blueprint each day's lessons fit.
- Have students write practice questions for cells on the blueprint as a way to review content taught.

We share more ideas for using assessment blueprints with students at the end of Chapters 5 and 6.

Watch Video Example 4.1 to hear how high school mathematics teacher Jennifer McDaniel incorporates test blueprints into her plan to make targets clear to her students.

MyEdLab **Application Exercise 4.3** Using an assessment blueprint

■ Summary: A Vision of Excellence in Classroom Assessment

In Chapter 2, we focused on Key 1: Clear Purpose by asking, "Why are we assessing?" In Chapter 3 we focused on Key 2: Clear Targets by asking, "What are we assessing?" In this chapter we began our exploration of Key 3: Sound Design by asking, "How should we assess?" Sound classroom assessments begin with a clear sense of purpose, have clear and appropriate learning targets, and rely on a proper assessment method. A proper method is one that provides the most accurate information from which we infer the actual level of achievement of the learning target.

We established four categories of assessment methods: selected response, written response, performance assessment, and personal communication. We discussed how we might use them selectively to assess student learning on different types of targets. Given the range of targets, we need to apply all of the assessment methods we have at our disposal—no single method can serve all of our assessment needs at all grade levels. We introduced the assessment development cycle with emphasis on the planning stage. We introduced the concepts of sampling and bias.

In the next four chapters, we continue learning about sound design by describing how to develop and use each method and then critique each for quality. We also will explore when and how to involve students in the assessment process while they're learning. This is a powerful teaching and motivational tool.

Chapter 4 Suggested Activities

End-of-chapter activities are intended to help you master the chapter's learning targets. They are designed to deepen your understanding of the chapter content, provide opportunities for personal reflection on ideas presented, and serve as a basis for discussion among peers. You may wish to do all of them or select those that you believe will be most useful to your learning. Each activity is correlated to one or more chapter learning targets to help with your selection.

Chapter 4 Learning Targets

As a result of your study of Chapter 4, you will be able to do the following:

1. Select the appropriate method(s) to assess specific learning targets
2. Follow the steps in the assessment planning process and create an assessment blueprint
3. Use an assessment blueprint with students as assessment for learning

Chapter 4 Activities

Activity 4.1   Keeping a Reflective Journal (All chapter learning targets)

Activity 4.2   Reflecting on Target–Method Match (Learning Target 1)

Activity 4.3   Practicing with Target–Method Match (Learning Target 1)

Activity 4.4   Auditing an Assessment for Clear Learning Targets (Learning Target 2)

Activity 4.5   Making an Assessment Blueprint (Learning Target 2)

Activity 4.6   Planning an Assessment for Learning Application (Learning Target 3)

Activity 4.7   Comparing Your Experiences with Information from the Chapter (All chapter learning targets)

Activity 4.8   Answering an Interview Question (All chapter learning targets)

Activity 4.9   Reflecting on Your Learning from Chapter 4 (All chapter learning targets)

Activity 4.10 Adding to Your Growth Portfolio (All chapter learning targets)

Activity 4.1: Keeping a Reflective Journal

Keep a record of your thoughts, questions, and insights as you read Chapter 4.

Activity 4.2: Reflecting on Target–Method Match

This is a follow-up activity to the Target–Method Match activity you completed using Figure 4.4.

1. After reading through the explanations of the various matches of target types to assessment methods, consider the cells you circled as mismatches between your answers and the answers in the text.
2. For each of the cells you circled, decide the following:
   - "Sticking Point" (It still doesn't fit with my thinking)
   - "Misconception" (I didn't understand it at first, but now it makes sense)
   - "Question" ("Yes but…" or "Yes and…")

   Mark your circled answers on Figure 4.4 with the key "S," "M," or "Q" to reflect your judgment.
3. Write a short reflection that explores each sticking point, misconception, and question you identified.

Activity 4.3: Practicing with Target–Method Match

Select a short unit that you have prepared to teach.

1. List the learning targets that will be the focus of the unit.
2. Classify each according to target type.
3. Determine which assessment method you would use for each, following the guidelines for target–method match.

Activity 4.4: Auditing an Assessment for Clear Learning Targets

Select an assessment that you have not personally developed. It may be one you have taken as a part of your studies, or it may be one that is a part of curriculum materials you are preparing to teach. In this activity you will work backward from an assessment to create the blueprint.

1. Create the assessment's blueprint by doing the following:
   - Identify and write down what learning target each item, exercise, or task assesses. Describe the learning in whatever terms you can. If two or more items, exercises, or tasks address the same learning target, use the same terms to describe that learning.
   - Determine how many points each item is worth.

2. Evaluate the blueprint for its match to instruction. Does it accurately represent what you think should be taught? (If this is one you have personally taken, does it accurately represent what was taught?)
   - Are some learning targets overrepresented? If so, which one(s)?
   - Are some learning targets underrepresented? If so, which one(s)?
   - Are any important learning targets left out? If so, which one(s)?
   - Do all items on the assessment align directly with the learning they are intended to assess?
3. Evaluate the blueprint for appropriate sampling.
   - Is the amount of evidence per learning target sufficient to serve the intended use of the information? If not, which ones need adjusting?
   - Is there too much evidence for any learning targets? If so, which ones need adjusting?
   - Does the number of points for each learning target represent its relative importance within the whole? If not, which ones are out of balance?
4. Write a short critique of the assessment noting the changes you would recommend, if any, based on what you discovered while creating its blueprint. If you discovered no problems, write a short rationale for your judgment.

Activity 4.5: Making an Assessment Blueprint

Select a unit you are preparing to teach and create a blueprint for an assessment you might use.

1. Decide whether the assessment information will be used summatively or formatively.
2. List the learning targets that will be the focus of instruction. Classify each target. Determine which assessment method(s) you will use.
3. Select or modify one of the assessment blueprints illustrated in this chapter. Write your learning targets on the assessment blueprint you have selected or modified.
4. Identify an appropriate sample size for each learning target following the considerations in this chapter.
5. Save your blueprint for use with activities in the upcoming chapters.

Activity 4.6: Planning an Assessment for Learning Application

Select a unit that you have prepared to teach and then complete the following activities.

1. Create an assessment blueprint for the unit following the instructions in Activity 4.5.
2. Choose one or more of the ideas described in the chapter for using an assessment blueprint with students. Write yourself instructions for what you would do.

3. Describe the effects on student motivation and achievement that you believe will result from engaging in the activity.

Activity 4.7: Comparing Your Experiences with Information from the Chapter

Select one "From the Classroom" entry from Chapter 4 and compare it to your experience as a student.

- How is it similar?
- What differences do you notice?
- What conclusions about the benefits of assessment planning might you draw?

Activity 4.8: Answering an Interview Question

Imagine that you are about to interview for a teaching position. The interview team (often a combination of administrators and teachers) is interested in understanding your level of classroom assessment literacy. Review Chapter 4's learning targets and think about what concepts and procedures were most significant to you from the chapter. Then think about what type of question an interview team might ask related to this significant learning. Write the question and draft a short response—one that you could give in one to two minutes orally.

Activity 4.9: Reflecting on Your Learning from Chapter 4

Review the Chapter 4 learning targets and select one that struck you as most significant. Write a short reflection that captures your current understanding. If you are working with a group, discuss what you have written.

Activity 4.10: Adding to Your Growth Portfolio

Any of the activities from this chapter can be used as portfolio entries. Select any activity you have completed or artifact you have created that will demonstrate your mastery of the Chapter 4 learning targets:

1. Select the appropriate method(s) to assess specific learning targets
2. Follow the steps in the assessment planning process and create an assessment blueprint
3. Use an assessment blueprint with students as assessment for learning

Selected Response Assessment

Chapter 5 Learning Targets

As a result of your study of Chapter 5, you will be able to do the following:

1. Make an assessment blueprint for a selected response assessment
2. Write propositions for knowledge and reasoning targets
3. Create selected response items for each format option
4. Audit a selected response assessment for quality
5. Use selected response assessments formatively with students

Based on the history of assessment in schools and our own collective experience as students, when we think of tests, we often envision selected response formats. Multiple-choice items, true/false questions, matching exercises, and fill-in-the-blank questions have played a prominent role in most students' educational experience. We often hear selected response assessment referred to as a "traditional" method because it made its appearance nearly one hundred years ago. Hailed as the new scientific measurement method, those at the forefront of educational innovation welcomed its objectivity, removing the subjectivity of teacher judgment inherent in the previously dominant method: essay assessment. Selected response has had staying power in the classroom and dominance in large-scale accountability testing for two reasons: it is easy to administer to large numbers of students at the same time and inexpensive to score.

As we have seen in Chapter 4, selected response methodology is well suited to a portion—and only a portion—of our content standards. So, if it is the only method used to gather data, only that portion of our valued learning targets will be assessed. Because it has been the dominant format in high-stakes testing, some schools have elected to rely predominantly on selected response formats in their classrooms as a way to prepare for the accountability exam. This has had the effect of severely narrowing the curriculum taught to only the content that can be tested with selected response formats. For those and other reasons, this method is sometimes viewed with distrust, even though it can be a valuable tool in every teacher's assessment repertoire, one tool among many.

In this chapter, we continue our exploration of Key 3: Sound Design (Figure 5.1) by learning how to create high-quality items for each of the four selected

figure 5.1 ■ Keys to Quality Assessment

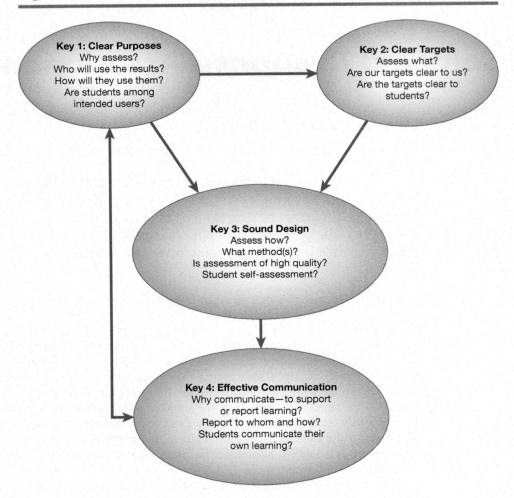

response formats, how to choose when to use which format, and how to use selected response assessments formatively to guide instruction.

■ The Myth of Objectivity

Almost from the time of their first appearance early in the 1900s, selected response assessments have carried a reputation for scientific precision because they appear to be free from the fallibility of human judgment that is required when evaluating responses with other assessment methods. In truth, however, subjectivity—that is, matters of teacher or assessor professional judgment—permeate selected response assessments too. Why? Because all assessments have two basic parts: (1) exercises designed to elicit some kind of response from examinees and (2) answer keys or scoring guides that allow the user to evaluate the quality of that response.

Objectivity in selected response assessment applies only to the scoring system. Well-written multiple-choice test items, for example, allow for just one best answer or a limited set of acceptable answers. This leads to the "objective" scoring of responses: they are right or wrong with no judgment required. However, professional judgment definitely comes into play during the process of writing items. The developer decides what learning targets to assess, how many questions to pose on a test, how to word each question, what the best or correct answers will be, and which incorrect answers to offer as choices, if needed.

All assessments, regardless of format, involve professional judgment. So good assessment requires sound judgment, a matter we will address in this and each of the following chapters. All assessments reflect the assessor's biases or perspectives: the key to your effective use of sound classroom assessment as a part of instruction is to make sure that your perspectives or instructional priorities are informed by current best thinking in the field and are clear and public for your students to see from the outset.

■ Considerations When Using Selected Response Assessment

This method is best used with learning targets calling for foundations of knowledge. It can also be a good choice for some forms of reasoning. A major advantage of this method is its efficiency: it can sample achievement broadly with great efficiency (because of the short response time per item), can be administered to large numbers of students at the same time, and can be scored in large numbers, also very quickly.

However, selected response assessment has limitations. For example, students' mastery of the content being assessed is always at risk of mismeasurement if they don't possess the level of reading proficiency required by the items. Therefore, this would not be an appropriate choice for anyone experiencing difficulty in reading and comprehending the language in which the assessment is written. When selected response assessment is unavoidable for these students, teachers can make adjustments such as reading the questions aloud to them. This is the only way to disentangle subject matter content mastery from reading proficiency and obtain an accurate estimate of achievement of the knowledge and reasoning in question. Keep in mind, however, if the selected response assessment is intended to measure reading proficiency (versus mastery of science or social studies content knowledge), such a remedy would lead to an inappropriate inference about student mastery of the intended target.

In another context, the reading proficiency barrier can be overcome in primary grades when the teacher asks the question of students and the answer choices are represented by pictures. For example, the teacher can ask, "Which of these pictures shows what this story is about?" or "Which set of pictures tells the story in the right order?" Students then select the picture corresponding to their answer choice.

■ Creating a High-Quality Selected Response Assessment

All assessments, regardless of intended use or method selected, need to go through the same development steps to ensure quality.

As we saw in Chapter 4, creating a high-quality assessment, regardless of method chosen, requires that we proceed through the same set of decision steps known as the Assessment Development Cycle (Figure 5.2). In this section we will examine how to carry out each of the steps to plan, develop, and evaluate a selected response assessment to ensure quality.

Step 1: Determining the Assessment Purpose

As with all assessments, the first decision questions that guide development are "Who will use the results?" and "What decisions will they make?" Typically assessment results serve one or more of the following purposes:

- For teachers to diagnose instructional needs prior to or during instruction
- For teachers to offer feedback to students and for students to offer peer feedback
- For students to self-assess and set goals for next steps
- For teachers to measure level of achievement for reporting on report cards

Each one of these purposes can be served with selected response assessments, but it is crucial to begin the design process with these decisions having been made.

figure 5.2 ■ The Assessment Development Cycle

Planning Stage
1. Determine the intended users and uses of the assessment information.
2. Identify and classify the learning targets to be assessed.
3. Select the appropriate assessment method or methods.
4. Determine the appropriate sample size.

Development Stage
5. Develop or select items, tasks, and scoring procedures.
6. Critique the overall assessment for quality.

Use Stage
7. Conduct and score the assessment, making note of difficulties.
8. Revise as needed for future use.

Step 2: Specifying the Intended Learning Targets

The second decision point is to list the learning target or targets that will be the focus of the assessment. We have established that target options for this method are limited to content knowledge and some patterns of reasoning. Begin assessment development with

When using a test you haven't developed, check its match to the learning targets you taught.

an outline of the content to be mastered and a description of each pattern of reasoning. Test exercises must sample these learning targets. If one or more targets are unclear or complex, clarify or deconstruct them as a part of this step.

Step 3: Selecting the Appropriate Assessment Method(s)

After having listed the learning target(s) to be assessed, we must verify that selected response assessment is the best choice for each. Consider the following:

1. Knowledge Targets: Some types of conceptual understanding may be captured with a selected response format, but others may not. For example, to assess conceptual understanding of multiplication, you could pose an item such as the following (Shepard, 1997, n.p.):

Which choice goes with:

$$
\begin{array}{cccc}
X & X & X & X \\
X & X & X & X \\
X & X & X & X
\end{array}
$$

A. $3 \times 4 =$
B. $3 + 4 =$
C. $3 \times 12 =$

As this example illustrates, selected response formats can measure some forms of conceptual understanding, if we think carefully about how to do so. On the other hand, this method is not the best choice for all forms of conceptual understanding. For example, if you want to test students' understanding of what constitutes a strong argument, you would be better to have them list the components and explain each—using an extended written response assessment format.

2. Reasoning Targets: Multiple-choice, true/false, matching, and fill-in test items can measure some, but not all, patterns of reasoning. This is a strong match when students can dip into their foundations of knowledge and reason with it to arrive at a correct or best answer. Examples of reasoning contexts and items appear in Figure 5.3.

3. Performance Skill Targets: While we can't use selected response test formats to assess student mastery of performance skills, we can use them to assess mastery of at least some of the procedural knowledge and understanding prerequisite to being able to demonstrate such skills. For instance, let's say we intend to use a

figure 5.3 ■ For Example: Multiple Choice Items That Measure Reasoning Learning Targets

Reasoning	Illustration
Analysis	Of the four laboratory apparatus setups illustrated below, which will permit the user to carry out a distillation? (Offer four diagrams, one of which is correct.)
Synthesis	If we combine what we know about the likely impact of strong differences in barometric pressure and in temperature, what weather prediction would you make from this map? (Accompany the exercise with a map and several predictions, one of which is most likely.)
Comparison	What is one important difference between igneous and sedimentary rocks? (Offer several differences, only one of which is correct.)
Classification	Given what you know about animal life of the arid, temperate, and arctic regions, if you found an animal with the following characteristics, in which region would you expect it to live? (Describe the case and offer regions as choices.)
Inference	From the evidence provided to you in the graph, if water temperature were to go up, what would happen to the oxygen content of that water? (Provide a graph depicting the relationship between the two and offer conclusions as choices.)

performance assessment to observe two students carrying on a conversation in a second language. We might first give them some selected response or fill-in-the-blank questions to test their knowledge of vocabulary and syntactic structure.

4. Product Targets: Selected response exercises cannot help us determine if students can create quality products. However, as with skills, selected response formats can test students' prerequisite knowledge of the attributes of a quality product. Students who cannot distinguish a quality product from an inferior one are unlikely to be able to create quality products. Selected response assessments can test these important prerequisites.

Figure 5.4 summarizes the appropriate uses of selected response assessment methodology.

figure 5.4 ■ Target Types Suited to Selected Response Assessment

Target Type	Suitability to Selected Response Methodology
Knowledge	Can assess mastery of elements of knowledge and some types of conceptual understanding
Reasoning	Can assess application of some patterns of reasoning
Performance Skill	Can assess mastery of prerequisite knowledge but cannot assess the skill itself
Product	Can assess mastery of prerequisite knowledge but cannot assess the quality of the product itself

Step 4: Determining the Appropriate Sample Size

At this step, identify how many problems will be assigned to each learning target. Pay attention to how much evidence you will need for each target to support the decision you intend to make. As the relative importance of the target or as the weight of the summative decision hanging in the balance goes up, it becomes more important that the assessment leads to a confident inference about student mastery. In those cases, the larger the sample is the better. If your purpose is formative, you would be better off considering the items for each learning target as a separate assessment. Such results reveal which targets need more attention. Figures 5.5, 5.6, and 5.7 provide examples of "blueprints" or sampling plans for assessments covering multiple learning targets in different contexts. You will notice that the blueprint in Figure 5.6 is set up differently from the others. This alternate form is appropriately used with learning targets for which you intend to probe more deeply into concepts through use of a pattern of reasoning.

figure 5.5 ■ For Example: Blueprint for Grade 5 Social Studies Quiz

Learning Target	Target Type	# of Points
1. Understand the concept of manifest destiny and its contribution to the migration of settlers in the development of the United States.	Knowledge	5
2. Identify significant individuals who took part in the westward expansion.	Knowledge	4
3. Understand the major effects of westward expansion on Native Americans and Mexicans.	Knowledge	4
4. Compare the lives of different Native American groups before and after westward expansion.	Reasoning	5
5. Understand how westward migration led to conflict between Native Americans and settlers and between Mexicans and settlers.	Knowledge	4

figure 5.6 ■ For Example: Blueprint for Secondary Social Studies Quiz

Content	Knowledge	Comparison
1. Identify characteristics of different systems of government	9	5
2. Understand the structure of U.S. government	4	5
3. Know rights and responsibilities of citizens in different systems of government	7	5
Total	20	15

figure 5.7 ■ For Example: Blueprint for Grade 3 Reading Quiz

Learning Target	Target Type	# of Points
1. Determine the lesson of a fable.	Reasoning	1
2. Identify key supporting details for the lesson of the fable.	Reasoning	2
3. Infer a character's feelings.	Reasoning	2
4. Determine how a character's actions contribute to the sequence of events.	Reasoning	2
5. Determine the meaning of words and phrases used in a text, distinguishing literal from nonliteral language.	Reasoning	3

MyEdLab **Self-Check 5.1**
MyEdLab **Application Exercise 5.1**   Making a blueprint for a selected response assessment

Step 5: Develop or Select Items, Exercises, Tasks, and Scoring Procedures

In this section, we describe a series of steps for transforming learning targets into quality selected response test questions. The process is as follows: identify the specific elements of content to be included on the test, write propositions depicting the most important learnings, choose which kinds of items to write, write the items, and assemble the test. These steps arise from our extensive experience in test development and promise to yield high-quality assessments with maximum efficiency. And they are time-savers in the long run.

Identifying Specific Content to Include   Once you complete the assessment blueprint, you are ready to identify what content you will test for each cell. In most instances, you won't include everything students are to have learned. Instead you will create questions that cover as much of the content standards as possible given the amount of testing time. Identifying this sample introduces an element of subjectivity into the assessment: anyone developing a test must decide what content to include within the frame of an array of possible choices. This subjectivity will not compromise the assessment's validity if the learning targets that underpin the content standards have been clearly stated, the content selected represents those targets accurately, and you are a confident, competent master of the material to be tested.

Writing Propositions   *Propositions* are declarative statements of important facts, concepts, and results of applying a pattern of reasoning that you want students to master. Writing propositions is an efficient way to (1) identify the content that will be on the test and then (2) generate any type of selected response item you choose to reflect that content.

A proposition can be thought of as a statement of a right answer. For example, in the blueprint in Figure 5.5, students are learning about the effects of westward expansion on Native Americans and Mexicans. One of your propositions might be the following: "Three effects of westward expansion on Plains Indians were increased disease, removal to reservation lands, and loss of food sources." This is a proposition because it states three effects you want students to know as a result of their study. To write propositions, first review the learning targets on your assessment blueprint. Then draft statements that capture the important facts, concepts, and understandings that will form the basis of your instruction and, hopefully, student learning. And remember the general sampling goal: for any given body of material, we want to collect enough test propositions to be able to confidently generalize from students' performance on the sample (represented by their score on the test) to their mastery of the whole. We know we can't ask everything, but we need to be sure to ask enough.

When your list of propositions for a given test is complete, step back and review it to be sure the most important content will be represented on your test. When your list of the propositions that will form the basis of your test is final, as you are about to see later, that test is 95 percent developed. While the work remaining is not trivial, it is not difficult. But before we get to that, we need to provide more details on proposition development.

> Writing propositions sharpens your focus and saves time.

Writing Knowledge Propositions   We will use the social studies assessment blueprint in Figure 5.6 as the basis for this example. This might be a plan for a final examination for a unit of study guided by several learning targets that, when considered in combination, hold students accountable for mastering content in civics and for demonstrating understanding through comparison. Under these circumstances, we can cross knowledge and reasoning expectations to yield a comprehensive test plan.

Reviewing this blueprint, you see that you need a total of 20 Knowledge items, nine of which will come from content related to different systems of government. Review the material you will use to teach about different systems of government and draft 15 to 20 statements that capture important facts, concepts, or enduring understandings that you think every student should know and understand. Even though you only need nine items, we suggest writing 15 to 20 propositions. A rule of thumb in proposition writing is to list about twice as many propositions as you will need to fill your final quota of test items. That way, if you need to replace some later or if you want to develop two parallel forms of the same test (as for pretest and posttest administrations, for example), you have additional propositions ready to go. As you write propositions, use clearly stated sentences like the following:

Three common forms of government are constitutional monarchies, dictatorships, and constitutional republics.

In constitutional republics, the power to govern is secured by the vote of citizens.

By the way, item writing is easier when you state propositions in your own words. Doing so helps deepen your own understanding of what it is you will emphasize in teaching and capture in the test questions. Try not to lift the statements verbatim from the text.

Likewise, the blueprint in Figure 5.6 calls for four questions in the *Knowledge* × *Understand structure of U.S. government* cell, so you will want to write eight to ten propositions. Here are two sample propositions:

> *The three branches of U.S. government are the legislative, judicial, and executive branches.*
>
> *Under the system of checks and balances, the executive branch balances the legislative branch through its ability to veto legislation.*

Writing Reasoning Propositions   Once you have written your knowledge propositions, move on to the next column, this time crossing the content categories with *Comparison*. Note from the blueprint that you need five items requiring comparative reasoning in each cell, for a total of 15. Given this expectation, try to identify and state ten important propositions for each cell. Here's an example from the row on *Understand structure of U.S. government*: "A difference between the U.S. Senate and House of Representatives is the term of office." And so you proceed through all nine cells of the table, seeking out and writing down more propositions than you will need. In effect, you are creating a list of elements of the material that it is important for students to learn.

An Important Note on Propositions Focused on Student Reasoning   When you wish to assess your students' ability to use their knowledge to figure things out—that is, to reason—the challenge is to state propositions reflecting the use of that pattern of reasoning with content in such a way that students are not simply giving back a learned response. For example, if you create the proposition "A difference between the U.S. Senate and House of Representatives is the term of office" and intend it to measure students' ability to compare, then you will only have evidence of their proficiency with comparison if you have not have explicitly taught that length of term is a difference between the two legislative bodies. So in this example, your reasoning propositions should represent the kinds of comparative inferences you want them to be able to draw using their own knowledge of government and their understanding of comparison—they apply the concepts of similarity and difference.

To test their ability to apply a pattern of reasoning to a body of content knowledge, then, you must present cognitive challenges at assessment time that demand more than remembering what was explicitly taught. To reach this goal, a relationship must exist between the questions that appear on the test and your preceding instruction: The item must present a problem for which students (1) have had the opportunity to master appropriate prerequisite knowledge but (2) have not had the opportunity to use it to solve this particular problem. The assessment exercise challenges them to reason it out right there on the spot. Certainly, students must access their bank of available knowledge. That is, they must retrieve the requisite information if they are to reason well. But the aim of these propositions is to convey more than retrieval from memory when the goal of instruction is more than just knowing. If you want students to make the leap, for example, from just knowing something to analyzing or comparing (that is, to reasoning), you must write propositions representing extrapolations you want them to be able to make. It is not acceptable for them to have solved the problem before and memorized the answer for later regurgitation. You want them to be able to use their knowledge to figure things out at assessment time. Otherwise, you have not taught or assessed the reasoning targets called for in your curriculum.

> To test mastery of a reasoning proficiency, the specific context in which it is applied can't be one students have already practiced.

Writing Reasoning Propositions for Interpretive Exercises   Here is another simple but effective assessment development idea. Let's say you wish to use selected response formats to assess student reasoning and problem-solving proficiency. But let's also say you are not sure all of your students have the same solid background in the content, or you want to see them apply content you don't expect them to know outright. In these contexts, you can turn to what is called an interpretive exercise. With this format, you provide information to respondents in the form of a brief passage, chart, table, or figure and then ask a series of questions calling for them to interpret or apply that material.

There are other very common instances when this method can be applied effectively. For instance, virtually every reading comprehension test relies on this format. We present students with passages that present the knowledge, ask them to read it, and then ask them inferential comprehension questions about that content. Such passages can deal with story comprehension or they can focus on particular content areas, such as science content. Or similarly in science, teachers often rely on table and graphs to present data and then ask students to interpret the data using analysis, comparison, or evaluation questions.

Propositions for interpretive exercises will be specific to the content to which the pattern of reasoning is to be applied. So to write them, you first have to locate the information they are to interpret. For example, the reading assessment blueprint in Figure 5.7 includes the learning target "Infer a character's feelings." To write propositions for this target, you would first select a reading passage. Let's say you have chosen a short text recounting Odysseus's experience with the Cyclops. Two of your propositions might look like the following:

> *Odysseus felt afraid in the cave of the Cyclops.*
> *Polyphemus felt angry toward the sailors.*

Of course, to qualify as an inference proposition, the text must provide evidence for the proposition without stating it outright.

Selecting Propositions for the Test   Once you have completed your collection of propositions tapping critically important learnings to be assessed—remember, you

figure 5.8 ■ For Example: Blueprint for a Grade 2 Mathematics Quiz

Learning Target	Target Type	Method	# of Points
1. Understand that the three digits of a three-digit number represent amounts of hundreds, tens, and ones.	Knowledge	Selected Response	3
2. Read numbers to 1,000.	Knowledge	Performance Assessment	2
3. Write numbers to 1,000.	Knowledge	Selected Response	4
4. Order numbers through three digits.	Knowledge	Selected Response	4
5. Compare numbers through three digits.	Reasoning	Written Response	2

have been writing more than you need—you must make the final cut. At this time, it is wise to step back from this list of propositions, review them one more time, and ask, "Do these really provide a composite picture of what I think are the important knowledge and reasoning targets of this unit?" When you really know and understand the material, weak propositions will jump out at you. If you find weak entries, remove them. When the list meets your highest standards of coverage, you are ready to select the specific number needed to actually fill the cells of the table. Just remember to keep the acceptable propositions that do not make the final cut.

When Writing Propositions is Unnecessary   For some learning targets, such as those in Figure 5.8, writing propositions is not needed. The target itself provides enough information to proceed directly to item writing or selection.

MyEdLab **Self-Check 5.2**
MyEdLab **Application Exercise 5.2** Writing propositions for learning targets

Building Test Items from Propositions   Previously, we noted that developing a high-quality test plan and specifying propositions represent 95 percent of the work in selected response test development. Complete the list of propositions and the test will almost develop itself from that point on. The reason lies in the fact that each proposition captures a complete and coherent thought. Professional test developers understand that the key to fast and effective item writing is to be sure to start with a complete and coherent thought about each fact, concept, general principle, or matter of inference that you intend to test.

Once you have a proposition in hand, you can spin any kind of selected response item out of it that you wish. Let us illustrate with the following proposition from the cell in Figure 5.6 that crosses *Characteristics of different systems of government* with *Knowledge*:

> *In a constitutional monarchy, the right to govern is secured through birth.*
> *To generate a true/false item out of this proposition that is true, you can simply include the proposition on the test as stated! The proposition is a true true/false test item as written. This is always the case with well-stated propositions.*

If you want a false true/false item, simply make one part of the proposition false:

> *In a constitutional monarchy, the right to govern is secured through the approval of those governed.*

To convert this proposition to a fill-in item, simply leave out the phrase dealing with the effect and ask a question:

> *How is the right to govern secured in a constitutional monarchy?*

If you desire a multiple-choice item, add a number of response options, only one of which is correct.

> *How is the right to govern secured in a constitutional monarchy?*
>   *a. With military power*
>   *b. Through birth*
>   *c. By vote of the citizens*
>   *d. Through purchase*

Here's the key: every well-conceived and clearly stated proposition, whether requiring retrieval of knowledge or its application in a reasoning context, is an automatic source of test questions. Here's another example, this time requiring *Comparison* using an understanding of *Structure of U.S. government*. In its initial statement, it is a true true/false question:

> *The executive and legislative branches of U.S. government differ in that the legislative branch is elected directly by the people.*

As a false true/false question:

> *Members of executive and legislative branches are both elected directly by the people.*

As a fill-in item:

> *Election of members of the executive and legislative branches differs in what way?*

As a multiple-choice item:

Election of members of the executive and legislative branches differs in what way?

    a. Legislators are restricted by term limits; presidents are not
    b. Legislators are elected directly; presidents are not
    c. One must register to vote for legislators but not for president

Invest your time and effort up front by learning the underlying structure of the material you teach and finding the important propositions. These are the keys to the rapid development of sound selected response assessments.

Choosing Item Formats   As you have seen, selected response assessment has four item formats from which to choose: multiple-choice, true/false, matching, and fill-in formats. Each has strengths and limitations. You can use the chart in Figure 5.9 to help you decide which item format is best suited to your assessment context (purpose and targets).

General Guidelines for Writing Quality Items   Once you have identified the format(s) you plan to use, a few simple keys will aid you in developing sound test items. Some of these guidelines apply to all formats; others are unique to each particular format. They all have the effect of helping respondents understand exactly what you, the item writer, are going for in posing the exercise. Be careful here—don't overthink this process. Just follow the six general guidelines offered here (and summarized in Figure 5.10) and item writing will become easy pretty quickly. The simplicity of these few suggestions belies their power to improve your tests.

1. Write clearly in a sharply focused manner. Good assessment development is first and foremost an exercise in effective writing and clear communication. Follow the rules of grammar—tests are as much a public reflection of your professional standards as any other product you create. Include only information essential to framing the question. Be brief and clear. Your goal is to test mastery of the material, not students' ability to figure out what you're asking.

Wrong:

When scientists rely on magnets in the development of electric motors they need to know about the poles, which are?

Right:

What are the poles of a magnet called?

    a. Anode and cathode
    b. North and south
    c. Strong and weak
    d. Attract and repel

figure 5.9 ■ Comparison of Selected Response Item Formats

Item	Used When	Advantage	Limitations
Multiple Choice	There is only one right answer. There are several plausible alternatives to the correct answer.	Can measure a variety of objectives. Easy to score. Can cover lots of material efficiently. Carefully crafted distracters can provide diagnostic information.	Guessing can skew score (up to 33% chance, depending on number of distracters). Can be hard to identify plausible distracters.
True/False	A large body of content is to be tested, requiring the use of many test items.	Can ask many questions in a short time. Easy to score.	Can be trivial or misleading if not written carefully. Guessing can skew score (50% chance).
Matching	There are many related thoughts or facts; you want to measure association of information.	Can cover lots of material efficiently. Easy to score. Can serve as several multiple-choice items in one (each response is a distracter for the others).	Process of elimination can skew score if not written carefully.
Fill in the Blank	A clear, short answer is required. You want to determine if students know the answer, rather than if they can select it from a list.	Assesses production of a response. Reduces the possibility of getting the right answer by guessing. Can cover lots of material efficiently.	Takes longer to score.

Source: Chappuis, Jan; Stiggins, Rick J.; Chappuis, Steve; Arter, Judith A., *Classroom Assessment for Student learning: Doing it Right–Using it Well*, 2nd Ed., ©2012. Reprinted and Electronically reproduced by permission of Pearson Education, Inc., New York, New York.

2. Ask a question. That is, when using multiple-choice and fill-in formats, minimize the use of incomplete statements as exercises. When you force yourself to ask a question, you force yourself to express a complete thought in the stem or trigger part of the question, which usually promotes respondents' clear understanding of what you are asking.

Wrong:

Between 1950 and 1965

    a. Interest rates increased.
    b. Interest rates decreased.
    c. Interest rates fluctuated greatly.
    d. Interest rates did not change.

Right:

> *What was the trend in interest rates between 1950 and 1965?*
>
> > *a. Increased only*
> > *b. Decreased only*
> > *c. Increased, then decreased*
> > *d. Remained unchanged*

3. Aim for the lowest possible reading level. This is an attempt to control for the inevitable confounding mentioned previously between reading proficiency and mastery of the content and reasoning students are to demonstrate. You do not want to let students' reading proficiency prevent them from demonstrating that they really know the material. Minimize sentence length and syntactic complexity and eliminate unnecessarily difficult or unfamiliar vocabulary. For an example, see the previous magnet questions.

4. Eliminate clueing. Sometimes the correct answer either within the question or across questions within a test can give away other answers. Other times, grammatical clues within items give away the correct answer. In either case, students get items right for the wrong reasons. The result is misinformation about their true achievement.

Wrong:

> *All of these are examples of a bird that flies, except an*
>
> > *a. Ostrich*
> > *b. Falcon*
> > *c. Cormorant*
> > *d. Robin*

(The article *an* at the end of the stem requires a response beginning with a vowel. As only one is offered, it must be correct.)

Also wrong:

> *Which of the following are examples of birds that do not fly?*
>
> > *a. Falcon*
> > *b. Ostrich and penguin*
> > *c. Cormorant*
> > *d. Robin*

(The question calls for a plural response. As only one is offered, it must be correct.)

5. Have a qualified colleague review your items to ensure their appropriateness. This is especially true of your relatively more important tests, such as big unit tests and final exams. No one is perfect. We all overlook simple mistakes. Having a willing colleague review your work takes just a few minutes and can save a great deal of time and assure accuracy of results.

6. Double check the scoring key for accuracy before scoring.

Guidelines for Multiple-Choice Items   When developing multiple-choice test items, keep these few simple yet powerful guidelines in mind.

1. Ask a complete question to get the item started, if you can. We repeat this for emphasis. This has the effect of placing the item's focus in the stem, not in the response options.
2. Don't repeat the same words within each response option; rather, reword the item stem to move the repetitive material up there. This will clarify the problem and make it more efficient for respondents to read. (See the "interest rate" example in the section on general guidelines.)
3. Be sure there is only one correct or best answer. This is where a colleague's independent review can help. Remember, it is acceptable to ask respondents to select a best answer from among a set of answers, all of which are correct. Just be sure to word the question so as to make it clear that they are to find the "best answer."
4. Word response options as briefly as possible and be sure they are grammatically parallel. This has two desirable effects. First, it makes items easier to read. Second, it helps eliminate grammatical clues to the correct answer. (See the second bird example given previously.)

Wrong:

Why did colonists come to the United States?

> *a. To escape heavy taxation by their native governments*
> *b. Religion*
> *c. They sought the adventure of living among Native Americans in the new land*
> *d. There was the promise of great wealth in the New World*
> *e. All of the above answers*

Right:

Why did colonists migrate to the United States?

> *a. For freedom of taxation*
> *b. For religious freedom*
> *c. For adventure*
> *d. All of the above*

5. Vary the number of response options presented as appropriate to pose the problem you want your students to solve. While it is best to design multiple-choice questions around three, four, or five response options, it is permissible to vary the number of response options offered across items within the same test. Please try not to use "all of the above" or "none of the above" merely to fill up spaces just because you can't think of other incorrect answers. In fact, sound practice suggests limiting their use to those few times when they fit comfortably into the context of the question.

Some teachers find it useful to include more than one correct answer and ask the student to find them all, when appropriate. Of course, this means those questions should be worth more than one point. They need to count for as many points as there are correct answers. For example:

Which of the labels provided represents a classification category for types of rocks? (Identify all correct answers.[*])

> *a. Geologic*
> *b. Metamorphic**
> *c. Sandstone*
> *d. Igneous**

By the way, here's a simple, yet very effective, multiple-choice test item writing tip: if you compose a multiple-choice item and find that you cannot think of enough plausible incorrect responses, include the item on a test the first time as a fill-in question. As your students respond, those who get it wrong will provide you with the full range of plausible yet incorrect responses you need the next time you use it.

Guidelines for True/False Exercises   You have only one simple guideline to follow here: make the item entirely true or false as stated. Complex "idea salads" including some truth and some falsehood just confuse the issue. Precisely what is the proposition you are testing? State it and move on to the next one.

Wrong:

> *From the Continental Divide, located in the Appalachian Mountains, water flows into either the Pacific Ocean or the Mississippi River.*

Right:

> *The Continental Divide is located in the Appalachian Mountains.*

Guidelines for Matching Items   When developing matching exercises, which are really complex multiple-choice items with a number of stems offered along with a number of response options, follow all of the multiple-choice guidelines offered previously. In addition, observe the following guidelines:

1. Provide clear and concise directions for making the match.
2. Keep the list of things to be matched short. The maximum number of options is ten. Fewer is better. This minimizes the information processing and idea juggling respondents must do to be successful.
3. Keep the list of things to be matched homogeneous. Don't mix events with dates or with names. Again, idea salads confuse the issue. Focus the exercise.
4. Keep the list of response options brief in their wording and parallel in construction. Pose the matching challenge in clear, straightforward language.

5. Include more response options than stems and permit students to use response options more than once. This has the effect of making it impossible for students to arrive at the correct response purely through a process of elimination. If students answer correctly using elimination and you infer that they have mastered the material, you will be wrong.

Wrong:

_____ 1. Texas	A. $7,200,000
_____ 2. Hawaii	B. Chicago
_____ 3. New York	C. Liberty Bell
_____ 4. Illinois	D. Augusta
_____ 5. Louisiana	E. Cornhusker
_____ 6. Florida	F. Mardi Gras
_____ 7. Massachusetts	G. 50th State
_____ 8. Alaska	H. Austin
_____ 9. Maine	I. Everglades
_____ 10. California	J. 1066
_____ 11. Nebraska	K. Dover
_____ 12. Pennsylvania	L. San Andreas Fault
	M. Salem
	N. 1620
	O. Statue of Liberty

Right:

Directions: The New England states are listed in the left-hand column and capital cities in the right-hand column. Place the letter corresponding to the capital city in the space next to the state in which that city is located. Responses may be used only once.

States' Capital Cities

_____ 1. Connecticut	A. Augusta
_____ 2. Maine	B. Boston
_____ 3. Massachusetts	C. Brunswick
_____ 4. New Hampshire	D. Concord
_____ 5. Rhode Island	E. Hartford
_____ 6. Vermont	F. Montpelier
	G. New Haven
	H. Providence

Guidelines for Fill-In Items   Here are three simple guidelines to follow:

1. Ask respondents a question and provide space for an answer. As stated previously, this forces you to express a complete thought. The use of incomplete statements as item stems is acceptable. But if you use them, be sure to capture the essence of the problem in that stem.
2. Try to stick to one blank per item. Come to the point. Ask one question, get one answer, and move on to the next question. Does the student know the answer or not?

Wrong:

> *In the percussion section of the orchestra are located _____, _____, _____, and _____.*

Right:

> *In what section of the orchestra is the kettledrum found? _____*

3. Don't let the length of the line to be filled in provide a clue as to the length or nature of the correct response. This may seem elementary, but it happens. Again, this can misinform you about students' real levels of achievement.

Mixing Formats Together   The creative assessment developer also can generate some interesting and useful assessment exercises by mixing the various formats. For example, mix true/false and multiple-choice formats to create exercises in which respondents must label a statement as true or false and select the response option that gives the proper reason it is so. For example:

> *As employment increases, the danger of inflation increases.*
>
> > *a. True, because consumers are willing to pay higher prices*
> > *b. True, because the money supply increases*
> > *c. False, because wages and inflation are statistically unrelated to one another*
> > *d. False, because the government controls inflation*

Or mix multiple-choice or true/false questions with the fill-in format by asking students to select the correct response and fill in the reason it is correct. As a variation, ask why incorrect responses are incorrect, too.

Summary of Building Test Items from Propositions   In this step, you transformed propositions into assessment questions. This can be very quick and easy. Regardless of the item format, however, clarity and focused simplicity must be hallmarks of your exercises. Always try to ask questions. Strive to eliminate inappropriate clues to the correct answer, seek one clearly correct answer whenever possible and appropriate, ask a colleague to review important tests, and follow just a few simple format-specific guidelines for item construction. Figure 5.10 presents a summary of

figure 5.10 ■ Selected Response Test Quality Checklist

1. **General guidelines for all formats**
   _____ Keep wording simple and focused. Aim for lowest possible reading level.
   _____ Ask a question.
   _____ Avoid providing clues within and between items.
   _____ Correct answer should not be obvious without mastering material tested.
   _____ Highlight critical words (e.g., _most, least, except, not_).
2. **Guidelines for multiple-choice items**
   _____ State whole question in item stem.
   _____ Eliminate repetition of material in response options.
   _____ Be sure there is only one correct or best answer.
   _____ Keep response options brief and parallel.
   _____ Make all response options the same length.
   _____ Limit use of "all" or "none of the above."
   _____ Use "always" and "never" with caution.
3. **Guideline for true/false items**
   _____ Make them entirely true or entirely false as stated.
4. **Guidelines for matching items**
   _____ Provide clear directions for the match to be made.
   _____ Keep list of trigger items brief (maximum length is 10).
   _____ Include only homogeneous items.
   _____ Keep wording of response options brief and parallel.
   _____ Provide more responses than trigger items.
5. **Guidelines for fill-in items**
   _____ Ask a question.
   _____ Provide one blank per item.
   _____ Do not make length of blank a clue.
   _____ Put blank toward the end.
6. **Formatting test items**
   _____ Be consistent in the presentation of an item type.
   _____ Keep all parts of a test question on one page.
   _____ Avoid crowding too many questions on one page.
   _____ Arrange items from easy to hard.
   _____ Try to group similar formats together.
   _____ Avoid misleading layout.
7. **Writing directions**
   _____ Write clear, explicit directions for each item type.
   _____ State the point value of each item type.
   _____ Indicate how the answer should be expressed (e.g., should the word true or false be written, or T or F? Should numbers be rounded to the nearest tenth? Should units such as months, meters, or grams be included in the answer?)
8. **Time**
   _____ Make sure the test is not too long for the time allowed.

Source: Adapted from _Student-Involved Assessment for Learning_, 5th ed. (p. 122), by R. J. Stiggins, 2008, Upper Saddle River, NJ: Pearson Education. Copyright © 2008 by Pearson Education, Inc. Adapted by permission of Pearson Education, Inc.

these guidelines collected for your convenient use. Further, remember to help students perform up to their potential by providing clear and complete instructions and making sure the test is readable.

Assembling the Test Finally, here are a few simple guidelines for setting up your test as a whole that will maximize the accuracy of the results:

1. Make sure your students know the point value for each assessment exercise. This helps them use their time wisely.
2. Start each test with relatively easy items. This will give students a chance to get test anxiety under control.
3. Present all questions of like format together (all multiple-choice items together, all fill-in items together, etc.).
4. Be sure all parts of a question appear on the same page of the test.
5. Make sure all copies are clear and readable.

If you are using the information diagnostically or if students will use the information to self-assess and set goals, consider grouping items by learning target instead. See Figure 5.11 for fourth-grade teacher Laura Anderson's explanation of how this formatting has helped her team and her students better analyze results.

Some Final Reminders As you plan your development and use of selected response assessments, attend carefully to the following issues:

- Be sure time and test length permit students to attempt all test items. Some need more processing time than others. If students don't get to try an item because time runs out, you have no way of knowing if they have mastered the material tested. You cannot automatically assume they would get it wrong. They might not—you don't know. To avoid the problem, give everyone every chance. If that means extending test time for some, extend it.
- Remember, as mentioned previously, *do not hand score* if optical scanning or other technology is available. It's a huge waste of time and more likely to lead to scoring errors.
- Use fill-in exercises when you wish to control for guessing. And make no mistake about it, guessing can be an issue. If a student guesses an item right and you infer that the right answer means the student has mastered the material, you will be drawing an incorrect conclusion. You have mismeasured that student's real achievement and this can lead to incorrect judgments regarding what comes next in a student's learning.
- Use multiple-choice items when you can identify one correct or best answer and a number of plausible incorrect responses (also known as distractors). On the surface, this might sound obvious. But think about it. If you formulate your distractors carefully to represent typical mistakes and misunderstandings you can use multiple-choice items to uncover those common misunderstandings and to diagnose students' needs. That is an assessment *for* learning way of thinking.

MyEdLab **Self-Check 5.3**
MyEdLab **Application Exercise 5.3** Creating a selected response assessment for each format option

figure 5.11 ■ From the Classroom: Laura Anderson

We used to . . .

Our fourth-grade team had always grouped for math, written our own unit assessments, and given tests within a similar time frame. Our test questions were not grouped and often either did not have enough or had too many questions. Teachers only received an overall test score and not enough specific data about which skills were not mastered. We also did not collect the data. Even when questions obviously need revisions, it was easier to put the test away until next year. Unfortunately, we did not remember the changes a year later and gave the same test over again. Our old team discussions were based on the logistics of the school day (i.e., schedules, upcoming events, and running of materials).

Now we . . .

New to us was the test format that challenged us to identify our learning targets and group "like questions" together by targets. This new format with a percent score by target really helps teachers and students quickly see which targets are met. Students indicate whether they feel they made a simple mistake or if they need more study.

Why we changed . . .

This feature really holds the kids accountable for their own learning. We saw signs of students becoming more invested in the test-taking process and taking more ownership of their learning. Also, our instruction has become more focused as we started posting learning targets in our classrooms. Our students are now clearer about the learning targets of our daily lessons.

What we notice as a result . . .

The most powerful change we have seen since starting the common assessment process is the team discussion piece after the test data collection. Now, we meet as a team and examine our student data and test questions. When many kids miss a particular test question, we discuss whether we feel it was a test question issue or a teaching issue. If a question needs revising, it is done right away. We have continued to improve our tests over the last three years rather than using the same flawed tests over again. These collegial discussions focusing on test data are like nothing we have ever been a part of. Now, we focus much more of our team time on instructional strategies, remediation ideas, and curriculum/test development. It wasn't always easy to make the time or feel comfortable sharing our weaknesses. But we have grown so much as teachers and have developed a professional community centered around improving our instruction.

Source: Reprinted with permission from Laura Anderson, 4th-grade Teacher, District 196, Rosemount, MN, 2011.

Step 6: Review and Critique the Overall Assessment before Use

You can work backward to verify test quality, either with tests you have developed or those you intend to use that have been developed by someone else—a colleague, a textbook company, or a third-party vendor. To do this, begin at the item level: Do the items themselves adhere to the quality control guidelines presented in this chapter? If they do not, there is obvious reason for concern about test quality. If they do, proceed to the next level of evaluation.

Transform the items into the propositions that they reflect. You accomplish this by doing the following:

- Combine the multiple-choice item stem with the correct response.
- Check that true true/false items already are propositions.
- Make false true/false items true to derive the proposition.
- Match up elements in matching exercises.
- Fill in the blanks of short-answer items.

Then analyze the resulting list of propositions, asking, *Do these reflect the priorities in my instruction?* Next, collect the propositions into like groups to determine the achievement standards or learning targets they represent or to create a table of specifications depicting the overall picture of the test, including the proportional representation of content and reasoning. Again, ask, *Do these reflect priorities as I see them?* This kind of reverse process can both reveal the flaws in previously developed tests and help you understand the nature of the revisions needed to bring the test up to your standards of quality.

Sources of Bias   Sources of bias represent categories of things that can go wrong—that can keep a student's test score from being an accurate reflection of that student's real level of achievement. Listed in Figure 5.12 are many of the sources of mismeasurement touched on in this chapter, together with actions you can take to prevent these problems. These remedies can help you develop sound selected response assessments.

Steps 7 and 8: Use and Refine the Assessment

When students don't have enough time to complete a test, we can't infer they didn't master the items they didn't attempt.

When you have the opportunity to administer the assessment, it will be important to watch for problems you may not have anticipated. Two things to monitor while students are taking your test:

1. *Some students don't have enough time to complete all items on the test.* When students run out of time before they have attempted all items, the test is not measuring their level of achievement accurately. Look for students frantically answering questions toward the end of the testing time. Also look for incomplete tests.
2. *Students are confused by an item.* When students ask clarifying questions, check to see if the confusion is due to some aspect of the item or the directions. Note the problem and revise the test prior to administering it again.

MyEdLab **Application Exercise 5.4** Auditing a selected response assessment for quality

figure 5.12 ■ Sources of Bias and Suggested Remedies

Potential Sources of Problems	Suggested Remedies
Lack of vision of the priority target(s)	Carefully analyze the material to be tested to find the knowledge and reasoning targets.
	Find truly important learning propositions.
Wrong method for the target	Use selected response methods to assess mastery of knowledge and appropriate kinds of reasoning only. Selected response can test prerequisites of effective skill and product performance, but not performance itself.
Inappropriate sampling: ■ Not representative of important propositions	Know the material and plan the test to thoroughly cover the target(s).
■ Sample too small	Include enough items to cover key concepts.
■ Sample too large for time available	Shorten cautiously so as to maintain enough items to support confident student learning conclusions.
Sources of bias: ■ Student-centered problems □ Cannot read well enough to respond	Lower reading level of test or offer reading support.
□ Insufficient time to respond	Shorten test or allow more time.
■ Poor-quality test items	Learn and follow both general and format-specific guidelines for writing quality items.
	Seek review by a colleague.
■ Scoring errors	Double check answer key; use it carefully.

■ Using Selected Response Assessment Formatively with Students

As you will recall from Chapter 2, formative uses of assessment information can involve both teachers and students. The following suggestions link the seven strategies of assessment for learning introduced in Chapter 2 to selected response instruments.

Where Am I Going?

Strategy 1: Provide Students with a Clear and Understandable Vision of the Learning Target. First, make sure that your learning targets are written in language that students will understand. If they have been transformed into a test blueprint, share it with them at the outset of instruction. Students can link the day's or week's lessons and assignments to particular targets or cells on the blueprint, thereby helping them to develop the understanding that learning is the goal of their effort.

You can also have students review their learning for each target by generating propositions for each cell on the blueprint.

Strategy 2: Use Examples of Strong and Weak Work.   As we saw in this chapter, the distractors on a well-designed multiple-choice item are plausible but incorrect answer choices. You can use a multiple-choice item to help students master the learning target by asking them to identify a wrong answer choice and explain why it is wrong.

Where Am I Now?

Strategy 3: Offer Regular Descriptive Feedback during the Learning.   Once you have your final list of learning targets or an assessment blueprint to be covered and a sufficient number of propositions, you can create two versions of the same test, "Form A" and "Form B." You can create a worksheet for students to use after having taken Form A, so that the quiz or test itself functions as feedback, as shown in Figure 5.13. Prepare the first part of the worksheet, "Reviewing My Results," by listing the learning target from your blueprint next to the problem number. Then have students take the quiz or test and hand it in. You correct their quizzes or tests simply by marking each answer as right or wrong and hand them back along with the worksheet "Reviewing My Results." Students then transfer the information from their quiz or test to the worksheet by marking the "Right" or "Wrong" column for each problem. Then review their wrong answers and decide whether their mistake was due to something they now understand and can correct without help or if they don't yet understand how to answer the problem. They mark the corresponding column "Fixable Mistake" or "Don't Get It" for each incorrect answer. Last, they complete the second part of the worksheet, "Analyzing My Results," by listing which learning targets or parts of a target they are good at (the targets for which they got all items correct), the targets or parts of a target they are pretty good at but which still need review (the targets for which they got one or more items wrong due to a fixable mistake), and the targets or parts of a target they still need to keep learning (the targets with items they got wrong and don't yet understand).

Strategy 4: Teach Students to Self-Assess and Set Goals for Next Steps.   By completing the form shown in Figure 5.13 and described in Strategy 3, students are using assessment information to self-assess. You can have them follow this with setting goals for further study by completing the part of "Analyzing My Results" that asks them to make a plan for what they will do to get better at the targets they have not yet mastered. If you have given students a copy of the assessment blueprint in advance, they can also "traffic light" the learning targets as you teach them. After a lesson or series of lessons on a learning target, students mark the target on the blueprint with highlighters: green for "got it," yellow for "partway there," and red for "not yet."

figure 5.13 ■ For Example: Reviewing and Analyzing My Results

Reviewing My Results

Name: _____ Assignment: _____ Date: _____

Please look at your corrected test and mark whether each problem is right or wrong. Then look at the problems you got wrong and decide if you made a mistake you can fix without help. If you did, mark the "Fixable Mistake" column. For all the remaining problems you got wrong, mark the "Don't Get It" column.

Problem	Learning Target	Right	Wrong	Fixable Mistake	Don't Get It
1					
2					
3					
4					
5					
6					
7					
8					
9					
10					

Analyzing My Results

I AM GOOD AT THESE!

Learning targets I got right:

I AM PRETTY GOOD AT THESE, BUT NEED TO DO A LITTLE REVIEW

Learning targets I got wrong because of a fixable mistake:

What I can do to keep this from happening again:

I NEED TO KEEP LEARNING THESE

Learning targets I got wrong and I'm not sure what to do to correct them:

What I can do to get better at them:

Source: Chappuis, Jan, *Seven Strategies Of Assessment For Learning*, 2nd Ed., ©2015. Reprinted and Electronically reproduced by permission of Pearson Education, Inc., New York, New York.

How Can I Close the Gap?

Strategy 5: Use Evidence of Student Learning Needs to Determine Next Steps in Teaching.   You can use Form A as a pretest and Form B as a posttest. You can use the sections on Form A pertaining to each learning target as quizzes to check for understanding and prepare further instruction as needed before moving on to the next learning target.

Strategy 6: Design Focused Instruction, Followed by Practice with Feedback.   When students have completed the worksheet "Reviewing and Analyzing My Results," you can use this information to better differentiate instruction. For students who have made fixable mistakes, the only follow-up needed may be for them to correct their answer and explain in writing what their mistake was. For students who have identified learning targets they don't yet "get," prepare activities that offer further practice with the learning targets on the assessment and then assign the specific activities to students according to how they have identified their needs. You can list the further learning activities on the board and let students use that information when filling out the "What I am going to do" section of "Analyzing My Results." You can also plan small-group instruction for those learning targets that students are still struggling with.

MyEdLab

Video Example 5.1

Self-Assessment and Goal Setting with Test Corrections

In Video Example 5.1, high school mathematics teacher Jennifer McDaniel explains how she has adapted this process for an activity she calls "test corrections." Once students have identified their fixable mistakes, they focus on the ones they need more time with. Ms. McDaniel's students also share how this practice contributes to developing a learning culture in her classroom. Figure 5.14 shows an example of the form her students use to guide their next learning steps.

Strategy 7: Provide Opportunities for Students to Track, Reflect on, and Share Their Learning Progress.   Set up a system for students to track their formative assessment information (the work that is for practice) and their summative assessment information (the work that is for a grade) organized by learning target. Periodically ask them to reflect on their progress: "I have become better at _____. I used to _____, but now I _____." Give them opportunities to share their progress with their parents or other significant adults in their lives.

In Figure 5.15, high school social studies teacher Myron Dueck explains how these formative assessment applications have changed his teaching and his students' achievement.

figure 5.14 ■ For Example Test Reflections and Corrections

AP Calculus Test Reflections and Corrections: Implicit Differentiation

Learning Target	Question Numbers	Simple Mistakes	Guess	Misconceptions
I can use implicit differentiation to find the derivative of a function.	1 2 3 4 5			
I can find dy/dx by implicit differentiation and evaluate the derivative at the indicated point.	6 7			
I can find the 2nd derivative in terms of x and y using implicit differentiation.	8 9 10			
I can find equations for the tangent and normal line to the graph at the indicated point.	11			
I can find dy/dx using both implicit and explicit methods and evaluate at a given point.	13 14			
Open Response: I can use implicit differentiation to find the derivative of a function. I can find a point P which the line tangent to the curve at P is horizontal.	14			

Test Corrections

What I did	What I should have done	What I used to think. . . but now I know

figure 5.15 ■ From the Classroom: Myron Dueck

I used to . . .

For the first decade of my teaching career, I constructed tests by section based on the type or style of the questions. For instance, my unit tests would have a structure such as this:

> Section 1: True & False   (10 pts)
> Section 2: Multiple Choice   (15 pts)
> Section 3: Short Answers   (10 pts)
> Section 4: Long Answer/Essay   (20 pts)

In each of the first three sections, I took a somewhat random sampling of concepts and facts from the unit being tested. Therefore, from each section I had a basic idea of what the student knew of the unit as a whole. The last section could be general or specific, depending on the unit of study.

These tests were fairly easy to make and even easier to mark. As well, I thought that this was the best type of test to produce, but this is probably based on years of seeing this as 'the standard' way to construct a test.

Now I . . .

I divide my test by the learning outcomes or standards I want to evaluate. Now a test on the USA in the 1920s is structured like this:

> Section 1: USA in the 1920s   (11 pts)
> Section 2: Causes of the Great Depression   (8 pts)
> Section 3: FDR's Efforts to End the Depression   (6 pts)
> Section 4: Reactions to FDR's Actions   (7 pts)
> Section 5: FDR's Overall Impact on the USA   (11 pts)

Once a student takes the test and I have evaluated it, the student notes his/her section scores on a custom tracking sheet. Each section is allotted a percentage score and this score is compared to the student's overall test score as well as his or her academic goal. Taking all of these numbers into account, the student determines which section(s) to retest. The student also has an opportunity to plan what he/she might do differently in preparation for the subsequent evaluation.

Why I changed . . .

1. Students are able to be evaluated according to each learning outcome and this has obvious benefits:
    a. I can reteach sections (learning outcomes) upon which the entire class scored poorly or below competency.
    b. An individual student can retest a single section or multiple sections depending on how he or she performed.
    c. A student can easily identify and focus on the areas in which they know they can improve.
    d. As the facilitator, I can effectively and efficiently administer retests as I am only retesting and remarking those sections that have been identified.

2. Struggling learners usually start with the section they know best, and research shows that success breeds success.
3. I am able to quickly evaluate if there is a strong correlation between the value of each section and the amount of time allotted to it in class.
4. I have constructed retests that have the same sections and values, but different questions or question formats. It is very easy to administer these retests and to determine if authentic learning has occurred.
5. This structure is a very good way to use both formative and summative assessments in the same way and at the same time.
6. Students feel a sense of ownership and control not present in conventional testing formats.

What I notice as a result . . .
1. Very positive student reactions to this system.
2. Incredible parent support and encouragement.
3. Increased student participation in 're-learning' activities.
4. Less stress and pressure at the time of the first evaluation.

Source: Reprinted with permission from Myron Dueck, High School Social Studies Teacher, SD 67 (Okanagan-Skaha), Penticton, BC, Canada, 2011.

MyEdLab **Application Exercise 5.5** Using selected response assessments formatively with students

■ Summary: Productive Selected Response Assessment

We established at the beginning of the chapter that these options often are labeled "objective" tests merely because of the manner in which they are scored. When test items are carefully developed, there is only one clearly best answer. No judgment is involved. However, the teacher's professional judgment does play a major role in all other facets of this kind of assessment, from test planning to selecting material to test to writing the test items. For this reason, it is essential that all those who develop selected response tests closely follow procedures for creating sound tests. Those procedures have been the topic of this chapter.

We discussed the learning target types that are considered a good match for selected response assessment. These can serve to assess students' mastery of content knowledge and understanding, ability to reason in important ways, and mastery of some of the procedural knowledge that underpins both the development of performance skills and the creation of complex products. Then we explored several context factors that extend beyond just the consideration of matching to the target that must be taken into account in choosing selected response assessment. These included factors related to students' reading abilities and to the kinds of support services available to the user.

To begin the test development process, we applied Steps 1 through 4 of the Assessment Development Cycle to selected response methodology: determining assessment purpose, identifying and classifying learning targets, verifying that selected response is a suitable choice, and selecting sample size.

Then we moved to Step 5 of the Assessment Development Cycle—item writing—beginning with how to write propositions for knowledge and reasoning targets. We showed how to use propositions to build four types of items: true/false, multiple-choice, matching, and fill-in items, providing guidance on when to use each format. We offered general guidelines for writing quality items and format-specific guidelines to ensure that items are of high quality. We concluded Step 5 with suggestions for assembling the test.

For Step 6, we explained how to review and critique the overall assessment before use, paying special attention to factors that can bias results. At Steps 7 and 8, we described what to watch for when administering the test and how to refine it for further use. And, last, we offered suggestions for how selected response items, quizzes, and tests can be used formatively with students to help increase their achievement.

Chapter 5 Suggested Activities

End-of-chapter activities are intended to help you master the chapter's learning targets. They are designed to deepen your understanding of the chapter content, provide opportunities for personal reflection on ideas presented, and serve as a basis for discussion among peers. You may wish to do all of them or select those that you believe will be most useful to your learning. Each activity is correlated to one or more chapter learning targets to help with your selection.

Chapter 5 Learning Targets

As a result of your study of Chapter 5, you will be able to do the following:

1. Make an assessment blueprint for a selected response assessment
2. Write propositions for knowledge and reasoning targets
3. Create selected response items for each format option
4. Audit a selected response assessment for quality
5. Use selected response assessments formatively with students

Chapter 5 Activities

Activity 5.1   Keeping a Reflective Journal (All chapter learning targets)

Activity 5.2   Practicing Writing Propositions (Learning Target 2)

Activity 5.3   Creating a Selected Response Assessment (Learning Targets 1, 2, and 3)

Activity 5.4   Critiquing a Selected Response Assessment (Learning Target 4)

Activity 5.5   Planning an Assessment for Learning Application (Learning Target 5)

Activity 5.6   Comparing Your Experiences with Information from the Chapter (All chapter learning targets)

Activity 5.7   Answering an Interview Question (All chapter learning targets)

Activity 5.8   Reflecting on Your Learning from Chapter 5 (All chapter learning targets)

Activity 5.9   Adding to Your Growth Portfolio (All chapter learning targets)

Activity 5.1: Keeping a Reflective Journal

Keep a record of your thoughts, questions, and insights as you read Chapter 5.

Activity 5.2: Practicing Writing Propositions

This activity has two parts. In the first part, you practice turning test items back into the propositions that underlie them. In the second part, you translate propositions into test items.

1. Transform each of the following test items into its basic proposition:
   - True true/false: One reason for declining numbers of Pacific salmon is the destruction of salmon habitat.
   - False true/false: A tariff is a tax on real estate.
   - Fill in: If we increase the radius of a ball by 3 inches, what will be the effect on its circumference?
   - Multiple choice: Which of the following is an example of a tariff?
     a. Income tax
     b. Tax on Chinese imports
     c. Real estate tax
     d. All of the above
2. Transform the following propositions into test items:
   - Automobiles and factories are the largest sources of air pollution.
   - The water cycle depends on evaporation and condensation.
   - In the United States, we have a bicameral legislature.
   - Our free market economic system is based on the law of supply and demand.

Activity 5.3: Creating a Selected Response Assessment

1. Select a short unit you have prepared to teach.
2. Determine how you intend to use the results of the assessment you will create.
3. List and classify the learning targets for the unit.
4. Create an assessment blueprint for the learning targets that can be measured by selected response methodology. Use one of the blueprint formats shown in this chapter.
5. Identify the content to be tested by writing propositions for each learning target, following the guidelines in this chapter.
6. Determine which item format you will use for each proposition. Refer to Figure 5.9, "Comparison of Selected Response Item Formats," for guidance.
7. Create your test items following the guidelines for writing quality items explained in this chapter.
8. Assemble the test and write the directions.
9. Review and critique the test for quality and revise it as needed.
10. If you created the test for formative use, use the blueprint to create a second version of it for summative use. If you created the test for summative use, use the blueprint to create a second version of it for formative use.

Activity 5.4: Critiquing a Selected Response Assessment

Retrieve a copy of a selected response test that you have taken in the recent past and do the following:

- Create an assessment blueprint for it by identifying the learning target each item assesses and indicating how many points each learning target is awarded.
- Transform each test item into its underlying proposition.
- Judge the quality of each item and the quality of the test as a whole, using the guidelines for item writing explained in this chapter.
- Write a summary of the assessment's strengths and weaknesses, if any.

Activity 5.5: Planning an Assessment for Learning Application

1. Select a unit that you have prepared to teach.
2. Create an assessment blueprint for the unit (or use the one you created in Activity 5.3).
3. Choose one or more of the ideas for using an assessment blueprint with students. Write yourself instructions for what you would do.
4. Describe the effects on student motivation and achievement that you believe will result from engaging in the activity.

Activity 5.6: Comparing Your Experiences with Information from the Chapter

Select one "From the Classroom" entry from Chapter 5 and compare it to your experience as a student.

- How is it similar?
- What differences do you notice?
- What conclusions about assessment design might you draw?

Activity 5.7: Answering an Interview Question

Imagine that you are about to interview for a teaching position. The interview team (often a combination of administrators and teachers) is interested in understanding your level of classroom assessment literacy. Review Chapter 5's learning targets and think about what concepts and procedures were most significant to you from the chapter. Then think about what type of question an interview team might ask related to this significant learning. Write the question and draft a short response—one that you could give in one to two minutes orally.

Activity 5.8: Reflecting on Your Learning from Chapter 5

Review the Chapter 5 learning targets and select one that struck you as most significant from this chapter. Write a short reflection that captures your current understanding. If you are working with a group, discuss what you have written.

Activity 5.9: Adding to Your Growth Portfolio

Any of the activities from this chapter can be used as portfolio entries. Select any activity you have completed or artifact you have created that will demonstrate your mastery of the Chapter 5 learning targets:

1. Make an assessment blueprint for a selected response assessment
2. Write propositions for knowledge and reasoning targets
3. Create selected response items for each format option
4. Audit a selected response assessment for quality
5. Use selected response assessments formatively with students

Written Response Assessment

Chapter 6 Learning Targets

As a result of your study of Chapter 6, you will be able to do the following:

1. Plan a written response assessment
2. Develop short-answer and extended written response items
3. Develop two types of scoring guides: checklists and task-specific rubrics
4. Audit a written response assessment for quality
5. Use written response assessment formatively with students

One of Rick's graduate students once described a final exam at the end of an undergraduate course. His major was Spanish language, literature, and culture. The final was an in-class essay exam with a 3-hour time limit. The entire exam consisted of one exercise, which posed the challenge in only two words: "Discuss Spain."

Many of us have experienced such prompts. One of the advantages often given for written response assessment relative to other test formats is that the items are considered much easier to develop. Unfortunately, users can turn that advantage into a liability by assuming that "easier to develop" means not much thought needs to go into it, as in the preceding example. As you can imagine, this also leads to trouble when it comes time to evaluate the responses. To succeed with this assessment format, we must invest thoughtful preparation time in writing items that challenge students appropriately and in crafting scoring guides that define in advance characteristics of acceptable responses. "I'll know it when I see it" does not have a home in assessing written responses.

Written response assessment includes both short-answer items and extended written response items. Short-answer items require only a brief response, with one or a limited number of possible right answers, whereas extended written response items call for a lengthier response generally having a greater number of possible correct or acceptable answers. Because state standards now include more complex reasoning and writing standards, the need to measure these types of standards accurately has renewed interest in assessment methods that can assess more deeply than can selected response assessment. One result has been an increased use of written response assessment—the method, by the way, that dominated student evaluation until the appearance of the multiple-choice format early in the 1900s. In this chapter we focus again on Key 3: Sound Design (Figure 6.1) by examining how to develop short-answer and extended written response items, how to score them accurately, and how to use written response assessment formatively with students.

figure 6.1 ■ Keys to Quality Assessment

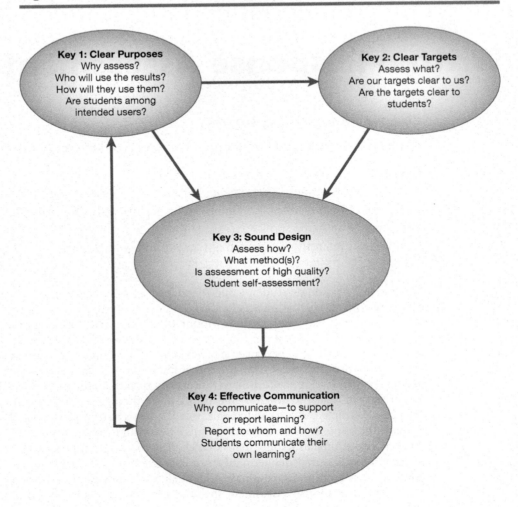

■ Considerations When Using Written Response Assessment

Remember, a valid assessment accurately reflects the desired learning, in part by using an appropriate assessment method. Written response methodology can be used to assess achievement of both knowledge-level and reasoning-level learning targets with some limitations.

Written Response Assessment of Knowledge-Level Learning Targets

Written response assessment is a *good match* for knowledge-level learning targets, which means there are some targets of this type that are not best assessed with this method. For example, when the targets are specific facts or concepts, selected response assessment formats provide a more efficient (faster and potentially less costly) means of assessment that, at the same time, allow for a more precise sampling. In other words, you can ask more multiple-choice questions than written response questions per unit of testing time because multiple-choice response time is so much shorter. So you can obtain an accurate measure of achievement on these types of knowledge targets while also providing a broader sample of performance per unit of time.

However, written response methodology is the better choice for assessing student mastery of content knowledge when the targets involve interrelated structures of knowledge or conceptual understanding. For example, we might want students to understand how the parts of a particular ecosystem in science interact with one another; understanding the relationships among different bodies of knowledge is what is important. A written response assessment can fit here. Or consider this exercise from a biology course final on the water cycle:

> Describe how evaporation and condensation operate in the context of the water cycle. Be sure to include all key elements in the cycle and how they relate to one another. (20 points)

A common problem with using selected response assessment for these types of knowledge targets is that it compartmentalizes learning—students can demonstrate mastery of discrete bits of knowledge but need not integrate them into a larger whole. Giving students written response assessments in this context helps them show what they know and it helps the teacher know *how* they know it and if they understand the connections.

Written Response Assessment of Reasoning-Level Learning Targets

Written response assessment is a *strong match* for reasoning-level learning targets. Reasoning occurs in the mind and is not directly observable. We cannot see processes of knowledge application or reasoning, but we can ask students to carry out and describe their reasoning processes and convey results in a written form. From this, we infer their level of mastery of a variety of reasoning competencies. For example, we can ask students to trace a line of argument in a political speech or to explain the process they used to arrive at a mathematics problem solution. Furthermore, we can pose problems that require the integration of information from two or more subjects or the application of more than one pattern of reasoning. Here is an example from a Science, Technology, and Society unit taught by a middle school teacher:

Using what you know about the causes of air pollution in cities, propose two potentially useful solutions. Analyze each in terms of its strengths and weaknesses. (20 points)

The key question here is, "Do students know how and when to use the knowledge they have to reason and solve problems?" Three keys to success in assessing student reasoning to keep in mind are the following:

1. Assessors must begin with a clear understanding of each reasoning pattern.
2. Assessors must know how to develop written response exercises and scoring criteria that reflect levels of quality specific to each reasoning pattern.
3. The exercises must present problems to students that are new at the time of the assessment (i.e., problems for which students have not previously memorized the response) and that require application of reasoning to address.

Assessing Student Writing as a Product

As you recall from Chapter 3, we define content standards that call for students to create different types of writing—arguments, informational/explanatory texts, and narratives—as product targets. It would seem logical that written response assessment would be a strong match for assessing students' ability to produce quality text. However, written response assessment is limited to addressing students' demonstration of content mastery and the quality of the reasoning presented. Proficiency at creating written products goes beyond this, including content standards related to organization, voice, word choice, sentence fluency, and conventions to which performance assessment methodology is better suited.

Limitations

Written response works only in situations in which students are proficient in the English language or in a different language if that is the focus of their learning. Students in the earlier primary grades, students with learning disabilities, or students who are not yet able to write will not be able to succeed in communicating what they know or think using this method of assessment. In these cases, another assessment method, such as personal communication, will be needed.

■ Creating a High-Quality Written Response Assessment

As we saw in Chapter 4, creating a high-quality assessment, regardless of method chosen, requires that we proceed through the same set of decision steps known as the Assessment Development Cycle (Figure 6.2). In this section, we will first explain how to carry out the four planning steps for a written response assessment. Then we

figure 6.2 ▪ The Assessment Development Cycle

Planning Stage
1. Determine the intended users and uses of the assessment information.
2. Identify and classify the learning targets to be assessed.
3. Select the appropriate assessment method or methods.
4. Determine the appropriate sample size.

Development Stage
5. Develop or select items, tasks, and scoring procedures.
6. Critique the overall assessment for quality.

Use Stage
7. Conduct and score the assessment, making note of diffculties.
8. Revise as needed for future use.

> All assessments, regardless of intended use or method selected, need to go through the same development steps to ensure quality.

will examine how to develop exercises and scoring guides and how to audit them for quality. Finally, we will describe what to watch for when giving the assessments to students and how to refine them after their first use.

Step 1: Determining the Assessment Purpose

Our first step is to answer the questions, "Who will use the results of this assessment?" and "How will they use them?" Typically, as we have seen in previous chapters, classroom assessment results serve one or more of the following purposes:

- For teachers to diagnose instructional needs prior to or during instruction
- For teachers to offer feedback to students and for students to offer peer feedback
- For students to self-assess and set goals for next steps
- For teachers to measure level of achievement for grading purposes

Each one of these purposes can be served with written response assessments, but it is crucial to begin the design process with this information in hand. The type of scoring guide you develop will be determined by which of these purposes or decisions you need to address in the instructional context of the assessment.

Step 2: Specifying the Intended Learning Targets

The second decision point is to list and classify the learning target or targets that will be the focus of the assessment. If one or more targets are unclear or complex, clarify or deconstruct them as a part of this step. Precisely what content or what kind of reasoning is the student to bring to bear in formulating and writing the response?

Step 3: Selecting the Appropriate Assessment Method(s)

After having listed the learning target(s) to be assessed, verify that written response assessment is the best choice for each. Consider the following:

1. Knowledge Targets: We can use written response assessment to measure knowledge targets involving interrelated structures of knowledge or conceptual understanding.
2. Reasoning Targets: We can use written response assessment to measure all reasoning targets, given consideration of the limitations described in the previous section.
3. Performance Skill Targets: While we can't use written response test formats to assess student mastery of performance skills, if we wish, we can use them to assess mastery of at least some of the procedural knowledge and understanding prerequisite to being able to demonstrate such skills. For instance, let's say we intend to use a performance assessment to observe and evaluate the quality of communication in two students' conversation in a second language. We might first use written response prompts to determine their knowledge of vocabulary and syntactic structure.
4. Product Targets: Written response exercises cannot help us determine if students can create quality products. However, as with skills, written response formats can test students' prerequisite knowledge of the attributes of a quality product. Students who cannot distinguish a quality product from an inferior one are unlikely to be able to create quality products. Written response assessments can test these important prerequisites.

Figure 6.3 summarizes the appropriate uses of written response assessment methodology.

Step 4: Determining the Appropriate Sample Size

When we determine the appropriate sample size for written response assessment, we establish priorities. Which of the learning targets or topics are most important, next most important, and so on? Which sections of content are relatively simple or more

figure 6.3 ■ Target Types Suited to Written Response Assessment

Target Type	Suitability to Written Response Methodology
Knowledge	Can assess conceptual understanding and understanding of relationships among elements of knowledge
Reasoning	Can assess understanding and application of all patterns of reasoning
Performance Skill	Can assess mastery of prerequisite conceptual understanding and reasoning but cannot assess the skill itself
Product	Can assess mastery of prerequisite conceptual understanding and reasoning but cannot assess the quality of the product itself

figure 6.4 ■ For Example: Blueprint for an Assessment on the Physics of Sound

Learning Target	Target Type	# of Points
1. Know what the term *vibration* means.	Knowledge	1
2. Understand that sound is produced by vibrations.	Knowledge	2
3. Know what the term *pitch* means.	Knowledge	2
4. Know how high and low pitches are produced.	Knowledge	2
5. Compare the rate of vibration to the pitch of a sound.	Reasoning	2

complex; which simply contain more material? These priorities will serve as the basis for your professional judgment regarding the distribution of points or ratings on your assessment blueprint. When identifying the relative importance of each learning target or topic, we seek consciously to match our emphasis in assessment to our emphasis in instruction. So, for example, if we spent 50 percent of our instructional time and practice on learning how to trace a line of argument in a political speech, then it makes sense to have roughly half of the assessment points come from one or more items assessing that learning target. If all learning targets on the assessment are of equal importance, then it makes sense to apportion the points evenly. Figure 6.4 is an example of a blueprint for a written response assessment in which the points are apportioned according to the relative importance given each learning target.

MyEdLab **Self-Check 6.1**
MyEdLab **Application Exercise 6.1** Planning a written response assessment

Step 5 Part I: Develop or Select the Items

One of the advantages of written response assessment is that these types of items are relatively easy to develop. However, as illustrated by the prompt "Discuss Spain," they can't just be thrown together at the last minute. Poorly framed written response items can be frustrating for students to answer and a nightmare for teachers to score. We want to design the prompt carefully so that students who have mastered the targets will be able to perform well and students who have not mastered the targets will not appear to have done so.

Short Answer or Extended Response?   Written response items can take one of two forms: short answer or extended response. Use short-answer items when the learning target calls for demonstration of conceptual understanding and the concept is fairly narrow, such as the learning target "Understand that Earth's rotation causes night and day." (A narrow concept is not necessarily easy to understand; it just has a straightforward rather than multifaceted explanation.) Some patterns of reasoning are also suited to short-answer items. For example, students can demonstrate their ability to summarize the main idea of a paragraph by writing a sentence or two at the most.

If, however, they are summarizing more complex material, the response could be one to several paragraphs in length. More complex learning targets requiring greater depth in an explanation or depth of reasoning are better suited to extended response items. "Discuss Spain" would be an example of a prompt that should be formatted as an extended written response item, if it weren't thrown away (which it should be).

> Learning targets requiring in-depth understanding or reasoning are well suited to an extended response format.

Devising Short-Answer Items   A short-answer item should be clearly worded and brief, giving students enough information to frame the desired response without providing so much information that they could produce an acceptable response without having mastered the target. If a high-quality response includes three examples, two characteristics, or four details, include that information in the item itself. Not doing so can compromise the accuracy of the results. For example, if a complete answer includes four details but you don't tell students that, you can't conclude that they don't know four details. Telling students to include four details doesn't help students who haven't mastered the target do better; they either can provide four details or they can't. On the other hand, without guidance on what constitutes a strong response, students who have mastered the target may provide only three details. If they knew you wanted four details they could have provided an extra one. Marking them down for not providing a fourth detail results in an inaccurate score.

Here are two examples of what to do and what not to do:

> *Grade 3 mathematics learning target:* Understand that shapes in different categories (e.g., rhombuses, rectangles, and others) may share attributes (e.g., having four sides) *(National Governors Association Center for Best Practices, 2010b, p. 26).*

Right: Name four ways that rhombuses, rectangles, and squares are alike.

Wrong: How are rhombuses, rectangles, and squares alike?

Also wrong: What do rhombuses, rectangles, and squares have in common?

> *Grade 4 social studies learning target:* Understand that human capital refers to the quality of labor resources, which can be improved through investments *(Council for Economic Education, 2010, p. 3).*

Right: Define *human capital* and give two examples of how you can improve your own human capital.

Wrong: What is human capital?

If your students do not yet write sentences, you can ask written response questions orally and students can respond orally. You can also ask them to draw a picture to supplement their explanation, if a picture will help show their thinking. If you do ask students to draw a picture, make sure that they understand the picture is supposed to show their thinking and is not supposed to simply illustrate the topic, as shown in the following examples:

> *Primary grades science learning target:* Understand that night and day are caused by Earth's rotation.

Right: Tell what you think causes us to have night and day. Draw a picture that shows the cause.

Wrong: Tell what you think causes us to have night and day. Draw a picture of day and night.

Also wrong: Explain night and day.

Devising Extended Response Items   "Discuss Spain." "Analyze *King Lear*." "Explain the causes of the Civil War." Examples of painful "essay" questions abound. What many of them have in common is a loose or absent connection to learning targets. High-quality extended response items, in contrast to these, carefully frame the task so that students who have mastered the intended learning targets know how to tackle the item.

Items Assessing Knowledge Mastery   Extended response items designed to assess factual and conceptual knowledge targets include three components: (1) a clear and specific context, (2) a statement of what students are to describe or explain, and (3) guidelines for an appropriate response. The *context* in items assessing knowledge mastery specifies the content students are to use in answering. It directs students' attention to the learning they are to be demonstrating. The *statement of what to describe or explain* helps students understand what they are to do with the knowledge set forth in the context. The *guidelines for an appropriate response* help students know what will be required in a complete and appropriate response.

To assess the learning target "Understand the importance of the carbon cycle and how it works," we can use this framework to create the item as follows:

1. *Set the context.*

> We have been studying the importance of the carbon cycle and how it works.

In this example the context is stated as a paraphrase of the learning target. This reminds students of the specific body of knowledge they are to access when drafting their responses. It's also helpful to remind students of the learning this item calls for when it is a part of a test that includes other learning targets.

2. *Tell what to describe or explain.*

> Based on your understanding of the carbon cycle, explain (1) why we need to know about it, and (2) how carbon moves from one place to another.

This is the task they are to carry out. With a knowledge or conceptual understanding learning target, students are generally explaining or describing something. Notice this sentence doesn't just say "Explain the carbon cycle," for two reasons. First, that wouldn't be sufficient to assess mastery of the complete learning target. Second, it doesn't give enough information—explain what? If you want students to explain its importance and how it works, tell them that specifically.

3. *Point the way to an appropriate response.*

> Be sure to include the following:
> - Why it is important to understand the carbon cycle (5 points)
> - The four major reservoirs where carbon is stored (4 points)
> - At least six ways that carbon gets transferred from one place to another (6 points)

Include enough information so students who know the material can show it, but not so much that students who don't can bluff.

This added information helps students know what will be considered an appropriate and complete response; students who know the material will be able to answer thoroughly, while students who don't will not be able to bluff their way through, hoping they include something that will be awarded points.

Items Combining Knowledge Mastery with Reasoning Competence Extended response items that combine knowledge and reasoning targets also have three components: (1) a clear and specific context, (2) a statement of the kind of reasoning needed, and (3) guidelines for an appropriate response. The context in items assessing knowledge mastery along with reasoning specifies the knowledge students are to use in answering. The statement of the kind of reasoning needed helps students understand what they are to do with the knowledge set forth in the context. The guidelines for an appropriate response help students know what will be required in a complete and appropriate response.

Let us say that the learning target underpinning the prompt "Discuss Spain" was as follows: *Understand the evolution of Spanish literature in the twentieth century and its relationship to Spain's changing political climate.* We can use the framework to craft the following item:

1. *Set the context.*

> During the term, we have discussed both the evolution of Spanish literature and the changing political climate in Spain during the twentieth century.

When we begin by referring to the specific content the item addresses, it reminds students to provide a response that demonstrates their mastery of the learning targets.

2. *Identify the pattern of reasoning.*

> Analyze these two dimensions of life in Spain, citing three instances where literature and politics may have influenced each other. Describe the mutual influences in specific terms.

In this example, "Analyze these two dimensions of life in Spain" would have been insufficient information. Remember, *analyze* (breaking down into component parts) can cover a lot of territory—student responses could be so divergent as to be impossible to score with a single preset scoring guide.

3. *Point the way to an appropriate response.*

> In planning your response, think about what we learned about prominent novelists, political satirists, and prominent political figures of Spain. (5 points per instance, total = 15 points)

In the last part of the item, we list the key elements of a good response without cueing the unprepared student on how to succeed.

Devising Interpretive Items Interpretive items allow you to assess mastery of reasoning proficiencies without expecting students to have learned the content outright. We do this by providing the knowledge needed in the form of a chart, graph, table, or text passage and then asking them to apply the pattern of reasoning to it. Interpretive items have three components: (1) a clear and specific context, (2) a statement of the reasoning task, and (3) guidelines for an appropriate response. To assess the learning target "Summarize text" in the elementary grades we can create the following item:

1. *Set the context.*

> In this quarter, we have been learning how to create summaries of lengthy text.

For interpretive exercises, the context is stated as a paraphrase of the learning target.

2. *Describe the reasoning task.*

> After reading (chapter or other relatively long text passage), write a paragraph that summarizes the plot.

Rather than just say "Summarize (the reading passage)," we give students a bit of guidance on what they are to summarize—one student could choose to summarize a character's actions, another to summarize the text in terms of lessons learned—there are as many ways to interpret *summarize* as there are students in your class. What do you want them to summarize?

3. *Point the way to an appropriate response.*

In your paragraph, be sure to do the following:
- Focus only on the main events. (2 points)
- Include enough information to cover all of the main events. (2 points)

Even with this guidance, there still is plenty of need for students at the elementary level to exercise their ability to summarize. We have not "over-helped" those students who are not proficient at the learning target.

Offering Choices   We recommend that you don't offer choices among response items. The assessment question we must always center on is, "Can you hit the agreed-on target?" It should never be, "Which part of the agreed-on target are you most confident that you can hit?" This latter question creates a sampling problem. It will always leave you uncertain about whether students have in fact mastered the material covered in exercises not selected, some of which may be crucial to later learning. When students select their own sample, it can misrepresent their true level of mastery.

Additionally, it's quite possible that the items will vary in difficulty, even if they are designed to measure the same learning target. Students who select the easier item (intentionally or unintentionally) may score well but may not have mastered the intended learning. Students who select the more difficult item may not score as well as students who chose the easier item even though their mastery was at a comparable, or higher level.

MyEdLab **Self-Check 6.2**
MyEdLab **Application Exercise 6.2** Developing short-answer and extended written response items

---

Step 5 Part II: Develop or Select the Scoring Guide

Some educators score written responses by applying what we call "floating standards," in which they wait to see what student responses look like before deciding what a good response should contain. A variation is the "connoisseur" assessor who contends, "I know it when I see it" and leaves the expectations for quality unstated. Not surprisingly, this practice violates the standards we've presented for high-quality assessment. The instructional and assessment philosophy that has guided everything we have discussed up to this point is this: *Students can succeed only if they understand what it means to succeed.* Part of our responsibility as teachers is to state the meaning of success up front, design instruction to help students attain our vision of success, and devise and use assessments that reflect that vision. That includes formulating scoring guides in advance before holding our students accountable for attaining the standards they represent.

The scoring of a written response item represents a classic example of one of the most important reasoning patterns that we discussed in Chapter 3: evaluative reasoning. In evaluative reasoning, you will recall, one makes a judgment about something based on the logical application of specified criteria. (*Criteria* are dimensions of quality upon which we base decisions. For example, one of your criteria for selecting a restaurant may be price. We can think of criteria as categories of "look-fors".) Theater critics evaluate plays according to certain (rarely agreed-on!) criteria and publish their reviews. Movie critics give thumbs up or down (an evaluative judgment) and explain why in terms of the criteria they feel are important. These are exactly the kinds of evaluative judgments teachers must make about responses to written response exercises. But, in all cases, the key to success is the clear development and communication of appropriate scoring criteria.

> Develop scoring guides that define success before beginning instruction.

Scoring Guide Options

Typically, we convey evaluative judgments about the quality of responses in terms of the number of points students attain. Three types of scoring guides are appropriate: checklists, task-specific rubrics, and general rubrics.

Checklists   A scoring guide in the form of a checklist identifies the possible correct responses or desired features of the response and specifies how points will be awarded. A checklist is useful when the desired answer has several parts and each one represents a specific category of knowledge or reasoning with knowledge.

For example, the item measuring the learning target "Understand the evolution of Spanish literature in the twentieth century and its relationship to Spain's changing political climate" can be appropriately evaluated with the following checklist:

> *3 points for each instance cited, maximum or 9 points*
> - *Quality of inferences about prominent novelists*
> - *Quality of inferences about political satirists*
> - *Quality of inferences about prominent political figures of Spain*

For the item assessing the learning target "Understands the importance of the carbon cycle and how it works," the checklist for the "how it works" part might look like the following:

> *1 point for any six of the following, maximum 6 points*
> - *Carbon moves from the atmosphere to plants through photosynthesis.*
> - *Carbon moves from the atmosphere to oceans by dissolving in places it is cold.*
> - *Carbon moves from the land to the atmosphere through fires.*
> - *Carbon moves from the land to the atmosphere through volcanic eruptions.*
> - *Carbon moves from the land to the atmosphere through burning fossil fuels.*
> - *Carbon moves from the land into oceans through erosion.*
> - *Carbon moves from plants/animals to the ground/sediments through decay.*

Creating Checklists   Checklists are fairly easy to create. They simply describe the specific information or components necessary for a strong response. In the "carbon cycle" example, the correct responses are propositions, which we learned to create in Chapter 5. A good way to create a checklist for an item such as this one is to follow the instructions for proposition development. Another way to create a checklist useful for scoring responses is to describe the features of a correct response and assign points to each.

Sharing Checklists   The written response item that students receive should include information about how their work will be scored. In the "Spanish literature and politics" example, it would be permissible to share the scoring checklist as written. In the "carbon cycle" example, however, the checklist functions as an answer key, so sharing it along with the prompt would not be a good idea. It would be appropriate to state the following: "6 points possible, one for each correct explanation."

Task-Specific Rubrics   As you recall from Chapter 3, a scoring guide in the form of a rubric is a detailed description of the features of a performance or product that constitute quality (also known as the criteria). The features are described at different levels of competence, representing a continuum of "novice" to "proficient" or "just beginning" to "strong." The levels can be labeled with words, symbols, or numbers. The level assigned to the response is known as the rubric score. A *task-specific rubric* is designed to score responses (that is, describe the features of quality) for one specific exercise. It is especially appropriate for assessing conceptual understanding. The task-specific rubric in Figure 6.5 is an example of a rubric that has been designed to identify the correct conceptualization and also to identify typical missteps and misunderstandings specific to the learning target, "Understand that Earth's rotation causes night and day."

Creating Task-Specific Rubrics   To develop a task-specific rubric, we refer back to selected response item development methodology for the "bones" of the task. Remember, first we create a proposition—a sentence that accurately states the conceptual understanding. Next we create statements representing *partial understanding* and *misunderstandings* typical to the particular concept. A response demonstrating partial understanding indicates the student has some of the information correct, or part of the concept correctly understood. It will have one or more of the following problems: information is missing, information is stated incorrectly, or information includes a minor misunderstanding. Responses that represent a misunderstanding can span a continuum of minor to major. A minor misunderstanding can be thought of as one that does not contradict the central concept; it is a small problem. A major misunderstanding is one that does contradict the central concept to be understood; it can be thought of as a "fatal flaw."

Finally we transform these statements (propositions, partial understandings, and misunderstandings) into rubric levels. Here is the process illustrated with the rubric for the "night and day" learning target.

figure 6.5 ■ For Example: Task-Specific Rubric

Learning Target:

Understand that the Earth's rotation causes day and night.

Item:

Everyone knows about day and night. Write what you think makes day and night. (Four lines are provided.)

Draw a picture to show what you think. (A 5 × 5-inch box is provided.)

Scoring Guide:

2 The response indicates that the Earth turns so that the same face is not always facing the sun.
Example: "The Earth turns every 24 hours and for 12 hours we are facing the sun."

1 The response indicates that the moon and sun are on different sides of the Earth and the Earth rotates facing one and then the other. There is no implication that the sun moves.
Example: "In the day we face the sun and in the night we turn to face the moon."

0 The response indicates that the sun moves to cause night and day (possibly across the sky).
Example: "The sun moves and makes way for the moon."

Source: "Day and Night" from Exemplary Assessment Materials–Science (p. 15), by Australian Council for Educational Research, Ltd., 1996, Hawthorn, Victoria, Australia. © VCAA, Reproduced by permission.

1. *Create a proposition—a sentence that accurately states the conceptual understanding.*

   Night and day are caused because Earth turns every 24 hours so the same side is not always facing the sun.

2. *Identify characteristics of partial understanding.*

   Night and day happen because the moon and the sun are on different sides of Earth.

   Night and day happen because Earth turns to face the sun and then the moon.

These are considered statements of partial understanding because, although incorrect, Earth's rotation does cause night and day. The misunderstandings represented do not contradict the explanation of Earth's rotation being the central cause. They are just a bit fuzzy on the mechanics.

3. *Identify typical misunderstandings. Also look for any egregious misconceptions that contradict the central understanding.*

   Night and day happen because the sun comes up and the sun goes down.

This is the fatal flaw—if the response indicates that the sun moves, we can conclude there is a complete lack of conceptual understanding.

4. *Determine how many levels the rubric will have.*

Levels (e.g., points): 2, 1, and 0

This concept doesn't have a lot of complexity. Basically Earth moves, or the sun moves. Students' explanation can earn partial credit for partial understanding but will earn no credit if they include reference to the sun moving, because that is considered the foundational misconception. Therefore, a three-level rubric will serve well. Notice also that this rubric has *instructional traction*, a feature introduced in Chapter 5, because it allows you to diagnose the specific error students are making, rather than just telling you who "gets it" and who doesn't.

For short-answer and extended response items assessing conceptual understanding that is not too complex, it makes sense to have three levels. You can use this formula to create one:

2 points: Statement describing correct explanation of the concept

1 point: Statement(s) describing explanations demonstrating partial understanding, but not including foundational misconceptions

0 points: Statement describing explanations showing complete lack of understanding and/or foundational misconceptionss

For conceptual understanding with more variables, it may make sense to use four levels, following this formula:

3 points: Statement describing correct explanation of the concept

2 points: Statement(s) describing explanations demonstrating partial understanding and statement of a simple misunderstanding, if appropriate

1 point: Statement(s) describing explanations showing partial understanding with some misunderstandings but no "fatal flaw"

0 points: Statement describing explanations showing complete lack of understanding and/or foundational misconceptions

A four-level rubric is often the best choice for an extended response item. However, if you find yourself struggling to differentiate between the descriptors for the middle levels, you will be better off using the three-point rubric. Remember, the number of levels on a rubric is primarily determined by the complexity of the learning target. If an assessment writer is not able to come up with four distinct levels of quality, the descriptors at levels 2 and 3 will not serve to discriminate between those two levels. Or details will be included to make the discrimination easier, but they will not be essential to the learning target to be assessed. In both instances, accuracy is at risk. The challenge in rubric writing is to articulate clear and appropriate levels of response quality in terms that you can consistently apply in scoring and that your students will understand upon seeing their results.

Sharing Task-Specific Rubrics   Task-specific rubrics can't be handed out to students in advance or along with the assessment item because that would remove all of the thinking from the task. They are like an answer key—they lay out exactly what the response needs to look like. Handing one out in advance turns the item into an exercise in following directions. You can, however, share them afterward to help students understand their missteps. This is especially useful if students will have an opportunity to engage in further practice followed by an opportunity to retest.

General Rubrics   A general rubric, like a task-specific rubric, is a detailed description of the features of a performance or product that constitute quality. In contrast to a task-specific rubric, however, a general rubric is designed to be used with any task measuring a given learning target. Figures 6.6 and 6.7 show examples of each

---

figure 6.6 ■ For Example: Task-Specific Rubric for Interpreting a Graph

---

This rubric is an example of a task-specific rubric. It can only be used on one task, the math problem "Going to School" (not included here).

4 points:

Has all five points on the graph labeled correctly. Indicates that Graham and Paul ride their bikes to school. Provides accurate and complete explanation of how those conclusions were drawn. Indicates that Susan walks and Peter takes a car as a part of the explanation.

3 points:

Has four or five points on the graph labeled correctly. Indicates that Graham and Paul ride their bikes to school. Explanation of reasoning is correct but incomplete and requires interpretation. May indicate that Susan walks and Peter takes a car as a part of the explanation.

2 points:

Has three points on the graph labeled correctly. Indicates that Graham or Paul rides a bike. Chooses the incorrect mode of transportation for the other. Explanation of reasoning is partially correct but also includes faulty reasoning. Explanation may indicate that information about Susan or about Peter was interpreted incorrectly.

1 point:

Has one or two points on the graph labeled correctly. Indicates that Graham or Paul rides a bike. Chooses the incorrect mode of transportation for the other. Explanation of reasoning, if offered, is incomplete and incorrect. Explanation may ignore information about Susan and Peter or have interpreted it incorrectly.

0 points:

Has no points on the graph labeled correctly. Indicates incorrect mode of transportation for Graham and Paul. Explanation of reasoning, if offered, is faulty.

Source: Chappuis, Jan; Stiggins, Rick J.; Chappuis, Steve; Arter, Judith A., *Classroom Assessment for Student learning: Doing it Right Using it Well,* 2nd Ed., ©2012. Reprinted and Electronically reproduced by permission of Pearson Education, Inc., New York, New York.

figure 6.7 ■ For Example: General Rubric for Interpreting a Graph

This is an example of a general rubric. It can be of use to judge responses to all problems requiring interpretation of a graph.

4 points:
Interprets information from graph to provide correct answers. Provides accurate and complete explanation of how conclusions were drawn.

3 points:
Interprets information from graph to provide correct answers. Provides accurate explanation of how conclusions were drawn, but explanation is incomplete and requires interpretation.

2 points:
Interprets information from graph to provide partially correct answers. Provides partially accurate explanation of how conclusions were drawn, but includes faulty reasoning. Explanation may also be incomplete and require interpretation.

1 point:
Interprets information from graph to provide partially correct answers. Explanation, if offered, consists of faulty reasoning and does not support correct conclusions drawn.

0 points:
Provides incorrect answers. Explanation, if offered, represents faulty reasoning.

Source: Chappuis, Jan; Stiggins, Rick J.; Chappuis, Steve; Arter, Judith A., *Classroom Assessment for Student learning: Doing it Right–Using it Well*, 2nd Ed., ©2012. Reprinted and Electronically reproduced by permission of Pearson Education, Inc., New York, New York.

type of rubric. Both rubrics assess the learning target "Interpret a graph." Figure 6.6 can only be used with one task. Figure 6.7 can be used with all tasks requiring interpretation of a graph. General rubrics are well suited to assessing more complex reasoning-level learning targets.

Creating General Rubrics   Here are a few key guidelines to keep in mind when developing rubrics to assess patterns of reasoning:

1. Begin with a clearly defined statement of what the pattern of reasoning looks like when it is done well. In Chapter 3, we began the explanation of each reasoning target with a definition. For example, we defined *inference* as *a reasonable guess or conclusion based on information.* This becomes the frame for the high end of your rubric.
2. Identify typical flaws in applying that pattern of reasoning. With *inference*, typical flaws include only considering part of the relevant information when drawing an inference, misinterpreting the information upon which the inference is based, and not considering any relevant information when drawing an inference.

figure 6.8 ■ For Example: General Rubric for Inference

Definition: An inference is a reasonable guess or conclusion based on information.

Level 3	Level 2	Level 1
The inference offered is logical. It is based on sufficient relevant evidence.	The inference offered is based on only part of the relevant information but does not take into account all of the relevant information. Or the inference may be based on a misinterpretation of the relevant information.	The inference offered is based on unverified or irrelevant evidence. Or the inference is a wild guess, based on no information. Or no inference is present.

3. Consider which of the flaws is most egregious, that is, which indicates a complete lack of understanding of how to apply the pattern of reasoning. In the case of *inference*, we suggest that not basing an inference on any available information is the indicator of complete misunderstanding of the type of thinking required. This becomes the frame for the low end of your rubric. The other flaws form the middle level or levels. Figure 6.8 shows a simple rubric for *inference* developed using this process.

Figures 6.9 through 6.13 offer rubrics for each of the other patterns of reasoning introduced in Chapter 3. Note that these rubrics are organized according to *indicators*, or subcategories. These subcategories are useful when matching the rubric to a learning target. Only a portion of the indicators may be appropriate for a simpler application at earlier grades, so you would only use the indicators that reflect expectations for that grade level. For example, when using the General Rubric for Comparison (Figure 6.10) with younger students, you may only want to assess for the indicator "Identification of similarities and differences" because that is the level of complexity called for in your grade-level content standards. Note also that when students are asked to analyze (Figure 6.9), it is often in service to evaluation (Figure 6.12), in which case indicators from both rubrics can be used to evaluate the respective reasoning processes. See Chapter 7, "Performance Assessment," for an in-depth explanation of the structure of general rubrics and a more detailed procedure for developing them.

As you read each rubric, it is a good idea to have an example of the pattern of reasoning in mind. Consider the following examples:

■ Inference: *Given the evidence provided in the reading (an article about the stock market), what is the relationship between interests rates and stock values?*

■ Analysis: *Using what you know about the causes of air pollution in cities, propose two potentially useful solutions. Analyze each in terms of its strengths and weaknesses.*

figure 6.9 ■ For Example: General Rubric for Analysis

Definition: Analysis is the examination of the components or structure of something to determine how the parts relate to each other or how they come together to form a whole.

Indicator	Level 3	Level 2	Level 1
Description of components	Identifies and describes all relevant components accurately.	Identifies and describes all relevant components with minor inaccuracies. Or identifies and describes some but not all of the separate components accurately.	Identifies and describes all components with major inaccuracies in some or all. Or does not succeed in identifying or describing the relevant components.
Explanation of contribution of each component to the whole	Explains the contribution that each component makes to the whole clearly and accurately.	Explains the contribution that each component makes to the whole with some omissions. Or explanation is somewhat lacking specificity.	Explains the contribution that each makes to the whole with major inaccuracies. Or explanation is missing altogether.
Explanation of relationships among components	Explains important patterns, distinctions, or comparisons clearly and accurately. Offers relevant and convincing evidence to support explanation of relationships.	Explains important patterns, distinctions, or comparisons with some omissions. Or explanation is somewhat lacking in specificity. Offers evidence in support of explanation of relationships that is not entirely relevant or is not entirely convincing.	Explanation of relationships among components offers no specifics, is inaccurate, or missing altogether. Offers irrelevant and/or unconvincing evidence in support of explanation of relationships. Or offers no evidence.

■ Comparison: *Given this early work and this late work by (author), how are they different in style?*
■ Classification: *Create a pie chart to show how you use your time in a typical 24-hour weekday.*
■ Evaluation: *Who do you believe is the best candidate for (office)? Why?*
■ Synthesis: *Write an original poem. (Note: this is a task constructed to evaluate a product target and would therefore be assessed only with performance assessment.)*

MyEdLab **Self-Check 6.3**
MyEdLab **Application Exercise 6.3** Developing scoring guides: checklists or task-specific rubrics

figure 6.10 ■ For Example: General Rubric for Comparison

Definition: Comparison involves describing the similarities or differences between or among items. In its more complex form, it involves first selecting appropriate items or features to compare, then selecting salient characteristics upon which to base the comparison, and last executing the comparison accurately.

Indicator	Level 3	Level 2	Level 1
Selection of items or features	The things to be compared are important and relevant to the comparison. Each item or feature to be compared is clearly defined. The rationale for choosing each is logical.	The things to be compared are important and relevant to the comparison. Definitions of some or all of the items or features are lacking in clarity. The rationale for choosing each is logical.	The things being compared are not important or relevant. Or it is not clear what is being compared. Or the rationale for why these things have been chosen is unclear, illogical, or missing.
Selection of criteria for comparison	The criteria to be used in comparing are appropriate and clearly define the specific features to guide thinking about similarity or difference.	The criteria to be applied are appropriate but some key features are overlooked or vaguely articulated.	Criteria are not specified or are inappropriate. Or poorly defined criteria are used. Or key criteria are missing.
Identification of similarities and differences	Similarities and differences are correct and defended with sound rationale.	Similarities and differences are partially correct and defensible. Or some are not drawn as clearly as they could be.	Similarities or differences are incorrect or vaguely drawn. Or important comparisons are missing.

Step 6: Review and Critique the Overall Assessment before Use

Figure 6.14 presents a checklist of factors to think about as you devise written response exercises. Answering these questions should assist you in constructing effective, high-quality written response exercises—those that avoid bias and distortion. Another good way to check the quality of a written response exercise is to try to write or outline a response yourself. If you can, you probably have a properly focused exercise. If you cannot, it needs work. Or ask a colleague to write a response and then discuss the item and its scoring guide together to see if either one needs revision. If your scoring guide takes the form of a general rubric, refer to Step 6 in the rubric development section of Chapter 7 for instructions on how to check it for quality.

Sources of Bias   Many factors can cause a student's score on a written response test to misrepresent that student's real level of achievement. Potential sources of bias appear in Figure 6.15, along with actions you can take to prevent or remedy them.

figure 6.11 ■ For Example: General Rubric for Classification

Definition: Classification is the process of sorting items into categories based on specified characteristics.

Indicator	Level 3	Level 2	Level 1
Identification of categories	Useful categories into which things are to be classified are identified and defined well in terms of key characteristics. Categories are independent of one another and are appropriate in scope and number to carry out the classification.	Some relevant categories are identified and characterized to carry out the classification. Some key categories are missing or not sufficiently distinguished from others to permit appropriate classification. Or one or more categories are too narrow or too broad to serve the comparison well. Or there are too many or too few categories than needed for the comparison.	Important categories are missing, not defined, or defined incorrectly. Or categories chosen are not suited to the comparison to be made. Or all categories are too broad or too narrow to serve the comparison well.
Sorting items	Items are sorted accurately into predetermined categories.	Some items are accurately sorted; others are misplaced.	Most or all items are misplaced.
Rationale for placement	The rationale for placement accurately identifies the salient features of the item that resulted in the classification made.	The rationale for placement of some items accurately identifies the salient features of the item that resulted in the classification made. The rationale for others may contain inaccuracies, miss some of the salient features, or include unimportant features.	The rationale for placement of items is missing. Or it focuses mainly on unimportant features of each item. Or it identifies features of each item that are inaccurate.

Steps 7 and 8: Use and Refine the Assessment

As with selected response assessment, it is not always possible to catch all problems with an assessment prior to its first use. Here are two things to watch for as you administer the assessment that will give you information you can use to refine the items:

■ Do students have enough time to complete their responses? If not, their scores will not be representative of their level of mastery. Watch for uncompleted items especially at the end of the test. For future use, either increase the testing time or reduce the number of items.

■ Do students ask for clarification of an item? Make notes of any clarifications you offer that may be caused by the working of the item or the directions and use your notes to revise the item for future use.

figure 6.12 ■ For Example: General Rubric for Evaluation

Definition: Evaluation is expressing and defending an opinion, point of view, judgment, or decision. It can be thought of as having three facets: an assertion, criteria the assertion is based on, and evidence that supports the assertion.

Indicator	Level 3	Level 2	Level 1
Assertion	The statement of position is clear. All key issues are identified and explained.	The position can be accurately inferred from what is said, but it is not explicitly stated. Or key issues are identified with some errors or confusion. Or some key issues are missing.	The position is vaguely stated or it changes as the evaluation progresses. Key issues are incorrectly identified or are not identified at all.
Criteria	The criteria upon which the position is evaluated are clear and appropriate.	Most of the criteria upon which the position is evaluated are clear and appropriate. Some are too vaguely defined, marginally relevant, or irrelevant.	The criteria upon which the position is evaluated are missing. Or they are inappropriate to the evaluation.
Evidence	The evidence offered is convincing and relevant to the position. It is clearly identified, accurately presented, and sufficiently explained.	Some of the evidence convincingly supports the position. Other evidence may be weak, irrelevant, or inaccurately presented. Or the evidence may be convincing and relevant but insufficiently explained.	The evidence offered is not relevant to the position. Or it does not support the position. Or evidence for the position is inaccurate. Or evidence is largely missing.
Refutation of other positions	Other positions are acknowledged and addressed by identifying and evaluating assumptions, citing limitations of evidence, or pointing out faulty reasoning. The refutation addresses the most salient elements of other positions. The refutation reflects facts and interpretations accurately.	Other positions are acknowledged, but they are not thoroughly addressed. Or parts of the refutation address trivial or irrelevant elements of other positions. Or the refutation includes some inaccuracies of fact or interpretation.	Other positions are not acknowledged or addressed. Or the refutation focuses on irrelevant elements of other positions. Or the refutation is a misrepresentation of facts or interpretations germane to other positions.

figure 6.13 ■ For Example: General Rubric for Synthesis

Definition: Synthesis is the process of combining relevant discrete elements or ingredients to create a new insight or idea. It involves identifying the relevant ingredients to combine and then combining them to create a pleasing or completely new inference, generalization, or insight.

Indicator	Level 3	Level 2	Level 1
Components to be combined	The components to be combined represent the most relevant information or elements to bring together into the synthesis.	Some of the information or elements brought to the synthesis are relevant, whereas others do not contribute effectively.	The components chosen are largely irrelevant to the synthesis to be created. Directly relevant information and/or elements are overlooked.
Combination of components	The components are interpreted accurately and blended successfully into a cohesive whole, yielding a distinctly new concept, performance, or product.	The components are blended in a way that is partially cohesive. Some elements have not been sufficiently or smoothly incorporated. Or some components have been inaccurately interpreted.	The components have not been sufficiently combined, resulting in a collection of distinct components rather than a new whole. Or the components have been inaccurately interpreted, resulting in an unusable new whole.

The following list of recommendations will help ensure accuracy and consistency in scoring responses.

1. Before scoring a class set of exercises, check your scoring guide against a few real responses to see if any last-minute adjustments are needed.
2. Refer to the scoring guide while scoring each student response.
3. Score all responses to one exercise before moving on to the next exercise. This does two things: it promotes consistency in your application of standards and speeds up the scoring process.
4. Score all responses to one exercise in one sitting without interruption to keep a clear focus on standards of quality.
5. Provide descriptive feedback based on the content of the scoring guide.
6. If possible, keep the identity of the respondent anonymous when scoring. This keeps your knowledge of the student's prior performance from influencing current judgments.
7. Although it is often difficult to arrange, try to have two independent readers use your scoring guide to score a few of the papers. In a sense, this represents the litmus test of the quality of the scoring guide. If two readers generally agree on the level of proficiency demonstrated by the respondent, then you have evidence of relatively objective or dependable subjective scoring. But if you and a colleague consistently disagree on the level of performance demonstrated, you may have uncovered evidence of problems in the appropriateness of the criteria.

figure 6.14 ■ Questions to Consider When Devising Written Response Exercises

_____ Do items call for brief, focused responses?

_____ Are they written at the lowest possible reading level? Double check at the time of administration to ensure understanding—especially among struggling readers.

_____ Do you have the confidence that qualified experts in the field would agree with your definition of a sound response? This is a judgment call.

_____ Would the elements in your scoring criteria be obvious to students who have learned the material?

_____ Have you presented the same set of items to all respondents? Don't offer optional questions from which to choose.

figure 6.15 ■ Sources of Bias and Suggested Remedies

Potential Sources of Problems	Counteraction
Lack of target clarity:	
■ Underlying knowledge unclear	Carefully study the material to be mastered and outline the knowledge structures to assess.
■ Patterns of reasoning unspecified	Define forms of reasoning to be assessed in clear terms.
Wrong target for essay	Limit use to assessing mastery of larger knowledge structures (where several parts must fit together) and complex reasoning.
Lack of writing proficiency on part of respondents	Select another assessment method or help them become proficient writers.
Inadequate sample of exercises	Select a representative sample of sufficient length to give you confidence, given your table of specifications.
Poor-quality exercises	Follow guidelines specified above.
Poor-quality scoring:	
■ Inappropriate criteria	Redefine criteria to fit the content and reasoning expected.
■ Unclear criteria	Prepare explicit expectations—in writing.
■ Untrained rater	Prepare all who are to apply the scoring criteria.
■ Insufficient time to read and rate	Find more raters or use another method.

When a high-stakes decision, such as promotion or graduation, rests on a student's score on a single written response assessment, double scoring is essential.

MyEdLab **Application Exercise 6.4** Auditing a written response assessment for quality

■ Using Written Response Assessment Formatively with Students

As you will recall from Chapter 2, formative uses of assessment information in the seven strategies of assessment for learning involve both teachers and students. The strategies connect assessment to instruction and learning in ways that can maximize both students' motivation to learn and their actual achievement. The following suggestions connect the strategies to written response applications.

Where Am I Going?

Strategy 1: Provide a Clear and Understandable Vision of the Learning Target. Begin by giving students a vision of the learning destination. Share with your students the learning targets, objectives, or goals either at the outset of instruction or before they begin an independent practice activity. Share a sample assessment blueprint as students complete practice exercises, asking them to determine which cell of the blueprint (learning target) the exercise addresses. If you will be using a general rubric to assess reasoning proficiency, introduce the language of the rubric by following the suggestions in Chapter 7.

Strategy 2: Use Examples and Models of Strong and Weak Work. Invite students to play a role in developing the scoring criteria for some sample exercises. Give them an excellent response and a poor-quality response to a past essay exercise and have them figure out the differences. Then have them actually score some sample responses. Discuss differences in scores assigned. Or if you are using a general rubric to assess reasoning proficiency, help students sort through what is and isn't quality work by using strong and weak models from anonymous student work, examples from life beyond school, and your own work. Ask students to use the rubric to evaluate these samples for quality and then to justify their judgments using the language of the rubric. A more detailed description of this protocol can be found in Chapter 7. See Figures 6.16 and 6.17 for explanations of how sixth-grade teachers Kelly Dye and Michele Buck use strong and weak work to help students improve their mathematics problem-solving proficiency.

Where Am I Now?

Strategy 3: Offer Regular Descriptive Feedback during the Learning. Design written response assessments so they can function as feedback to students. Make sure they are aware of the criteria that constitute quality and use the language of the rubric to provide strength and next-step feedback on their practice work. If you build scoring guides in ways that reflect common misunderstandings, misconceptions, or flaws in reasoning associated with specific score levels, then students' scores on practice assessments can serve as diagnostic feedback to you and to them.

figure 6.16 ■ From the Classroom: Kelly Dye

I used to . . .

On tests and quizzes, I would give an extended response or short-answer question and assess it based on my idea and criteria of what a 4-point, 3-point, 2-point, 1-point, and 0-point response would be. I would score the students' work and give it back with an attached rubric. We would discuss it briefly and I would attach comments as to what was well done and what needed improvement in their answers.

Now I . . .

The students learn how to answer extended response and short-answer questions by practicing and by assessing each other's work. I show strong and weak models of the different answers and we discuss what criteria are needed to achieve the different point values. Students then have a chance to practice answering questions on their own. I scan them into the electronic whiteboard anonymously and we as a class assess them. This can be done in pairs, groups, or a whole class.

Why I changed . . .

I feel that student involvement is a key piece in having them understand and focus on the learning target. I believe that students needed to have a more active role in their learning and academic growth, as well as their weaknesses. When they take ownership and responsibility, they are more likely to achieve and feel confident in their work.

What I notice as a result . . .

Students have a clearer picture of the learning target and have much more success when answering extended response and short-answer questions. Frequent practice of scoring and repeated exposure to strong and weak examples allow them to better assess their own work. This has led them to more accurately answer these types of questions not only in my classroom but also on the state test.

Source: Reprinted with permission from Kelly Dye, 6th-grade Mathematics Teacher, Olmsted Falls City Schools, Olmsted Falls, OH, 2011.

Strategy 4: Teach Students to Self-Assess and Set Goals for Next Steps.   Have students predict their performance in each cell in the assessment blueprint and then compare their prediction with the actual score. Were they in touch with their own level of achievement? If you are using a general rubric, let students use the rubric to self-assess, making note of their own strengths and areas for improvement. See Figure 6.18 for an explanation of how middle school science teacher Jeff Overbay helps students self-assess on specific learning targets.

How Can I Close the Gap?

Strategy 5: Use Evidence of Student Learning Needs to Determine Next Steps in Teaching.   Examine student responses to determine the cause of incorrect or low-quality responses. Was the cause incomplete understanding, flawed reasoning,

figure 6.17 ■ From the Classroom: Michele Buck

I used to . . .

I used to show students examples of work after a summative assessment.

Now I . . .

Now I do an activity we call "Scoring Camp for Kids." First, the students complete math problems relating to a specific learning target using real-life problems. Upon completion of the pretest the student and teacher use student models to create a rubric to score the student answers. Finally, the kids rate the models while discussing the strong and weak points for each math problem. When the "Scoring Camp for Kids" lesson is complete the students attempt and score additional practice problems.

Why I changed . . .

I changed my teaching focus to include formative assessments and clear learning targets. I found that many of my students questioned why I was taking off points on the extended response questions on the chapter tests. A few students did not even attempt the essay questions because they were not able to make a connection between a math skill and how it relates to a real-life math story.

What I notice as a result . . .

Now my students understand how to read a question and determine what they need to include in their answer in order to get a perfect score. Most importantly, the students now know why points are taken off of their score. Clear learning target instruction directly impacts student achievement, because my students are earning higher scores on summative assessments.

Source: Reprinted with permission from Michele Buck, 6th-grade Mathematics Teacher, Olmsted Falls City Schools, Olmsted Falls, OH, 2011.

or a misconception? Use this information for actions described in Strategy 6. In addition, use your analysis of problems encountered to adjust instruction the next time you teach these learning targets.

Strategy 6: Design Focused Instruction, Followed by Practice with Feedback.

If you are working on a learning target having more than one aspect of quality, build competence one block at a time by addressing one component at a time. After delivering instruction targeted to an area of need, let students practice and get better before reassessing and grading. Give them opportunities to revise their responses based on feedback focused just on that area of need prior to the graded event.

figure 6.18 ■ From the Classroom: Jeff Overbay

I used to . . .

In the past I would use the combined curriculum document as a guide for teaching. I never felt confident that I was covering the necessary content or that I was being effective in the classroom. It was more of a topical approach to teaching content. Having objectives has always been a part of my teaching but having clear learning targets for both myself and my students was something that seemed to always be out of reach.

Now I . . .

I now use the deconstructed standards to design a student-friendly self-assessment of the learning targets. These are broken down into knowledge, reasoning, and skills targets.

	Knowledge Targets: "What do I need to know?"		
1.	Yes _____	No _____	1. I can <u>give examples</u> of **adaptations** that allow organisms to survive in their environment.

	Reasoning Targets: "What can I do with what I know?"		
1. _____	_____		1. I can <u>use models</u> to show how energy flows through an ecosystem (food chains, food webs, and energy pyramids).

Why I changed . . .

The use of learning targets ensures assessment accuracy. The targets are much clearer and guide the day-to-day learning.

What I notice as a result . . .

Students now know where we are going and can self-assess along the way. This process helps students to quickly recognize areas that they are struggling with. These templates can also be used as a guide to create more accurate assessments. They actually become the guide for designing the assessments.

Source: Reprinted with permission from Jeff Overbay, 7th/8th-grade Science Teacher , Bell County School District, Pineville, KY, 2011.

Strategy 7: Provide Opportunities for Students to Track, Reflect on, and Share Their Learning Progress.   Give students a list of misconceptions and design instruction to address the misconceptions. As students are able to correct each misconception, have them date the list and write the correct understanding (Figure 6.19).

figure 6.19 ■ For Example: Correcting Misconceptions

Misconception	Date	Correction
1.		
2.		
3.		

Source: Chappuis, Jan, *Seven Strategies Of Assessment For Learning,* 2nd Ed., ©2015. Reprinted and Electronically reproduced by permission of Pearson Education, Inc., New York, New York.

Set up a system for students to track their formative assessment information (the work that is for practice) and their summative assessment information (the work that is for the grade), organized by learning target. Periodically ask them to reflect on their progress: "I have become better at _____. I used to _____, but now I _____." Give them opportunities to share their progress with their parents or other significant adults in their lives.

> MyEdLab **Application Exercise 6.5** Using written response assessment formatively with students

■ Summary: Tapping the Potential of Written Response Assessment

In this chapter, we have explored ways to use the written response method of assessment. We began by describing considerations for using this method—it is a good match for knowledge and reasoning targets with some limitations.

We then applied the eight steps of the Assessment Development Cycle to the creation of high-quality written response exercises. We described when to use short-answer items, when to use extended response items, and how to devise items of each type. Next, we discussed scoring guide options—checklists, task-specific rubrics, and general rubrics. We offered guidance for selecting among the options and presented guidelines for devising each type of scoring guide. We concluded the discussion of assessment development with suggestions for critiquing the overall exercise before use, problems to look for during administration of the assessment, and recommendations for scoring responses to ensure accuracy and consistency.

In the final section of the chapter we addressed formative use of this method by explaining how to apply the seven strategies of assessment for learning to written response exercises, thereby increasing student motivation and achievement.

■ Chapter 6 Suggested Activities

End-of-chapter activities are intended to help you master the chapter's learning targets. They are designed to deepen your understanding of the chapter content, provide opportunities for personal reflection on ideas presented, and serve as a basis for discussion among peers. You may wish to do all of them or select those that you believe will be most useful to your learning. Each activity is correlated to one or more chapter learning targets to help with your selection.

Chapter 6 Learning Targets

As a result of your study of Chapter 6, you will be able to do the following:

1. Plan a written response assessment
2. Develop short-answer and extended written response items
3. Develop two types of scoring guides: checklists and task-specific rubrics
4. Audit a written response assessment for quality
5. Use written response assessment formatively with students

Chapter 6 Activities

Activity 6.1   Keeping a Reflective Journal (All chapter learning targets)

Activity 6.2   Evaluating a Written Response Item for Quality (Learning Target 4)

Activity 6.3   Evaluating a Written Response Scoring Guide for Quality (Learning Target 4)

Activity 6.4   Creating a Written Response Assessment (Learning Targets 1, 2, and 3)

Activity 6.5   Planning an Assessment for Learning Application (Learning Target 5)

Activity 6.6   Comparing Your Experiences with Information from the Chapter (All chapter learning targets)

Activity 6.7   Answering an Interview Question (All chapter learning targets)

Activity 6.8   Reflecting on Your Learning from Chapter 6 (All chapter learning targets)

Activity 6.9   Adding to Your Growth Portfolio (All chapter learning targets)

Activity 6.1: Keeping a Reflective Journal

Keep a record of your thoughts, questions, and insights as you read Chapter 6.

Activity 6.2: Evaluating a Written Response Item for Quality

In the chapter we learned guidelines for developing different types of items. Using those guidelines, evaluate the two written response items for quality.

1. For the first item, use the guidelines for devising interpretive items. For the second item, use the guidelines for devising items combining knowledge mastery with reasoning competence.
2. Identify the item's strengths by noting the parts that adhere to the guidelines.
3. Identify weaknesses (if any) by noting parts that deviate from the guidelines. Make recommendations for how the item developer could improve the item.

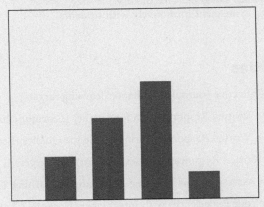

Item 1: Elementary Mathematics Task

Learning Target: Draw a scaled bar graph to represent a data set with several categories (National Governors Association Center for Best Practices, 2010b,CCSS Mathematics, grade 3, p. 25). *Note: This task is intended to extend the learning target by challenging students to think more deeply about the types of comparisons to which bar graphs are suited.*

1. What might this be a graph of? Put titles and numbers on the graph to show what you mean.
2. Write down everything you know from your graph.

Item 2: Secondary English Language Arts Task

Learning Target: Cite strong and thorough textual evidence to support analysis of what the text says explicitly as well as inferences drawn from the text, including determining where the text leaves matters uncertain (National Governors Association Center for Best Practices, 2010a,CCSS English Language Arts, p. 38).

Read each of the statements below and put a check if Emerson would most likely complete the activity or put an X if he would disagree or not do the listed activity. For each answer, find a statement from Emerson's work to support your check or X. Be sure to quote the statement directly and give the page number in parentheses. Use the introduction to *Nature & Self Reliance.*

1. _____ Reject organized religion
2. _____ Look to the past for guidance
3. _____ Claim that religious truth comes from intuition
4. _____ Rely on others for his success and happiness
5. _____ Join a popular "civic organization"

Source: Reprinted with permission from Thomas Mavor, 1999, Brother Martin High School, 4401 Elysian Fields Ave., New Orleans, LA 70122.

Activity 6.3: Evaluating a Written Response Scoring Guide for Quality

1. Retrieve a written response test item that you have answered in the recent past.
2. If you did not receive a scoring guide either before or after answering the item, create one based on the feedback you received on your item. Compare the scoring guide you created to the guidelines for quality in this chapter. Describe the scoring guide's strengths and weaknesses (if any).
3. If you did receive a scoring guide either before or after answering the item, compare it to the guidelines for quality in this chapter. Describe the scoring guide's strengths and weaknesses (if any).

Activity 6.4: Creating a Written Response Assessment

1. Select a short unit you have prepared to teach. Alternatively, you can select one of the learning targets from this chapter for the content of your exercises.
2. Determine how you intend to use the results of the assessment you will create.
3. List and classify the learning targets for the unit.
4. Create an assessment blueprint for the learning targets that can be measured by written response methodology.
5. Determine whether you will create a short-answer or extended response item for each learning target; then create the item following the guidelines in this chapter.
6. Determine which scoring guide option is best suited to each item; then create the scoring guides following the guidelines in this chapter.
7. Review and critique the items and scoring guides for quality and revise them as needed.

Activity 6.5: Planning an Assessment for Learning Application

1. Select a unit that you have prepared to teach.
2. Identify a learning target that can be assessed with written response methodology.
3. Select one or more of the ideas from the seven strategies of assessment for learning applied to written response assessment described in this chapter.

4. Write instructions for what you would do.
5. Describe the effects on student motivation and achievement that you believe will result from engaging in the activity.

Activity 6.6: Comparing Your Experiences with Information from the Chapter

Select one "From the Classroom" entry from Chapter 6 and compare it to your experience as a student.

- How is it similar?
- What differences do you notice?
- What conclusions about the benefits of student involvement with written response tasks and scoring guides might you draw?

Activity 6.7: Answering an Interview Question

Imagine that you are about to interview for a teaching position. The interview team (often a combination of administrators and teachers) is interested in understanding your level of classroom assessment literacy. Review Chapter 6's learning targets and think about what concepts and procedures were most significant to you from the chapter. Then think about what type of question an interview team might ask related to this significant learning. Write the question and draft a short response—one that you could give in one to two minutes orally.

Activity 6.8: Reflecting on Your Learning from Chapter 6

Review the Chapter 6 learning targets and select one that struck you as most significant from this chapter. Write a short reflection that captures your current understanding. If you are working with a group, discuss what you have written.

Activity 6.9: Adding to Your Growth Portfolio

Any of the activities from this chapter can be used as portfolio entries. Select any activity you have completed or artifact you have created that will demonstrate your mastery of the Chapter 6 learning targets:

1. Plan a written response assessment
2. Develop short-answer and extended written response items
3. Develop two types of scoring guides: checklists and task-specific rubrics
4. Audit a written response assessment for quality
5. Use written response assessment formatively with students

Performance Assessment

Chapter 7 Learning Targets

As a result of your study of Chapter 7, you will be able to do the following:

1. Plan a performance assessment
2. Develop performance tasks
3. Audit performance tasks for quality
4. Develop general rubrics
5. Audit general rubrics for quality
6. Use performance assessment formatively with students

When we want to hear music in its truest form, we go to hear it live. So it is with performance assessment. To evaluate certain types of achievement in their truest form, we ask students to execute a performance or create a product so we can observe and judge it. We evaluate public speaking proficiency, oral proficiency with a foreign language, musical performance, science investigative processes, and writing proficiency, for example, in this manner.

Performance assessments begin with tasks that require students actually to demonstrate performance of certain skills or to create products that demonstrate mastery of certain standards of quality. Then we judge level of achievement by comparing each student's performance or product to predetermined levels of proficiency. Our goal is to make these subjective judgments as objective (free of bias) as possible. We accomplish this by devising clear and appropriate rubrics or rating guides that describe the range of quality from weak to strong and then by learning to apply rubrics with consistency.

In this chapter we continue our focus on Key 3: Sound Design (Figure 7.1) by examining how to develop performance tasks and rubrics, how to evaluate them for quality, and how to use performance assessment formatively with students.

figure 7.1 ■ Keys to Quality Assessment

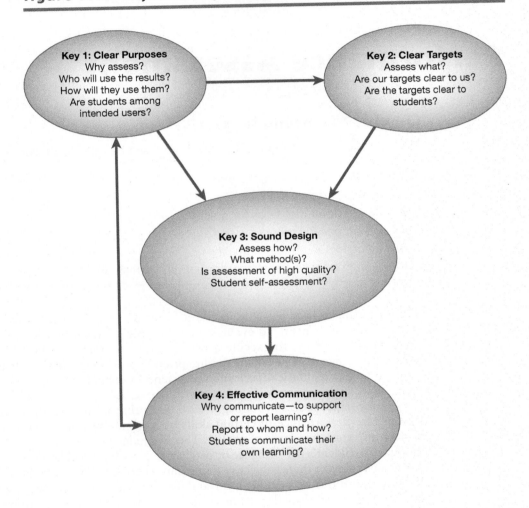

Key 1: Clear Purposes
Why assess?
Who will use the results?
How will they use them?
Are students among
intended users?

Key 2: Clear Targets
Assess what?
Are our targets clear to us?
Are the targets clear to
students?

Key 3: Sound Design
Assess how?
What method(s)?
Is assessment of high quality?
Student self-assessment?

Key 4: Effective Communication
Why communicate—to support
or report learning?
Report to whom and how?
Students communicate their
own learning?

■ Considerations When Using Performance Assessment

Remember, a valid assessment accurately reflects the desired learning, in part by using an appropriate assessment method. Performance assessment methodology can be used to assess achievement of knowledge, reasoning, performance skill, and product learning targets with some limitations.

Performance Assessment of Knowledge-Level Targets

Performance assessment of knowledge-level targets is only a *partial match* at best. It is true that applying knowledge in context helps us learn it more deeply and remember it longer, and it is fine to engage your students in a performance assessment for that purpose. However, if your purpose is to elicit evidence of knowledge-level mastery, observing and judging complex performances or products that call for the use of that knowledge may not be the best way to find out if students succeeded. It's not that we can't assess knowledge and understanding with this method. Under certain conditions, we can; mastery of conceptual understanding can be assessed with a performance task, if we control for elements of the task that might interfere with students' ability to demonstrate their understanding accurately. And recall from Chapter 4 that it is an acceptable choice with primary students and with older students who cannot read or write.

In all other instances, it is a good match for knowledge targets only when the student performs well. A performance assessment calls for the use of knowledge in some context—as the basis for reasoning, in a demonstration such as an oral presentation, or in the creation of a product such as a graph or research paper. If the student is successful at the task (and if the task requires the knowledge we are intending to test), then we can conclude that the student has mastered the underpinning knowledge target(s). However, if the student doesn't perform well, it is difficult to say that the problem was lack of knowledge. Other factors beyond knowledge are involved in success, so a lack of success cannot be attributed to a lack of knowledge. If the learning target in question is truly a knowledge target, we are better off using one of the other three methods— selected response, written response, or personal communication—due to considerations of accuracy, efficiency, and usefulness of information.

Performance Assessment of Reasoning-Level Targets

Performance assessment is a *good match* for assessing student reasoning and problem-solving proficiency. We must always rely on outward manifestations of having reasoned well to infer proficiency. For example, we can give chemistry students unidentified substances to identify and observe as they set up the apparatus and carry out the investigation. The scoring rubric would then reflect the proper order of activities for conducting such experiments—an example of analytical reasoning. In this case, the reasoning process is as important as getting the right answer—the reasoning process is what you're assessing.

Student products also can provide insight into their reasoning proficiency. Consider the example in which students are to carry out a science experiment calling for them to draw and defend an inference or take a position on a controversial science-related issue and defend it (evaluative reasoning) in a written report. You would evaluate these reports in terms of the standards of a good report, if those criteria have been clearly and completely articulated. But in addition, the resulting products would be evaluated in terms of the students' reasoning by using rubrics for reasoning proficiencies such as those presented in Chapter 6. You would rely on a two-part set of performance criteria with one part reflecting the proper structure of a report and the other part reflecting the quality of the reasoning demonstrated.

Performance Assessment of Performance Skill Targets

This is a *strong match*: the power of this methodology lies in its ability to provide a dependable means of evaluating skills as students demonstrate them. Communication skills such as speaking and oral reading fall into this category, as do the performing and industrial arts, physical education, and oral proficiency in speaking a foreign language. Observing students in action for these types of learning targets is the most accurate source of useful information about their level of achievement.

Performance Assessment of Product Targets

Herein lies the other great strength of performance assessment; this is another *strong match*. Certain content standards call for the creation of products such as research reports, pieces of art, displays of data, and so on. The quality of those products indicates the creator's level of achievement. If we develop sound scoring rubrics that reflect the key attributes of these products and learn to apply the criteria well, performance assessment can serve us as both an efficient and effective tool.

Figure 7.2 provides a simple summary of the alignments among performance assessment and the various kinds of achievement that we expect of our students.

Limitations

If the learning target in question can be assessed by more than one assessment method, then select performance assessment only when there is time to conduct it well. It is a labor-intensive method. The more performance tasks you need to administer, the longer it will take to conduct and score. For performance skill and product targets, it is your only choice. So make sure you plan sufficient time for students to complete the task. We will discuss the time issue again in the section on developing tasks later in this chapter.

figure 7.2 ■ Target Types Suited to Performance Assessment

Target Type	Suitability to Performance Assessment Methodology
Knowledge	Not generally a good choice for this method
Reasoning	Can assess reasoning and problem-solving proficiencies
Performance Skill	Can assess all performance skill targets
Product	Can assess the quality of the product required by product targets

■ Planning a High-Quality Performance Assessment

All assessments, regardless of intended use or method selected, need to go through the same development steps to ensure quality.

As we saw in Chapter 4, creating a high-quality assessment, regardless of method chosen, requires that we proceed through the same set of decision steps known as the Assessment Development Cycle (Figure 7.3). In this section, we will explain how to carry out the four planning steps for a performance assessment.

Step 1: Determining the Assessment Purpose

Our first step is to answer the questions, "Who will use the results of this assessment?" and "How will they use them?" Typically, as we have seen in previous chapters, classroom assessment results serve one or more of the following purposes:

- For teachers to diagnose instructional needs prior to or during instruction
- For teachers to offer feedback to students and for students to offer peer feedback
- For students to self-assess and set goals for next steps
- For teachers to measure level of achievement for grading purposes

Each one of these purposes can be served with performance assessments, but it is crucial to begin the design process with this information in hand. The scope of the task and the structure of the rubric you select or develop will be determined by these decisions.

Step 2: Specifying the Intended Learning Targets

The second decision point is to list and classify the learning target or targets that will be the focus of the assessment. If targets are unclear or complex, clarify or deconstruct

figure 7.3 ■ The Assessment Development Cycle

Planning Stage
1. Determine the intended users and uses of the assessment information.
2. Identify and classify the learning targets to be assessed.
3. Select the appropriate assessment method or methods.
4. Determine the appropriate sample size.

Development Stage
5. Develop or select items, tasks, and scoring procedures.
6. Critique the overall assessment for quality.

Use Stage
7. Conduct and score the assessment, making note of difficulties.
8. Revise as needed for future use.

them as a part of this step. Without a clear vision of the specific learning targets, it is not possible to develop a task that will elicit the correct evidence or design a rubric that captures levels of mastery accurately.

Step 3: Selecting the Appropriate Assessment Method(s)

After having listed the learning target(s) to be assessed, verify that performance assessment is the best choice for each one.

Step 4: Determining the Appropriate Sample Size

As we have seen in previous chapters, the sampling challenge is to gather just enough evidence to make a relatively confident judgment of level of achievement without wasting time gathering too much evidence. How do you know how many tasks to include within any particular assessment to give you confidence that you or your students are drawing dependable conclusions about proficiency?

To understand this assessment challenge within the context of performance assessment, let's say we are members of a licensing board charged with responsibility for certifying the competence of commercial airline pilots. One specific skill we want them to demonstrate, among others, is the ability to land the plane safely. So we take candidates up on a bright, sunny, calm day and ask them to land the plane, clearly an authentic performance assessment. And let's say the first pilot does an excellent job of landing. Are we ready to certify?

Obviously, no. Our assessment reflected only one narrow set of circumstances within which we expect our pilots to be competent. What if it's night, not a bright, clear day? A strange airport? Windy? Raining? An emergency? These represent realities within which pilots must operate routinely. So the proper course of action in certifying competence is to see each pilot land under various conditions to ensure safe landings on all occasions. To achieve this, we hang out at the airport waiting for the weather to change, permitting us to quickly take off in the plane so we can watch our candidates land under those conditions. And over the next year we exhaust the landing condition possibilities, right?

No again. We have neither the time nor the money to go through all of that with every candidate. So what do we do? We compromise. We operate within our existing resources and sample pilot performance. We have each candidate land the plane under several different conditions. And at some point, the instances of landing proficiency (gathered under strategically selected conditions) combine to lead us to a conclusion that each pilot has or has not mastered the skill of landing safely.

This example frames the performance assessment sampling challenge in a real-world situation that applies just as well in your classroom. How many "landings" must you see under what kinds of conditions to feel confident your students can perform according to your criteria? The science of such sampling is to have thought through the relevant conditions within which you will sample performance. The art is to use your resources creatively to gather enough different instances under varying conditions to bring you and your students to a confident conclusion about proficiency.

With performance assessment, sampling issues concern both the number of tasks to be given and the scope of the task. To make these determinations, we consider four factors:

1. The decision the evidence will inform
2. The complexity of the learning target
3. The consistency of student performance
4. The proximity of the student's performance to the cut-off mark

Sampling Consideration 1: Decision the Evidence Will Inform   How you intend to use the results is the first sampling consideration. If it will be in the context of a low-stakes formative classroom assessment, a small sample will often do. For example, if you are deciding how to regroup for instruction, a short task may provide sufficient information to make a decision. In a low-stakes context, if the small sample leads you to an incorrect decision, it is relatively easy to notice and fix it in the moment. In a high-stakes summative assessment context, it is important to avoid the consequences of an incorrect decision and enlarge the sample to minimize that possibility. For example, if you are deciding on students' final report card grades, you are going to want more rather than fewer samples to be sure you are making the correct inference about level of proficiency. An incorrect decision in this situation is far harder to fix after it has been made.

Sampling Consideration 2: Complexity of the Target   If the target is a relatively simple one, it may require fewer tasks to judge level of achievement than a more complex target even for summative purposes. For example, you may be able to judge a primary student's reading rate with one or two performances because this target is relatively narrow and sharply focused. On the other hand, if you want to judge proficiency at reading aloud with fluency, you may need several performances because the target has more dimensions to it. The definition of *reading fluency* often includes *accuracy*, *phrasing*, and *expression* and you may need several demonstrations to hear and evaluate all of the parts.

Sampling Consideration 3: Consistency of Student Performance   If the student's work shows that he has clearly mastered or clearly not mastered the learning target, then we need fewer tasks to infer with confidence about that student's level of achievement. A student whose assessment results are consistently at one level of proficiency on a given learning target can with some confidence be said to be at that level. However, having results that vary considerably for a given learning target doesn't engender the same level of confidence. If the student's performance fluctuates, it may be necessary to assign one or more additional tasks until we are able to make a stable estimate of level of achievement. Here is the rule of thumb: we have gathered enough evidence if we can confidently predict how that student would do if we gave him one more task.

Sampling Consideration 4: Proximity of Performance to the Cutoff Mark When a student's level of achievement is very close to or on the dividing line between two levels of proficiency, such as very close to a judgment of "meets the standard" or teetering between two grades, it is helpful to have more samples to justify assigning the level or grade. (As we will explain in Chapter 10, the extra samples should provide evidence of current achievement and not come from an earlier, less proficient phase of the student's learning.) If a student's performance is consistent and considerably above or below a defining cutoff point, having more data is not likely to change the judgment.

MyEdLab **Self-Check 7.1**
MyEdLab **Application Exercise 7.1** Planning a performance assessment

Step 5: Develop or Select the Task

Although performance assessment tasks can be highly motivational, lots of fun, and great learning experiences for students, they can also pose difficulties, such as when the results provide less information than needed to support the intended use or when students misinterpret what they are supposed to do, create the wrong performance or product, or run out of time and can't finish. These problems compromise the accuracy of the assessment results and often cause students to give up in frustration.

Characteristics of a High-Quality Performance Task We can avoid these difficulties and others like them by carefully working through three design features, which we will refer to as *criteria*:

- The specific content of the task
- Issues of feasibility and fairness
- The number of tasks needed to sample performance sufficiently

Figure 7.4 shows each of these criteria along with their underlying requirements.

Criterion 1: Content of the Task The bottom line for performance tasks is that they have to elicit from students the kind of response that will permit you to dependably assess proficiency. Whether you are selecting, creating, or revising a task, the content of the task is the first criterion to consider. What learning will completion of this task demonstrate, and what information will you provide? What context will be given for the task?

Target Alignment The requirements of the task should produce evidence of the learning target(s) the task is intended to assess. This is known as *content validity*. Even if the task is engaging and offers a great learning experience, if it doesn't align

figure 7.4 ■ Characteristics of a High-Quality Performance Task

Criterion 1: Content of the Task
- Target Alignment
- Information Provided
  - The Learning Students Are to Demonstrate
  - The Form the Performance or Product Should Take
  - The Materials to Be Used
  - Time Line for Completion
  - The Evaluation Criteria
- Context

Criterion 2: Feasibility and Fairness
- Time Allowed
- Resources Required
- Instructions Provided
- Level of Scaffolding
- Help Allowed
- Choice
- Avoidance of Bias

Criterion 3: Sample Size
- Use of Information
- Coverage of the Target

directly to the learning targets you are teaching, it will not provide evidence of level of mastery of those learning targets. For example, you might give students a task that has them pack a suitcase with items the main character in a story might need to overcome the difficulties that lay ahead of him and then explain why they chose each item. While the assignment offers an opportunity for creative, divergent thinking, if the learning targets you are teaching focus on summarizing the plot or inferring characters' motivation, this task will not be a good match.

Information Provided   When we structure a task, we need to provide students with specific information in order for them to know what they are to do. Imagine in a science class students have received this task: *build a mousetrap car and explain how it works.* While the task outlines the basic challenge, without more information, many students will be at a loss to sort through where to begin or to know what to do next, requiring the teacher to repeatedly explain the task in more detail.

Compare that task to the following one:

Building a Mousetrap Car

A mousetrap car converts one snap of the trap to forward motion. For this task, you are to use your knowledge and understanding of how to convert energy into motion, along with your understanding of the principles of mechanics, to design and diagram a plan for a mousetrap car. Then you are to build and demonstrate your car. After the demonstration, you will give a brief oral presentation in which you point out your key design features and explain why you included each feature.

Materials and Time Line

Use only material provided in class (followed by a list of the materials). You will have four class periods to design and diagram your plan, construct the car itself, and prepare to explain your key design features and why you included them.

Evaluation Criteria

Your performance will be evaluated on the following criteria:
- Clarity and completeness of your diagrammed plan
- The match between your plan and the car you built
- The accuracy of your explanation of your design features

The scoring rubric is attached.

We and our students are better served when the description of the task includes the following information:

- The learning students are to demonstrate
- The form the performance or product is to take
- The materials to be used (if any)
- The time line for completion
- A reminder of the criteria that will be used for evaluation

The Learning Students Are to Demonstrate   Good tasks specify the knowledge, reasoning, and skills (if any) students are to bring to bear in completion of the task, thereby reminding them of which parts of all they have been studying they are to focus on. It provides them with a clear vision of the targets the task will assess. Chances are in the first version of the Mousetrap Car task, the underlying learning target was not to build a mousetrap car. That is the *activity*. What *learning* will the activity demonstrate? The learning targets to be demonstrated by building the mousetrap car from the second version of the task are the following:

- Knowledge and understanding of how to convert energy into motion
- Understanding of the principles of mechanics

The Form the Performance or Product Should Take   Most tasks include some version of describing the performance or product that will ultimately be evaluated, but the description may not include enough detail. In the first version of the Mousetrap Car task, "build a mousetrap car and explain how it works" does not give enough specific information to elicit evidence of the learning targets. If you need the diagram to see if the student intentionally used principles of mechanics, then students need to be required to create one. When students are explaining, will they be creating

explain a healthy diet. It would be an appropriate accommodation to allow the students who are non-writers to use pictures to illustrate a balanced diet. While this may seem to be an aspect of choice, the students aren't making the choice from a list of options, the teacher is, and the accommodations are intended to control for a source of bias unrelated to the mastery of the learning target to be assessed.

Avoidance of Bias   Successful completion of the task cannot depend on unrelated knowledge or skills, such as intensive reading in a task intended to evaluate a mathematics learning target or complex mathematical problem solving in a task intended to evaluate reading. Nor can the task depend on having one particular cultural or linguistic background for successful completion. This can happen when a task uses a context such as sewing or baseball that is not familiar to some students. Including unrelated skills or a context relying on cultural or linguistic background can interfere with the accuracy of results for groups of students due to conditions beyond their control.

Criterion 3: Sample Size

As discussed earlier in this chapter, quality tasks provide enough evidence—a sufficient number of examples of the desired performance—to lead to a confident conclusion about the student's proficiency. The conservative position to take in this case is to err in the direction of oversampling to increase your level of confidence in the inferences you draw about student competence. If you feel uncertain about the conclusion you might draw regarding the achievement of a particular student, you have no choice but to gather more information. To do otherwise is to knowingly mismeasure that student's learning, which is never in the student's best interest. Two factors guide our determination of the sample size needed: how the information will be used and the scope of the learning target to be assessed.

Use of Information   In this first sampling consideration we focus on the purpose for the assessment. What decision will the results inform—summative or formative? Will the decision carry high stakes or low stakes? Different uses of the information will call for different sample sizes, as described earlier in this chapter. There are three ways that tasks can sample adequately for the intended use. The first is to adjust the breadth of the task, that is, its complexity and coverage. Sometimes one sufficiently broad task can provide enough information for its intended use. The second way to sample adequately has to do with the number of tasks you prepare. For some purposes, you may need to see only one performance or product while for others you may need to see several separate performances or products to adequately sample for the intended use. (Think back to the example of certifying airplane pilots.) The third way is to assign repeated instances of the same performance. In this case you may be able to use one task and ask students to carry it out as many times as needed to support the intended use of the information.

Coverage of the Target   In the second sampling consideration we focus on the learning target to be assessed. How complex is it? The breadth of the task or the number of tasks should adequately cover the breadth of the target(s). Is the task broad enough to cover the important dimensions of the learning target? If the target is a complex content standard, you may need several tasks, each focusing on one part of the content standard. One way to gather samples that show both student progress and achievement status is to have students collect work in a portfolio. If we carefully outline the types of entries along with the learning target(s) each represents, we can amass a strong sample. With a portfolio, we can gather evidence over time, creating a sample that adequately reflects the breadth and depth of the learning target(s) being assessed. In Chapter 10 we describe how to assemble and use portfolios to accomplish this purpose.

MyEdLab **Self-Check 7.2**

MyEdLab **Application Exercise 7.2** Developing performance tasks

---

Step 6 Part I: Review and Critique the Task before Use

We have developed a Rubric for Performance Tasks (Figure 7.6) to help you evaluate any performance task for the degree to which it meets the standards of quality on the three criteria described in this section:

- Content of the task
- Feasibility and fairness
- Sample size

We strongly recommend that you spend time studying this rubric as a concise summary of this section before moving on to the next section.

MyEdLab **Application Exercise 7.3** Auditing performance tasks for quality

---

Step 5 Part II: Develop or Select the Scoring Rubric

This is the part of the performance assessment design where we describe what "counts." The challenge is not only to describe what "outstanding" performance looks like but also to map each of the different levels of performance leading up to the highest levels. We must do this with both descriptive language and with examples of student work illustrating each level of proficiency. In this sense, rubrics provide the vocabulary and illustrations needed to communicate expectations to our students regarding successful performance. Our rubrics cannot exist only in our minds. We must translate them into student-friendly language, with examples, for our students, their parents, school leaders, and the community to see and understand.

figure 7.6 ■ Rubric for Performance Tasks

Criterion 1: Content of the Task

Indicator	Level 3: Ready to Use	Level 2: Needs Some Revision	Level 1: Needs Major Revision OR Don't Use
Target Alignment	All requirements of the task are directly aligned to the learning target(s). The task will elicit a performance or product that could be used to judge proficiency on the intended learning target(s).	Some requirements of the task are not aligned to the learning target(s). There is extra work in this task not needed to assess the intended learning target(s). Some, but not all, aspects of the learning target(s) have been tapped by this task.	Requirements of the task are not aligned to the learning target(s). The task will not elicit a performance or product that could be used to judge proficiency on the intended learning target(s).
Information Provided	The task includes the following information: ■ The knowledge the students are to use in creating the performance or product ■ The form the product or performance should take ■ The materials to be used, if any ■ Time line for completion ■ A description of, or reference to, the criteria by which the performance or product will be judged in language students are familiar with	Some of the following information is clear; some is unclear or missing: ■ The knowledge the students are to use in creating the performance or product ■ The form the product or performance should take ■ The materials to be used, if any ■ Time line for completion ■ A description of, or reference to, the criteria by which the performance or product will be judged in language students are familiar with	The task is missing most or all of the following information: ■ The knowledge the students are to use in creating the performance or product ■ The form the product or performance should take ■ The materials to be used, if any ■ Time line for completion ■ A description of, or reference to, the criteria by which the performance or product will be judged in language students are familiar with
Context	The task provides as realistic a context as possible, given the learning target and the intended use of the information. The conditions model application of the learning to a situation found in life beyond school.	The task provides an artificial context, which could be made more realistic. The conditions do not provide a clear link to application of the learning to situations found in life beyond school.	The task either provides no context, when it would be appropriate to provide one, or the context does not lead students to see how the learning could apply to situations found in life beyond school.

Criterion 2: Feasibility and Fairness

Indicator	Level 3: Ready to Use	Level 2: Needs Some Revision	Level 1: Needs Major Revision OR Don't Use
Time Allowed	The time allowed for the task is sufficient for successful completion.	The time allowed is too long or too short, but either the time line or the task can be adjusted.	The task will take considerably longer than the time allowed for many students to complete it and neither the task nor the time line can be adjusted.
Resources	All resources required to complete the task successfully are available to all students.	Some students may have difficulty obtaining the resources required to complete the task successfully, or one or more of the resources will be difficult for most students to obtain.	Many or most students will have difficulty accessing the resources required to complete the task successfully.

(Continued)

figure 7.6 ■ Rubric for Performance Tasks (*Continued*)

Criterion 2: Feasibility and Fairness

Indicator	Level 3: Ready to Use	Level 2: Needs Some Revision	Level 1: Needs Major Revision OR Don't Use
Instructions Provided	The instructions are clear and unambiguous.	The instructions may leave room for erroneous interpretation of what is expected.	The instructions are confusing and frustrating to students.
Level of Scaffolding	The task information is sufficient to let students know what they are to do without giving so much information that the task will no longer accurately measure the complexity of the learning target. The content of the task points the way to successful completion without doing the thinking for the student.	Some parts of the task give students too much help. In some places, the content of the task removes the thinking or the work from the student, compromising the accuracy of results or the learning.	The task is too heavily scaffolded. If used for summative purposes, the task cannot measure students' ability to create the performance or product independently because the content is so explicit that students can follow it like a recipe. If used formatively, students can satisfactorily complete the task without having learned anything. The task measures only students' ability to follow directions.
Help Allowed	Multiday tasks specify the type of help from others that is allowed. If no help is allowed, that is stated clearly.	Although there is some reference to the type of help allowed on multiday tasks, it could be misinterpreted.	Multiday tasks do not specify the type of help from others (if any) that is allowed.
Choice	If the task allows students a choice of tasks, it is clear that all options will provide evidence of achievement on the same intended learning target(s). All options represent the same level of difficulty.	If the task allows students a choice of tasks, all options will provide evidence of achievement on the same intended learning target(s). There may be some variance in the level of difficulty represented among the options.	If the task allows students a choice of tasks, not all of the options address the same intended learning target(s) or there is considerable variance in the level of difficulty represented among the options.
Avoidance of Bias	Successful completion of the task does not depend on skills unrelated to the target being assessed. The task is culturally robust. Successful completion does not depend on having one particular cultural or linguistic background.	Successful completion of the task may be slightly compromised by skills unrelated to the target being assessed. Successful completion of the task may be slightly compromised by having one particular cultural or linguistic background.	Successful completion of the task is dependent on skills unrelated to the target being assessed (e.g., intensive reading in a mathematics task). The task is not culturally robust. Successful completion depends on having one particular cultural or linguistic background.

figure 7.6 ■ Rubric for Performance Tasks (*Continued*)

Criterion 3: Sample Size

Indicator	Level 3: Ready to Use	Level 2: Needs Some Revision	Level 1: Needs Major Revision OR Don't Use
Use of Information	The breadth of the task, the number of tasks, or the number of repeated instances of performance is sufficient to support the intended use of the information.	The task is broader than needed to support the intended use of the information. Or there are more tasks or repeated instances of performance than are needed to support the intended use of the information.	The breadth of the task, the number of tasks, or the number of repeated instances of performance is not sufficient to support the intended use of the information.
Coverage of Target	The breadth of the task, the number of tasks, or the number of repeated instances of performance is sufficient to cover the breadth of the learning target to be assessed.	The task is broader than needed to cover the breadth of the learning target to be assessed. Or there are more tasks or repeated instances of performance than are needed to cover the breadth of the learning target to be assessed.	The breadth of the task, the number of tasks, or the number of repeated instances of performance is not sufficient to cover the breadth of the learning target to be assessed.

If you search on the Internet for scoring rubrics, you will find hundreds of options, some of which are well constructed and some of which are not. Whether you decide to use one of these existing rubrics or create one yourself, it is important to understand the characteristics of rubrics that ensure quality. In this section, we'll review the basic structure of a rubric, introduce the terminology used to describe features of a rubric, and examine the dimensions of a high-quality rubric.

Rubric Structure Rubrics can be thought of as falling into one of two categories: *holistic* or *analytic*. A holistic rubric has only one rating scale—all features of quality are considered together when determining the score, and only one rating results. The rubric for a summary shown in Figure 7.7 is an example of a holistic rubric. An analytic rubric has two or more rating scales—features of quality have been organized into separate categories and are rated independently from one another. Analytic rubrics yield a separate rating for each category. The rubric for oral presentations shown in Figure 7.8 is an example of an analytic rubric.

Holistic rubrics are best suited to evaluating learning targets that are not complex or multidimensional. For example, a rubric for a summary is generally holistic because there are only four separate, relatively straightforward features to evaluate: a good summary states only main points, states them accurately, covers all material to be summarized, and is written in the student's own words. These features can be combined into a rubric with only one rating scale without losing any detail.

figure 7.7 ■ For Example: Holistic Rubric for a Summary

Level 4:
The summary states the main idea and/or major points of the material to be summarized.
No small detail or extraneous information, such as personal reflections or opinions, is included.
All statements are accurate.
The summary covers all of the material to be summarized.
The summary is written in the writer's own words.

Level 3:
The summary states most of the main ideas and/or major points of the material to be
    summarized.
A few smaller details may be included, but no extraneous information, such as personal
    reflections or opinions, is included.
All statements are accurate.
The summary covers all of the material to be summarized.
The summary is written in the writer's own words.

Level 2:
The summary includes a portion of the main ideas and/or major points of the material to be
    summarized, or only a portion of the material is represented by the summary.
Small details and/or extraneous information such as personal reflections or opinions may
    make up a portion of the summary.
The summary may include inaccurate statements.
The summary may not be written entirely in the writer's own words; passages may be copied
    from the text.

Level 1:
The summary does not represent the main ideas and/or major points of the material to be
    summarized.
Or the summary consists entirely of small details, unrelated ideas, and/or extraneous
    information such as personal reflections or opinions.
The summary may contain inaccurate statements.
The summary may not be written entirely in the writer's own words; passages may be copied
    from the text.

Analytic rubrics are best suited to complex, multidimensional learning targets such as "Write arguments to support claims with clear reasons and relevant evidence" (National Governors Association Center for Best Practices, 2010a, CCSS English Language Arts, Writing Grade 8, p. 42), or "Develop a uniform probability model by assigning equal probability to all outcomes, and use the model to determine probabilities of events " (National Governors Association Center for Best Practices, 2010b, CCSS Mathematics, Statistics and Probability Grade 7, p. 51).

The context of the assessment may also be a consideration in deciding about the level of detail needed in the criteria. Analytical scales tend to be more helpful in formative assessment contexts where highlighting student strengths and weaknesses is the goal. However, when in a summative context such as assigning a grade for report card purposes, a single holistic rating may suffice.

figure 7.8 ■ For Example: Analytic Rubric for an Oral Presentation

Oral Presentation Criterion 1: CONTENT

Level 5:

- My presentation had a clear main topic.
- All of the information in my presentation related to and supported my topic.
- The information I included was important to understanding my topic.
- I chose facts, details, anecdotes, and/or examples to make my topic come alive for my audience.

Level 3:

- My topic was fairly broad, but the audience could tell where I was headed.
- Most of my details related to and supported my topic, but some might have been off-topic.
- Some of my information was important, but some details might have been too trivial to be included. Maybe I should have left some details out.
- Some of my information may not have been interesting or useful to my audience.

Level 1:

- I wasn't sure what the focus of my presentation was, or I got mixed up and changed topics during my presentation. I think I wandered through a few topics.
- I didn't really know how to choose details to share, so I just used whatever came into my mind.
- I forgot to think about what information might be most interesting or useful to my audience.

Oral Presentation Criterion 2: ORGANIZATION

Level 5:

- The opening of my presentation introduced my topic in a way that caught the audience's interest.
- I chose a sequence for the content of my presentation so that it was easy to follow. My audience could easily make a mental outline of the content.
- I used transition words to guide the audience. I don't think anyone got lost listening to me.
- My conclusion wrapped up my topic and left the audience feeling satisfied.

Level 3:

- My presentation had a recognizable opening, but it may have been a little plain.
- Most of my ideas were in an order that was easy to follow, but there may have been an instance or two where ideas seemed out of place.
- In some places I may have jumped from one idea to the next without helping the audience follow me.
- I had a conclusion. My audience knew when my presentation was over, but I could have done a better job of leaving them with a feeling of satisfaction.

Level 1:

- I just plunged into my ideas without setting the audience up to hear about my topic.
- I wasn't sure what order to put my ideas in, so they came out in a jumble. I think my audience would have had trouble making a mental outline of the content.
- I left out transitions. I didn't help the audience follow along with my thoughts.
- When I finished, the audience didn't know it was the end. I forgot to make a closing statement.

(Continued)

figure 7.8 ■ For Example: Analytic Rubric for an Oral Presentation *(Continued)*

Oral Presentation Criterion 3: DELIVERY

Level 5:

- I maintained eye contact with the audience throughout my speech.
- My voice was loud enough for the audience to hear.
- I varied my voice level and intonation to emphasize meaning.
- I articulated clearly so the audience was able to understand every word.
- I spoke at a pace that kept the audience engaged without racing through my speech.
- I avoided repeatedly using "filler" words between my ideas (e.g., "and," "uh," "um," "you know," "like").
- I used gestures and movement to enhance the meaning of my words.
- I knew my speech well enough so that I could just glance at my notes to help me remember what to say.
- If I used visual aids or props, they helped make my meaning clearer.

Level 3:

- I made eye contact with my audience part of the time. Or I only made eye contact with a few people in the audience and I forgot to look around at everyone.
- My voice was loud enough for the audience to hear part of the time, but it also was too quiet at times.
- I varied my voice level and intonation a few times to emphasize meaning, but I may have spoken in a monotone part of the time, too.
- I articulated clearly some of the time, but some of the time I mumbled.
- I spoke at a fairly good pace, but there were times when I spoke too quickly.
- Sometimes I used "filler" words between my ideas (e.g., "and," "uh," "um," "you know," "like").
- My gestures and movement might have been a little stiff or unnatural, but they didn't distract the audience from the meaning of my presentation.
- I gave parts of my presentation without having to read my notes but had to read them quite a bit in places.
- If I used visual aids, they were understandable, but they may not have added much to my meaning.

Level 1:

- I had a hard time making eye contact with my audience. I mostly looked up, away, or down.
- My voice was too quiet for everyone to hear me.
- I may have spoken in a monotone with no variance in intonation. Or I may have tried to vary my voice level and intonation on certain words, but I wasn't sure which ones to emphasize.
- I mumbled frequently, so the audience had a hard time understanding what I was saying.
- I had a hard time with the speed of my talking—I either raced or dragged through my presentation.
- I used a lot of "filler" words between my ideas (e.g., "and," "uh," "um," "you know," "like").
- My gestures and movement seemed stiff or unnatural, or I moved around so much it distracted the audience from the meaning of my presentation.
- I had to read my notes for most or all of my presentation.
- If I used visual aids, they were confusing. I wasn't sure how to explain them or how to link them to the ideas I was talking about.

figure 7.8 ■ For Example: Analytic Rubric for an Oral Presentation *(Continued)*

Oral Presentation Criterion 4: LANGUAGE USE

Level 5:

- I chose words and phrases that created a precise understanding of my message with the needs of my audience in mind.
- I used language techniques such as humor, imagery, similes, and metaphors effectively as appropriate to my topic, purpose, and audience to enhance my message.
- If I used any vocabulary that was unfamiliar to my audience, I explained it or used it in a context that helped listeners understand the meaning.
- I matched the level of formality in my language and tone to my audience and purpose.
- I used words and phrases accurately.
- My oral presentation was grammatically correct.

Level 3:

- In some parts of my presentation the words and phrases I used created a precise understanding of my message. There may have been places where my language did not communicate as clearly as it could have. I may have used some clichés.
- I tried to use language techniques such as humor, imagery, similes, and metaphors as appropriate to my topic, purpose, and audience, but I'm not sure how effective they were in enhancing my message.
- I may have used one or two unfamiliar terms that puzzled my audience.
- My language or tone may have been a little too formal or too casual in places to match the audience or purpose for my presentation.
- I used words and phrases accurately most of the time, but there may have been a few places where I used a word or phrase incorrectly.
- Most of my presentation was grammatically correct. I only had a few problems with usage or syntax.

Level 1:

- Many of my words and phrases were too general to convey meaning precisely. My presentation included a number of clichés. Maybe I'm not sure what it means to use precise language.
- I wasn't sure which language techniques to use. My presentation may have sounded repetitive and dull because I used the same words over and over again.
- I didn't realize (or I forgot) that my audience would not know the meaning of some of the vocabulary I used. I think listeners were confused by my terminology.
- I didn't know how to change my language or tone to match the audience or purpose for my presentation. It was either too formal or too casual.
- I may have used a number of words incorrectly. I just don't know.
- I think I may have made a number of grammar mistakes.

Rubric Terminology   When judging a rubric for quality, we will refer to the following four features: *criteria, indicators, levels,* and *descriptors.* On first pass, this next section may seem to be a complex analysis of the parts of a rubric. You may want to read it more than once. Considering these four features when examining (or creating) a rubric will become second nature to you and, we can tell you from long experience, you will find them very helpful in your pursuit of quality performance assessment. We will use the Oral Presentation Rubric shown in Figure 7.8 as the illustration of each of these features.

Criteria   The categories of quality that comprise an analytic rubric are known as *criteria* (also sometimes referred to as *traits*). Criteria represent key, independently varying dimensions of quality. Each criterion has its own scoring scale. You can teach each criterion separately at first so students can practice and receive feedback on each criterion separately. Thus, they can self-assess on each criterion separately. Further, you can assign grades to each criterion separately, if desired. The Oral Presentation Rubric has four criteria:

- Content
- Organization
- Delivery
- Language use

Indicators   Criteria for complex performances or products can be broken down further into subcategories called *indicators*. Indicators can be formatted as bulleted lists of the features assessed in each criterion and take the form of a word or a phrase. Sometimes they aren't called out on published rubrics as a separate list, but we find it quite helpful to create a list of indicators to show what each criterion will assess. If you look back to the Rubric for Performance Tasks in Figure 7.6, you will see the indicators listed in the left-hand column. Including indicators helps organize the content of the rubric and makes it easier to understand. The indicators for the Rubric for a Summary are not shown, but they are the following:

- States only main ideas
- Is accurate
- Covers all material
- Is written in student's own words

The indicators for the Oral Presentation Rubric are shown in Figure 7.9. If you compare the indicators to the rubric, you will see that each indicator matches a description at each level. In essence, the indicators are a summary of the content of each criterion.

Levels   *Levels* on a rubric are the points on a scale defining range or degrees of quality. They can be labeled with numbers (e.g., 1, 2, 3, 4), phrases (e.g., "Just Beginning," Making Progress," "Proficient"), and/or symbols or pictures (e.g., using a picture of a pizza crust to represent "basic"; a picture of the crust with tomato sauce to represent "making progress"; and a picture of the crust, the sauce, and the toppings to represent "proficient"). On an analytic rubric, the various criteria generally each have the same number of levels. The Rubric for a Summary in Figure 7.7 has four levels. The Oral Presentation Rubric in Figure 7.8 has five levels. (We'll discuss how to determine the number of levels a rubric should have later in this section.)

figure 7.9 ■ For Example: Indicators for the Oral Presentation Rubric

Content
- Makes main topic clear
- Shows how all information relates to and supports topic
- Includes information that is important to understanding the topic
- Uses facts, details, anecdotes, and/or examples to make topic come alive for audience

Organization
- Introduces topic and catches audience's interest in the opening
- Uses sequence of ideas that supports meaning and is easy to follow
- Includes transition words to guide audience
- Concludes by wrapping up topic and leaves audience feeling satisfied

Delivery
- Maintains eye contact with audience throughout
- Uses voice that is loud enough for audience to hear
- Articulates clearly
- Speaks at a pace that keeps audience engaged without racing
- Avoids "filler" words ("and," "uh," "um," "you know," "like")
- Uses gestures and movement to enhance meaning
- Uses notes only as reminders
- Uses visual aids or props, if appropriate, to enhance meaning

Language Use
- Chooses words and phrases to create a clear understanding of the message
- Uses language techniques (e.g., humor, imagery, simile, and metaphor) effectively as appropriate to topic, purpose, and audience
- Explains unfamiliar terminology, if used
- Matches level of formality in language and tone to purpose and audience
- Uses words and phrases accurately
- Uses correct grammar

Descriptors   *Descriptors* refer to the sentences or phrases representing each indicator at each level. Descriptors provide the detail used to flesh out the indicators at each level. When rubrics are used formatively, the descriptors diagnose specific strengths and weaknesses, provide effective feedback to students, and allow students to engage in accurate self-assessment.

Characteristics of a High-Quality Rubric   Now that we have established the terminology associated with rubric design, we can use that terminology to describe the characteristics of a high-quality rubric. Whether you are selecting a rubric, revising one, or creating it from scratch, there are three main features to pay attention to in order to ensure that the rubric will give an accurate picture of student achievement and that it can be used for the purposes you intend: the content, the structure, and the descriptors. Each of these represents a criterion for rubric quality. Figure 7.10 shows each of these criteria along with the underlying requirements.

figure 7.10 ■ Key Attributes of a High-Quality Rubric

Characteristic	A Quality Rubric:
Criterion 1: Content of the Rubric	*Blends with the task to define the learning target*
■ Target Alignment	Criteria focus only on key factors in performance
■ Match to Essential Elements	Everything of importance is included; unimportant left out
Criterion 2: Structure of the Rubric	*Organized for easy use*
■ Number of Criteria	Match complexity of the learning target and use context
■ Independence of Criteria	Meaning of criteria are truly different from one another
■ Grouping of Descriptors	Descriptors align only with their assigned criterion
■ Number of Levels	Each level defines a separate step toward proficiency
Criterion 3: Descriptors in the Rubric	*Relies on descriptive language*
■ Kind of Detail	Descriptions reference attributes of performance without judgment
■ Content of Levels	Content is consistent across levels of the same criterion
■ Formative Usefulness	In formative contexts, descriptions point out the way to better performance

Criterion 1: Content of the Rubric   When you are deciding whether a rubric is of high quality or not, the first criterion to consider is its *content*. What are you assessing? What features of a student's performance or product will the assessment measure? A good rubric defines the intended learning target by what is required to do it well. If the rubric misrepresents the intended learning, students will work toward producing evidence of something other than what you desire—what students see on the rubric is what they will attempt to achieve. To evaluate a rubric's content, we pay attention to two factors: *target alignment* and *match to essential elements*.

Target Alignment   Just as the task should align to the learning target(s) to be assessed, so should the rubric. The rubric's criteria and descriptors should not focus on features that do not contribute to achieving at a high level on the learning target. Sometimes rubrics stray from their focus, such as when students are asked to produce a poster to demonstrate a reasoning target and the rubric includes features of the poster more closely related to following directions ("has three colors") or art. "Home-grown" rubrics, absent careful consideration of the intended learning, often suffer from this problem. If we are evaluating a pattern of reasoning, the rubric should represent levels of quality for the salient features of the type of reasoning. Unrelated features should be left out or assessed separately for another purpose.

Match to Essential Elements   The rubric's criteria, indicators, and descriptors should represent best thinking in the field about what it means to perform well on the intended learning target. Everything of importance for students at your level should be included. Three unfortunate things happen when important components are omitted: (1) we send the message (wrongly) that what is left out is unimportant; (2) results offer incomplete information on which to plan future instruction; and (3) students receive no feedback on the valued yet missing elements of competence.

By the same token, trivial features related to the target, those *not* important to success, should be left out. For example, the rubric may stipulate one way of demonstrating competence, but the requirement may not be essential to competence. It may be a matter of a particular teacher's preference. In this case, the rubric has inaccurately limited the definition of what it means to do well and has penalized students who demonstrate their achievement of the intended learning target in an equally compelling yet different way. If the feature is essential to the learning target, leave it in. If not, leave it out.

Criterion 2: Structure of the Rubric

The second criterion for a high-quality rubric is the structure of the rubric. In this context, *structure* refers to how the rubric is organized. Good clear structure makes the rubric easier to use. Once criteria are defined to represent important dimensions of quality, the criteria and their associated descriptors are organized in ways that enable the evaluator to create an accurate profile of strengths and areas for further work. To evaluate a rubric's structure, we pay attention to four factors: the *number of criteria*, the *independence of the criteria*, the *grouping of the descriptors*, and the *number of levels*.

Number of Criteria   The number of criteria should be sufficient to reflect the complexity of the learning target and should also be determined by considering the intended use. If it is summative, several important dimensions may be combined into one category, resulting in fewer criteria. If the intended use is formative, it is better to keep the dimensions discrete, resulting in more criteria. If the rubric is holistic, the single scale needs to sufficiently represent all important parts of the target in one scale. If the target is complex, the rubric needs to include whatever number of criteria is needed to appropriately define all important categories of proficiency.

Independence of Criteria   If there are multiple criteria, they should be independent of one another. Similar descriptors should appear only in one criterion. This is where the indicators come in handy. If you have created a "bulleted list" of the features the criterion is to include, this will help you ensure you don't evaluate what is basically the same characteristic in two different places. When the same feature is rated in more than one criterion, it may indicate that the criteria aren't separable and should be combined. If they are separable, they can be rated independently. Each feature should be assigned to only one criterion.

Grouping of Descriptors   If there are multiple criteria, all descriptors should fit under the criterion to which they are assigned. In other words, the categories defined by the criteria should suit the descriptors contained within them. Grouping of descriptors is a classification challenge. If the descriptors don't fit where they're placed, they should be moved or the categories should be redefined.

Number of Levels   The number of levels usually ranges from three to about six or seven. Each level represents a defined step toward proficiency. The number of levels is dependent on the complexity of the learning target and the purpose for the assessment—will it be a summative use or a formative use? When the use is formative, the levels should be useful in diagnosing student strengths and next steps: there should be enough of them to reflect typical stages of student understanding, capabilities, or progress. However, there should not be so many of them that it is difficult or impossible to define each or to distinguish among them.

Some simpler learning targets truly only need to be divided into three levels of proficiency, so it makes sense to have only three levels. The following rubric, created to evaluate elementary students' proficiency with making inferences from what they read, is an example of a learning target suited to three levels.

3: Guess based on enough evidence, accurately interpreted

2: Guess based on insufficient evidence or on an inaccurate interpretation of the evidence

1: Wild guess based on no discernible evidence

More complex learning targets such as those represented in the Oral Presentation Rubric (Figure 7.7) can be divided into five levels. This rubric has three defined levels, but it is easy to see that a student's performance may have some features of the "5" level and some features of the "3" level or some features of the "3" level and some from the "1" level. With such rubrics, when a performance falls between two of the defined score points, you can highlight the phrases that describe it from each of the defined levels and then assign it the intermediate score, in this case, either the "4" or the "2."

Many rubrics designed for large-scale accountability testing will have a four-point structure. When the purpose of the rubric is to determine overall level of proficiency, this structure is often used. In this context, it doesn't matter what the specific strengths and weaknesses of an individual's performance are, nor does it matter if any of the description of the "2" or the "3" matches the performance. Some students will have some elements of the "4" and some elements of the "1" and will be given either a "2" or a "3" depending on the severity of what is lacking. This is not necessarily wrong, but it is immensely unhelpful for classroom assessment purposes. Not all four-point rubrics have that problem. In the classroom, we need the levels to be attached to the correct descriptors. The Rubric for a Summary (Figure 7.7) is an example of how a four-point rubric can be designed so that the score at each level links to a well-defined waypoint on the journey to mastery.

Criterion 3: Descriptors in the Rubric   The last criterion to consider when judging a rubric's quality relates to the *descriptors*—the "goes-unders" in each criterion. These are the details that flesh out the indicators at each level. To evaluate a rubric's descriptors, we pay attention to three factors: the *kind of detail*, the *content of the levels*, and the *formative usefulness*.

Kind of Detail   The wording should be descriptive of features of the work. Example 1 shows a rubric using descriptive language to evaluate *Display of Information*, one criterion of a rubric for scientific investigation (Chappuis, 2015, pp. 52–53).

> *Example 1: Descriptive Language*
>
> 4: *Display of information is accurate, complete, and organized so that it is easy to interpret.*
> 3: *Display of information is accurate, mostly complete, and is mostly organized so that it is easy to interpret. It may have one or two omissions.*
> 2: *Display of information is partially accurate, partially complete, and may have some organizational problems.*
> 1: *Display of information is inaccurate, incomplete, and not well organized.*

Evaluative language, where the words in the descriptors simply repeat the judgment of the level, should be avoided because the descriptors add no useful information to help the evaluator distinguish among the levels. Example 2 shows a rubric using evaluative language to evaluate *Display of Information* (Chappuis, 2015, p. 53).

> *Example 2: Evaluative Language*
>
> 4: *Excellent display of information*
> 3: *Good display of information*
> 2: *Fair display of information*
> 1: *Poor display of information*

Quantitative language, where the descriptors simply specify a number of items or the frequency of events, should also be avoided unless it is truly the number of instances that determines level of quality. In the Rubric for a Summary (Figure 7.7), you will see an example of when a frequency count does contribute to quality: the greater the amount of extraneous information in the summary, the lower the performance level. In the Oral Presentation Rubric, for the criterion *Delivery*, you will see that a greater number of disfluencies contributes to a lower score. Example 3 shows a rubric for *Display of Information* in which the quantitative descriptors do not accurately reflect what quality looks like.

> *Example 3: Quantitative Language*
>
> 4: *Displays four pieces of information*
> 3: *Displays three pieces of information*
> 2: *Displays two pieces of information*
> 1: *Displays one piece of information*

Descriptive language identifies in specific terms what students are doing well and what needs work. Evaluative language offers no insight into features of quality present or absent. Quantitative language substitutes number counts for explanations of level of quality and runs the risk of inaccurately representing the learning target.

Content of Levels   The descriptors at each level of the rubric should be parallel in their references to elements of quality. Creating indicators helps with this; you simply make sure you have a descriptor at each level for each indicator. If an indicator is mentioned at one level, it generally should be mentioned at all others. For example, in a writing rubric, if "focus" is described at the highest level, it should be described at the other levels. If a descriptor for an indicator is missing at one or more levels, there should be a logical explanation.

Formative Value   If a rubric is intended for formative use, its number of levels and descriptors should work together to function as effective feedback to the student and the teacher, leading to clear conclusions about strengths and areas needing work. Teachers should be able to use the rubric to determine what to teach next, to identify needs for differentiated instruction, or to identify topics for whole-group reteaching. Teachers should be able to use the language of the rubric to offer feedback to students. Students should be able to use the language of the rubric to self-assess, to revise their own work, to plan their own next steps in learning, and to offer feedback to peers. Rubrics that can be used in these ways are said to have *instructional traction*, that is, the power to provide sufficient detail to guide action directed at further learning. Rubrics with instructional traction for student use are written in language students can understand.

> Rubrics that have instructional traction for student use are written in language they can understand.

Process for Developing Rubrics   When your search for previously developed rubrics draws a blank or none of the available options seem to meet your needs—that is, when it's clear that original development on your part is the only answer—there is a straightforward process you can follow. Further, you can do this development work alone, with a colleague, or with a team of teachers. As long as all involved are masters of the learning target(s) to be reflected in the performance assessment, rubric development with a partner or team can be both engaging and productive. The steps in the process (also shown in Figure 7.11) are as follows:

1. Establish your knowledge base.
2. Collect samples of student work and sort them according to levels of quality.
3. Identify the key characteristics that differentiate levels of quality.
4. Determine whether you will create an analytic or a holistic rubric.
5. Define levels of quality and identify anchor papers.
6. Practice applying the rubric, revising it as needed.

figure 7.11 ■ Steps in Creating a Rubric

1. Establish your knowledge base.
2. Collect samples of student work and sort them according to levels of quality.
3. Identify the key characteristics that differentiate levels of quality.
4. Determine whether you will create an analytic or a holistic rubric.
5. Define levels of quality and identify anchor papers.
6. Practice applying the rubric, revising it as needed.

Please keep in mind that, even though this process appears complex at first blush, once a high-quality rubric is completed the cost of its development is amortized over the life of its use. And a really good one lasts a long time and will help your students achieve successfully.

Step 1: Establish a Knowledge Base   The first task is to become clear ourselves about what the performance or product to be evaluated looks like when it is done well. As mentioned previously, this requires that developers bring an appropriate level of pedagogical content knowledge to the table. With this foundation of expertise to rely on, along with access to appropriate professional literature, text materials, and previously developed rubrics, you can begin. Start by creating a list of what you believe are the characteristics of a high-quality performance or product, as described by the content standard or learning target the rubric will assess. (If you find yourself stymied at this first step, considering enlisting someone more familiar with the learning target to work through the steps with you.) Next, read through previously developed rubrics that assess the content standard or learning target, if you have them. As you proceed, accumulate a list of characteristics that you believe represent key dimensions of the learning target.

Step 2: Collect Samples of Student Work and Sort Them According to Levels of Quality   Success in completing this step hinges on having access to student samples demonstrating a range of quality from weak to strong for the reasoning proficiency, performance skill, or product target that is to be the focus of the evaluation. Good sources are your own students' work; samples obtained from a colleague; samples found in textbooks, professional literature, or online; and samples provided by your district or state department of education. When you have assembled those samples, first randomly sort them into two piles. One is to be used to help you with rubric development. The other will be used later in the process to help you refine the rubric.

After selecting one pile to work with, number the samples. (Don't number them by rank order at this point; just number them in the order they show up in the pile.) Then sort the samples according to quality, writing down your reasons for placement of each sample as you go. These reasons will be used in the next step, so make sure you note them carefully. We suggest that you sort the samples into three categories:

strong, medium, and weak. If development is being done by a team, have all members sort independently, noting at that time why they placed each sample in its category.

If you are faced with new rubric development without access to samples of student work, obviously you will have to rely heavily on your mastery of the achievement target in question. You will need a sharp focus on that specific target. If you lack that understanding, then it will be essential that you solicit help from a colleague who has that strong academic background. If you feel you are qualified to carry out the initial development of a rubric, then as you work on it, it will be important that you find or create a context in which you can have students participate in the assessment so you can generate some samples for use in the later steps.

Step 3: Identify the Key Characteristics That Differentiate Levels of Quality The challenge at this step is to discover the key features of student work that capture the important differences among strong, medium, and weak work. As a team, compile all of the reasons you placed samples into the "strong" pile, all of the reasons you placed samples into the "medium" pile, and all of the reasons you placed samples into the "weak" pile. This should provide you with three lists: features the samples in the "strong" pile have in common, features the samples in the "medium" pile have in common, and features the samples in the "weak" pile have in common.

Step 4: Determine Whether You Will Create an Analytic or a Holistic Rubric Your next task is to look at those three lists and decide whether separate categories of quality are emerging. This is the point at which you can decide whether the rubric should be holistic or analytic. If you can identify broad, independently varying categories of strengths and weaknesses, these indicate separate criteria and you may want to create a rubric that is analytic in structure. Use the information from this chapter to help you think through this decision. Once you have tentatively identified the criteria, it's time to refine them. You might discover that two criteria really refer to the same thing or that one criterion is too broad and really needs to be divided into two criteria. Most analytic rubrics go through several iterations of criteria definition and organization. The Rubric for Rubrics (Figure 7.12) offers guidelines to help with this work.

Step 5: Define Levels of Quality and Identify Anchor Examples Next you need to describe levels of quality within each key criterion. Refer to the reasons you listed for each level, sorting them into the separate categories represented by your criteria if your rubric is analytic in structure. These reasons become your descriptors. Refine the collection of descriptors at each level until you are satisfied that the descriptors are assigned to the correct criterion and that they adhere to the guidelines for descriptors set out in the Rubric for Rubrics (Figure 7.12).

As you go, identify samples of student work that clearly illustrate the key attributes of performance at each level for each criterion. These will become your *anchor examples*. Anchors can be used to help other teachers better understand how to differentiate among the levels of quality you have established and how to score student work consistently. They can also be used with students to help them understand the language of the rubric, as described in the last part of this chapter.

Step 6: Practice Applying the Rubric, Revising It as Needed When you began working with samples of student work, we had you make two piles. The first served you in completing the preceding steps and can be set aside. Now turn to the other pile—still in random order in terms of quality. Practice evaluating each of them using your new rubric. This step really is most effectively carried out with more than one rater. Partners can independently judge each work sample and then compare ratings, discussing any resulting differences in evaluative judgment. We know of no more powerful way to refine a new rubric than this one.

As you proceed through this pilot application of the rubric, note places where you experience difficulties either due to a lack of precision in criterion definition, an overlap between criteria, or difficulty differentiating levels of quality, for example. It is even possible at the stage that you may realize that you have missed an apparent key to quality that must be added to the rubric or you may sense that a criterion or descriptor is unnecessary and can be eliminated or subsumed into another. This is the purpose of this pilot test.

MyEdLab **Self-Check 7.3**

MyEdLab **Application Exercise 7.4** Developing general rubrics

---

Step 6 Part II: Review and Critique the Rubric Before Use

We have developed the Rubric for Rubrics (Figure 7.12) to help you evaluate any rubric for the degree to which it fulfils the standards for the three criteria described in this section: *content*, *structure*, and *descriptors*.

Understanding Reliability: Inter-Rater Agreement Because of the subjective nature of performance assessment, you, the rater, become a potential source of distortion in ratings due to your bias. If the rubrics you apply in evaluating student work are incorrect, imprecise, or subject to influence by factors unrelated to the student's actual achievement (such as gender, prior performance, etc.), the filters through which you see and evaluate that work can lead you to inaccurate judgments about level of proficiency.

To prevent this, we must first find or create high-quality rubrics, as described in the preceding section, and second, we must learn to apply them consistently. The gauge of consistency that we apply in such assessment contexts is that of *inter-rater agreement*. Rubrics are being applied consistently when two raters evaluate the same performance or piece of work using the same criteria and, without conversing

figure 7.12 ▪ Rubric for Rubrics

Criterion 1: Content of the Rubric

Indicator	Level 3: Ready to Use	Level 2: Needs Some Revision	Level 1: Needs Major Revision OR Don't Use
Target Alignment	Criteria and descriptors align directly with the content standards or learning targets they are intended to assess.	The rubric includes one or two small features that are not related to the intended content standards or learning targets.	The rubric focuses on features unrelated to the intended content standard or learning targets. One or more of the following apply: ▪ The criteria and descriptors inappropriately focus on dimensions of the task rather than the learning targets. ▪ The learning targets are not clearly evident or represented.
Match to Essential Elements	Criteria and descriptors represent best thinking in the field about what it means to perform well on the content standards or learning targets. ▪ Everything of importance for students at your level has been included. Trivial and unrelated features have been omitted. ▪ If the rubric is a developmental continuum, the content represents the best thinking in the field about how proficiency develops over time.	A few descriptors are irrelevant or unimportant for defining quality for the content standard or learning target, but most are relevant and important.	Many important descriptors of quality are not present. The criteria and/or the content of the descriptors focus on irrelevant features.

Criterion 2: Structure of the Rubric

Indicator	Level 3: Ready to Use	Level 2: Needs Some Revision	Level 1: Needs Major Revision OR Don't Use
Number of Criteria	The number of criteria reflects the complexity of the learning target and is suited to the intended use of the results. ▪ If the rubric is holistic, a single scale sufficiently represents the target. Or if the use is summative, a single scale is sufficient to inform a judgment of proficiency. ▪ If the target is complex the rubric is analytic. The number of criteria appropriately defines categories of proficiency.	For an analytic rubric, the number of criteria needs to be adjusted. Either a single criterion should be divided into two or more criteria, or two or more criteria should be combined.	The rubric is holistic when it needs to be analytic to accurately reflect the complexity of the content standard or learning target to be assessed or to support the intended use of the results.

figure 7.12 ■ Rubric for Rubrics (*Continued*)

Criterion 2: Structure of the Rubric

Indicator	Level 3: Ready to Use	Level 2: Needs Some Revision	Level 1: Needs Major Revision OR Don't Use
Independence of Criteria	If there are multiple criteria, they are independent of one another—the same or similar features are represented in only one criterion.	The criteria are mostly independent of one another, but in some cases features are represented in more than one criterion.	The same or similar features are represented in multiple criteria throughout the rubric, to the extent that the criteria do not function as separate categories.
Grouping of Descriptors	If there are multiple criteria, indicators and descriptors are grouped logically within each criterion. All descriptors fit under the criterion in which they are placed.	Most indicators and descriptors under a criterion are placed correctly, but a few need to be moved to a different criterion.	Indicators and descriptors that go together are not placed together. Descriptors that do not go together are placed within the same indicator. The categories represented by the criteria don't work.
Number of Levels	The number of levels fits the complexity of the target and the intended use of the results. There are enough levels to reflect typical stages of student understanding, capabilities, or progress but not so many that it is impossible to distinguish among them.	There are more levels than needed. The number of levels makes it difficult to distinguish between or among two or more levels, so some levels will need to be merged. Or there are not quite enough levels to reflect typical stages of student understanding, capabilities, or progress, so more will have to be created.	The number of levels is inappropriate for the learning target being assessed or the intended use of the results. One or both of the following are true: ■ There are so many levels it is impossible to reliably distinguish among them. ■ There are far too few levels to be useful in reflecting typical stages of student understanding, capabilities, or progress.

Criterion 3: Descriptors in the Rubric

Indicator	Level 3: Ready to Use	Level 2: Needs Some Revision	Level 1: Needs Major Revision OR Don't Use
Kind of Detail	Wording is descriptive of the quality of the work. There is enough detail that it is possible to match a student performance or product to the appropriate level. Descriptors provide an accurate explanation of the characteristics of quality.	Wording is mostly descriptive of the quality of the work but has one or more problems: ■ The rubric includes a few terms that are vague. ■ Some language is evaluative rather than descriptive.	Wording is not descriptive. One or more problems exist: ■ Descriptors consist of vague terms without clarification (e.g., "extremely" or "insightful"). ■ Descriptors rely heavily on evaluative language to differential levels of quality (e.g., "mediocre," "clever," or "above average").

(*Continued*)

figure 7.12 ■ Rubric for Rubrics (*Continued*)

Criterion 3: Descriptors in the Rubric

Indicator	Level 3: Ready to Use	Level 2: Needs Some Revision	Level 1: Needs Major Revision OR Don't Use
	If counting the number or frequency of something is included as an indicator, changes in such counts *are* indicators of changes in quality.	■ Only the top level of quality is described sufficiently; the other levels include insufficient or no descriptive detail. ■ The rubric mostly avoids frequency counts, but in a few instances counts are used even though changes in counts do not equate to changes in quality.	■ The rubric is little more than a list of categories and a rating scale. ■ Descriptors consist almost solely of counting the number or frequency of something when quantity does not equate to quality.
Content of Levels	The rubric is parallel in content across levels. If a feature is present in one level, it is present in all levels. If a feature is missing at one or more levels, there is a logical rationale.	The rubric is mostly parallel in content across levels. One or a few descriptors of quality at one level are missing at other levels when they should be present.	The rubric is not parallel in content across levels. Most descriptors of quality are not represented at all levels and there is not adequate rationale for their omission.
Formative Usefulness	If the rubric is intended for formative use, its language can function as effective feedback to the student and the teacher, describing strengths and areas needing work in sufficient detail to guide further action: ■ Students can easily use the rubric to revise their own work and plan their own next steps. ■ Teachers can easily translate results into instruction.	If the rubric is intended for formative use, some descriptors can function as effective feedback to the student and the teacher, describing strengths and areas needing work in sufficient detail to guide further action. Other descriptors need refining to accomplish this purpose.	If the rubric is intended for formative use, its language does not function as effective feedback to the student and the teacher because it doesn't describe strengths and areas needing work in sufficient detail to guide further action.

about it, draw the same conclusion about the level of proficiency demonstrated in that performance or work. Surely you can see that, if they disagree, the judgment of student proficiency would be a function of who does the judging, not the actual level of achievement. That would be unfair. Our goal always is to be so clear about the attributes of good performance and so crisp and clean in our description of levels of quality in the rubric that consistency in judgment will be possible.

There is a simple way to check for bias in your evaluations: compare them with the judgments of another trained and qualified evaluator who independently observes and evaluates the same student performances or products using the same rubric. Now, you may be saying, it's just not practical to determine inter-rater agreement by having two raters evaluate all samples of student work. And, unless an extremely high-stakes decision is to be made, it's not necessary. But still, you will need to ensure that you and your colleagues are applying the criteria in the rubric consistently across students and across time. So it is a good idea to work with one or more colleagues periodically to rate a small sample of student work (a few samples at each level of quality) you each have already rated, and then sit down for a few minutes and talk about commonalities and differences in your ratings, one sample at a time. Do you both see the sample about the same way? If so, go on to the next one. If not, try to resolve differences, adjusting your rubric as needed.

Please understand that our goal here is not to have you carry out this test of objectivity every time you conduct a performance assessment. An important part of the art of classroom performance assessment is the ability to sense when your rubric and anchor papers are sufficiently clear that, if another judge were to pick them up and use them, they could learn to do so quite effectively.

The more important the performance assessment (that is, the greater its potential impact on students, such as when it is used for promotion decisions, graduation decisions, and the like), the more important it becomes that you verify inter-rater agreement. Schools that ask students to do exhibitions and demonstrations, such as senior projects, science fairs, and music competitions, must routinely verify the level of inter-rater agreement. In all such cases, it is essential that raters be fully trained and qualified to apply in a dependable manner the rubrics that underpin the evaluation.

Steps 7 and 8: Use and Refine the Assessment

As with all other assessment methods, it is not always possible to anticipate every problem with a performance assessment task prior to administering it. Likewise, when using a rubric for the first time, you may discover some refinement is needed. Keep notes of any difficulties students have with understanding or completing the task. Also note any issues your rubric may have. You can use the Rubric for Tasks and the Rubric for Rubrics to help identify the problems and also to guide revisions.

MyEdLab **Application Exercise 7.5** Auditing general rubrics for quality

Using Performance Assessment Formatively with Students

As you will recall from Chapter 2, formative uses of assessment information, described in the seven strategies of assessment for learning, involve both teachers and students. The strategies connect assessment to instruction and learning in ways that can maximize both students' motivation to learn and their actual achievement. The following suggestions translate the strategies to performance assessment contexts.

Where Am I Going?

Strategy 1: Provide a Clear and Understandable Vision of the Learning Target
Create a student-friendly version of your rubric; then introduce the concepts of quality represented on it by using the following protocol (Chappuis, 2015, pp. 60–61):

Step 1: Ask students what they think a good _____ (whatever it is the rubric describes) looks like. Record all responses on chart paper. Keep the list in their language.

Step 2: Share one or more examples of the performance or product that have definite strengths. (They don't need to be perfect.) Ask students to notice what the example does or doesn't do that is important to quality. Add their comments to the chart paper list. Don't worry if extraneous ideas show up.

Step 3: Tell students this is a good list and they have done exactly what the experts have done to create a rubric to judge quality. Let them know that their list includes many of the same things that experts came up with.

Step 4: Introduce the "expert" list (this will be the criteria and indicators for the rubric you are preparing to share with them) by saying that the experts came up with lots of ideas just like they did. There were so many ideas that they knew no one could keep them all in their head at one time, so the grouped their ideas into categories, which are called *criteria* (or *traits*—you decide which term to use). Then show the list of criteria represented in your rubric. (If it is a holistic rubric, just share the list of indicators.)

Step 5: Show the bulleted list of indicators one criterion at a time. As you do this, ask students to check for a match to something on the chart paper list. If they find one, write the criterion next to the word or phrase they found on the chart paper. If they find no matches, tell students they will be learning about that criterion later.

Step 6: Hand out the student-friendly version of the rubric. It will not seem so daunting to students after going through steps 1 through 5. We want students to leave their first encounter with the rubric thinking "I already know some of this and I think I'll be able to learn the rest of it."

MyEdLab
Video Example 7.1
Using Strong and
Weak Models: Middle
School Science

Strategy 2: Use Examples and Models of Strong and Weak Work   Carefully chosen examples of the range of quality can create and refine students' understanding of the learning target by helping them answer the questions, "What defines quality work?" and "What are some problems to avoid?"

- Have students use the rubric to evaluate anonymous strong and weak student work samples and then share their reasons, using the language of the rubric to justify their scores.
- Share published strong work (and weak work, if available). Let students comment on the quality of these examples using the language of the rubric.
- Share a draft of your own work, showing students how you would revise it using the rubric.

Watch Video Example 7.1 to see Ken Mattingly using a range of samples to clarify a rubric to middle school science students.

See Figure 7.13 for an explanation of the impact clear targets have on students in Bruce Herzog's fifth-grade class. See Figure 7.14 for an explanation of how high school science teacher Stephanie Harmon uses strong and weak work with her students.

Where Am I Now?

Strategy 3: Offer Regular Descriptive Feedback during the Learning   Create or revise rubrics so that they function as feedback to students. Make sure they are aware of the criteria that constitute quality and use the language of the rubric to provide strengths and next-step feedback on their practice work.

- Highlight phrases on the rubric that describe strengths and areas needing further work.
- Let students use a blue highlighter to mark phrases on the rubric that they believe describe their performance or product's strengths and areas needing improvement. Then have them turn their work in along with the highlighted rubric. You mark the phrases representing strengths and areas needing further work with a yellow highlighter. Where you and the students agree, the phrases will be green. Where you don't agree, they will be blue and yellow. Pass the work and the highlighted rubrics back. Let the students with lots of green work together or alone to revise their work, based on the feedback from the rubric. Group the students with lots of blue and yellow and provide further instruction on what quality looks like, perhaps doing more with Strategy 2.
- Prepare students to offer each other feedback by giving them sufficient practice with examining strong and weak anonymous samples.

figure 7.13 ■ From the Classroom: Bruce Herzog

I used to ...

I have been an elementary school teacher for over twenty-five years. For the first fifteen years of my career I ended every year feeling disheartened by the fact that most of the students who were not meeting grade-level standards when they entered my room the previous fall were still below grade-level standards when the year ended. So each new year I worked even harder to improve my instruction because, throughout my career, I had been told over and over that good instruction would lead to good learning. I embraced new strategies and new programs of instruction that promised to lead to high achievement for all students, yet success still remained out of reach for far too many of my students.

Now I ...

When I first heard about formative assessment I was skeptical, but when I read the research that showed that effective assessment practices could lead to unprecedented achievement gains it convinced me to give it a try. I began by having my students set goals and reflect on their learning. It became immediately apparent that most students weren't exactly sure about what they were supposed to be learning. This led me to focus on making sure that the learning targets I expected students to meet were clear. I did this through the use of rubrics, study guides, and continued student goal setting and reflection. Having clear learning targets helped me focus my instruction on those clearly identified learning targets and enabled me to refine my assessments to reflect exactly what students were learning.

What I notice as a result ...

I saw almost immediate results. Within the first month that I began using formative assessment practices in my classroom I saw achievement gains from virtually all students with the greatest gains being made by the lowest-achieving students. Using these practices has completely changed the learning environment in my classroom. Good instruction is still important, but the focus has shifted from teaching to learning and from the teacher to the student. Now that learning targets are clear to students they are able to take responsibility for meeting those learning targets. By regularly reflecting on where they are in relation to the targets they are able to decide what action they need to take or what help they need in moving toward meeting those targets. Formative assessment has removed the barriers to learning in my classroom.

Do all students reach grade level standards in my room now? No, but many more do now than before I began using formative assessment practices and I am seeing dramatic improvement in those students who still have a way to go. More importantly, all students now know that, when they take responsibility for their own learning, they can be successful. One of my students probably put it best when he wrote in one of his reflections, "Now I know what I need to know and I know when I know it."

Source: Reprinted with permission from Bruce Herzog, 5th-grade Teacher, Nooksack Valley School District, Nooksack Valley, WA, 2011.

figure 7.14 ■ From the Classroom: Stephanie Harmon

Strategy #2: Criteria for Strong/Weak Models

What We Do

At the beginning of the course, the students and I talk about what quality work looks like. We divide into small groups and develop criteria for what makes a strong model strong and what makes a weak model weak. Then as a whole class, we use ideas from the small group discussions to develop common criteria for strong/weak models.

As we go through the course and use the criteria to assess our work, we also reevaluate our criteria and revise it as necessary. We have whole-class discussions using anonymous samples of student work to discuss whether the samples are strong or weak. We make a point to use the language of our criteria in these discussions so that the focus is the quality of the work.

Impact on Learning

Students take ownership of this process. They become proficient in self-assessing and peer-assessing work samples. They make insightful comments, and the quality of their work has improved. They use what I call the "language of quality" from the language we used in our class criteria for strong models. This is evident in their feedback comments and also their self-assessments.

Source: Used with permission from Stephanie L. Harmon, Science Teacher, Rockcastle Country High School, Mt. Vernon, KY.

See Figure 7.15 for an explanation of how high school English teacher Michael Doman conducts peer review in his class.

Strategy 4: Teach Students to Self-Assess and Set Goals for Next Steps   Have students use the language of the rubric to identify their own strengths and areas for improvement. Then have them make a revision plan detailing what they will do to strengthen the areas needing work. Contribute ideas to the revision plans as needed.

How Can I Close the Gap?

Strategy 5: Use Evidence of Student Learning Needs to Determine Next Steps in Teaching   Evaluate their practice work with the rubric and use the information to figure out which students need reteaching, which students will be able to move forward with feedback, and which students only need the opportunity to self-assess and plan their own next steps.

Strategy 6: Design Focused Instruction, Followed by Practice with Feedback
If you are working on a learning target having more than one component of quality (often represented as separate criteria on a rubric), consider focusing instruction on

figure 7.15 ■ From the Classroom: Michael Doman

In grades 9–12 (in our school), individual teachers tend to have their own way to handle peer review, but there are some universal trends. Typically, peer review is used to create student learning conversations during the middle phase of the writing process. For some teachers, once students have working drafts, they meet in partnerships or small teams to review their work. The review process is focused on ideas and content, organization and structure, and voice. Many teachers adapt the 6+1 trait rubric so that it can be used by the kids to formatively assess the work of their peers.

After providing time in class to review, students use the comments to revise their drafts. At this time, many teachers formally collect the revised drafts (or specific paragraphs) to offer their comments. When the paper is returned, students use the teacher's comments (and writing conferences) to start working on their final drafts. Several days before the due date, students get back in their peer review partnerships/ groups and look at their essays again. This time grammar and conventions are evaluated along with the other traits. Throughout the process, students complete metacognitive reflection tasks that ask them to think about the strengths and weaknesses of their drafts. Our Creative Writing class uses a workshop approach that involves one full week per unit devoted to peer review.

Source: Reprinted with permission from Michael L. Doman, Naperville Community Unit School District 203: Naperville, IL.

just one aspect of the learning target (or one criterion of the rubric), giving students practice with that one aspect and offering feedback on their practice work for just that one aspect of quality, before moving on to the next component (or criterion).

Strategy 7: Provide Opportunities for Students to Track, Reflect on, and Share Their Learning Progress   Set up a system, such as a portfolio, that lets students track their learning along the way. Have them include their work, the feedback they received, the revisions they made, their own self-assessments, and any goals they set for further work. Have them reflect on the contents of their portfolio, summarize their progress, and comment on it. What changes have they noticed? What is easier to accomplish now? What insights into themselves as learners have they discovered? See Chapter 10 for more guidance on setting up portfolios and having students reflect on them.

MyEdLab **Application Exercise 7.6** Using performance assessment formatively with students

■ Summary: Thoughtful Development Yields High-Quality Performance Tasks and Rubrics

This chapter has been about the great potential of performance assessment, with its array of design possibilities. Performance assessment, like other methods, brings with it specific rules of evidence.

To ensure quality, we began with a consideration of the types of learning targets for which this method will yield accurate results, concluding that strong matches can be developed for reasoning, performance skill, and product targets. We then reviewed the four assessment planning steps in the context of performance assessment: (1) determine the assessment purpose, (2) specify the intended learning targets, (3) select the appropriate assessment method, and (4) determine the appropriate sample size. We explained the sampling challenge in depth as it applies to performance tasks.

Clearly, the heart of this chapter was our exploration of the two assessment development steps for performance tasks and rubrics: develop or select the task and develop or select the scoring rubric.

We described three dimensions of quality necessary for our performance tasks to generate an accurate picture of student achievement: the content of the task, its feasibility and fairness, and the sample size. We then synthesized the discussion of each of these three dimensions into the Rubric for Tasks, which can be used to evaluate the quality of existing tasks and also to guide their development.

To begin the discussion of high-quality rubrics, we explained the two basic structure choices for rubrics—*holistic* or *analytic*—and the terminology needed to understand rubric quality: *criteria*, *levels*, *indicators*, and *descriptors*. We described three dimensions of quality necessary for our rubrics to generate accurate results and to support the use of those results, both formatively and summatively: the content of the rubric, its structure, and its descriptors. We discussed each dimension in depth and then described a six-step protocol for designing your own rubrics, urging collaboration with colleagues for this activity. We offered the Rubric for Rubrics as a tool to be used when evaluating the quality of existing rubrics and when developing a rubric from scratch.

We addressed one additional factor crucial to accuracy of results, inter-rater agreement, suggesting ways to verify that your own ratings are consistent with those of other trained raters.

Finally, we applied the seven strategies of assessment for learning to performance tasks and rubrics, describing ways to introduce standards of quality represented in our rubrics to students, giving them practice with applying those standards to anchor papers, receiving feedback based on the language of the rubrics, and then using the rubrics to offer peer feedback, to self-assess, and to set goals for further learning. We offered suggestions for using the rubric to diagnose and reteach to student learning needs. And we recommended that students use tasks and rubrics to track their progress, reflect on it, and share it with others.

As curriculum continues to evolve to prepare students for the world beyond their K–12 education, we will come to rely increasingly on performance assessment as part of the basis for our evaluation of student achievement. Yet it is not sufficient that we measure these valued proficiencies accurately; we must also find the time to integrate performance assessment and instruction. Let us strive to structure our teaching time so that it also allows students the opportunity to engage with practice tasks, receiving feedback from high-quality rubrics and using those rubrics to assess their own learning progress.

■ Suggested Activities

End-of-chapter activities are intended to help you master the chapter's learning targets. They are designed to deepen your understanding of the chapter content, provide opportunities for personal reflection on ideas presented, and serve as a basis for discussion among peers. You may wish to do all of them or select those that you believe will be most useful to your learning. Each activity is correlated to one or more chapter learning targets to help with your selection.

Chapter 7 Learning Targets

As a result of your study of Chapter 7, you will be able to do the following:

1. Plan a performance assessment
2. Develop performance tasks
3. Audit performance tasks for quality
4. Develop general rubrics
5. Audit general rubrics for quality
6. Use performance assessment formatively with students

Chapter 7 Activities

Activity 7.1   Keeping a Reflective Journal (All chapter learning targets)

Activity 7.2   Evaluating a Performance Task for Quality (Learning Target 3)

Activity 7.3   Creating a High-Quality Performance Task (Learning Targets 1, 2, and 3)

Activity 7.4   Evaluating a Rubric for Quality (Learning Target 5)

Activity 7.5   Creating a High-Quality Rubric (Learning Targets 1, 4, and 5)

Activity 7.6   Planning an Assessment for Learning Application (Learning Target 6)

Activity 7.7   Comparing Your Experiences with Information from the Chapter (All chapter learning targets)

Activity 7.8   Answering an Interview Question (All chapter learning targets)

Activity 7.9   Reflecting on Your Learning from Chapter 7 (All chapter learning targets)

Activity 7.10 Adding to Your Growth Portfolio (All chapter learning targets)

Activity 7.1: Keeping a Reflective Journal

Keep a record of your thoughts, questions, and insights as you read Chapter 7.

Activity 7.2: Evaluating a Performance Task for Quality

Work independently, with a partner, or with a team to carry out this activity.

1. Find a performance task you have used with students, one you will use with students, or one that you have been assigned during the past few years.
2. If you are working alone, make a copy of the Rubric for Tasks. If you are working with others, make a copy of the task for each person. Also make a copy of the Rubric for Tasks for each person.
3. Evaluate the task for each of the three criteria in the Rubric for Tasks. Refer to the text in Chapter 7 for clarification of the concepts referred to in the rubric. Note any features of the task needing improvement and make suggestions for revision. If you are working with others, complete this step independently and then share your evaluation and notes with each other.
4. Revise the task so that it meets all applicable standards of quality as described in the Rubric for Tasks.

Activity 7.3: Creating a High-Quality Performance Task

Work independently, with a partner, or with a team to carry out this activity.

1. Select a learning target from the content you are preparing to teach for which performance assessment is a recommended method.
2. Identify the intended use and the intended users of the assessment results the task will provide.
3. Draft the task by following the guidelines explained in the section "Develop or Select the Task."
4. Consider the intended use and the learning target to answer the following questions:

   - How many tasks will be needed to sample well?
   - How broad will the task have to be to sample the complexity of the learning target well?

5. Identify the criteria that will be used to judge the performance or product. If you do not have a high-quality rubric available, revise or create one following the instructions in Activity 7.4 or 7.5.
6. Evaluate your task using the Rubric for Tasks. Note any features of the task needing improvement and make suggestions for revision.
7. Revise the task so that it meets all applicable standards of quality as described in the Rubric for Tasks.

Activity 7.4: Evaluating a Rubric for Quality

Work independently, with a partner, or with a team to carry out this activity.

1. Find a rubric you have used or will use to assess student achievement. Or find one that has been used to assess your performance or work during the past few years.
2. If you are working alone, make a copy of the Rubric for Rubrics. If you are working with others, make a copy of the rubric for each person. Also make a copy of the Rubric for Rubrics for each person.
3. Evaluate the rubric for each of the three criteria in the Rubric for Rubrics. Refer to the text in Chapter 7 for clarification of the concepts referred to in the rubric. Note any features of the rubric needing improvement and make suggestions for revision. If you are working with others, complete this step independently and then share your evaluation and notes with each other.
4. Revise the rubric so that it meets all applicable standards of quality as described in the Rubric for Rubrics.

Activity 7.5: Creating a High-Quality Rubric

Work independently, with a partner, or with a team to carry out this activity.

1. First decide if you (and your partner or team members) have the expertise necessary to develop a rubric in a content area you are preparing to teach. If you don't yet have that, choose a nonschool performance or product that you are good at to evaluate with the rubric you will create. Otherwise, select a learning target from the content you are preparing to teach for which performance assessment is a recommended method.
2. Work through the first five steps explained in the section titled "Process for Developing Rubrics" to create a draft rubric. Use the information in the section titled "Characteristics of a High-Quality Rubric" to guide your decisions.
3. Make note of what aspects of your rubric need revising after using your draft to evaluate work samples (Step 6). If you are working with others, do this independently and then share your thoughts.
4. Revise your draft.
5. Evaluate your revised rubric for each of the three criteria in the Rubric for Rubrics. Note any features of your rubric needing improvement and make suggestions for revision. If you are working with others, complete this step independently and then share your evaluation and notes with each other.
6. Revise your rubric so that it meets all applicable standards of quality as described in the Rubric for Rubrics.

Activity 7.6: Planning an Assessment for Learning Application

1. Select a unit that you have prepared to teach.
2. Identify a learning target that can be assessed with performance assessment methodology.
3. Select one or more of the ideas from the seven strategies of assessment for learning applied to performance assessment described in this chapter.

4. Write yourself instructions for what you would do.
5. Describe the effects on student motivation and achievement that you believe will result from engaging in the activity.

Activity 7.7: Comparing Your Experiences with Information from the Chapter

Select one "From the Classroom" entry from Chapter 7 and compare it to your experience as a student.

- How is it similar?
- What differences do you notice?
- What conclusions about the benefits of student involvement in performance assessment might you draw?

Activity 7.8: Answering an Interview Question

Imagine that you are about to interview for a teaching position. The interview team (often a combination of administrators and teachers) is interested in understanding your level of classroom assessment literacy. Review Chapter 7's learning targets and think about what concepts and procedures were most significant to you from the chapter. Then think about what type of question an interview team might ask related to this significant learning. Write the question and draft a short response—one that you could give in one to two minutes orally.

Activity 7.9: Reflecting on Your Learning from Chapter 7

Review the Chapter 7 learning targets and select one that struck you as most significant from this chapter. Write a short reflection that captures your current understanding. If you are working with a group, discuss what you have written.

Activity 7.10: Adding to Your Growth Portfolio

Any of the activities from this chapter can be used as portfolio entries. Select any activity you have completed or artifact you have created that will demonstrate your mastery of the Chapter 7 learning targets:

1. Plan a performance assessment
2. Develop performance tasks
3. Audit performance tasks for quality
4. Develop general rubrics
5. Audit general rubrics for quality
6. Use performance assessment formatively with students

Personal Communication as Assessment

Chapter 8 Learning Targets

As a result of your study of Chapter 8, you will know how to do the following:

1. Understand issues to consider when assessing via personal communication
2. Use questioning strategies to gather diagnostic information and to deepen students' content understanding and reasoning proficiencies
3. Structure class discussions for formative and summative use
4. Conduct conferences, interviews, and oral examinations to obtain accurate information about student achievement
5. Use student journals and logs as formative assessment

Teachers gather a great deal of valuable information about student achievement by talking with them. While we don't tend to think of this personal interaction as "assessment," it often is. At different times during teaching and learning, we ask questions, listen to answers, and evaluate achievement. Unlike some other forms of assessment, if a student's response is puzzling, we can ask follow-up questions immediately to understand the knowledge they are relying on or their reasoning. A few strategically placed questions can help to monitor and adjust teaching for students collectively or individually. For instance, if a student does not perform satisfactorily on a performance assessment, we can search for the cause with a few carefully phrased questions and use the student's responses to guide further instruction.

Assessment via personal communication can take many forms: questions and answers during instruction, conferences and interviews with students, student contributions during class discussions, oral examinations, and student journals and learning logs. As with all assessment methods, personal communication can be used formatively or summatively. When used formatively, it can probe students' knowledge and understanding in order to diagnose problems and misconceptions, allowing teachers to adjust instruction accordingly. Equally important is its ability to affect student learning directly: done well, assessment via personal communication can deepen students' conceptual understanding and strengthen their reasoning proficiencies. With careful attention to rules of accuracy, some personal communication options can serve to make summative decisions about students' level of achievement.

figure 8.1 ■ Keys to Quality Assessment

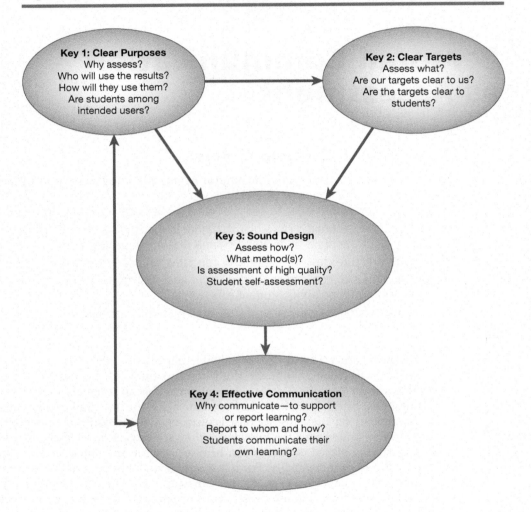

In this chapter, we complete our focus on Key 3: Sound Design (Figure 8.1) by examining accurate and effective use of each of the personal communication options. However, we will not follow the same format as we did in the three preceding "methods" chapters. Each form of personal communication has its own guidelines for accurate and effective use. So after we discuss when to use this assessment method and conditions affecting reliability and validity in a general sense, we will explain the development and use of each form of personal communication.

■ Considerations When Assessing Via Personal Communication

Personal communication–based assessments can provide direct evidence of proficiency in three of our four kinds of targets and can provide insight into the student's readiness to deliver on the other. This is a versatile assessment option.

Assessing Knowledge-Level Learning Targets with Personal Communication

Assessing knowledge-level learning targets can be done with personal communication, but you need to be cautious, especially when using the information summatively, such as for a grade. Obviously, you can question students to see if they have mastered the required knowledge or can retrieve it through the effective use of reference materials. To succeed, however, you must have placed limits on the content domain of knowledge you are assessing. And, if that domain is large, if you cannot ask all possible questions using this labor-intensive method, your questions must sample and generalize in a representative manner. And, remember, knowing and understanding are not the same thing. So you will want to tailor questions that get at the types of knowledge you are assessing.

Assessing Reasoning-Level Learning Targets with Personal Communication

Herein lies a strength of personal communication as a means of assessment. Carefully targeted questions can probe student reasoning and problem solving, both while students are thinking out their answers and, retrospectively, to analyze how students reached a solution. Additionally, you and your students can use questioning interactively to understand and enhance each other's understanding and reasoning. Asking your students to "think out loud" while they're involved in the reasoning process can provide a window into their reasoning. For example, you can ask students to talk through their thought processes as they analyze events or objects, describing component parts. You can ask questions to probe their abilities to draw meaningful comparisons, to make simple or complex inferences, or to express and defend an opinion or point of view. There is no more powerful method for exploring and thus developing student reasoning and problem solving than a conversation while students are actually trying to solve the problem.

As another example, mathematics teachers often ask students to talk about their thinking while proceeding step by step through the solution to a complex math problem. This provides insight into students' mathematical reasoning that cannot be attained in any other way. Further, as students talk through a process, you also can insert follow-up questions: "Why did you take (or omit) certain steps?" "What would have happened if you had . . . ?" "Do you see any similarities between this problem and those we worked on last week?" When students are unable to solve the problem, tactical questions can tell you why. Did they lack prerequisite knowledge? Analyze the problem incorrectly? Misunderstand the steps in the process? In a formative assessment context, these probes permit you to find student needs and link your assessment to instruction almost immediately. Effective tactical questions can also prompt students to think more deeply about problems in their work and to generate their own solutions. For example, a primary student may be trying to measure a 9" line with a 6" ruler. The question "What do you notice about your ruler compared to the line?" can prompt the student to think of how best to address the problem.

Well-designed instructional questions can reveal gaps in knowledge and reasoning errors.

One common way of using personal communication to assess reading comprehension with primary students is to have them retell a story they have just read. As the retelling proceeds, you can ask questions to probe students' understanding of characters or events as needed.

Assessing Performance Skill Targets with Personal Communication

In the previous chapter, we established that the only way to obtain direct information about student performance skills is to have students actually engage in the performance so we and they can compare their work to established standards of quality. If the performance skill is one of oral communication, then the assessment method is both performance assessment and personal communication. They are one and the same in this case. The strength of direct personal interaction with students in this category is in the assessment of their oral communication skills—their ability to use the language to convey their ideas.

But even in other performance areas, you can ask students to talk through a hypothetical performance, asking a few key questions along the way, and know with a certain degree of confidence whether they are likely to be proficient or less than proficient performers. While admittedly an approximation of actual performance, this can work well formatively to focus further instruction and it will result in a stronger performance when it comes time for the summative assessment.

Assessing Product Targets with Personal Communication

Although personal communication cannot be used to assess product targets, it can be used to check students' understanding of key features of quality. As with many performance skill targets, this will not yield an assessment of the target but will help you to focus further instruction, which will result in a higher-quality product in the end.

Figure 8.2 provides a summary of the alignments among assessment via personal communication and the various kinds of achievement that we expect of our students.

figure 8.2 ■ Target Types Suited to Assessment via Personal Communication

Target Type	Suitability to Assessment Via Personal Communication
Knowledge	Can ask questions, evaluate answers, and infer mastery
Reasoning	Can ask students to "think aloud"; can ask questions to probe reasoning processes
Performance Skill	Can assess some types of oral communication proficiency; can assess mastery of prerequisite knowledge to skillful communication
Product	Can probe procedural knowledge and knowledge of attributes of quality products but cannot assess product quality

Understanding the Quality Control Issues

Professional judgment and, therefore, subjectivity permeate all aspects of assessments that rely on personal communication. Consider the depth of your involvement and, therefore, the extent of your control of the assessment: you set the achievement targets and the criteria used to judge level of mastery, compose and store records of performance, summarize and interpret results, and make key instructional decisions based on what you see and hear. This subjectivity makes it imperative that, as with other assessment methods, you know and understand your achievement target and know how to translate it into clear, specific questions and other probes to generate focused information.

As with the other three assessment methods we have studied, the validity and reliability of a personal communication–based assessment depend on its use in appropriate contexts and on your ability to manage effectively the subjectivity inherent in this method. There are several issues to understand to ensure both validity and reliability of results:

- Ensuring common language and cultural awareness
- Creating a safe learning environment
- Attending to content validity
- Meeting the record-keeping challenge
- Becoming aware of personal "filters"
- Understanding students' communication preferences
- Meeting the sampling challenge

Ensuring Common Language and Cultural Awareness   Teacher and student must share a common language for this mode of assessment to work effectively, for in its absence bias can creep in, rendering the evidence undependable. By common language, we don't just mean a shared vocabulary and grammar, although these obviously are critical to sound assessment. We also mean a shared understanding of the manner in which a culture communicates meaning through verbal and nonverbal cues. For example, in some cultures where social emphasis is placed on the collective good, it is unseemly for students to hold themselves up publicly as appearing to know more than others. This can give rise to a culturally based reluctance to answer questions in class: students may be proficient but not be willing to volunteer evidence of that fact. Or, similarly, in some cultures it is a sign of disrespect for children to make eye contact with those of an older generation, and yet without eye contact, we may judge that something is amiss. While we may be tempted to draw inferences about student learning based on such nonverbal behaviors, we must take care to avoid doing so. When we lack understanding of culturally based communication norms, we risk misjudging students' level of achievement.

> Understanding the culturally based communication patterns of students in your class contributes to establishing a common language.

Creating a Safe Learning Environment   One of the principal tasks for a teacher is to create a classroom environment that welcomes error, which is a necessary part of learning. We make it clear to our students that learning is the goal of school and that making mistakes is a natural part of learning when we do the following:

- Offer feedback rather than summative judgment on work that is for practice
- Respond to students' comments in ways that communicate it's okay to not know, it's good to ask questions, and it's great to venture responses without being certain they are correct
- Establish classroom norms that help students treat each other's learning, including mistakes, with respect

Personal communication works best as assessment when students feel they are in a safe learning environment. Without it, we are unlikely to have a high-quality assessment experience due to the personal nature of this assessment method. Students must understand and believe it's essential during their learning that they are honest about what they know and don't know—what they can and cannot do. Students must know that if they offer a response that hides what they don't understand, we will be less able to help them. When we create a safe learning environment, we promote the belief that "I don't know" is an acceptable answer and we make it emotionally comfortable for students to reveal their learning needs honestly.

A note of caution regarding sarcasm: Although some students enjoy humor with a sarcastic edge to it, any form of sarcasm in a teacher's comments makes the learning environment feel unsafe to some students. If sarcastic humor is part of your communication style, we advise that you save it for your personal life and don't let it creep into your professional life as a teacher. It is not appropriate to engage in a behavior that entertains some students and hurts others.

Attending to Content Validity   Even though personal communication is often used off the cuff to gather information about what students do and don't understand, we still need to be clear about the learning targets we are addressing with our questions. We can easily gather unhelpful information by asking the wrong questions. The classic example is asking knowledge recall questions when what you really need to assess is students' ability to use their knowledge to reason in a particular manner. If the question doesn't flow from a clear vision of the learning target, the actions we take based on the students' responses may be unproductive.

Meeting the Record-Keeping Challenge   Most often, there are no tangible assessment products (e.g., test papers or essays) resulting from assessments conducted via personal communication, which can pose record-keeping problems if we are not careful. When the interaction takes a few minutes, focuses on narrow targets, and the evidence triggers immediate action, record keeping is unnecessary. But when the context includes many students, complex targets, and several samples of responses that we intend to use later, we absolutely must maintain some record of results beyond what is in our memory. The human mind is fallible as a recording device. Not only can we forget and lose things in there, but also the things we try to remember about a student's performance can change over time for various reasons, only some of which are within our control. This presents validity concerns. We must act purposefully to counteract this by recording results before they get lost or are changed in our minds. Handheld digital technology can help with this. If you have no access to such assistance, rely on some sort of recorded or written record. Or revise your assessment plans to rely on another assessment method.

Becoming Aware of Personal "Filters"   We must remain aware of and strive to understand those personal and professional filters through which we hear and process student responses. They represent preconceived expectations, views, or even attitudes arising from our own experiences or norms. Those filters provide the basis for our interpretation and evaluation of student responses as well as the actions we recommend to respondents. If not managed effectively, these screens hold the potential for distorting—in other words, biasing—assessment results.

If we set our expectations of a particular student, not on the basis of a clear understanding of the learning targets and the student's current achievement status, but rather on the basis of a preconceived perception or stereotype, we almost certainly will mismeasure achievement. The insidious aspect is that we can remain unaware of our own biases. We don't go around saying, "Athletes never study and don't care," or "I have a feeling that Sarah has mastered this, even though she didn't demonstrate it this time," yet biases are subtle and we must remain vigilantly aware of them in our own minds.

> Identifying your own personal filters is necessary to ensure that you interpret student responses accurately.

Being Aware of Students' Personal Communication Preferences   Some students tend to be reticent to speak out much or at all in class. Some are uncomfortable speaking in front of others. Some cultures consider it inappropriate for one to appear stronger or more "knowing" than others in public. Some students who have struggled to find success in the past may fear public failure again. Any of these propensities can pose a problem in obtaining an accurate representation of learning. We may want to engage such students in assessment via personal communication in a one-on-one setting or in a smaller group setting to ensure that they feel safe and are able to respond fully and freely.

Meeting the Sampling Challenge   As we have seen in previous chapters, the sampling challenge is to gather just enough evidence to make a relatively confident judgment of level of achievement without wasting time gathering too much evidence. And as with other forms of assessment, we can make sampling mistakes that invalidate the assessment. One sampling error is to gather too few bits of information to lead to confident conclusions about proficiency. Our sample can be too small. This is a risk with personal communication when we draw conclusions about student achievement by only asking one question or by only hearing from a few students who may not be representative of the range of achievement in the class. Because personal communication assesses students one at a time, the tendency may be to overgeneralize from too small a sample.

Another sampling error, paradoxically, can arise from spending too much time gathering too many bits of evidence. This is a problem of inefficiency. We eventually reach a point of diminishing returns, where collecting additional information is unlikely to change our conclusion about proficiency. This is less likely to happen with personal communication.

To avoid such sampling problems, we must be crystal clear about targets and purposes and gather just enough information. Remember, any assessment represents only a sample of all the questions we could have asked if the assessment could have been infinite in length. The key to successful sampling in the context of personal communication is to ask a representative set of questions that is robust enough to give us confidence in the generalizations we draw. If our purpose is formative, we can generally work with a smaller sample, but if the purpose is summative, we need to be sure our sample accurately reflects the domain we are assessing.

Example of an Easy Fit   Mr. Lopez, an elementary teacher, tells this story illustrative of a time when sampling challenges were relatively easy to meet:

> *I was about to start a new science reading activity on fish with my third graders. As a pre-reading activity, I wanted to be sure all my students had sufficient background information about fish to understand the reading. So I checked the story for vocabulary and concepts that might be stumbling blocks for my students. Then I asked a few strategic questions of the class, probing understanding of those words and ideas and calling on students randomly to answer. As I sampled the group's prior knowledge through questions and answers, I made mental notes about who seemed not to know some of the key material. There were only three or four. Later, I went back and questioned each of them more thoroughly to be sure. Then I helped them to learn the new material before they began reading.*

In this scenario, the performance arena is quite small and focused: vocabulary and concepts from within one brief science story. Sampling by means of personal communication was simple and straightforward, and there are no real record-keeping challenges presented. Mr. Lopez simply checked for understanding on the part of the students before proceeding. He made a mental note to follow up with those students who had the most difficulty but decided that all other information gathered during the questioning period could be "deleted."

MyEdLab **Self-Check 8.1**

■ Example of a More Challenging Fit

Next we examine a scenario in which the assessment challenges are more formidable. A high school health teacher wants to rely extensively on small- and large-group discussions. She announces at the beginning of the year that she will be listening to students' comments in discussion to gather evidence of their mastery of health-related content and reasoning and of the quality of their contributions. This evidence will be factored into each student's grade. She is careful to point out that she will call on people to participate and that she expects them to make solid contributions.

This achievement target is broader than that of Mr. Lopez in two ways: it contains many more elements (the domain is much larger), and it spans a much longer period of time. Not only does the teacher face an immense challenge in adequately sampling each individual's performance, but also her record-keeping challenge is much more complex and demanding. Consider the record-keeping dilemma posed by a class schedule that includes, say, four sections of eleventh-grade health, each including 30 students! Mental record keeping is not an option: When we try to store such information in our gray matter for too long, it can get lost. Besides, this qualifies as a series of summative assessments, so the pressure is on to ensure accuracy. These are not unsolvable problems, but they take careful preparation to assess. In this sense, they represent a significant challenge to the teacher.

These two scenarios capture the essence of the quality control challenge you face when you choose to rely on personal communication as a means of assessing student achievement. You must constantly ask yourself, "Is my achievement target narrow enough in its scope and short enough in its time span to allow for conscientious sampling of the performance of an individual student or students as a group?" If the answer is yes in your opinion, proceed to the next question: "Is the target narrow enough in its scope and short enough in its time span to allow me to keep accurate records of performance?" If the answer again is yes, proceed. If the answer to either question is no, choose another assessment method or abandon the target.

Summary: Avoiding Quality Control Problems We can avoid problems due to the fallibility of the human mind and bias only by attending to those seven recommendations just described as they apply in the context of personal communication. Whether we plan or are spontaneous in our personal communication with students, we must bear these quality standards in mind.

■ The Many Forms of Personal Communication as Assessment

As with the other three modes, this one includes a variety of assessment formats: questioning, conferences and interviews, class discussions, oral examinations, and journals and logs (Figure 8.3). We will define each format and identify several keys to its effective use in the classroom.

Instructional Questions and Answers

Asking questions has long been a foundation of the education process. As instruction proceeds, the teacher poses questions for students to answer, listens to responses, and adjusts next steps accordingly. Done well, this activity can promote thinking and learning. Done poorly, it can cause students to tune out completely. The following keys to successful use will help you take advantage of the strengths of instructional questioning as an assessment format while overcoming the weaknesses.

Establishing the Purpose In a group setting information gathered through instructional questioning is best used formatively (Chappuis et al., 2012). One formative use is to gauge level of student understanding in order to plan or adjust

figure 8.3 ■ Personal Communication Assessment Formats

Format	Description	Primary Use	Target Types		
Instructional Questions and Answers	Teacher poses questions for students to answer or discuss. Students pose questions and respond to each other.	Formative	K	R	
Class Discussions	Students engage in a discussion. Can be either teacher-led or student-led.	Formative or Summative	K	R	S
Conferences and Interviews	Teacher meets with students to talk about what students have learned and have yet to learn.	Formative	K	R	
Oral Examinations	Teacher plans and poses questions for individual students to respond to.	Summative	K	R	S
Journals and Logs	Students write to explain, explore, and deepen their own understanding; teacher and/or other students respond.	Formative	K	R	

Source: Chappuis, Jan; Stiggins, Rick J.; Chappuis, Steve; Arter, Judith A., *Classroom Assessment for Student learning: Doing it Right - Using it Well,* 2nd Ed., ©2012. Reprinted and Electronically reproduced by permission of Pearson Education, Inc., New York, New York.

MyEdLab

Video Example 8.1

Commit and Toss
Activity: Grade 4

instruction. A second formative use is to trigger further thinking and to deepen learning. Watch Video Example 8.1 to see fourth-grade teacher Crystal Thayer engage her students in a formative assessment activity designed to elicit evidence of their misconceptions in science. If you intend to use information gathered through instructional questions summatively, it is better to ask the questions in a one-on-one setting. For this use, refer to the guidelines in the section "Oral Examinations."

There is one purpose for which instructional questioning is *never* appropriate. It is always inappropriate as a disciplinary tool. You may have witnessed or experienced this in your own education—the teacher believes certain students are not prepared or are not paying attention and calls on them to answer questions purposely to embarrass them as punishment. The misguided belief behind this action is that shame will cause students to come to class prepared or to pay attention in the future. However, feelings of shame do not direct attention to the intended learning; rather they move these students into an ego state, which can create an adversarial relationship in the students' minds. Additionally this practice contributes to creating an unsafe learning environment, which helps no one. If students' off-task or unprepared behavior is to be addressed, it is much better to do so privately with actions directed at helping the students become better learners.

Never call on students with the intention of embarrassing them.

The questions you develop should be worth asking—they should enhance learning in specific ways (which you have identified in determining your purpose). They are not simply a way to check on who has done the work and who has not. That is a waste of learning time for the class.

Framing the Question   Instructional questions designed to gauge level of student understanding generally focus on *knowledge* and *reasoning* learning targets. These questions can be thought of as an oral version of either selected response assessment or written response assessment. We recommend that you plan questions in advance to ensure that they align with the target and with its level of complexity. When crafting a question, make sure it is clearly worded and posed in a straightforward syntax. If it is a knowledge-level question, make sure it helps students focus on a relatively narrow range of acceptable responses. If it is a reasoning-level question, label the type of reasoning you are looking for and include the specific reasoning verb in the questions. You can use the suggestions in Chapters 5 and 6 as further guidance in the development of knowledge and reasoning questions to be posed orally.

If your objective is to determine what students know and understand, direct questioning of content, coupled with questions that elicit summaries or key points of the learning will suffice. When you want to help students use information to reason strategically, the wording of the questions posed is critical for their success. Figure 8.4 offers question stems that will elicit the various patterns of reasoning described in previous chapters.

figure 8.4 ■ Reasoning-Level Question Stems

Analyze:

- What are the important components, parts, or ingredients of _____ ?
- What is the order in which _____ happened? What are the steps?
- What is the main idea of what you read or saw? What details support this main idea?
- What familiar pattern do you notice? (Examples include familiar story structure and numerical sequence.)
- What is this question asking?
- What kind of reasoning is being called for here?
- What information do you need to solve this problem or approach this task?

Compare/contrast:

- What are some characteristics that would help us discriminate (or distinguish) between _____ and _____ ?
- How are _____ and _____ alike and/or different?
- Create an analogy for _____.
- Can you think of something else that is similar? (For example, what other stories have similar openings, characters, plots, or themes?)

Synthesize:

- What do you conclude from _____ and _____ ?
- How would you combine, blend, or organize _____ and _____ ?
- How might you adapt or modify _____ to fit _____ ?
- How would you describe _____ to someone else?
- How might you formulate a response or answer to _____ ?

Classify:

- Find an example of _____ (a group or category).
- What is _____ an example of?
- How might you sort _____ into groups or categories?
- What characteristics of _____ tell us what group it belongs to?

Infer/deduce:

- What do you think will happen next? (predict)
- Why did the author do _____ ?
- What are the implications of _____ ?
- What can you conclude from the evidence or pieces of information? *For example, "What does that tell us about numbers that end in five or zero?"* (generalize)

Evaluate:

- Take a position on _____ and justify, support, defend, or prove your position.
- What is your opinion on _____ ? What evidence do you have to support your opinion?
- Appraise, critique, judge, or evaluate _____. Support your appraisal, critique, judgment, or evaluation with evidence.
- Dispute or judge this position. Is it defendable or not? Why or why not?
- Is this argument sound? What evidence supports your judgment?
- Is this _____ successful? What evidence supports your opinion?
- Could _____ be better? Why or why not?
- Which is better? Why?

Source: Chappuis, Jan; Stiggins, Rick J.; Chappuis, Steve; Arter, Judith A., *Classroom Assessment for Student learning: Doing it Right - Using it Well*, 2nd Ed., ©2012. Reprinted and Electronically reproduced by permission of Pearson Education, Inc., New York, New York.

If your purpose in engaging in questioning is to promote deeper thinking and to further learning, more open-ended questions can be useful. For example, Johnston (2004) has developed the following question stems to encourage students to think aloud about their reasoning and learning:

- *What did you notice about _____?*
- *Remember how you used to _____? Now you _____. What differences do you notice?*
- *What kind of _____ is this?*
- *What about _____ surprised you?*
- *What problems did you notice in today's _____?*
- *How are you planning to go about this?*
- *What parts are you sure about? What parts are you unsure about?*
- *Would you agree with _____? (pp. 13–59 passim)*

Asking the Question   Prior to asking the question, review your purpose—that is, the intended use of the information. This will help you know how you will ask students to respond. There are two basic options (Walsh & Sattes, 2005): *directed questions* where we ask the question of a specific student, and *undirected questions*, where we create a protocol for answering. With directed questions, we craft a question with a specific student in mind for the purpose of probing the level of understanding. Using directed questions helps us distribute questions across a range of students rather than relying on volunteers, who may be the same few students each time. It also helps ensure that all students are engaged in thinking about a response. With undirected questions, we may either call on volunteers or still call on students at random. Undirected questions are suited to checking for understanding and to deepening thinking.

Whether you are using directed or undirected questions, be sure to pose the question in a manner that communicates that the answer matters to you and that you are genuinely interested in what students have to say. While posing the question, make eye contact with various students around the room before calling on a respondent.

> Ask questions with your full attention, as though the answer matters.

Think Time   Often referred to as *wait time*, think time is a period of three to seven seconds after you have asked the question and before you invite responses. It is not uncommon for teachers to wait less than one second before calling for a response (Walsh & Sattes, 2005). This lack of thinking time causes students to offer quick, right-answer-type responses rather than reflective well-reasoned responses, even when the question calls for something beyond a brief right answer. Research on the effect of increasing thinking time in science classes at elementary and secondary levels found that when teachers pause after asking a question, students responded with deeper levels of thinking (Rowe, 1972, 1978).

> It's not *wait* time for *students*. It's thinking time.

Other research has shown that increasing thinking time to between three and seven seconds resulted in an increase in the following:

- *Length of student response*
- *Number of unsolicited responses*
- *Frequency of student responses*
- *Number of responses from lower-achieving students*
- *Student-to-student interaction*
- *Speculative responses (Akron Global Polymer Academy, 2011, n.p.)*

Unless your goal is to test automaticity of responses, such as having memorized math facts, pause for between three and seven seconds after posing a question. This thinking time will increase the instructional value of the question for all students.

Calling on Students to Answer   All students deserve the opportunity to participate in answering instructional questions. The challenge here is twofold: to maximize engagement and to make sure we are not oversampling the understanding of a few students and undersampling the understanding of the rest.

If you are engaged in directed questioning, ask the question, wait three to seven seconds, and then call on the student you have in mind. Make sure you keep track mentally of those you have called on so the same few students don't feel singled out for your special questions. If you need a more extensive sample of achievement from any one student, it can be more effective to use selected response or written response assessment rather than to keep one student in the "hot seat" publicly for an extended period of time.

If you are engaged in undirected questioning, you can call on both volunteer and nonvolunteer respondents. Use the volunteer approach sparingly, for if you use it too often, you risk developing a group of "target" students (Walsh & Sattes, 2005), a small group of students who participate while the rest of the class looks on from the sidelines or checks out mentally. Active participation in asking and answering questions is correlated with higher achievement; if we use the volunteer approach too often, we are allowing the majority of our students to miss out on a valuable learning opportunity.

Randomizing Respondents and Keeping All Students Engaged   To keep all students actively engaged, we recommend using one or more methods of randomizing who gets called on to reply. One simple way to do this is to have all students write their names on tongue depressors, which you put in a cup and draw from after the three- to seven-second think time has elapsed. The name you draw is the person who answers. To keep all students engaged, put the "drawn" names in a separate cup, but periodically dip back into it, so no one thinks they are finished after one answer.

Another way to keep all students actively engaged during a question and answer period is known as "Think-Pair-Share." In this protocol, you pose the question, wait three to seven seconds (the "think" part), and then ask students to discuss their thoughts with a partner. The thoughts could be answers, questions, or reflections on the question. Students may form groups of four and share their partner discussions. You can randomly call on students to share with the whole class, or you can ask for volunteers to share.

The following strategy, described by Walsh and Sattes (2005, pp. 64–65), was shown in a research study to eliminate failure on content-related tests. Put students in groups of three or four, number the students in each group (e.g., each group of three has a "1," a "2," and a "3"), pose the question, pause for think time, then ask each small group to discuss the question. After allowing sufficient discussion time, call out a number and have each student with that number put their hands up. Then call on one or more of these students to share their group's thinking.

A fourth way to maximize engagement is to ask all students to write a response on a piece of paper; then collect them and read them aloud (without names). Ask students to listen for similarities and differences and then use their responses as a touchstone for further questions and discussions of novel answers, mistakes, and misconceptions.

Listening to Responses   Your students may believe that the purpose of instructional questioning is to elicit the answer that is in the teacher's mind rather than the answer that is in their minds. Whether or not students offer a correct response, be aware that the interchange is an opportunity for learning. Listen carefully to what a student actually says. Keep your body language "open," interested, and neutral—too much nonverbal encouragement can be as distracting as folded arms and a frowny face. Also be careful not to interrupt or cut a student's answer short.

> *Kids will participate in classes where they feel respected, where there is mutuality of discourse (i.e., the teacher and student feel they will learn something from one another—it's not a one-way street). . . . So if we want more kids to "talk" in class, and to do so thoughtfully, and be listened to with respect by peers, we need to treat them like people who have ideas worth sharing, people whose interpretations of ideas, based on their life situations, are interesting to us. (Fried, 2001, p. 191, as cited in Walsh & Sattes, 2005)*

When students respond, listen as though the answer matters.

Responding to Responses   First and foremost, do not reply the instant the student has stopped speaking. Walsh and Sattes (2005) recommend pausing for a moment, adding a second "think time" opportunity. It signifies that the teacher has indeed listened to the student's answer and is taking a moment to compose a thoughtful follow-on statement. This second pause contributes to students' developing more complete and correct answers. It is also useful to teach students to pause and think before adding their response or replying to one another's comments.

At this juncture you have multiple response options. You can acknowledge correct or high-quality responses and question incorrect ones for underlying reasons. You can pose questions to understand incomplete or unfocused responses and offer probes to guide student thinking. You can also follow up correct answers with questions to get at underlying reasons. For example, Johnston (2004) has developed the following question stems to elicit further thinking:

- *How did you figure that out?*
- *Remember how you used to _____? Now you _____. Notice the difference?*
- *How else might you _____?*

- *What parts are you sure/not sure about?*
- *What if _____ changed?*
- *How do you know we/you got this right?*
- *I hadn't thought about it that way. How did you know?*
- *Would you agree with that?*
- *How could we check? (pp. 13–59 passim)*

Preparing Students   As stated previously, creating a safe learning environment is a necessary precondition to the accuracy of assessment via personal communication. We create safe learning environments when we treat student responses with respect and require them to do the same. To help accomplish this, you can do the following (Chappuis et al., 2012):

1. *Make sure students understand that one of the purposes of question-and-answer interchanges is to clarify what they understand and do not yet understand and then to proceed with further learning.*
2. *Tell students you are looking for honest responses, and that it's fine to respond even though they may not have confidence in the accuracy or completeness of their answers. Help them understand that a response that misrepresents the truth about their understanding only gets in the way of their success as learners.*
3. *Establish expectations that students will honor each other's contributions (as will you), welcoming mistakes and misconceptions as opportunities for the whole class to gain deeper understanding. (p. 271)*

Beyond creating a safe learning environment, we can maximize the learning students experience by doing the following (Chappuis et al., 2012):

1. *Explain "thinking time." When students first experience an extended pause after a question, they have a tendency to wait rather than to think. It is a good idea to explain that the pause isn't really "wait time"—we're not all waiting for a count of three or seven before launching answers. Instead, it is intended to honor students' need to think a bit—to ponder the question, turn it over in their minds, and then formulate a response, which may be an answer, a question, or a comment that offers further reflection on the question.*

2. *Model the response patterns that you'd like to see from students.*

   - *Speculate on a given topic. This encourages students to explore ideas and to understand that uncertainty is a normal stage in the thinking process.*

   - *Reflect on topics. For example, say, "I sometimes wonder ... ." This encourages students to explore the topic rather than to seek a single quick answer. Encourage them to ask "wondering" questions.*

   - *Cheerfully (or calmly, if that is more your style) admit when you don't have an answer and model what to do about it. Follow "I'm not sure" with "What could we do to find out?" Sometimes a class member or two will be able to answer a question you can't, so encourage students to weigh in.*

3. *Teach students the question stems that elicit the different patterns of reasoning you are teaching. Have them use the question stems with each other in small- or large-group discussions. (pp. 269–271)*

MyEdLab **Self-Check 8.2**

MyEdLab **Application Exercise 8.1** Using questioning strategies

---

Class Discussions

When students participate in class discussions, the things they say reveal a great deal about their level of knowledge, conceptual understanding, and reasoning capabilities. Discussions can be teacher- or student-led group interactions in which a topic, question, or content is explored from various perspectives. Teachers listen to the interactions, evaluate the quality of student contributions, and infer individual student or group achievement.

Whether we use this mode of assessment formatively or summatively, the evaluation of student contributions requires forethought about the criteria by which we will judge the quality of those contributions. And, as with all assessment development, we begin with the question of *purpose*: How do you want to use the information? Who else will use it? To do what?

Then we move to *target*: What learning target(s) will be the focus of the assessment? Class discussions can have the simultaneous effect of enhancing understanding and developing reasoning proficiency while strengthening communication skills. Class discussions have serious sampling limitations if you intend to use the information about knowledge, mastery, or reasoning proficiency for summative purposes. Because there are better options in most cases for evaluating knowledge and reasoning learning targets when the intended use is summative, we recommend that class discussions be used formatively, as assessment for learning, to diagnose problems and deepen knowledge, understanding, and reasoning.

If, however, your curriculum includes a communication skill target that calls for students' being able to engage productively in discussions, you may need to assess it for a grade, in which case the class (or group) discussion will be the most likely assessment format. An example of such a standard is the following: "Prepare for and participate effectively in a range of conversations and collaborations with diverse partners, building on others' ideas and expressing their own clearly and persuasively" (National Governors Association Center for Best Practices, 2010a, CCSS English Language Arts, p. 48). The grade-level standards that flesh this content standard out at eighth grade state the following:

a. *Come to discussions prepared, having read or researched material under study; explicitly draw on preparation by referring to evidence on the topic, text, or issue to probe and reflect on ideas under discussion.*

b. *Follow the rules for collegial discussions and decision-making, track progress toward specific goals and deadlines, and define individual roles as needed.*

c. *Pose questions that connect the ideas of several speakers and respond to others' questions and comments with relevant observations and ideas.*

d. *Acknowledge new information expressed by others and, when warranted, justify or qualify their own views in light of the evidence presented. (p. 49)*

And, just as with all skill targets, assessing this standard will require a scoring rubric that clearly describes each component at several levels of competence. It would also be wise to engage students in practice discussions with opportunities for feedback, self-assessment, and opportunities to improve before the graded event. The seven strategies of assessment for learning can be used to develop proficiency with skill targets such as this one. Figure 8.5 shows an example of a rubric designed to address both the quality of thinking and discussion skills in a seminar-type discussion setting. This rubric was not designed to match the content standard described previously but rather to be used as a general rubric for both text interpretations and assertions as well as discussion skills. It can be used formatively to diagnose learning needs, to offer feedback, or for students to self-assess. It can also be used summatively to grade level of achievement of discussion skills. (Remember from Chapter 7 that a rubric is only suited for your use if it accurately represents content standards you will be teaching.)

To take advantage of the strengths of this method of assessment, while minimizing the impact of potential weaknesses, follow these keys to successful use:

- Prepare questions or discussion issues in advance—focus sharply on the intended achievement target.
- Be sure students are aware of your focus in evaluating their contributions. Are you judging the content of students' contributions or the form of their contribution, that is, how they communicate? Be clear about what it means to be good at whatever you are judging.
- Remember, the public display of achievement or lack thereof is risky in the eyes of some students. Provide those students with more private means of demonstrating achievement if the learning target isn't related to discussion skills.
- In contexts where achievement information derived from participation in discussion is to be used summatively, keep dependable records of performance. Rely on more than your memory of students' contributions.

MyEdLab **Application Exercise 8.2** Developing a high-quality rubric for structuring group discussions

figure 8.5 ■ For Example: Seminar Discussion Rubric

CCSS Speaking and Listening Standards Grades 11–12

1. Initiate and participate effectively in a range of collaborative discussions (one-on-one, in groups, and teacher-led) with diverse partners on grades 11–12 topics, texts, and issues, building on others' ideas and expressing their own clearly and persuasively.

1a. Come to discussions prepared, having read and researched material under study; explicitly draw on that preparation by referring to evidence from texts and other research on the topic or issue to stimulate a thoughtful, well-reasoned exchange of ideas.

1c. Propel conversations by posing and responding to questions that probe reasoning and evidence; ensure a hearing for a full range of positions on a topic or issue; clarify, verify, or challenge ideas and conclusions; and promote divergent and creative perspectives.

1d. Respond thoughtfully to diverse perspectives; synthesize comments, claims, and evidence made on all sides of an issue; resolve contradictions when possible; and determine what additional information or research is required to deepen the investigation or complete the task.

Text Interpretations and Assertions (1.a)	Level 4	Level 3	Level 2	Level 1
	The student's comments	*The student's comments*	*The student's comments*	*The student's comments*
	■ Demonstrate insightful thought about ideas in the text. ■ Make connections between experiences/events within the text and experiences/events in other texts or situations. ■ Are supported credibly with sufficient evidence from the text.	■ Reflect consideration of ideas in the text. ■ Occasionally make connections between experiences/events within the text and experiences/events in other texts or situations. ■ Are supported with evidence from the text.	■ Sometimes focus on ideas found in the text but other times include unrelated ideas with little or no explanation of the perceived relevance. ■ Are supported with evidence that does not go far enough, is only loosely related to the interpretation or assertion, or is partially inaccurate.	■ Appear significantly unrelated to ideas found in the text with no explanation of the perceived relevance. ■ Offer interpretations or make assertions with no attempt at support. Or if support is attempted, it reveals a lack of understanding of what constitutes credible support.

(Continued)

figure 8.5 ■ For Example: Seminar Discussion Rubric (*Continued*)

Discussion Skills (1.b, 1.c)	Level 4	Level 3	Level 2	Level 1
	The student	*The student*	*The student*	*The student*
	■ Asks open-ended questions that stimulate discussion. ■ Offers comments that build on ideas expressed by others during the discussion. ■ Offers questions to probe others' interpretations; elaborates challenges to others' ideas with reasoned evidence. ■ Responds to challenges and questions with further information or refines own interpretations to accommodate new perceptions or information. ■ Speaks directly to other students during discussion. ■ Selects words, phrases, and terminology to enhance intended meaning. ■ Maintains engagement throughout the discussion.	■ Offers questions to probe others' interpretations and assertions. ■ Responds to challenges and questions with further information or refines own ideas to accommodate new perceptions or information. ■ Speaks directly to other students during discussion. ■ Uses words, phrases, and terminology that communicate intended meaning. ■ Maintains engagement throughout the discussion.	■ Sometimes interrupts others while they are speaking. ■ Offers comments that ignore previous contributions or appear unrelated to the flow of ideas in the discussion with no attempt to connect them. ■ Offers no response when interpretations or assertions are challenged or responds to questions by reasserting the idea being questioned. ■ Sometimes speaks directly to other students during discussion; at other times, directs comments or questions to the teacher when it would be more appropriate to speak to discussion participants. ■ Uses words, phrases, and terminology in a way that sometimes confuses other participants. ■ Maintains engagement in parts of the discussion but disengages in other parts.	■ Consistently interrupts others while they are speaking. ■ Expresses criticism focused on attributes of the speaker rather than on attributes of the ideas presented. ■ Makes no attempt to interact with questions or challenges to an interpretation or assertion. ■ Consistently directs comments or questions to the teacher when it would be more appropriate to speak to discussion participants. ■ Uses words, phrases, and terminology in a way that obscures meaning. ■ Disengages from the discussion repeatedly or completely.

Conferences and Interviews

With this option, the teacher meets with students individually. Generally, student–teacher meetings serve as structured or unstructured audits of student achievement, in which the objective is to talk about what students have learned and have yet to learn. The teacher and student talk directly and openly about levels of student attainment, comfort with the material the student is in the process of mastering, and specific needs, interests, desires, and/or any other achievement-related topics that contribute to an effective teaching and learning environment.

Conferences or interviews need not be structured as standardized events, with each meeting a carbon copy of the others. You might, for example, schedule a conference with only one student to fill an information gap. Also conferences or interviews will vary in their focus with students who have different needs. You can accomplish a lot in a short one-on-one meeting with some preparation. The following are keys to your successful use of conference and interview assessment formats:

- Carefully think out and plan your questions in advance. In some cases, you may want students to share in the preparation.
- Avoid asking questions that will elicit a simple "yes" or "no" answer.
- Develop questions that focus attention on student progress toward established learning goals.
- Have samples of student work available, if needed, to add specificity to the discussion. Make sure students understand how different samples provide evidence of specific learning targets. Also have the rubric used to judge quality available, if applicable.
- Plan for enough uninterrupted time to conduct the entire interview or conference.
- Conclude each meeting with a summary, perhaps of the lessons learned, information gleaned, or implications for how you and the student will work together in the future. Students can also participate in the summary or be tasked with providing it.

One important strength of the interview or conference as a mode of assessment lies in the impact it can have on your student–teacher relationships. When conducted in a context where the students understand the expectations and the achievement target, conferences have the effect of empowering students to take responsibility for at least part of the assessment of their own progress. These meetings can help you establish the expectation that everyone is committed to success, probe for ways to maximize achievement, and motivate students to work toward a desired goal.

Oral Examinations

With this form of personal communication assessment, teachers plan and pose exercises for their students, who reflect and provide oral responses. Teachers listen to and interpret those responses, evaluating quality and inferring levels of achievement.

Although the oral examination tradition lost favor in the United States with the growing use of selected response testing during the 1900s, it still has great potential for use today, especially given the increasing complexity of our valued educational targets.

Oral examinations are generally used summatively: in a very real sense, they are versions of the other three assessment methods, discussed in Chapters 5, 6, and 7, but with the added benefit of being able to ask follow-up questions. Questions are structured similarly to selected response items, short-answer and extended written response items, and performance assessment tasks, depending on the type of learning target being assessed. Oral examination questions can reliably measure *knowledge* and *reasoning* targets and can also measure *performance skill* targets that require one-on-one communication, such as assessing correct pronunciation when speaking a second language.

To develop questions for this use, follow the guidelines for quality for the assessment method (selected response, written response, or performance assessment) that is appropriate for the type of target you are assessing. In addition, keep the following guidelines in mind (adapted from Chappuis, Stiggins, Chappuis, & Arter, 2012, pp. 280–281):

- Develop questions that focus on the desired learning target(s).
- Ask questions using the easiest possible vocabulary and grammatical construction. Don't let the language or syntax get in the way of allowing students to communicate their learning.
- If the question is to be used to assess mastery of a combination of knowledge and reasoning targets, use the formula explained in Chapter 6: identify the knowledge to be brought to bear, specify the kind of reasoning students are to use, and identify the standards you will apply in evaluating responses.
- When assessing a content standard for summative purposes, present one set of questions to all students; don't offer choices of questions to answer.
- Develop scoring checklists or rubrics that describe levels of quality in a response in advance of the assessment. Be sure that qualified experts in your field would agree with the features of a sound response. See Chapters 6 and 7 for guidance on how to do this.
- In addition, your scoring checklists or rubrics should allow you to separate achievement on knowledge and reasoning targets from facility with verbal expression so students aren't able to do well on the exam without having mastered the targets.
- Prepare in advance to accommodate the needs of any student who may confront language proficiency barriers.
- Have a method of recording results ready to use at the time of administration.
- If necessary, audiotape responses for later reevaluation.

MyEdLab **Application Exercise 8.3** Using oral examinations to obtain accurate information about student achievement

Journals and Logs

Sometimes personal communication–based assessment can take a written form. We classify this as personal communication assessment when the purpose of the writing is to engage in conversation. Although journals and logs are used for a variety purposes in the classroom, this section addresses their use as a structured interaction with the teacher or with another student, where students share important learnings, views, experiences, reactions, understandings, confusions, and misunderstandings relative to the learning targets they are working on. Many see these methods as most useful in formative assessment contexts, that is, in supporting student learning as it is happening.

Journals and logs can function as written conversations.

Journals   Dialogue journals capture conversations between students and teachers in the truest sense of that idea. As teaching and learning proceed, students write messages to you conveying thoughts and ideas about the achievement expected, self-evaluations of progress, points of confusion, important new insights, and so on, and periodically give you their journals. You then read the messages and reply, clarifying as needed, evaluating an idea, amplifying a key point, and so on, and return the journals to the students. This process links you and each of your students in a personal communication partnership as they grow.

Personal journals represent a less structured journal option. Teachers give students time during each day or week to write in their journals. As with other options, it is important to establish a clear purpose and audience for personal journals at the outset. In this specific application, the purpose can either be to provide insight into each student's level of understanding or to give students the chance to reflect on the day's or week's learning targets.

When the purpose is to provide insight into understanding, specify a topic or question focused on the learning target, have students write about it, and then read each student's journal entry to determine what instruction to provide next. You may comment on a journal entry or not, depending on what you will do with the given information. For example, if only a few students have a misunderstanding and you can clear it up with a comment, you may choose to do so. Or you may be able to use the information to structure a follow-up lesson for some or all students.

When the purpose of the journal is to track, reflect on, or question, the writing task can be more open-ended and if we read the journal entries, we comment at the invitation of the student. The advantage of students recording this information in a personal journal is they can keep the journal and review their thoughts, questions, and progress periodically. In Figure 8.6, classroom teacher Jody Petry explains how clear targets have contributed to her students' ability to communicate about their learning successes and needs.

Learning Logs   Learning logs ask students to keep ongoing written records of one or more of the following aspects of their studies:

- Achievement targets they have mastered
- Targets they have found useful and important

figure 8.6 ■ From the Classroom: Jody Petry

I used to . . .

I used to "drive through" my curriculum. When planning classroom activities and assignments, I would plan them with me (the teacher) in mind. I used my lesson plans as simply a list of things to do. Once an assignment or activity was taught, I would move on—keep driving and not look back. I was essentially the driver, with the map, and my students were in the backseat. Since I was in charge of the learning, conversations during learning were shallow. The students didn't have the knowledge of their learning to talk about.

Now I . . .

Assessment *for* learning practices has given me the tools to hand over the learning to my students, essentially putting them in charge. They are the drivers and I am in the backseat. They are holding the "map" (learning targets). My students know where their learning is headed. Learning targets have given my students the knowledge they need to have in order to talk about what they are learning and what they need to work on. Using "I can" statements, my students know what it is they are supposed to know.

Why I changed . . .

Before, students were unable to tell me what they were not understanding in relationship to a concept we were working on. I could see how they weren't sure of what they were supposed to know. After learning more about assessment *for* learning, I noticed all of the holes in my instruction. I found out how to connect my teaching with students' learning.

What I notice as a result . . .

Students can now name their learning. Using learning targets has given my students the power when it comes to their learning. They are able to tell what it is they need to know and what it is that they need to improve. My students have more in-depth conversations about learning, using rich academic vocabulary in group discussions. My students are now equipped to give focused feedback about where they are in their learning. Using a 1 through 4 scale, students can gauge their understanding of the material.

Source: Reprinted with permission from Jody Petry, Northwest R-I School District, House Springs, MO, 2011.

- Targets they are having difficulty mastering
- Learning experiences, lessons, or instructional strategies that worked particularly well for them with an explanation of their thoughts about why they worked
- Experiences, lessons, or strategies that were confusing or difficult with an explanation of their thoughts about what the problem might be
- Questions that have come up along the way and where they might want help
- Ideas for study topics or learning strategies that they might like to try in the future

The goal in the case of learning logs is to have students reflect on, analyze, describe, and evaluate their learning experiences, successes, and challenges, writing about the conclusions they draw.

MyEdLab **Application Exercise 8.4** Using journals and logs as formative assessment

---

■ Summary: Person-to-Person Assessment

With personal communication assessment, we use our interactions with students to assess important achievement targets, including knowledge mastery, reasoning proficiency, and mastery of certain communication-based skills. We also can assess student mastery of knowledge and reasoning prerequisites to performance skills and product development capabilities. But, remember, to tap the skills and products themselves, performance assessment is required.

We have five personal communication options at our disposal: instructional questions and answers, class discussions, conferences and interviews, oral examinations, and journals and logs. One key to success in using this method to assess student achievement is to remember that, just because assessment is sometimes casual, informal, unstructured, and/or spontaneous, this does not mean we can let go of concern about standards of assessment quality. In fact, we must be equally careful not to allow personal filters, poor sampling techniques, insufficient thinking time, and/or inadequate record keeping to interfere with the accuracy of our conclusions. And more importantly, remember that, in this case, we rely completely on oral language to collect evidence of achievement. That means teacher and student must share a common vocabulary and awareness of the cultural nuances in which that language is embedded.

As with the other three modes of assessment, this one is quite flexible. Even though we typically don't refer to personal communication as assessment, if we start with a clear and appropriate vision, translate it into thoughtful probes, sample performance appropriately, and attend to key sources of bias, we can generate quality information in this manner. So can students. Whether participating in whole-class discussions, smaller collaborative groups, or with a partner, students can be assessors, too. They can ask questions of each other, listen to responses, infer achievement, and communicate feedback to each other. But we must be aware that the ability to communicate effectively in an assessment context is not "wired in" from birth. Both you and your students must practice it to hone it as an assessment skill.

■ Suggested Activities

End-of-chapter activities are intended to help you master the chapter's learning targets. They are designed to deepen your understanding of the chapter content, provide opportunities for personal reflection on ideas presented, and serve as a basis for discussion among peers. You may wish to do all of them or select those that you believe will be most useful to your learning. Each activity is correlated to one or more chapter learning targets to help with your selection.

Chapter 8 Learning Targets

As a result of your study of Chapter 8, you will be able to do the following:

1. Understand issues to consider when assessing via personal communication
2. Use questioning strategies to gather diagnostic information and to deepen students' content understanding and reasoning proficiencies
3. Structure class discussions for formative and summative use
4. Conduct conferences, interviews, and oral examinations to obtain accurate information about student achievement
5. Use student journals and logs as formative assessment

Chapter 8 Activities

Activity 8.1   Keeping a Reflective Journal (All chapter learning targets)

Activity 8.2   Creating Diagnostic Questions (Learning Target 2)

Activity 8.3   Using Questioning Strategies to Deepen Understanding (Learning Target 2)

Activity 8.4   Drafting a Class Discussion Rubric (Learning Target 3)

Activity 8.5   Developing Oral Examination Questions (Learning Target 4)

Activity 8.6   Using Journals and Logs in the Classroom (Learning Target 5)

Activity 8.7   Comparing Your Experiences with Information from the Chapter (All chapter learning targets)

Activity 8.8   Answering an Interview Question (All chapter learning targets)

Activity 8.9   Reflecting on Your Learning from Chapter 8 (All chapter learning targets)

Activity 8.10   Adding to Your Growth Portfolio (All chapter learning targets)

Activity 8.1: Keeping a Reflective Journal

Keep a record of your thoughts, questions, and insights as you read Chapter 8.

Activity 8.2: Creating Diagnostic Questions

Work independently or with a partner to complete the following activity.

1. After reading the section titled "Instructional Questions and Answers," list one to three learning targets that you will be preparing to teach. Choose targets that you believe students will have some pre-existing misconceptions and/or misunderstandings about.
2. List two or three misunderstandings and/or misconceptions students might have when studying the learning target(s).
3. Create two questions you could ask in a whole-class setting to diagnose one or more of the misunderstandings and/or misconceptions you listed.
4. Use the guidelines for item quality from Chapters 5 and 6 (as applicable) to refine your questions. Briefly describe any revisions you made to each question.

Activity 8.3: Using Questioning Strategies to Deepen Understanding

Work independently or with a partner to carry out the following activity.

1. After reading the section titled "Instructional Questions and Answers," identify one or more questioning strategies (e.g., think time, randomizing respondents) you want to practice in the classroom.
2. Record yourself as you are practicing the strategy(ies) in the classroom. Analyze the recording, making note of instances of successful use and any improvements you would like to make.
3. Practice with the strategy(ies) again, and then reflect individually or with a partner on the following questions: What effect did the questioning strategy(ies) have on your instruction? What effect did you notice on student engagement and learning?
4. If possible and appropriate, ask the students you have practiced with for feedback on your use of the strategy(ies) you have used.

Activity 8.4: Drafting a Class Discussion Rubric

This activity can be done independently, with a partner, or with a team. It is a good idea to do it with at least one other person, if possible.

1. Identify the learning targets that define the group discussion expectations for students in the grade or subject you are preparing to teach.
2. Collect a sample of class/group discussion checklists and/or rubrics that relate to the learning targets you have identified.

3. Select one or more to revise/combine so that they adhere to standards of quality for a rubric as explained in Chapter 7. Or develop your own rubric for class/group discussion skills using the process described in Chapter 7.
4. Evaluate your rubric for quality using the Rubric for Rubrics (found in Chapter 7). Ask others to do the same for your rubric. Note and discuss any revisions needed.
5. Revise your rubric based on your notes.

Activity 8.5: Developing Oral Examination Questions

Work independently or with a partner to complete the following activity.

1. After reading the section titled "Oral Examinations," select a learning target or short collection of learning targets suited to assessment via oral examination. Assume that you will use the information generated summatively.
2. Create a test blueprint for the oral examination using one of the two forms explained in Chapter 4 (or a version of one of them).
3. Use the assessment development guidelines from Chapters 5 and/or 6 (as appropriate to your learning targets) to create questions for your examination. Also create the scoring guide, which could be an answer key, a list of acceptable responses, or a rubric, depending on the learning target to be assessed.
4. Determine how you will record your judgments of student responses. Plan for how you will share results with the students.

Activity 8.6: Using Journals and Logs in the Classroom

Work independently or with a partner to complete the following activity.

1. After reading the section titled "Journals and Logs," select a learning target or short collection of learning targets, such as those from a unit of study, as the focus for journal or learning log entries.
2. Identify your purpose for asking students to keep the journal or log.
3. Read through Chapter 10 for options for prompts and instructions you might give students.
4. Reflect on how much individuality, freedom, and choice students might be given and still accomplish the desired outcome of the journal or log.
5. Decide which form their journals or logs will take (e.g., booklet, folder of loose pages, online file, or other).
6. Estimate how often students will make entries. Determine who will respond and approximately how often.
7. Write the instructions you will give students to guide their entries. Include the following:

   - The intended learning targets and the rationale for keeping a journal or log
   - The types of entries you will ask them to make and the frequency
   - Who will read and respond to them and how often
   - What types of responses their entries will receive

- What you will do with the information they share
- Any other guidance you think students might need

Activity 8.7: Comparing Your Experiences with Information from the Chapter

After reading through the ideas for student involvement in Chapter 8, select one and compare it to your experience as a student.

- How is it similar?
- What differences do you notice?
- What conclusions might you draw about the benefits of student involvement?

Activity 8.8: Answering an Interview Question

Imagine that you are about to interview for a teaching position. The interview team (often a combination of administrators and teachers) is interested in understanding your level of classroom assessment literacy. Review Chapter 8's learning targets and think about what concepts and procedures were most significant to you from the chapter. Then think about what type of question an interview team might ask related to this significant learning. Write the question and draft a short response—one that you could give in one to two minutes orally.

Activity 8.9: Reflecting on Your Learning from Chapter 8

Review the Chapter 8 learning targets and select one that struck you as most significant from this chapter. Write a short reflection that captures your current understanding. If you are working with a group, discuss what you have written.

Activity 8.10: Adding to Your Growth Portfolio

Any of the activities from this chapter can be used as portfolio entries. Select any activity you have completed or artifact you have created that will demonstrate your mastery of the Chapter 8 learning targets:

1. Understand issues to consider when assessing via personal communication
2. Use questioning strategies to gather diagnostic information and to deepen students' content understanding and reasoning proficiencies
3. Structure class discussions for formative and summative use
4. Conduct conferences, interviews, and oral examinations to obtain accurate information about student achievement
5. Use student journals and logs as formative assessment

Record Keeping: It's More Than Paperwork

Chapter 9 Learning Targets

As a result of your study of Chapter 9, you will be able to do the following:

1. Separate formative from summative assessment information
2. Organize the entries in a gradebook according to the learning represented
3. Track information about work habits and social skills separately from achievement information
4. Record achievement information so you can interpret it accurately

One of the surprises of your first month of teaching will be the amount and diversity of student information you will have to manage. In a few short weeks after welcoming your students, you will have hundreds of bits of information to juggle. What information will you keep? What should you keep track of? How will you keep track of it? How will you use it? This chapter prepares you with decision points, organizing structures, and recording recommendations that will help you manage assessment information as it comes in and know what to do with it. You will learn how to create an accurate record ready to use either formatively while learning is occurring or summatively when the time comes to complete report cards.

With this chapter, we shift our focus to Key 4: Effective Communication (Figure 9.1) by examining options for keeping track of student learning so that we can communicate accurately to whomever needs the information. In Chapter 10, we explore ways for students to track and share their learning progress, a foundation of assessment FOR learning. In Chapters 11 and 12 we address effective communication through report card grades and conferences. So, in effect, here in Chapter 9 we lay the groundwork for communicating in each of those ways.

figure 9.1 ■ Keys to Quality Assessment

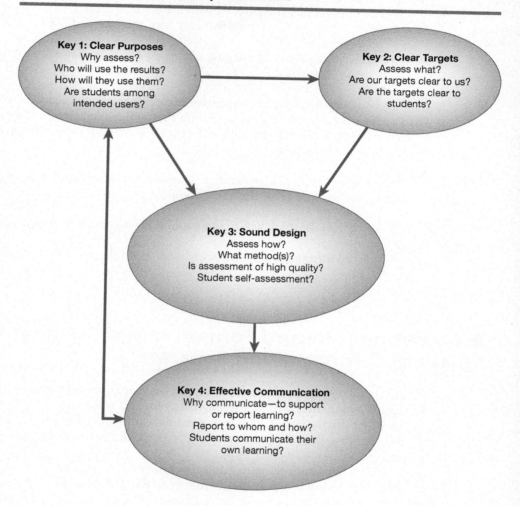

■ From Records to Useful Information

Assessment information guides instructional decisions. It is only useful to the extent that it is organized and recorded so that you and others can use it to make informed decisions. However, it should be self-evident that no record-keeping guidelines can make inaccurate information useful. Accuracy is a nonnegotiable prerequisite. To summarize what we have learned in the previous chapters, accuracy requires the following:

- Aligning instruction directly with the learning targets
- Aligning assessments directly with the learning targets
- Selecting or developing assessments with the intended use in mind (formative or summative)
- Gathering evidence of learning relying on practices that adhere to standards of assessment quality

Once you are confident that your assessment information is accurate, you are ready to address the record-keeping guidelines that will make communicating about student learning, including deriving end-of-term grades, efficient and effective. Those guidelines are as follows:

1. Record formative and summative assessment information separately.
2. Organize entries in the gradebook according to the learning target represented.
3. Keep track of work habits and social skills separately from achievement information.
4. Record information by raw score when possible.

■ Guideline 1: Record Formative and Summative Assessment Information Separately

Your first record-keeping decision will be to determine what part of the information you gather will be used formatively and what part will be used summatively. As discussed in Chapter 4, these decisions will be made initially while you are planning instruction and then revisited and refined throughout a unit of study.

One important thing to remember when separating formative and summative assessment information is that, while everything students do counts for learning, only some of it counts for the grade. Figure 9.2 illustrates how you might categorize and use all of the evidence you will collect. Figure 9.3 shows a form you can use to keep track of the intended use of information from each assignment and assessment. Remember, it is impossible to plan for the intelligent gathering of information without a sense of why you are gathering it, that is, its purpose. In Figure 9.4, middle school English language arts teacher Elizabeth Schroeder explains how she balances and tracks formative and summative assessment information and the effect it has on her students.

■ Guideline 2: Organize Entries in the Gradebook According to the Learning Target Represented

This guideline is concerned with the labels and categories you establish for your records. Your instruction and assessments will both be driven by and tightly linked to your content standards, so it will be a fairly straightforward task to record the assessment results according to the learning target assessed.

Adhering to this guideline will allow you to track student progress by learning target, which is essential to diagnosing and addressing learning needs, planning whether or how to reteach if necessary, or offering students feedback on their

figure 9.2 ■ Deciding What to Keep Track of and What to Report

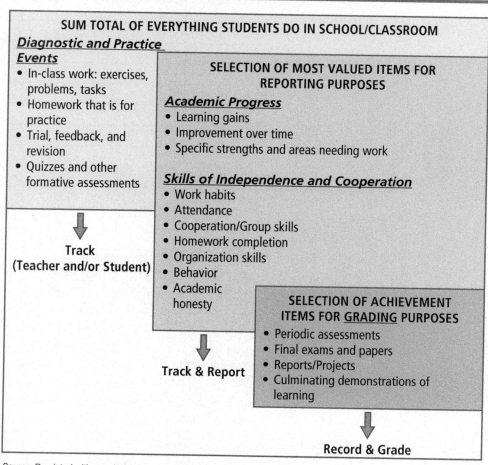

Source: Reprinted with permission from Ken O'Connor.

figure 9.3 ■ Formative and Summative Assessment Plan

Chapter/Topic(s)/Unit of Study: _____

Time Frame: _____

Learning Target	Assignments & Assessments		
	Date	Type	Description

Type:

E = End of term grade (summative)
TC = Teacher check for learning (formative)
SC = Student check for learning (formative)
P = Practice (formative)
O = Other (formative)

figure 9.4 ■ From the Classroom: Elizabeth Schroeder

I used to . . .

First, I used to grade every piece of work that my students completed. I was of the mindset that work is not valued unless it is acknowledged . . . and I thought that acknowledgment was a letter grade. Second, I used to use what I call a "tracking sheet" that students could use to follow their progress on learning targets, formatives, and summative—an organizer to remind them of the goals, take part in their own learning, and give them a way to evaluate their own work and progress. However, it was "hit or miss" with the tracking sheet and it was hard to keep it up to date and was eventually placed in their binder unfinished. Lastly, I used to let everyone take the summative test at the end of the unit, regardless of their completion or understanding of their practice work. This procedure resulted in many incomplete assignments and lower scores on the summative exam.

Now I . . .

I still acknowledge every piece of work that my students complete. However, I have developed a new way to look at standards, learning, and grading. I began educating students, parents, and ME that everything does not need to be given a letter grade. I now show formative work as "collected" in the gradebook. I still check their assignments to make sure that they understand the learning goal before moving on; but I check student work with them, individually, giving them direct feedback—as they do the work and while it is fresh in their mind instead of by me on my sofa at home. The value is now my time instead of a grade.

The next thing I changed was the unit tracking sheet. I kept the main portions of the document to gauge their learning, tweaking a few words here and there; but the major change came in the use of the page. The students now refer to it every day, bringing it with them as we check their practice work. I make initials on the work they complete and then at the end of the summative exam they evaluate their progress, charting their course of work.

The last thing I changed was the requirements to take the summative exam. Previously, I would allow students to take the test if some of their formative work was not turned in. I had a certain day that it was scheduled and everybody took it. Now, I have a "test day," but only the students who have successfully completed the formative work are allowed to take it. If students do not get to take the test that day, it is their responsibility to finish their practice work and then take the test on their own time.

Why I changed . . .

I knew the pieces were not working right. I learned a new way of making it happen as I envisioned it through reading the book *Classroom Assessment* for *Student Learning*.

What I notice as a result . . .

WOW! So many things to report as change! My students are more engaged in their learning. They enjoy showing me their work instead of placing it in a box for a grade. They put more effort in their practice, knowing that I will be reviewing it with them, and they enjoy the one-on-one attention. Secondly, I now have a tracking sheet that is used as a personal assessment piece, a quick look for a parent/conference meeting, and a gauge for standards-based learning. Lastly, my students WANT to complete their practice—because lack of effort or incomplete means NO GRADE in my class. And the biggest change has been the numbers of "incomplete work" to report. **It is now nonexistent.**

Source: Reprinted with permission from Elizabeth Schroeder, 7th-grade English language arts teacher, Jerome School District, Jerome, ID, 2011.

learning strengths and needs. Organizing your evidence by learning target is also valuable in discussing student strengths and needs with parents during the grading period and at its end in conferences.

Standards-Based Grade Reports

Many schools and districts have developed *standards-based* grade reports. This means that you will be reporting student achievement according to your district's or state's content standards. In many cases, you will be reporting on the level of mastery or proficiency each student has attained on content standards listed on the grade report. When you record information according to the learning target it reflects, it makes it much simpler to transfer the data into the report card format.

Using Computer Programs for Grade Management

Many schools and districts have adopted computerized information management systems to manage school processes and student data. These systems vary widely in the nature of the records they can store and receive as well as in what they permit the user to do by way of summarizing evidence for grading purposes. What they have in common is that student grade reports are generated electronically from the data you enter. The grade report may or may not be standards based, depending on how the school or district has set it up. However, within these systems you are most often able to set your own categories, so you can create standards-based records to populate the grade report categories, even if they only refer to the subject (e.g., language arts, mathematics, or music).

Level of Detail

With formative assessment information, how much detail you record is up to you and is determined by what you want to do with the information. In general, you will want more rather than less detail about specific learning targets to guide formative decisions about who needs what and when and what to do about it. With summative assessment information, we can combine scores about separate learning targets into the larger content standards to which they contribute or even into strands (larger categories) representing several content standards because the purpose is to sum up overall level of achievement.

Figure 9.5 shows an example of a teacher's gradebook entries organized by content strand and then by individual learning targets. *Syn/Ant* is an abbreviation for "Identify synonyms and antonyms," *Pre/Suf* is an abbreviation for the learning target "Identify the meaning of prefixes and suffixes," and *Fluency* refers to the learning target "Read aloud with fluency." The content strands "Applies skills and strategies to read" and "Understands what is read" are two categories on the report

figure 9.5 ■ For Example: Formative and Summative Data Reported in Separate Sections

Reading	Applies Skills & Strategies to Read									Understands What Is Read									Test: Skills & Strategies			Test: Understands		
Learning Target	1 Syn/Ant	2 Syn/Ant	3 Syn/Ant	4 Pre/Suf	5 Pre/Suf	6 Pre/Suf	7 Fluency	8 Fluency	9 Fluency	1 Inference	2 Inference	3 Inference	4 Summary	5 Summary	6 Summary	7 Comp/Cont	8 Comp/Cont	9 Comp/Cont	Syn/Ant	Pre/Suf	Fluency	Inference	Summary	Comp/Cont
Assignment																								
Date																								
First																								
Last																								

Source: This has been adapted so much that the credit is not applicable

figure 9.6 ■ For Example: Elementary Gradebook Arranged by Learning Target

Number Sense					
	Identifies place value to 10,000s	Reads, writes common fractions	Reads whole numbers through 4 digits	Writes whole numbers through 4 digits	Orders and compares whole numbers through 4 digits
Date					
Task					
F/S					
Students					
1.					
2.					
3.					

Computation							
	Addition	Subtraction	Multiplication		Division		Uses calculator to + or − 4 or more digits	Estimation Skills
	+ with 3 or more digits	− with 3 or more digits	Facts to 10	Fact Families	Facts to 10	Fact Families		
Date								
Task								
F/S								
Students								
1.								
2.								
3.								

Task:	SR = Selected Response; PA = Performance Assessment; O = Oral; HA = Homework Assignment; Q = Quiz
F/S:	F = Formative; S = Summative

Source: Reprinted with permission from Ken O'Connor.

card under the heading of *Reading*. The teacher has organized the entries so that the results of formative practice events are recorded in the two sections with multiple entries and the summative results are recorded in the columns marked "Test." There is also a place for the teacher to note the assignment and the date. Figure 9.6 shows an example of a teacher's gradebook organized by learning targets and categorized by content strands in mathematics. There is a place for the teacher to note the assignment, the date it was assigned, and whether the data will be used formatively or summatively. Figure 9.7 shows an example of how one teacher has set up an electronic gradebook according to learning targets.

MyEdLab **Application Exercise 9.2** Using a gradebook to record formative and summative assessment information

figure 9.7 ■ For Example: Electronic Gradebook Page

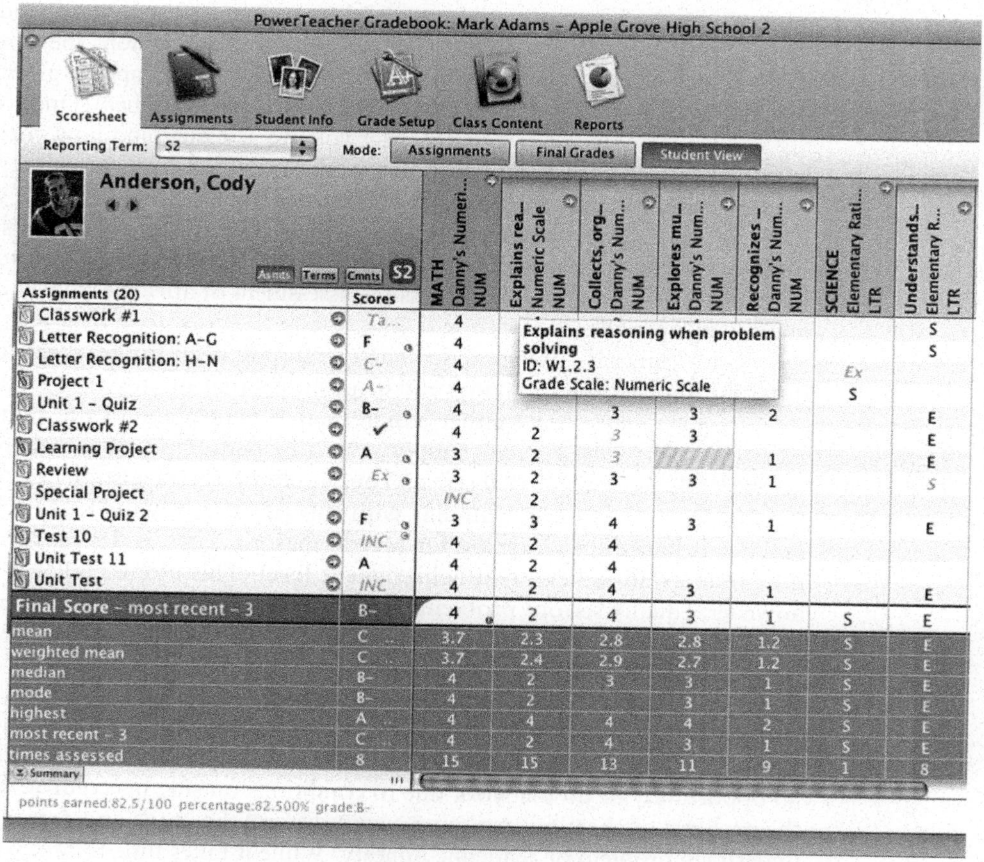

Source: NCS Pearson. (2007–2011). PowerTeacher 2.3 [computer software]. Minneapolis, MN: NCS Pearson.

■ Guideline 3: Keep Track of Work Habits and Social Skills Separately from Achievement Information

Student behaviors and dispositions such as class participation, academic honesty, timeliness of work turned in, attendance, cooperation, and attitude all contribute to success at learning. They are all important; part of your job as a teacher will be to help students to develop productive behaviors and dispositions toward learning, that is, to teach them to be successful learners.

If the behaviors and dispositions you select to track and report on are broad, such as "effort" or "work habits," you will need to define the actions that underpin them. For example, is effort signified by work turned in on time? Doing extra work? Something else? We recommend that you select and define important work habits and social skills with colleagues—as a grade-level team, a department, a school, or a district—so that (a) they can be shared with and understood by students and (b) students can experience consistency of expectations across contexts.

After clarifying the underlying actions for each behavioral expectation, you will need to identify how you will assess each one. Remember that all students need to understand the behaviors and actions they are expected to learn and have opportunities to improve prior to being held accountable for having mastered them. Once you know specifically what you are assessing and how you are assessing it, you can set up a tracking system that works for you, keeping in mind your intended use of the information. For example, if some of your students struggle with different work habits, you can analyze your records to identify trends and devise solutions with students and their parents. Figure 9.8 provides a template you can use to help implement this guideline. In addition, we discuss the assessment of affective student characteristics in detail in Appendix A.

Part of your job will be to teach students successful learner behaviors.

Unfortunately, past practice has commonly been for teachers (or schools or districts) to select the behaviors and dispositions that matter most to them and then either assign them a percentage of the summative grade or simply award or deduct points for their presence or absence. You would be the rare student if you were not familiar with this practice in your K–12 schooling. This practice is harmful to learning for several reasons. First, it destroys the accuracy of the grade as an indicator of achievement level. This alone makes it a nonstarter; however, equally serious problems relate to what happens to the student as a result.

It is not ethical to knowingly misrepresent a student's level of achievement.

Let's take, for example, the problem of late or missing work. Lowering a grade does nothing to change the behavior of students who have adopted an indifferent stance to poor grades. And it does not address the underlying problems. Is the student not completing homework because he doesn't understand the assignment? Does she think she won't be able to succeed and therefore doesn't try? Did the student not have an opportunity to do the work due to conditions outside his control? Similarly, with the problem of cheating, assigning a zero distorts the grade and does not address the underlying problem of academic honesty. While it takes time to talk with individuals about underlying causes, we can't help them if we don't correctly identify the problem

figure 9.8 ■ Template for Tracking and Assessing Work Habits and Social Skills

1. What work habits and/or social skills do you want to keep track of?

Work Habit or Social Skill	Actions That Define Competence

2. How will you assess and judge level of attainment of each?

Work Habit or Social Skill	Assessment Method and Plan

3. What system will you set up to track this information?

4. How will you summarize student attainment of work habits and social skills? How will you report it?

   Summarize:

   Report:

5. How will you make clear to students the work habits and social skills they are expected to demonstrate? How will you help them understand the ways in which their performance will be assessed and reported?

   Making the target clear:

   Making the criteria for competence clear:

   Making the assessment plan clear:

   Making the reporting system clear:

Source: Chappuis, Jan; Stiggins, Rick J.; Chappuis, Steve; Arter, Judith A., *Classroom Assessment for Student learning: Doing it Right - Using it Well*, 2nd Ed., ©2012. Reprinted and Electronically reproduced by permission of Pearson Education, Inc., New York, New York.

they face. Left unaddressed, they are developing habits that will not serve them well in their future as students and as adults. If we encounter these problems, it is our responsibility to help students overcome them.

Extra Credit Work

Extra credit has often been offered as a way for students to raise their grade, yet when students are awarded points simply for completing the work or for such unrelated acts as bringing a can of food for the food drive, the meaning of the grade has been compromised. It has been raised by the student's willingness to do extra work, a disposition, rather than by evidence of further learning. For the grade to be an accurate representation of the student's current level of achievement, the work must be evaluated on its quality relative to the learning target it represents. If you are going to offer extra credit, make sure students understand that only evidence of higher levels of learning will contribute to increasing their grade. Learning first, grades second.

MyEdLab **Application Exercise 9.3** Tracking student work habits and social skills

■ Guideline 4: Record Information by Raw Score When Possible

We retain the most flexibility and the most accuracy in interpretation when we record assessment information in raw score form, when raw scores are available. Raw scores provide a reference to the sample size, which is lost when they are translated to a percentage, a grade, or a proficiency level before being recorded. For example, consider a score of two out of three correct answers. It could be recorded as 2/3 (the raw score), as 67%, as a D (a grade), or as 1 (a proficiency level). Now consider a score of 12 out of 18 correct answers, which could be recorded as 12/18, 67%, D, or 1. If these two assessments measure the same learning target, the one with the larger sample will provide the more stable estimate of student level of achievement. With raw scores you are better able to review a collection of data to accurately interpret it. And, when you are combining information to derive a final grade, you are better able to make weighting decisions (which we will discuss in Chapter 12). Rubric scores should also be recorded in raw score form for reference when combining rubric scores with other information (also discussed in Chapter 12).

MyEdLab **Application Exercise 9.4** Recording student achievement

■ Summary: Going for the Record

The quality of our communication about student learning is only as good as the information that forms the foundation of the message being delivered. In standards-driven schools, those records need to arise from assessments that reveal how each student has done, or is doing, in mastering each relevant achievement target. Once we know that our information is accurate, its usefulness will be influenced by the records we keep. Therefore, we recommend adhering to four guidelines. First, keep records separately by purpose—formative or summative—to meet the different communication tasks each will serve. Second, organize assessment data according to classroom learning target or standard. Third, keep track of work habits and social skills separately from academic achievement information. If we don't do this, our grades will not serve as accurate reflections of student achievement levels. This guideline also affects what we do with extra credit work, with missing or late work, and with work displaying evidence of academic dishonesty. Fourth, record information in raw score form, when available, rather than by percent, grade, or proficiency level, to retain the most options for accurate use of the data. With a well-thought-out record-keeping system in place, we are better able to interpret the information we collect and to make decisions that support learning.

■ Suggested Activities

End-of-chapter activities are intended to help you master the chapter's learning targets. They are designed to deepen your understanding of the chapter content, provide opportunities for personal reflection on ideas presented, and serve as a basis for discussion among peers. You may wish to do all of them or select those that you believe will be most useful to your learning. Each activity is correlated to one or more chapter learning targets to help with your selection.

Chapter 9 Learning Targets

As a result of your study of Chapter 9, you will be able to do the following:

1. Separate formative from summative assessment information
2. Organize the entries in a gradebook according to the learning represented
3. Track information about work habits and social skills separately from achievement information
4. Record achievement information so you can interpret it accurately

Chapter 9 Activities

Activity 9.1   Keeping a Reflective Journal (All chapter learning targets)

Activity 9.2   Planning Formative and Summative Assessment Events (Learning Target 1)

Activity 9.3   Tracking Work Habits and Social Skills (Learning Target 3)

Activity 9.4   Comparing Your Experiences with Information from the Chapter (All chapter learning targets)

Activity 9.5   Answering an Interview Question (All chapter learning targets)

Activity 9.6   Reflecting on Your Learning from Chapter 9 (All chapter learning targets)

Activity 9.7   Adding to Your Growth Portfolio (All chapter learning targets)

Activity 9.1: Keeping a Reflective Journal

Keep a record of your thoughts, questions, and insights as you read Chapter 9.

Activity 9.2: Planning Formative and Summative Assessment Events

Select a unit that you have prepared to teach. Work independently or with a partner to map out the formative and summative assessment events you might schedule by doing the following:

1. Use the form "Formative and Summative Assessment Plan" (Figure 9.3) as is or modify it to fit your context.
2. Identify the unit of study and how many days or weeks it will cover.
3. List the learning targets that will be the focus of instruction during the unit in the order you will teach them.
4. Describe the assignments and assessments that will serve a summative purpose (e.g., end-of-term grade) for each learning target. Descriptions can take the form of page numbers in a text or other resource, assignment or assessment names, or other information that works for you. Note the approximate date for each and mark it with the letter "S" for "Summative" in the column labeled "Type."
5. Identify the formative assessments you would give. Describe them with whatever reference works for you (page numbers, assignment or activity titles, etc.). Use the key to identify the specific purpose for the formative assessment and mark it in the column labeled "Type."

Activity 9.3: Tracking Work Habits and Social Skills

Work independently, with a partner, or with a team to complete the following activity.

1. Using the form "Template for Tracking and Assessing Work Habits and Social Skills" (Figure 9.8), decide which work habits and social skills you will want to keep track of.
2. Then for each decide which behaviors or actions will define competence. If you are working with colleagues, discuss this until you come to consensus.
3. Determine how you will assess and judge level of attainment for each.
4. Create a system for tracking this information.
5. Make a plan for how you will make clear to students the work habits and social skills they are expected to demonstrate.
6. Make a plan for how you will help students understand the ways in which they will be assessed and how you will report their performance.
7. Note ideas for interventions to help students improve for each work habit and social skill you have listed.

Activity 9.4: Comparing Your Experiences with Information from the Chapter

Read the "From the Classroom" entry in Chapter 9 and compare it to your experience as a student.

How is it similar?

What differences do you notice?

What conclusions might you draw about the benefits of tracking formative assessment results separately from summative assessment results?

Activity 9.5: Answering an Interview Question

Imagine that you are about to interview for a teaching position. The interview team (often a combination of administrators and teachers) is interested in understanding your level of classroom assessment literacy. Review Chapter 9's learning targets and think about what concepts and procedures were most significant to you from the chapter. Then think about what type of question an interview team might ask related to this significant learning. Write the question and draft a short response—one that you could give in one to two minutes orally.

Activity 9.6: Reflecting on Your Learning from Chapter 9

Review the Chapter 9 learning targets and select one that struck you as most significant from this chapter. Write a short reflection that captures your current understanding. If you are working with a group, discuss what you have written.

Activity 9.7: Adding to Your Growth Portfolio

Any of the activities from this chapter can be used as portfolio entries. Select any activity you have completed or artifact you have created that will demonstrate your mastery of the Chapter 9 learning targets:

1. Separate formative from summative assessment information
2. Organize the entries in a gradebook according to the learning represented
3. Track information about work habits and social skills separately from achievement information
4. Record achievement information so you can interpret it accurately

Students Collecting and Reflecting on Evidence of Their Learning

Chapter 10 Learning Targets

As a result of your study of Chapter 10, you will be able to do the following:

1. Create tracking systems for students to use to record their assessment data
2. Select the types of portfolio(s) best suited to your students' needs
3. Prepare students to reflect on their learning progress

Whenever students are engaged in learning, they are operating on two levels (Black, 2013). On the more obvious level they are developing mastery of a learning target, but on the less visible level they can be learning self-regulation processes. Giving students regular opportunities to notice and reflect on progress helps them develop the inner dialogue of self-monitoring necessary to becoming an independent learner.

Several benefits accrue when students are engaged in keeping track of their progress and reflecting on it, all of which contribute to increased achievement. First, it develops their ability to think metacognitively. In one well-known study (Allen & Hancock, 2008), researchers divided classes of elementary students in grades 4, 5, and 6 into three groups. At the outset of instruction, all groups received personalized information about their reading strengths and weaknesses, based on the Woodcock Johnson III test. The first group used their profiles to reflect in writing about their strengths as readers regularly during the unit of instruction. The second group did not engage in self-reflection, and the third group experienced a different intervention. The self-reflection group attained significantly greater learning gains on the posttest of reading comprehension than did the other two groups (Andrade, 2013).

Tracking and self-reflection can have a positive motivational benefit, too. One outcome is that they cause students to notice incremental gain, which feeds motivation to continue putting forth effort. You are most likely familiar with computer games built on this premise. Players play again and again to get a little farther. At the end of a round, as long there is the promise of progress, they will return. In computer games where players "die" every round, they don't return to play the next time because they think they'll "live;" they play to "die" a little later. Even when experiencing a setback, players will keep at it until they reach a point where they repeatedly fail to make progress. Then they tend to look for a different game that will allow them to make incremental gains and will provide regular evidence of those gains. In much the same way, noticing progress in the classroom helps students attribute success to effort. We can build this motivational cycle into classroom learning experiences by setting up one or more systems to let students track their learning and watch themselves grow.

With this chapter, we continue our focus on Key 4: Effective Communication (Figure 10.1) by exploring ways for students to track and reflect on their learning progress. We begin with the prerequisite conditions and then examine three categories of tracking options: recording information from assignments and

figure 10.1 ■ Keys to Quality Assessment

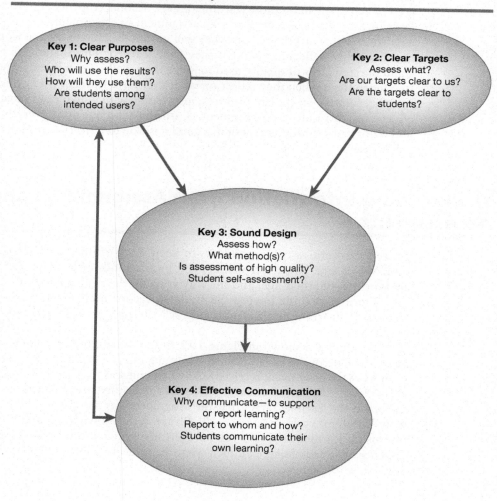

assessments, keeping learning journals, and collecting evidence in portfolios. Along the way we offer suggestions to help you manage the process without doing all of the work for the student, and last we discuss how to engage students in self-reflection.

Prerequisites to Successful Student Record Keeping

There are four prerequisites, all of which will be familiar to you at this point in your study of classroom assessment. First, all assignments and assessments must accurately reflect achievement of intended learning targets. If students are to track their progress toward mastery, the results they are tracking must accurately represent level of achievement on those learning targets. Second, students need to know which learning target is represented by each assignment or assessment—or which parts are aligned to which targets–because they will need to be able to use the work itself as a resource when reflecting on what they have learned. Third, students must understand the standards of quality used to judge their work, again because they will need to refer to them when they reflect on what they have learned. And, fourth, teachers must keep an eye on student progress, intervening with guidance or reteaching when efforts do not result in advancement. A student who has done everything assigned and is not making progress is not in a good position to reflect on growth or improved achievement.

Recording Information from Assignments and Assessments

There are several ways for students to keep track of information for later reflection. Which one you select will depend on the kinds of learning targets students are working on, their age, and the way you and the students will use the information. Options include having the students record their results either by assignment or by learning target and then track their progress by writing, coloring, or graphing.

On the form shown in Figure 10.2 the student records the name of the assignment, the date of the assignment, the learning target associated with the assignment, what score the assignment received, and whether it was formative or summative. Then, in the "stars and stairs" column the student notes her strengths and next steps with respect to the learning target that the assignment has shown. ("I did _____ well. Now I need to work on _____.") On the form shown in Figure 10.3 the student records the learning target (or you have already written it on the form), the date of the evidence he is examining, and then what the evidence tells him he has done well and needs to work on next.

figure 10.2 ■ For Example: Tracking Progress by Assignment

Tracking Progress by Assignment

Assignment	Date	Target	Score	F/S	★⌐

Source: Chappuis, Jan, *Seven Strategies Of Assessment For Learning,* 2nd Ed., ©2015. Reprinted and Electronically reproduced by permission of Pearson Education, Inc., New York, New York.

MyEdLab

Video Example 10.1

Students Keeping Track of Their Learning

Figure 10.4 shows a form that can be used when a content standard is developmental; that is, each learning target builds on the previous one. The students simply color the star on the top of the step once they have mastered it, also entering the date of mastery. The form in Figure 10.5 illustrates tracking progress by graphing. In this example, there are three practice tasks for each of the learning targets shown, two with ten points possible and one with five points possible. (Oral fluency is evaluated with a five-point rubric.) The teacher either notes the task number or gives the task a name. Students graph their scores after each practice task in the left-hand columns. The right-hand columns provide a place for students to graph their summative test results.

Watch Video Example 10.1 to hear students and a teacher discuss the value of students tracking their own learning.

figure 10.3 ■ For Example: Tracking Progress by Learning Target

Learning Target	Date	What I did well	What I need to work on
1. I can explain the constitutional structure of our government.			
2. I can describe the processes that have been used to create, amend, and repeal laws.			

Source: Chappuis, Jan, *Seven Strategies Of Assessment For Learning,* 2nd Ed., ©2015. Reprinted and Electronically reproduced by permission of Pearson Education, Inc., New York, New York.

figure 10.4 ■ For Example: Tracking Progress by Coloring

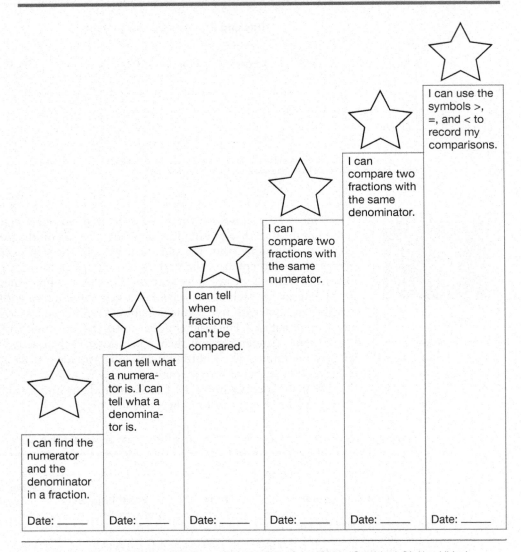

I can use the symbols >, =, and < to record my comparisons.

I can compare two fractions with the same denominator.

I can compare two fractions with the same numerator.

I can tell when fractions can't be compared.

I can tell what a numerator is. I can tell what a denominator is.

I can find the numerator and the denominator in a fraction.

Date: _____   Date: _____   Date: _____   Date: _____   Date: _____   Date: _____

Source: Reprinted by permission from Rick Croom, San Juan Unified School District: Carmichael, CA. Unpublished classroom materials.

■ Writing in Learning Journals

Two types of learning journals that work well for tracking progress are the dialogue journal and the learning log. Dialogue journals are conversations about learning between students and the teacher. They are flexible in structure but usually involve the students recording the following:

figure 10.5 ■ For Example: Tracking Progress by Graphing

	PRACTICE									TEST		
	Synonym/ Antonym			Prefix/Suffix			Oral Fluency			Synonym/ Antonym	Prefix/Suffix	Oral Fluency
	(Task #)	(Task #)	(Task #)	(Task #)	(Task #)	(Task #)	(Task #)	(Task #)	(Task #)			
10												
9												
8												
7												
6												
5												
4												
3												
2												
1												
Date												

Learning targets: I can identify synonyms and antonyms.
I can tell the meaning of prefixes and suffixes.
I can read aloud with fluency.

Source: Chappuis, Jan, *Seven Strategies Of Assessment For Learning,* 2nd Ed., ©2015. Reprinted and Electronically reproduced by permission of Pearson Education, Inc., New York, New York.

■ What they think they are supposed to be learning
■ Their sense of the progress they have made
■ Anything they are confused about
■ Questions they have

The teacher responds in writing, orally, or with further instruction. Writing in dialogue journals helps keep students in touch with connections between what they are doing and what they are learning.

With a learning log, students keep ongoing documentation over the course of a project or unit. Notations include the following: :

- Actions they have taken
- Helpful processes and resources they have used
- The learning progress they are making over the course of the project or unit

The learning log is different from a dialogue journal in that its primary purpose is for students to keep a record of everything they do so they can strengthen their learning processes and strategies. In Figure 10.6, high school science teacher Andy Hamilton explains how learning logs function in his classes.

figure 10.6 ■ From the Classroom: Andy Hamilton

Learning Logs

What I Do

My primary mode of in-class assessment these days is a variation of the learning log. Students include all of their practice work and notes, and it helps them keep track of which things we do to provide evidence for specific targets. They self-evaluate throughout, and if they run into difficulty, they can easily find the notes and practice that match the target they are struggling with. Practice quizzes are correlated to specific learning targets so they can evaluate their evaluations from time to time. The entire learning log is assembled throughout a unit and collected at the end of a grading cycle. Labs are about the only thing excluded from the logs. These are graded with quality in mind. For this reason, they are collected as we go, a few days after the lab is completed in class.

Impact on Learning

I have noticed that my students are more independent as learners with a learning log in hand. They spend time using the learning log to figure out problems and rely less on outside help at first. They know where to go to find information and are generally more willing to do the assignments when they see exactly what targets they relate to. When the evaluations are honest, they are able to spend time studying what they need most. It also provides a way for me to track their learning without constantly collecting or checking homework. I can see with a glance how they have been doing on practice quizzes and what their self-evaluations say. I can easily determine which students are struggling or which concepts are causing widespread confusion. The time I save processing homework daily allows me to do more formative assessment.

What My Students Say

Some of my students say they used to spend hours studying but now get better results with less time because they know exactly what they need to study.

Source: Used with permission from Andy Hamilton, West Ottawa Public Schools, Holland, MI. Unpublished classroom materials.

MyEdLab **Self-Check 10.1**
MyEdLab **Application Exercise 10.1** Using tracking systems for student learning

■ Collecting Evidence in a Portfolio

A portfolio is a collection of work assembled so that it tells a story. Just as artists assemble portfolios of their work to convey their talents and journalists assemble collections of their writings to represent their capabilities, so too can students collect examples of their work to tell a variety of stories about their learning.

Benefits of Portfolios

We gather a great deal of information about student achievement over an entire semester or year. Visualize a file drawer full of information on student mastery of content knowledge, reasoning proficiencies, performance skills, and product development capabilities. When we assign a grade, we force the file drawer contents through a narrow-diameter funnel. What comes out as a letter grade has lost all of the detail. This is where portfolios can help: they allow us to document the story behind the grade.

The range of contents a portfolio can hold includes the following:

- Artifacts such as examples of student work with feedback about quality
- Student self-assessments on the quality of the work
- Multiple drafts with revisions
- Student reflections on their growth as learners

This collection provides students, teachers, and parents with the detail that underpins the grade.

Misconceptions about Portfolios

As portfolios have increased in popularity in recent years, they sometimes have been confused with an assessment method, as when they are referred to as "portfolio assessment." Portfolios are correctly thought of as collections of assessments, not as an assessment method in and of themselves. Illustrating another point of confusion, some people have limited portfolio contents to artifacts from performance assessments. There is precedent for this. When artists assemble portfolios of their work, they collect the artistic products they have created. When journalists collect samples of their articles, they too gather their work into a coherent whole. These are products. As you know, they can serve as the basis for product-based performance evaluations. However, within the classroom we have four forms of assessment at our disposal—selected response, written response, performance assessment, and personal communication. Each can contribute to the story of student achievement. So they all can appear in portfolios. Additionally, portfolios can hold many other types of artifacts, such as photos, letters, rough drafts, schedules, lists (such as of books read), and other evidence relevant to telling a complete story of achievement status or growth. The greatest power of a portfolio in classroom assessment in our opinion resides in its ability to make incremental changes in achievement visible over time.

The effective use of portfolios requires that we apply them in a thoughtful and purpose-driven way. In the past, some local and state education agencies have liked the portfolio idea so much that they mandated that teachers start one for each student, without asking or answering the question, "Why?" Envision the universal, all-encompassing "mega-portfolio" starting in primary grades and building through to graduation. Each year, teachers accumulate evidence of achievement and each subsequent teacher adds more. The file folder becomes a file drawer, then a file cabinet, and then a closet stuffed with material. By the end of grade 12, the collection is akin to boxes of work stored in an attic.

Of course this is foolish. Even keeping a digitized version of the contents is not the solution to this problem. Imagine an "electro-mega-super-portfolio," still completely devoid of purpose. It is a truckload of information wherever it is stored. Under any circumstances, portfolios can easily become overwhelming if we don't understand how to cull student work to tell the story we intend to tell. We need to begin with an understanding of the range of purposes for portfolios and the requirements that need to be in place for them to enhance learning or to function as a communication tool. If we start with no purpose, no story to tell, or no clear achievement targets, we end up with a useless and unmanageable mass of evidence, whether on paper or in a cloud.

Types of Portfolios

A portfolio is merely an organizing tool for a collection of artifacts intended to tell a story. Whether you will digitize the contents or keep them in file folders, the design principle "Form follows function" applies. The portfolio story, like all other stories, requires a theme. The theme, or its *purpose* (its function), guides the selection of artifacts. Spandel and Culham (1995) provide a productive way to think of this by suggesting four types of portfolios: the celebration portfolio, the growth portfolio, the project portfolio, and the achievement status portfolio. Figure 10.7 summarizes the four types of portfolios, their purposes, and the kinds of artifacts they include.

Celebration Portfolios   The purpose of a celebration portfolio is to showcase a student's best work, what the student is most proud of, or what the students likes the best. It can be used as a keepsake, which you invite students to create as a personal collection of favorite works and special academic mementos. They might use this portfolio to communicate to families the things they are most proud of or to show positive examples of their learning experiences or classroom activities. In this case, the students are selecting the contents, guided by the question, "What work have I done that is special to me?" This is a wonderful place for young students to begin their portfolio development experience by just collecting favorite pieces of work and then culling the collection for the really special works. The decisions are all made by the students, according to their own vision of why the piece is important.

Students can use this experience to begin to identify the attributes of classroom work that are important to them and to generate personal insights about their own meaning of quality. Over time and through interaction with their teachers and

figure 10.7 ■ Types of Portfolios

	Purpose	Artifacts Included
Celebration	To showcase best work or what the student is most proud of	Student choice based on quality of work or personal preference
Growth	To show progress toward one or more learning targets	Work samples from before, during, and after learning
Project	To document the trajectory of a project	All drafts of work during the creation of the product or performance
Achievement Status	To demonstrate level of achievement with respect to one or more learning targets	Work samples demonstrating the highest level of achievement

classmates, they can begin to connect these elements of quality into a growing framework that ultimately helps them understand their own sense of what represents "good work." In this sense, the celebration portfolio can begin to put students in touch with their own strengths and interests and can help them learn to make choices.

Growth Portfolios   The purpose of the growth portfolio is to illustrate progress toward mastery of one or more learning targets. In the growth portfolio, students collect samples of work periodically to show how their level of proficiency has increased for a specified learning target. For example, students might keep samples of their writing from the beginning of the year and add samples to their collection periodically over the course of a semester or year. With this type of portfolio, the evaluation criteria need to be held constant over time so that students are able to point out ways in which their work has improved according to stable criteria. Growth portfolios include periodic written self-reflections describing changes they see in their achievement and capabilities. The span of time covered can range from a brief cycle of mastery lasting only a few days to one lasting a full year, depending on the complexity of the learning target.

Project Portfolios   The purpose of a project portfolio is to document the completion of steps in a project conducted over time. Entries chosen provide evidence of engaging in each stage of the project's work. For example, students completing a major science project might show how they arrived at a hypothesis, how they determined the apparatus to use for gathering the needed data, how they conducted the tests, the test results, and the analysis and interpretation of those results.

A project portfolio is an ideal format to use to describe such work carried out over an extended period. The evaluative judgments made in this case may be based on two sets of performance criteria. The first set of criteria reflects the steps students must have completed within a specified time frame. These typically provide highly structured guidelines for what to collect as proof of work completion. They teach students lessons about the necessity of planning a task and sticking to a timeline. You might also hold students accountable for periodically reviewing progress with you. The second set of criteria may focus on the quality of work completed at each step along the way. Of course, this demands that students not merely provide evidence of having done the activity but also provide evidence that they did it well. An alternative to judging the quality of work at each step is to have students use their documentation to reflect on what they learned from completing the project. As with growth portfolios, the span of time covered can range from a brief project lasting only a few days to one lasting a full year or longer, depending on the context.

Achievement Status Portfolios   Yet another use of portfolios can be to demonstrate level of achievement with respect to one or more learning targets. Here, either we or our students make a case within the portfolio for having attained certain levels of proficiency with respect to specified content standards. Therefore, the intended achievement targets determine the guidelines for content selection. Several applications of this kind of portfolio are relevant in school. As students move through the learning progression of the math curriculum, for example, we might maintain portfolios depicting their current achievement status. So at any point in time, decision makers could check this record and know what comes next. In this case, when a sample of student work is collected that reveals a new high level of achievement, the old evidence previously held in the portfolio—now outdated—would be discarded. This portfolio format might accompany a student across grade levels over the years. In another kind of application, in some districts, students present a portfolio of evidence of having attained certain essential proficiencies in order to qualify for graduation. In a much simpler context, we might ask students to assemble evidence of having mastered all requirements for completing a particular course. In all of these cases, the guidelines for selecting material will be highly structured and driven by specific academic requirements that provide evidence that students have mastered prerequisites and are ready to move on.

Work Sample Annotations

When a portfolio consists solely of a collection of work samples, no matter who has assembled them, it will not work well as a communication tool without some way of indicating why each sample was chosen and what it is intended to illustrate. Without this component, a student-involved parent conference can go something like this: "Here's my work." The parents' job is to flip through pages of assignments, projects, quizzes, and tests, most of which they may have seen before. More thought is needed to bring the artifacts to life—to create a compelling story line.

Work sample annotations are comments students make about each piece of evidence selected for the portfolio. They can be very short—their purpose is to link the work to the intended learning in some way. When students are required to articulate why they have chosen a selection, it helps them be clear about why they are choosing the piece and whether it is the best choice for the purpose. If there will be an audience for the portfolio beyond the student, annotations help the audience understand the intent behind the artifact's inclusion. When students are required to annotate each portfolio entry, when the time comes to share the portfolio, nervousness or other distractions will not cause them to forget what the particular entry was selected to demonstrate.

There are several ways to structure annotations. One relatively unstructured form is the "pause and think" comment, offered in response to prompts such as the following:

- Why is this learning important to you?
- What about this learning is important to you?
- What do you notice about yourself as a learner?
- What is a key point you have learned from completing this assignment?

Annotations can also take the form of "I can" statements attached to entries, along with a short explanation of how the entry demonstrates the learning. Or they can consist of student self-assessments against established criteria. In this case, students point out features of their work that match phrases in the criteria and make judgments about level of quality, growth, strengths, and/or areas for improvement. Frequently, annotations are written on a cover sheet for each entry. Figure 10.8 shows two examples of portfolio entry cover sheets.

Involving Students in Selecting Portfolio Entries

Let's say you were assembling a job application portfolio. Clearly it would be important for you to take responsibility for selecting the material to be included for two reasons. First, you know yourself best and can best ensure the telling of a complete and accurate story. Second, selecting the content allows you to present yourself in the most positive light called for in this competitive situation. Our students are driven, Covington (1992) tells us, by a desire to maintain and to present to the world a sense that they are academically capable. We support and encourage that positive self-image by involving students in recording their own story through their portfolios. But to make this work, they must also actively participate in selecting the artifacts for the portfolio.

While the teacher generally decides what type of portfolio the students will assemble, the teacher, the students, or both make the rest of the decisions. In the celebration portfolio, the story is essentially the student's to tell. There is much room for student involvement in the growth, project, and achievement status options as well. Keep in mind that the more effort students put in to deciding on the portfolio contents, the more ownership they will have. Here's how one teacher friend of ours handles this process: Her sixth graders maintain files of all work completed, one for each discipline. When it comes time to assemble a growth portfolio in preparation for a student-led parent conference (discussed in Chapter 12), she advises her students on how to select the artifacts, but the students make the ultimate choices, for they will be the ones explaining the selections and what they demonstrate. Figure 10.9 summarizes the options for teacher and student decisions about portfolio contents.

figure 10.8 ■ For Example: Portfolio Entry Cover Sheets

Form A

Date:_____   Title of Entry: _____

Learning target(s) this entry demonstrates:

What this entry shows about my learning:

Why I chose this entry:

Form B

Date:_____   Title of Entry: _____

What this shows I am good at/have mastered/know how to do:

What this shows I need to keep working on:

Source: Chappuis, Jan, *Seven Strategies Of Assessment For Learning,* 2nd Ed., ©2015. Reprinted and Electronically reproduced by permission of Pearson Education, Inc., New York, New York.

figure 10.9 ■ Who Decides?

	Learning Targets	Number and Kinds of Entries	Artifacts	Kinds of Annotations
Celebration	Student or both	Student	Student	Student or both
Growth	Teacher or both	Teacher or both	Teacher, student, or both	Teacher or both
Project	Teacher	Teacher or both	Teacher, student, or both	Teacher or both
Achievement Status	Teacher	Teacher or both	Teacher, student, or both	Teacher or both

MyEdLab **Self-Check 10.2**
MyEdLab **Application Exercise 10.2** Using portfolios

■ Periodic Student Self-Reflection

A powerful way to help students develop a clear sense of themselves as learners is to have them write or talk about their accumulating evidence and what it says to and about them. The evidence can take the form of student records, notes in a journal or log, or a collection of artifacts assembled into a portfolio. Figure 10.10 offers prompts that you can use to help students reflect on what they have learned, how they have learned it, and who they are as learners.

   It can be difficult for students to be accurately and constructively self-reflective, at least at first. This is risky business for most, especially for those with a history of academic failure. Research reminds us that students will go to great lengths to

figure 10.10 ■ For Example: Prompts to Activate Self-Reflection

Portfolio Type	Starters
Celebration	I am happiest/proudest of _____ because _____.
	I really liked doing _____ because _____ .
	What this portfolio says about me…
	Here is the impact assembling this portfolio has had on my interests, attitudes, or views of _____ (content, learning target, or process).
Growth	I have become better at _____ . I used to _____ , but now I _____ .
	Here is what has helped me improve: _____ .
	Here is what has helped me as a learner: _____ .
	Here is what I learned about myself as a learner: _____ .
	Here is what gets in my way as a learner: _____ .
	Here is what is difficult for me: _____ .
	This used to be hard, but now it's easy: _____ . Here is what made it easier: _____ .
	Here are "before" and "after" pictures of my learning. The first one shows _____ . The second one shows _____ .
Project	Here is what I learned about myself as a learner while doing this project: _____ .
	I developed the following skills as a result of doing this project: _____ .
	Here is what I liked least/most about doing this project _____ . Here's why: _____ .
	Here is how my thinking changed about _____ because of doing this project: _____ .
	This project has affected my interest in _____ . It has caused me to _____ .

(Continued)

figure 10.10 ■ For Example: Prompts to Activate Self-Reflection (*Continued*)

Portfolio Type	Starters
Achievement	My selections have shown I have mastered _____ . Here is how they show that: _____ .
	My strengths in (subject or learning target) are _____ .
	I still need to work on _____ .
	Here is how I achieved mastery of _____ (learning target): _____ .
	Here is how I would change what I did if I had it to do over: _____ .
	Here is what doing _____ has taught me about myself as a learner: _____ .

Source: Adapted from Seven Strategies of Assessment for Learning (pp. 159–166) by J. Chappuis. 2009, Upper Saddle River, NJ: Pearson Education.

maintain a positive internal sense of academic ability, even to the point of denying or being unable to see, let alone face, the flaws in their work (Covington, 1992). For this reason, guided practice in a safe environment is a necessity.

You can help establish that safe environment by modeling the process; that is, consider analyzing and reflecting on some of your own work in front of the class. Or consider having the class collaborate in teams to compose a hypothetical self-reflection on a collection of evidence. This is the best way we know to show students that your classroom is a safe place. Both success and struggles point the direction, not to a judgmental grade, but to a specific path for continued growth. In Figure 10.11, elementary teacher Laura Grayson shares how she structures a year-long self-reflection activity with her students.

figure 10.11 ■ From the Classroom: Laura Grayson

Gifts of Learning

What I Do

One thing that I have tried new this year is a yearlong reflection of learning in my classroom. I have hung nine canvases on my wall (one for each month of the school year) and titled it as "Gifts of Learning." At the end of the month, in a class meeting format my students reflect on their personal learning for that month, and we decide how we might represent that learning for that month.

Impact on Learning

This has been a powerful piece for the students in my classroom in terms of reflecting on their own learning, working collaboratively with classmates, and finding ways to represent the learning. It has also allowed us to reflect back on previous learning. We have these on our wall the whole year to include in our discussion.

figure 10.11 ▪ From the Classroom: Laura Grayson (*Continued*)

> **What My Students Say**
>
> I have heard students say, "Oh remember in November when we studied the states and capitals. That fits with what we are learning now."

Source: Reprinted with permission from Laura Grayson, Kirkwood School District: Kirkwood, MO. Unpublished classroom materials.

MyEdLab **Application Exercise 10.3** Student self-reflection

▪ Summary: Student-Involved Record Keeping and Reflection

We help our students become increasingly efficacious when we teach them to improve the quality of their work one key attribute at a time, when we help them learn to see and keep track of changes in their own capabilities, and when we help them reflect on the relationships between those improvements and their own actions.

Portfolios offer ways to communicate about student achievement in much greater detail than is permitted by report card grades. In these cases, the communication arises from and focuses on actual examples of student work. Unlike grades, portfolios can tell a more detailed story of a student's achievement. This does not mean that portfolios should replace grades, but rather that we should see them as serving different purposes—different users and uses. Portfolios have gained popularity in recent years because of their potential as a teaching tool that offers many opportunities for student involvement. They can encourage students to take responsibility for their own learning, track that learning, and gain an enhanced sense of academic progress and self-worth. Portfolios help students learn to reflect on their own work, identify strengths and weaknesses, and plan a course of action—critically important life skills.

But with all these pluses, these ways of communicating take very careful planning and dedication to use well. Unfortunately, many educators (and students) have drowned in the sea of papers collected to serve an externally mandated "mega-portfolio" system. We can avoid problems that have plagued portfolios and other student-involved record-keeping systems in the past by doing the following:

- ▪ Gather dependable evidence so as to create an accurate picture of achievement, with students as partners in that process.
- ▪ Interact with students regularly about their evidence of achievement, checking to be sure they are in touch with and feeling in control of their progress.

- Think intentionally about what students should be tracking and how they should be tracking it.
- Give students regular opportunities to track and reflect on their learning and on themselves as learners.

The possibilities of student-involved record keeping are bounded only by the imagination of the users, meaning you and your students. The methods of conveying information explored in this chapter hold the promise of allowing students to tell their own story of academic success. This, in and of itself, represents one of the most powerful learning experiences we can offer them.

■ Suggested Activities

End-of-chapter activities are intended to help you master the chapter's learning targets. They are designed to deepen your understanding of the chapter content, provide opportunities for personal reflection on ideas presented, and serve as a basis for discussion among peers. You may wish to do all of them or select those that you believe will be most useful to your learning. Each activity is correlated to one or more chapter learning targets to help with your selection.

Chapter 10 Learning Targets

As a result of your study of Chapter 10, you will be able to do the following:

1. Create tracking systems for students to use to record their assessment data
2. Select the types of portfolio(s) best suited to your students' needs
3. Prepare students to reflect on their learning progress

Chapter 10 Activities

Activity 10.1   Keeping a Reflective Journal (All chapter learning targets)

Activity 10.2   Planning a Tracking Option for Students (Learning Target 1)

Activity 10.3   Planning a Portfolio Option for Students (Learning Target 2)

Activity 10.4   Selecting Options for Reflecting on Learning (Learning Target 3)

Activity 10.5   Comparing Your Experiences with Information from the Chapter (All chapter learning targets)

Activity 10.6   Answering an Interview Question (All chapter learning targets)

Activity 10.7   Reflecting on Your Learning from Chapter 10 (All chapter learning targets)

Activity 10.8   Adding to Your Growth Portfolio (All chapter learning targets)

Activity 10.1: Keeping a Reflective Journal

Keep a record of your thoughts, questions, and insights as you read Chapter 10.

Activity 10.2: Planning a Tracking Option for Students

Select a unit you have prepared to teach. Work independently or with a partner to plan one or more ways for students to track their progress.

1. Make a list of the learning targets that will be the focus of the unit.
2. Decide for each learning target which tracking option will work best. You may use one option for all targets or a combination of options. Options discussed in this chapter include recording progress by assignment or by learning target (in writing, by coloring, or by graphing); through keeping a learning journal; and through collecting and annotating evidence in a portfolio.
3. Determine the frequency with which students will track their learning.
4. Create the forms students will use.
5. Write an explanation that you could use to introduce the purpose of keeping track of learning to your students. How will it benefit them as learners? With whom will they share their records?
6. Write an explanation that you could use to introduce the purpose of students' keeping track of their learning to parents. How will it benefit their children as learners? With whom will their children share their records?

Activity 10.3: Planning a Portfolio Option for Students

This activity takes Activity 10.2 a step further. In it you will make a more detailed plan for setting up a portfolio with students.

1. Decide which portfolio option you would like to plan—celebration, growth, project, or achievement status.
2. Identify the learning targets that will be represented by the portfolio.
3. Determine the length of time students will have to create and add to the portfolio.
4. Determine what decisions students will make and what decisions you will make in creating the portfolio. Refer to Figure 10.9 for suggestions.
5. Identify the artifacts or types of artifacts that will go into the portfolio. If students are to decide what goes in, write a set of guidelines you will share with them to help them choose.
6. Identify how each entry will be annotated. Create the form or forms students will use for their annotations.

Activity 10.4: Selecting Options for Reflecting on Learning

This activity follows either of the two previous activities.

1. Select one or more self-reflection prompts (or create your own) that best suit the type of record-keeping system you have planned, your learning targets, and the age of your students.

2. Create the form students will use to conduct their self-reflection.
3. Determine what evidence students will need to refer to during their reflection.
4. Write an explanation of the purpose for having students engage in self-reflection that you could share with your students. How will it benefit them as learners? With whom will they share their reflections?
5. Write an explanation of the purpose for having students engage in self-reflection that you could share with their parents. How will it benefit their children as learners? With whom will their children share their reflections?

Activity 10.5: Comparing Your Experiences with Information from the Chapter

Read one of the "From the Classroom" entries in Chapter 10 and compare it to your experience as a student.

How is it similar?

What differences do you notice?

What conclusions might you draw about the benefits of students tracking and reflecting on their learning?

Activity 10.6: Answering an Interview Question

Imagine that you are about to interview for a teaching position. The interview team (often a combination of administrators and teachers) is interested in understanding your level of classroom assessment literacy. Review Chapter 10's learning targets and think about what concepts and procedures were most significant to you from the chapter. Then think about what type of question an interview team might ask related to this significant learning. Write the question and draft a short response—one that you could give in one to two minutes orally.

Activity 10.7: Reflecting on Your Learning from Chapter 10

Review the Chapter 10 learning targets and select one that struck you as most significant from this chapter. Write a short reflection that captures your current understanding. If you are working with a group, discuss what you have written.

Activity 10.8: Adding to Your Growth Portfolio

Any of the activities from this chapter can be used as portfolio entries. Select any activity you have completed or artifact you have created that will demonstrate your mastery of the Chapter 10 learning targets:

1. Create tracking systems for students to use to record their assessment data
2. Select the types of portfolio(s) best suited to your students' needs
3. Prepare students to reflect on their learning progress

Report Card Grading: Summarizing Achievement at a Point in Time

Chapter 11 Learning Targets

As a result of your study of Chapter 11, you will be able to do the following:

1. Understand the purpose for report card grades
2. Select information about a student's current level of academic achievement for inclusion in the report card grade
3. Summarize assessment information accurately
4. Combine rubric ratings with other assessment information to arrive at an accurate, fair, and defensible end-of-term grade

Grading is the process of condensing a great deal of information into a single symbol for ease of communication. While assessment plays an active role in both teaching and learning, grading does not: teaching and learning can happen just fine without it. In fact often elementary teachers say, "We don't grade our students. We use '3,' '2,' and '1' instead." Or "We use 'A' for *Advanced*, 'P' for *Proficient*, 'B' for *Basic*, and 'BB' for *Below Basic*." Of course, in reality, these are summary symbols, too. Grading—the act of summarizing information about what students have done and representing that summary with a symbol—is a part of our education system.

But if teaching and learning can succeed without grading, why do we do it? It is a more complex question than it may seem. How would you answer it? If you asked five people outside of education what they think is the purpose of grades, you could get 5 to 50 different answers. If you asked the same question of five people in the education field, you could also get 5 to 50 different answers. Chances are throughout your career as a student you have experienced a number of very different approaches to how your grades were figured. And chances are many of your teachers have been quite strongly committed to their various grading beliefs and practices. Why is grading so emotionally charged? And why are there so many different beliefs guiding grading practices?

In this chapter we will assert that the only legitimate purpose of grades is to *communicate*, continuing our focus on Key 4: Effective Communication (Figure 11.1). Our goal here is to show you how to create fair and defensible grades. We begin with the issues educators currently face in identifying the purpose for report

figure 11.1 ■ Keys to Quality Assessment

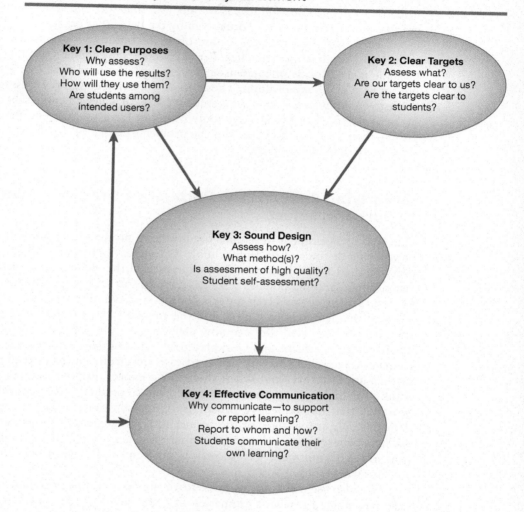

card grades. Then we examine the factors commonly included in determining a grade and discuss which should be used. Last we will show you how to combine information from a variety of sources into one symbol or number.

■ What Is the Purpose of Grades?

Beliefs about the intended purpose of grades and what they can be used to accomplish drive grading policies from the classroom to the boardroom. There is general agreement that one of the main functions of grades is to communicate about student performance. However, you will also find in some grading practices the underlying belief that the purpose of grades is to rank and thus sort and select students. Other grading practices in use today are driven by the belief that grades should be used as motivators. The resulting policies are often in conflict with themselves and with what we know to be best practice. Let us reiterate the chapter's opening statement: Grading is the process of condensing a great deal of information into a single symbol for ease of communication. Those on the receiving end of the message expect a grade to communicate accurately a student's level of achievement in school. In order for it to do so, that has to be its only purpose. Here we examine the other purposes—their underlying beliefs and the problems caused by trying to make grades serve more than one purpose.

Underlying Belief 1: The Purpose of Grades Is Also to Sort and Select

One goal of assessment in schools used to be to produce a dependable rank order of students at the end of high school. As long as there was a valedictorian and everyone had a "rank in class," few questioned the effectiveness of the school's functioning. Grading policies were designed to sort and select students. That may seem surprising to you given today's definition of the mission of schools. Over the years as the demands of society and the economy have changed, the mission of schooling has evolved. We are now called to prepare all students for successful participation in college and workplace training. Our society now requires that all students leave school having mastered essential proficiencies in reading, writing, mathematics, science, and social studies. We expect dropout rates to decline and want a far higher proportion of our students to graduate from college. The consensus is that our collective prosperity hinges on our success in meeting these demands. We see vestiges of the former rank-order mission of assessment when teachers believe that a bell curve distribution in grades indicates their grading policies are working well. Yet society is no longer served by bell curve–shaped achievement results.

We also see a shadow of this leftover mission in other grading practices. For example, when a teacher's estimation of a student's aptitude, intelligence, or academic ability influences the grade given to that student, students with a perceived higher intelligence will receive a higher grade. Teachers sometimes do this with the belief that grades are most accurate when they reflect a rank order of students' perceived aptitudes.

Producing a dependable rank order requires that we "fiddle" with the raw achievement data. When we impose this extra purpose on our grading system, we recalibrate raw data to spread the results along a continuum. The resulting grades no longer serve to communicate about an individual's achievement in regard to expectations for mastery: any one student's grade is dependent on who else is in the class and how well they have done (or how "capable" their teacher has judged them to be).

Underlying Belief 2: The Purpose of Grades Is Also to Motivate

It is very common today to encounter classroom grading policies that include practices designed to motivate and control student behavior. For example, let's say a teacher uses homework grades as a motivator to compel students to practice because this teacher believes that those who do the work learn more—a reasonable position, to be sure. So in his class failure to turn in a homework assignment is entered as an F in the gradebook.

Now let's say there are two students in this class, both of whom have a high level of mastery of the material. Each has demonstrated a high level of achievement on all tests, quizzes, and projects. Yet one student has consistently failed to complete practice assignments and so has accumulated many Fs for homework in the gradebook. At report card grading time, one student has been assigned an A, while the other is assigned a D (the result of averaging in all those Fs).

The resulting communication problem becomes apparent when we realize that both students have achieved at the same level. The message the grade is intended to communicate is garbled: parents, other teachers, and other institutions won't know or understand the subtleties of meaning hidden within the grade and may draw inappropriate conclusions about one student's achievement. Thus, a reporting process designed to promote greater effort yields miscommunication about this student's achievement.

> Grades should not be used to reward or punish behavior.

The Power of Formative Assessment   Assessment can motivate, but that motivation is not achieved best through the manipulation of grades. Remember, it is our formative assessment practices that have the greatest impact on student effort and it is those formative assessment practices that we should rely upon to cause students to try harder. In Figure 11.2, high school science teacher Ben Arcuri describes how he balances formative and summative assessment to increase motivation and achievement.

The Sole Purpose of Grades Is to Communicate

This is precisely why we argue that, when it comes to grades, accuracy of communication demands that we choose one purpose only. One set of summary symbols cannot communicate an understandable message if it is used for all three purposes: communicating about level of student achievement, rank ordering students, and motivating behavior. The purpose for grades must be first and foremost to communicate accurately about level of achievement. This is crucial to school success because, in standards-driven schools and classrooms where students consistently strive to ascend preset learning progressions, the question of the moment for student and teacher always is, "What comes next in the learning?" When grades can be linked directly back to academic standards,

> The purpose of grades must be first and foremost to communicate accurately about level of achievement.

figure 11.2 ■ From the Classroom: Ben Arcuri

Balancing Formative and Summative Assessment

What I Do

In my senior chemistry classes there is a balance between formative and summative assessment. The summative assessment is only used for grading. The formative assessment is strictly used as a guide for each individual student.

Quizzes are specifically designed for practice. Students complete the quiz individually, then I mark it and return it the next day. The feedback is immediate and effective and is used to improve learning. The quiz results directly guide my teaching practice. I address common problems in a variety of ways, sometimes reteaching a concept to the whole class. The quiz results show students which concepts they know and don't know. They use checklists to organize their study and complete specific questions from the textbook and worksheets on the concepts they don't yet know. The students complete the practice they feel is most beneficial to them individually. I record the practice that students are completing in my grade book, but it is not calculated in the grade. The answer keys to every worksheet can be found on my website. Students come to me with questions, and we discuss them individually or as a class. Following practice, students have an opportunity to complete an optional re-quiz. The re-quiz is made up of different questions on the same concepts. I mark the re-quiz and return it to the student. The hope is that the students' level of understanding has increased. A higher score on the re-quiz is a powerful way to increase the level of motivation, confidence, and overall disposition of the students.

Students complete many quizzes and re-quizzes throughout the chapter to prepare for the important chapter test. The chapter test is worth 70% of the grade. Laboratory work makes up the other 30%. Doing well on the test is completely determined by the work completed to prepare for the quizzes because the test questions mirror the quiz questions. I don't like surprises on tests. If the students complete the quizzes, review or relearn specific concepts, and re-quiz on the concepts to check their new level of understanding, they will be successful on the tests.

Impact on Learning

This system has been shown to create a positive, motivating, and confidence-building environment. The fact that the quiz score is not used in calculating the grade allows students to answer the questions without the fear of failing and also reduces test anxiety. Students understand that the system is in place to help them through the course and that they are in full control of their learning.

I no longer assign the entire class worksheets and assignments. I no longer spend hours marking questions and corrections. I no longer have to deal with late work slowing down classroom progress. There are no longer deadlines, late marks, or any other factors that can skew the students' grade. The grade at the end of the semester represents the students' level of understanding.

I can say with confidence that teachers have the ability to increase the overall motivational and confidence level of their students by incorporating characteristics of formative assessment into their classroom, resulting in more students striving to maximize their success in the class.

I have documented positive changes in my classroom and students in the following areas:

- More questions asked in class and outside of class
- Increased participation in classroom discussions

figure 11.2 ■ From the Classroom: Ben Arcuri (*Continued*)

- Better preparation for quizzes and tests
- A reduction in test anxiety
- More practice and review completed
- More confidence in ability to achieve higher grades and maintain higher grades
- Less competition
- An increase in intrinsic motivation

What My Students Say

One of the best comments I have ever received from a student is "This class makes me feel better about myself."

Source: Used with permission from Ben Arcuri.

they show us where each student is now in the learning and, therefore, what comes next. Anything that gets in the way of that purpose must be dealt with through another means.

MyEdLab **Self-Check 11.1**

MyEdLab **Application Exercise 11.1** Understanding the purpose of report card grading

■ Communicate about What?

If we are to devise report card grading approaches that meet our communication needs, while contributing to a supportive and motivating environment, the first issue we must confront is, What do we wish to use grades to communicate about? We must decide which student characteristics should be factored into the academic grade. Currently there is no debate about whether achievement should be considered. It is a major goal of schooling and it is what we are expected to communicate about. However, frequently, teachers include one or more of the following three factors as well:

- Aptitude—Those who "overachieve" in relation to their aptitude, intelligence, or academic ability receive higher grades than those who fail to work up to their "potential."
- Effort—Those who try harder receive higher grades.
- Compliance—Those who follow school and classroom rules (e.g., those who behave) receive higher grades than those who don't.

As you recall, we addressed this issue in Chapter 9 in the section titled "Guideline 3: Keep Track of Work Habits and Social Skills Separately from Achievement Information." In that section we briefly discussed what can happen when that guideline is violated. Now we need to look at what happens when teachers use information about factors other than achievement to determine the academic report card grade because it is still a common practice for many teachers, some of whom may become your colleagues. So, in this section we will examine what inclusion of each factor looks like and the rationale typically offered for its inclusion. Then we will share the reasons why it shouldn't be done. Figure 11.3 summarizes the options.

figure 11.3 ■ Which Factors Should Be Included in the Grade?

Factor	Definition	Track?	Include in Grade?
Achievement	Level of student mastery on preestablished content standards	Yes	Yes
Aptitude	Level of aptitude, intelligence, or academic ability	No	No
Effort	How hard the student tries	Define first, then track	No
Compliance	How well the student adheres to rules and requirements	Define first, then track	No

Aptitude as a Grading Factor

Assume two students demonstrate exactly the same level of achievement, and that level happens to be right at the cut-off between two grades. If you judge one student to be an overachiever in relation to ability, aptitude, or intelligence and judge the other to be an underachiever, you would assign them different grades. Or "Student X is capable of so much more, so even though for Student Y, this work would receive an A, for Student X it is a B." And conversely, "Student Y's work demonstrates achievement at the C level but because he is less capable than his peers, he will receive a B." When aptitude is factored into the grade, achievement scores are adjusted to reflect the level of performance expected based on a judgment of the individual student's potential.

Rationale for Including Aptitude   If we consider intelligence, ability, or academic aptitude in the grading equation, we hold out the promise that every student will be judged according to his or her potential. Those who are slacking will be motivated to put forth their best effort and those who are struggling will be rewarded for doing the best they can do. These are compelling arguments for factoring aptitude or ability into the grading process.

Reasons Not to Include Aptitude   There are significant counterarguments. First, the definition of aptitude or intelligence is far from clear. Scholars who have devoted their careers to the study of intelligence and its relationship to achievement do not agree among themselves as to whether each of us has one of these or many, whether this is a fixed or mutable human characteristic, or whether it is stable at some points in our lives and fluctuating at others. Not only do they disagree fundamentally about the definition of these characteristics, but they also are at odds regarding how to assess them (Gardner, 1993; Sternberg, 1996).

Our second argument against factoring aptitude into a grade is the difficulty of accurate measurement. Given these uncertainties among experts, we, who have no background in the study of intelligence, are not likely to be able to assess any student's true potential. That is not to say that all students come to school with the same intellectual preparedness. We know they do not. But it is one thing to sense this to be true and another matter to assume that we possess enough refined wisdom about intelligence to be able to measure it dependably (however we define "it"), turn it into a single quantitative index, and then factor it in when computing report card grades. Additionally, when we attempt to do this, we are assuming that intelligence is a fixed quantity and students' experiences in our classrooms will not alter their "potential," when in fact that "potential" can be developed by what we and our students do.

Even if teachers were to come up with (and agree on) an accurate definition, they would face the severe difficulty of generating the classroom-level aptitude and achievement data needed to classify students according to their potential and thus to categorize them as over- or underachievers. That is, each teacher would need a formula for deciding precisely how many units of achievement are needed per unit of aptitude to label a student as an over- or underachiever, and that formula would have to treat each and every student in exactly the same manner to ensure fairness. We do not possess the conceptual understanding and classroom assessment sophistication to enable us to make such judgments.

A Brief Note About Aptitude   A brief comment is in order about aptitude as something separate from achievement. It is tempting to use students' records of prior achievement as a basis from which to infer ability, intelligence, or aptitude. But achievement and aptitude are not the same. Many things other than intellectual ability influence achievement, such as home environment, school environment, and disposition. Inferring level of ability from prior achievement is very risky. Resist this temptation. It is actually one of the things that students do that gets in the way of them believing they can succeed. "I failed at this in the past, so I'm no good at it or not smart enough to succeed at it now." They need us to counter the claim, not factor it into our expectations of their present performance.

> Students need to see evidence that counters the claim "I'm not smart enough."

Third, there is the issue of harm done due to an inaccurate perception of aptitude. What if you label a student as an underachiever on the record and you are wrong? That student may be misclassified for years and suffer serious consequences. Such a misjudgment may well become a self-fulfilling prophecy.

Fourth, is there not a danger of backlash from the student who is labeled as being a bright high achiever? At some point, might this student ask, "Why do I always have to strive for a higher standard to get the same grade as others who have to do less?" Consider the motivational implications for these students.

Fifth, there is the certainty, if we consider aptitude when grading, that the same level of achievement attained by two students in the same class will receive different grades, especially in borderline cases. We know of no one who wants to try to explain this one to those students or their parents.

And, sixth, there is the dilemma of muddled communication. Because different teachers define intelligence or ability or aptitude differently, assess it differently, and factor it into the grade computation equation differently, those who try to interpret the resulting grade later cannot hope to sort out those teachers' intended messages. *What does a "B" mean?* This only works to make our grades useless as communicators.

Should Aptitude Be Included?

To justify incorporating aptitude into a grade, we must be able to take concrete and specific action to overcome all arguments against it. Can we devise a definition of academic aptitude that translates into sound assessment and that promises to treat each student equitably? Perhaps someday but not today. We lack a defensible definition and the measurement tools needed to know students' aptitudes. We can't even say for sure whether it's a stable human characteristic. There is no place for aptitude, ability, or intelligence in the report card grading equation. For now, these problems are insurmountable.

But, you might ask, what about the compelling arguments in favor of this practice? What about our desire to individualize so all students and teachers can be motivated by the potential of success? What about the hope this practice seems to offer to perennial low achievers? Must we set aside these desires? No. We must individualize on the basis of a student characteristic that we can define clearly, assess dependably, and link effectively to learning. There is a far better candidate, a candidate that does not fall prey to the problems we experience in struggling with aptitude or intelligence. That individualizing factor is students' prior achievement.

Think of it this way: if we know where a student stands along the continuum of ascending levels of competence, then we know from our carefully planned continuous-progress curriculum what comes next for that student. Thus, we can tailor instruction to help that student move on to that next step in mastery of knowledge, demonstration of reasoning proficiency, performance of required skills, and/or creation of required products. Each student's success in hitting those next targets, then, becomes the basis for the report card grades we assign. Think of it as a contract between teacher and student where all agree on targets and definition of mastery at the outset and then monitor progress continually together until mastery is achieved.

Effort as a Grading Factor

In this case, the issue is framed as follows: assume two students demonstrate exactly the same level of achievement, and that level happens to be right on the borderline between two grades. If one student obviously tried harder to learn, demonstrated more seriousness of purpose, or exhibited a higher level of motivation than did the other, that student will receive the higher grade. Another example is when a teacher adds (or subtracts) points for any effort-related factor: length of a paper (quantity versus quality), amount of time spent studying or completing a project, evidence of a pattern of conscientiousness, or extra care with neatness. A third example is offering extra credit for extra work without regard to the level of achievement demonstrated. A fourth example is when teachers award extra points when students bring in food for the canned food drive, bedding for the hamster, or tissue boxes.

Rationale for Including Effort Many teachers factor effort into their grading for apparently sound reasons. They see effort as being related to achievement: those who try harder learn more. So by including effort in the grade, in effect, they believe that they are driving students toward greater achievement. This is often also the underlying reason that some teachers factor their interpretation of a student's aptitude into the grade—to reward effort (from the perceived low-aptitude student) and punish lack of it (from the perceived high-aptitude student).

As a society, we value effort in its own right. Those who strive harder contribute more to our collective well-being. School is an excellent place to reinforce what is, after all, one of life's important lessons. A subtle but related reason for factoring effort into the grade is that it appears to encourage risk taking, another characteristic we value in our society. A creative and energetic attempt to reach for something new and better should be rewarded, even if the striving student falls short of actual achievement success. This may be especially important for low achievers, who may not have mastered all of the prerequisite knowledge needed to achieve in their current class. The one thing within their control is how hard they try. Even if students are trapped in a tangle of failure because of their academic history, at least they can derive some rewards for putting forth effort. Thus, the compelling reason for using effort as one factor in grades is to keep students engaged in trying hard.

Reasons Not to Include Effort The first problem we face is that definitions of what it means to "try hard" vary greatly from teacher to teacher. Some definitions are relatively easy to translate into sound assessments, for example, *Those who complete all homework put forth effort.* But other definitions are not, for example, *Trying hard means making positive contributions to the quality of the classroom learning environment.*

Second, some teachers may say student participation in class is an indicator of their level of effort. But who most often controls who gets to contribute in class? The teacher. Even when students are free to speak, lack of contribution cannot be interpreted as lack of involvement. (To be sure, in some classes such as second language studies, oral participation is necessary for learning. We would prefer to regard that as a requirement of the course and not as a variable left up to the student, which is what it comes down to if it defined as effort.)

A third problem with including effort in the grade is that students can manipulate their apparent effort to attain more points. If students know you grade in part on the basis of level of effort shown, they can behave in ways that make you believe they are trying hard, whether they are or not.

A fourth problem crops up when points are awarded for effort in terms of work completion: work completion, rather than learning, becomes students' overarching goal. Whether learning occurs is less important than getting the assignment done and turned in on time. This is an example of the task-completion orientation discussed in Chapter 2. In Figure 11.4, high school science teacher Sara Poeppelman describes how shifts in her grading practices have moved away from rewarding students who "play school well" and toward accurately representing their levels of achievement without sacrificing student motivation to try.

A fifth problem creeps in when we award points for effort in lieu of achievement. The student tried hard but didn't succeed. Rather than identifying and addressing the reasons for lack of success, when we award points for effort and move on, we are sweeping some very real learning issues under the carpet.

A sixth problem is that factoring effort into the grade may send the wrong message to students. In life beyond school, trying hard to do a good job is ultimately not sufficient. If we don't deliver relevant, practical results in the end, we will not be deemed successful, regardless of how hard we try. Besides, from the perspective of basic school philosophy, what is it we really value—achieving or knowing how to make it look like we tried hard? What if the student didn't have to try hard in order to master what we are teaching? That is not the student's fault.

A seventh problem arises when teachers judge students' effort by their level of assertiveness in the learning environment. Those who actively seek teacher attention and participate enthusiastically in learning activities are judged to be motivated. But what about quieter students? Effort is less likely to be exuberantly visible in their behavior regardless of its level. And this also may carry with it gender and/or cultural differences, yielding the potential of systematic bias in grades as a function of factors unrelated to achievement. Members of some groups value cooperation over competition or blending in as opposed to standing out. Such values do not stand in the way of learning and should not stand in the way of attaining a grade reflective of that learning. Gender, ethnicity, and personality traits have no place in the report card grading equation.

And, finally, to the extent that teachers differ in their definition, assessment, and manner of integrating information about effort into the grading equation, we muddle communication once again. *What does a "B" mean?* Those who try to interpret the resulting grade later cannot hope to sort through the variety of teachers' intended messages. This again only works to make our grades ineffective as communicators.

Should Effort Be Included?   First, as a matter of general principle, we can value both effort and achievement. When we value achievement, we define it clearly, assess it accurately, and build our reporting systems to communicate information about it accurately. When we value effort too, we create a mutually acceptable definition, devise

Effort is not reliably induced through the manipulation of grades.

figure 11.4 ■ From the Classroom: Sara Poeppelman

I used to ...

Like many teachers, I used to give summative quizzes and tests and assignments that may or may not have assessed the most important aspects of what the students were supposed to have learned as a result of the instruction that was taking place in my classroom. If the students scored well, that was wonderful for them and if the students did not score well, too bad, and we went on with content that needed to be covered by the end of the year. Breaking down standards into meaningful targets that were useful to the students and myself rarely occurred. Formative assessment? I did not have a clue what that was either and how it could be any more useful than the summative assessments that I was already utilizing.

Grades generally reflected and favored those students who turned in assignments on time and did not really assess students' knowledge and understanding of key science concepts.

Now I ...

Daily, students and I utilize learning targets to move the class toward the critical learning that will result from that day's instruction. Formative assessment is regular and ongoing. Instruction is modified as a result of formative assessments, sometimes for the whole class and sometimes differentiated for groups with specific challenges related to the formative assessment results. Feedback is now king. Students receive frequent feedback and utilize the feedback to make improvements on their work. Grades focus predominantly on student knowledge, skills, and understanding related to the learning targets, rather than being predominantly a measure of which students "played school well."

Why I changed ...

I was at my first training on formative assessment practices, and this just made so much more sense than the way that I had been practicing the art and science of teaching up to that point, especially the importance of feedback rather than "grades." Up to this point in my career, one of the things that really bothered me was that students were often too concerned about their grade rather than what they were learning. As a teacher my philosophy has always been to focus on the learning, but I realized that my assessment practices were not promoting learning and it seemed that use of formative assessment and feedback would be a practical method to promote learning rather than a grade-driven focus.

What I notice as a result ...

As a result of changing my assessment practices (what I assess, how I assess it, what my students or myself do as a result), I have noticed more students are engaged in the process of learning without the focus on the grade. By focusing in on the critical content and skills that I assess and reporting those to derive a final grade, rather than habits, such as turning homework in, I have significantly fewer students who have to be retained. Providing specific feedback with students on the other end attending to that feedback has helped motivate students to attempt to do better on assessments and other challenges in the future. I feel that I am now helping to develop learners who have the skills and confidence to take on challenges with intrinsic motivation rather that students who focus on the "once and done," grade and extrinsic motivation.

Source: Reprinted with permission from Sara Poeppelman, High School Science Teacher, Lewis County Schools, Vanceburg, KY.

appropriate assessment tools and procedures to measure it accurately, and build our reporting systems to communicate about it accurately as well. When we value both enough to track progress on each, we don't combine them into the same grading equation. It's not complicated to devise reporting systems that present separate information on each.

A Note on Assessing Effort   After we define effort, we must assess it well. As we have established, the assessment must arise from a clear target, rely on a proper method of assessment, sample effort in a systematically representative manner, and control for all relevant sources of bias that can distort our assessment and mislead us. But if we use behavioral indicators of students' level of effort and most of the "trying hard" behaviors take place outside of our presence (i.e., at home), how can we know that we are sampling well or controlling for bias?

For example, here's one form of bias that is hard to overcome: when students set out purposely to game the system with respect to their real level of effort, they can seriously bias our assessment. This may be impossible to eliminate as a problem. If we see 30 students per day all day for a year and some are misleading us about their real level of effort, we may well see through it. But as the number approaches and exceeds 150 students for one hour a day and sometimes only for a few months, as it does for many middle and high school teachers, there is no way to confidently and dependably determine how hard each student is trying.

Think about the issue of student motivation. Let's say that you gather undependable evidence and conclude that a student is not trying hard and, in fact, this is incorrect. That student is giving maximum effort but you conclude the opposite. What message does that send to the student? What effect is this turn of events likely to have on her desire to continue trying hard and learn? Also consider the other error. What if you say that a student is trying hard and, in fact, he is not? What message does this send and what impact is that message likely to have?

Moreover, if effort influences the grades of some, equity demands that it have the same influence on all. The assessment and record-keeping challenges required to meet this standard are immense, to say the least. But a more serious challenge again arises from the personality issue. Less outgoing people are not necessarily trying less hard. Quiet effort can be diligent and productive. As teachers, we really do have difficulty knowing how much effort most students are putting forth. And we have few ways of overcoming this problem, especially when most of the effort is expended outside the classroom.

If you can define effort clearly, assess all students consistently, and meet the standards of sound assessment, then gather your data and draw your inferences about each student's level of effort. Just be very careful how you communicate those results at report card grading time.

Compliance as a Grading Factor

The question in this case is, What role should adherence to school and classroom rules play in determining students' report card grades? If two students have demonstrated exactly the same level of achievement, but one disobeys the rules, should that student's grade be lowered? Or if you establish rules and deadlines with which you expect students to comply, should points that are figured into the grade be awarded or deducted for compliance or lack of it?

Rationale for Including Compliance   Consider the kinds of compliance that we absolutely must address. What if students fail to come to school? The law says they must attend. If they're not in class, their learning suffers. The threat of reduced or failing grades can compel attendance, as well as punctuality. Students are expected to learn important lessons of personal responsibility. Fail to come to work for your job after school and you get fired. We can use grades to teach students to show up.

Another problematic behavior that we can address with the threat of grade reduction is cheating. If you cheat on a test, you get a zero. When averaged in at the end of the term, this will have the effect of radically reducing the final average and grade. This punishment will deter cheating and teach an important lesson about dishonesty.

Additionally, without factoring compliance into grading, some teachers have difficulty managing the classroom. Their behavior management system relies on issuing sanctions for misbehavior by connecting compliance with the rules to the grade. In life beyond school, society expects us to follow the rules—to obey our agreed-on laws. It's the way we preserve the social order. Schools are supposed to be conveying to young people the lessons of behavior in a civil culture. Connecting grades to behavior helps us to teach students obedience.

Compliance with the rules does generally lead to greater student learning. As teachers, we know that learning is maximized when everyone does what they are supposed to do. A well-managed class permits everyone to benefit the most. If one or two students fail to follow the rules, everyone's learning opportunities can be reduced.

Finally, although students are not in control of the academic ability that they bring to school, they are in complete control of whether they follow the rules and meet deadlines. If they wish to influence the grades they receive, this is one concrete way for them to do it.

Reasons Not to Include Compliance   Before citing the counterarguments, we need to establish that we agree it is important for students to obey school and class-room rules. Not only can those rules affect student learning, but also they protect student safety and well-being. Surprising as it may seem, that's not the issue in this case. When behaviors such as truancy, tardiness, cheating, and not paying attention in class come up, they spark passionate debate. These behaviors are counterproductive and need to be addressed. But what is the best way to do so? When our desire is to deter students from engaging in these counterproductive behaviors, punishing them through lowered grades does not work for a number of reasons.

First, we don't address the underlying problems of attendance, lateness, academic dishonesty, and attention in class when we give them a consequence and move on. And for too many of our students, the threat of a lowered grade does nothing to change the behavior.

Second, the accuracy of the information about student achievement contained within the grade suffers and miscommunication is assured. Let's say a student has taken four of five exams during a grading period and averaged 93 percent correct across all of them. Then this student is accused of sharing answers with another student on the fifth exam and is given a zero. If we wanted to communicate accurately about the achievement of this student, we would assign an A on the report card to deliver a message to all message receivers of almost total mastery of the material.

However, when we factor the zero into the average, the result is 74 percent (93 times 4 on the first four exams plus zero on the fifth exam equals 374, divided by 5 equals 74), or a C on the report card. The effect is a misrepresentation of the student's actual level of achievement—intentional miscommunication. We have no way to let the various message receivers know the subtle message hidden in this grade.

Third, if every teacher defines standards of compliance differently, gathers evidence of different sorts, and gives compliance issues different weight when determining their particular grades, message receivers will always have difficulty determining what the report card grade communicates about level of achievement. *What does a "B" mean?*

Should Compliance Be Included?   We agree that unacceptable behaviors should be addressed and minimized or eliminated if possible. Sometimes stiff penalties should be imposed. However, the decisions that will be made based on the achievement information contained in report card grades are too important to permit that information's accuracy to be sacrificed by lowering grades as punishment for behaviors unrelated to actual achievement.

There is strong legal precedent for this stance. Many states have passed laws that disallow grading policies that, for example, permit grade reduction for poor attendance. You should check for such laws in any state in which you teach. Let us hasten to add that the courts also have upheld the school's right to administer consequences for violating truancy laws. It's just that the punishment cannot lead to a distortion of the student's record of achievement. The courts compel us to separate the punishment, whatever that is, from our achievement records. In the case of cheating cited here, the school is justified in administering fair punishment. But that punishment cannot involve the student's academic record. The only acceptable action is to administer another fifth exam, average the resulting score with the other four, and assign the grade indicated by that average.

When the use of grade reduction as punishment has the effect of distorting the student's academic record, we violate the student's *constitutional* guarantees to equal access to future educational opportunities (Bartlett, 1987). We have many appropriate punishment options at our disposal that don't distort the record and violate student rights, including detention, limiting access to desirable activities, community service, and so on. There is no need to sacrifice the accuracy of the academic record.

Communicate about Achievement Only in the Academic Grade

When we use evidence of achievement as the sole basis for determining students' report card grades, in effect, our contract with students says that their grade will reflect what they have learned with respect to preestablished learning targets. The content standards that comprise the work of the grading period will be the basis for standards-based teaching, standards-based assessing, and standards-based reporting. This is what it means to be *standards based: a "B" should reflect a student's level of achievement on a given set of content standards*. Period.

Report on Other Factors Separately

Attendance, classroom behavior, academic honesty, work completion habits, skills of cooperation, and the like are valued outcomes of schooling. Many reporting systems have a place for this information on the report card. However, as you know, the report card is no place for your best guess at reporting time. If we value these factors in our own classrooms, we must clearly define them, teach them, plan to help students improve them, and track them. When we have done that, we can report student progress on them. However, as we have seen, when we figure one or more of these factors into the academic grade, the meaning of the academic grade is lost and so is the message about the degree of presence or absence of whichever factors we are including.

A Word about Grading in a Cooperative Learning Context

In brief: don't do it. The rule is this—report card grades must provide dependable information about the actual achievement of the student to whom they are assigned. This means that, even in contexts where students cooperate during learning, assessments must yield a clear and unencumbered indication of how well each individual student mastered the desired learning target. Only evidence derived in this way should contribute to determining each student's report card grade.

MyEdLab **Self-Check 11.2**

MyEdLab **Application Exercise 11.2** Selecting information to include in the report card

---

■ Summarizing Assessment Information

Now that we have addressed the purpose of grades (to communicate) and the information to be included (achievement only), we can turn our attention to selecting and combining information into one summary score.

The summarizing process picks up where we left off in Chapter 9. As you recall, we recommended that you first decide what information will be used summatively and what will be used formatively. We discussed systems that you can use to differentiate the two in your record book. Then we presented four record-keeping guidelines:

- Record formative and summative assessment information separately.
- Organize entries in the gradebook according to the learning targets represented.

- Keep track of information about work habits and social skills separately from achievement information.
- Record achievement information by raw score, when possible.

By following the guidelines in Chapter 9, your data will be organized so that you can easily convert them to a common scale, weight them as desired, and combine them to arrive at one overall number. Now we examine five steps in the process of summarizing grades as shown in Figure 11.5.

figure 11.5 ■ Process for Summarizing Grades

Step 1: Use the Most Current Information

Step 2: Verify Accuracy of Data

Step 3: Convert Entries to a Common Scale

Step 4: Weight Information as Needed

Step 5: Combine Information Thoughtfully

Step 1: Use the Most Current Information

Your records may include multiple assessments measuring the same learning target. In a standards-based environment, grade reports must reflect our best measure of student achievement at the time they are completed. If more recent information about student achievement on a given learning target shows a higher level of learning, then the report card grade should be based on the newer evidence. Averaging the newer information with the old, outdated information has the effect of lowering the grade for the student who had the farthest to come and did so. It provides an incorrect picture of student achievement at that point in time, which can lead to ill-informed instructional and support decisions. It also reinforces the notion that it's better to already know than to learn. Grading expert Ken O'Connor (2011) reminds us it's not where a student starts on a given learning target that matters at grading time but where the student finishes. Let the formative assessment record clearly show progress and growth and include that in conferencing about student achievement, but let the report card grade communicate about level of achievement at the end of the grading period.

As an example, let's say your assessment plan includes five unit assessments focused on particular standards and a comprehensive final exam that covers the entire set of standards for the grading period. A particular student starts slowly, scoring very low on the first two unit assessments, but gains momentum and attains a strong score on the comprehensive final exam, revealing, in effect, subsequent mastery of the standards covered in those first two unit assessments. The key grading question is the following: Which piece of information provides the most accurate depiction of that student's real achievement at the end of the grading period, the final exam score or that score averaged with all five unit tests? If the final is truly comprehensive, averaging it with those first two unit assessments will produce a misleading result.

If students demonstrate achievement at any time that, in effect, renders past assessment information inaccurate, then you must drop the former assessment from the record and replace it with the new—even if the new information reflects a lower level of achievement. To do otherwise is to misrepresent that achievement. However, a better solution is to give a practice form of the final and use the process explained in Chapter 5 wherein students identify what they have mastered, what they need to brush up on, and what they still need to focus on. Give them a few days (or as much time as you can) to review their targeted problems before administering the final exam. That way, if the problem of forgetting has crept in, they can refresh their memory. If the problem is that they hadn't mastered it even though the earlier assessment indicated they had, there is time to rectify that, too.

Step 2: Verify Accuracy of Evidence

As we identify which assessment evidence provides the most recent indication of mastery of a given learning target, it is a good idea to confirm its accuracy. Discard any inaccurate information from grading records. (And remember that outdated information is inaccurate information at grading time.) No one has yet developed an information management and communication system that can convert inaccurate information—misinformation about a student's achievement—into an accurate grade. Chapters 1–8 offer the guidance you need to ensure that accuracy.

Step 3: Convert Entries to a Common Scale

Once you have identified which information you will use, you will need to convert each score to a common scale. You may have recorded summative information in a variety of forms: raw scores, percentages, rubric scores, letters, and/or other evaluative symbols.

If your entries are in the form of raw scores (number correct out of number possible) and percentages (percent correct), we recommend two traditional combination procedures. You can convert all scores to percentages or you can convert all entries to raw scores. In either case, remember to use only the most current available evidence and to make sure you have enough evidence to sample the learning targets adequately. If the target in question requires use of rubric scores, you will want to follow an additional procedure, explained in the section "Converting Rubric Scores to Grades" later in this chapter. If you have letters or other symbols as summative data, you will need to go back to the underlying assessments and replace the letters or symbols with raw scores, percentages, or rubric scores.

Step 4: Weight Information as Needed

If you wish to give greater weight to some assessment results than to others, you can accomplish this by multiplying those scores by a weighting factor. For instance, if one score is to count twice as much as others, the weighting factor for that score is 2. Simply multiply the score by two before moving on to the next steps of combining information.

An additional consideration in applying weights to grades is the structure of the grade report. Will you figure one grade to cover all of the learning targets you taught in a subject or does your report card grade have separate categories within the subject? As a preservice teacher-to-be you will not know this now, but when you get your first job, you will need to find this out at the beginning of the grading period. It will help you to set up your record book so your data are tracked according to those categories. If you will be reporting in several categories, first apply the weighting factors as desired for the data in each category. If, in addition, you must combine those grades into a single summary grade, determine if and how the categories will be weighted.

Step 5: Combine Information Thoughtfully

Using the appropriate measure of central tendency—mean or median—for the type of data, combine information from assessments into a final grade. (Figure 11.5 provides definitions and examples of mean and median.) We traditionally combine individual pieces of achievement evidence into a final summary by calculating the mean. When the data are consistent—that is, when they fall within a narrow score range—the mean will yield an accurate representation of level of achievement. But when data include extreme scores—when they collectively span a range of score points—calculating the mean will skew the resulting score, as shown in Figure 11.6. To counter this problem, many grading experts advocate using median scores rather than mean scores to summarize achievement. O'Connor (2011) encourages us to think of this process as *determining* a grade rather than *calculating* it because the measure of central tendency should be chosen to suit the data at hand.

figure 11.6 ■ Measures of Central Tendency

Here is a set of numbers from a precalculus student's quarter grade report. Notice how the summary score derived changes according to the measure of central tendency.

55, 80, 42, 89, 83, 85, 91, 70, 91

Term	Definition	Result
Mean	The average score	76.2
Median	The middle score	83

Source: Chappuis, Jan; Stiggins, Rick J.; Chappuis, Steve; Arter, Judith A., *Classroom Assessment for Student learning: Doing it Right - Using it Well*, 2nd Ed., ©2012. Reprinted and Electronically reproduced by permission of Pearson Education, Inc., New York, New York.

MyEdLab **Self-Check 11.3**
MyEdLab **Application Exercise 11.3** Summarizing assessment information for the report card

■ Converting Rubric Scores to Grades

In Chapter 7 we established that rubrics are useful as formative assessment tools to help students understand and master complex learning targets. They can also be used summatively to assign a grade or determine level of student mastery of key standards. In this section we describe how to convert ratings from rubrics to grades or to mastery levels.

To begin, any rubrics used to evaluate student work for grading (summative) purposes need to satisfy the quality criteria described in detail in Chapter 7. If those standards of quality are not met, then the resulting grade is not likely to provide an accurate reflection of the student's achievement.

The transformation of rubric ratings into grades, like so much of the classroom assessment process, involves a major helping of professional judgment. The challenge is to turn a profile of several ratings for each student into a single grade in a consistent manner that ensures accuracy and complete understanding by the grade recipient. There are two ways to do this. One relies on average ratings and the other on defining patterns of ratings.

Note at the outset that these processes can be applied either in assigning a grade to (1) a summative assessment during the grading period that will later be combined with other evidence to feed the determination of a final grade or (2) a "final exam" assessment that is the culminating demonstration of proficiency on which the final grade will be based.

Average Ratings

For each student, calculate the average rating (the mean) of ratings across the profile of scales within the rubric. The average rating is the total of the ratings the student received divided by the total number of ratings. What we're doing here is figuring out the typical rating by calculating an average. We want to know what the ratings taken together tell us about how well the student performs. For grading purposes, use only the scores from work toward the end of the grading period to determine a grade for a given content standard because the later scores will be more representative of the student's current achievement level.

Look at the rubric and decide logically what range of average ratings would match to each grade or level of mastery. (Grades and levels of mastery are accompanied by an explanation of what each level means in terms of achievement, so use those descriptions to make your determination.) We recommend that you work with your teaching colleagues to make sure you have considered your judgment carefully. Then create a conversion table that stipulates the range for each grade or level of mastery. Use the table to determine the appropriate grade for each student. Figure 11.7 illustrates one way to convert average ratings from a four-point rubric into a summary grade and into a percentage. (If you need to combine rubric information with other kinds of assessment information, you will need the percentage information, as explained in the following section.)

figure 11.7 ■ Logical Grade Conversion Table for Average Ratings

Rubric Rating Average	*Logical Grade* Conversion	*Logical Percentage* Conversion
3.5–4.0	A	95%
2.9–3.4	B	85%
2.3–2.8	C	75%
1.7–2.2	D	65%
1.6 and below	F	55%

Source: Chappuis, Jan; Stiggins, Rick J.; Chappuis, Steve; Arter, Judith A., *Classroom Assessment for Student learning: Doing it Right - Using it Well,* 2nd Ed., ©2012. Reprinted and Electronically reproduced by permission of Pearson Education, Inc., New York, New York.

Identifying a Pattern of Ratings

The second option is to work with a team of teaching colleagues to fashion a means for converting profiles of ratings on each particular assessment into grades. First, for example, we decide that to get an A, the preponderance of student work has to be at the highest level of ratings. So we decide that at least 50 percent of the ratings must be a 4 on a set of four-point rubrics. From here, the team established the pattern of ratings needed for each of the other grades, creating a conversion table to be used consistently in assigning grades. Figure 11.8 illustrates one way to use the *pattern of ratings* option to create a conversion table for linking student scores to grades.

figure 11.8 ■ Logical Conversion Table for Patterns of Ratings

If the student's pattern of ratings is:	The *logical grade* is:	The *logical percentage* is:
At least 50% of the ratings are 4, and not more than 5% are lower than 3	A	95%
75% of the ratings are 3 or better, and no more than 5% are lower than 2	B	85%
40% of the ratings are 2 or better and no more than 5% are lower than 2	C	75%
40% of the ratings are 2 or better and no more than 50% are lower than 2	D	65%
More than 50% of the ratings are lower than 2	F	50%

Source: Chappuis, Jan; Stiggins, Rick J.; Chappuis, Steve; Arter, Judith A., *Classroom Assessment for Student learning: Doing it Right - Using it Well,* 2nd Ed., ©2012. Reprinted and Electronically reproduced by permission of Pearson Education, Inc., New York, New York.

You will notice in both conversion charts (Figures 11.7 and 11.8) that the percentages are a somewhat simplified representation of the range of scores that each grade represents. When using or reporting percentages rather than grades, we recommend that you create a more precise equation table, such as that shown in Figure 11.9. Note that the grade-to-percentage conversions in Figures 11.7, 11.8, and 11.9 are intended as examples. We encourage you to work with your colleagues to devise conversions that match your expectations. These become the preset standards you can share with students and parents to help them understand how the numbers or individual summative assessments will be used to determine a final grade.

figure 11.9 ■ Grade to Percentage Conversion Table for a Four-Level Rubric

Rubric Rating Average	*Logical Grade* Conversion	*Logical Percentage* Conversion
3.9–4.0	A+	99
3.7–3.8	A	95
3.5–3.6	A–	91
3.3–3.4	B+	88
3.1–3.2	B	85
2.9–3.0	B–	81
2.7–2.8	C+	78
2.5–2.6	C	75
2.3–2.4	C–	71
2.1–2.2	D+	68
1.9–2.0	D	65
1.7–1.8	D–	61
1.5–1.6	F	55
1.3–1.4	F	48
1.0–1.2	F	40

Source: Chappuis, Jan; Stiggins, Rick J.; Chappuis, Steve; Arter, Judith A., *Classroom Assessment for Student learning: Doing it Right - Using it Well*, 2nd Ed., ©2012. Reprinted and Electronically reproduced by permission of Pearson Education, Inc., New York, New York.

To set this up appropriately and apply it consistently, obviously the underlying ratings need to provide an accurate reflection of the student's achievement and the conversion must be done consistently. This requires that each teacher possess sufficient knowledge of levels of quality represented in the rubric to assign scores accurately and consistently with other teachers. You will be able to do this if you practice doing it with your colleagues over the first few years of your teaching career. Then in the following years you will be able to help new teachers develop this expertise. It is a part of becoming a better teacher every year.

■ Combining Rubric Ratings with Other Assessment Information

To illustrate this straightforward four-step process, we'll use the scores of one student, Isaiah.

Step 1: Use the logical conversion table you have created to convert the rubric scores to a logical percentage. Let's say you have done this for Isaiah's rubric scores and his logical percentage is 85 percent.

Step 2: For the "nonrubric" portion of the grade, determine one final percentage that represents the assessment information from other sources. Let's say you gave several selected response tests that each yielded a percent correct score. You have combined these percentages using the measure of central tendency that best fits the data and Isaiah's resulting score is 93 percent.

Step 3: Decide if the rubric percentage (from Step 1) will have the same weight as the nonrubric percentage (from Step 2). More? Less? Assign a weighting factor as appropriate. Assume for Isaiah's class that you want the rubric percentage to count twice as much as the nonrubric percentage (because you have deemed the learning targets represented in each merit that relative importance). So the weighting factor for the rubric percentage would be 2.

Step 4: Use the weighting factor to combine the rubric percentage with the nonrubric percentage. Combine the weighted percentages to determine a final average. In Isaiah's case, it would look like the following (we'll add the rubric percentage of 85 twice to reflect its weighting factor):

$$(85 + 85 + 93) \div 3 = 263$$

$$263 \div 3 = 88\%$$

Isaiah's combined final score is 88 percent.

Figure 11.10 summarizes the recommendations for converting rubric scores to grades.

figure 11.10 ■ Recommendations for Converting Rubric Scores to Grades

1. *Don't convert rubric scores to letter grades at all if you can help it.* The descriptions associated with each score point give a clearer picture of students' level of achievement.

2. *Use a decision rule to convert a set of rubric scores to a final grade.* Look at the rubric and decide what level on the rubric describes "excellent work," "good work," "fair work," and "poor work." Then come up with a decision rule for combining the rubric scores.

3. *Replace out-of-date evidence with more recent evidence.* Keep in mind, however, that you still need a large enough sample of work to provide a stable estimate of achievement.

4. *Be careful when combining rubric scores with percentage information to form a final grade.* Decide how much weight the percentage and rating portions of the grade will get. Combine letter grades directly using these weights. Or use a decision rule to convert the resulting rubric grade back to a percentage and then combine the percentage with other percentage scores using your weighting scheme.

Source: Chappuis, Jan; Stiggins, Rick J.; Chappuis, Steve; Arter, Judith A., *Classroom Assessment for Student learning: Doing it Right - Using it Well*, 2nd Ed., ©2012. Reprinted and Electronically reproduced by permission of Pearson Education, Inc., New York, New York.

■ Reporting the Final Grade

Reporting the final percentage score on the report card has the benefit of preserving some detail about a student's level of achievement, but most districts require teachers to convert the academic achievement summary score to a letter grade, a number grade (e.g., 4, 3, 2, 1), or a proficiency scale (E=Exceeds, M=Meets, etc.). Standards for setting cutoffs vary from district to district, school to school, or in some cases, teacher to teacher. The range for an A in some places may be 94 to 100 percent, for example, and in others it may be 89 to 100 percent.

Although these differences cannot be eliminated, we can acknowledge the lack of precision they carry and wok to ensure consistency in our own organizations. It is also important to communicate to parents in commonsense terms the level of achievement represented by each of our report card symbols. Figure 11.11 shows a common rule for converting percentages to letter grades. Your school or district will most likely have an agreed-on conversion rule that allows all teachers to translate summary numbers into your report card's symbols with consistency.

Keep the Link to Learning Targets

Keep the big communication picture in mind as you think about reporting. The grading process begins with you articulating a set of achievement expectations in the form of clear learning targets. You then carefully translate these standards into high-quality assessments capable of informing you about how well each student has mastered each standard. You keep achievement records classified by learning target.

figure 11.11 ■ For Example: Rule for Converting Percentages to Letter Grades

A+	= 97–100%	C	= 73–76%
A	= 93–96%	C–	= 70–72%
A–	= 90–92%	D+	= 67–69%
B+	= 87–89%	D	= 63–66%
B	= 83–86%	D–	= 60–62%
B–	= 80–82%	F	= 59% and below
C+	= 77–79%		

Source: Chappuis, Jan; Stiggins, Rick J.; Chappuis, Steve; Arter, Judith A., *Classroom Assessment for Student learning: Doing it Right - Using it Well*, 2nd Ed., ©2012. Reprinted and Electronically reproduced by permission of Pearson Education, Inc., New York, New York.

Finally you combine evidence of learning across assessments into a summary grade. But that grade isn't merely a summary of scores. It is also a summary of student success at mastering the standards reflected in your assessments. For this reason and given the records you have kept, we strongly recommend that whenever you report a grade, that grade be accompanied by a listing of these standards, indicating which ones the student did and did not master. This link brings the reporting process full circle from expectations to achievement and adds to the clarity of the message the grade is intended to communicate.

Inform Students in Advance of Your Grading Procedures

MyEdLab
Video Example 11.1
Grading Revisited

One final critically important guideline to follow is to be sure all students know and understand in advance the procedures you will use to derive their grades. What assessments will you conduct, when, and how will you factor each into your grading? What are students' time lines, deadlines, and important responsibilities? If students know their responsibilities up front, they have a better chance of succeeding. Watch Video Example 11.1 to hear students and teachers discuss the impact of grading practices that allow for learning prior to summative evaluation.

MyEdLab **Application Exercise 11.4** Combining rubric ratings and assessment information to determine final grades

■ Summary: Communicating with Report Card Grades

For the foreseeable future, parents and communities still expect their children to be assigned report card grades in school, especially at high school levels. They know, as we should too, that grades will play a key role in decisions that influence students' lives. This may not remain true forever, because we are constantly struggling with the limitations of grades as a communication system. But it is true now. This means our challenge is to do the very best job we can of assigning accurate, interpretable grades.

In an era of standards-driven schools, if report card grades are to serve decision makers, they must reflect student attainment of the specific knowledge, reasoning, skill, and product creation achievement targets leading up to state or local standards. Only then can we teachers, for example, know where students are now in relation to where we want to take them. For this reason, grading systems must include indicators of student achievement unencumbered by other student characteristics, such as aptitude, effort, and compliance. This is not to say that we should not report information about factors other than achievement, if definition and assessment difficulties can be overcome, which is no small challenge. But under any circumstances, aptitude, intelligence, and ability have no place in grade reporting.

The reference point for interpreting a report card grade should always be the specific material to be learned. Students deserve to know in advance how you will accomplish this in their class, and they need to know the standards you expect them to meet. If you are assessing characteristics other than achievement, you must follow appropriate rules of sound assessment and should report results separately from achievement grades.

As you conduct assessments and accumulate results, you must take care to record as much detail about student achievement as is available. To be sure, nearly all of this useful detail ultimately will be sacrificed by the necessity of communicating the rich complexity of student achievement in the form of a single letter grade. But don't give up the detail until you absolutely must. And when report card grading time arrives, share as much of the detail as you can with your students, so they understand what is behind the single little symbol that appears on the report card. Then boil the richness of your detail away only grudgingly.

Grades are not the primary reason for assessment and they are not the primary purpose of education. As you formulate your own grading guidelines, keep in mind the goal of standards-based education: to teach, assess, improve, and communicate about student learning in relation to academic learning standards. Remember that while teaching, learning, and improving all require formative assessment information, they do not require grading. However, if we are going to grade student work, we also need to keep in mind that the first audience for grades is the students themselves and for them it is personal. Their learning *is* harmed when we adopt unexamined or ill-informed grading practices. Few people choose to become teachers because of the lure of assessment—grading may not be why you are becoming a teacher, but doing it accurately *will* contribute to student well-being, which is surely a part of every teacher's desire.

■ Suggested Activities

End-of-chapter activities are intended to help you master the chapter's learning targets. They are designed to deepen your understanding of the chapter content, provide opportunities for personal reflection on ideas presented, and serve as a basis for discussion among peers. You may wish to do all of them or select those that you believe will be most useful to your learning. Each activity is correlated to one or more chapter learning targets to help with your selection.

Chapter 11 Learning Targets

As a result of your study of Chapter 11, you will be able to do the following:

1. Understand the purpose for report card grades
2. Select information about a student's current level of academic achievement for inclusion in the report card grade
3. Summarize assessment information accurately
4. Combine rubric ratings with other assessment information to arrive at an accurate, fair, and defensible end-of-term grade

Chapter 11 Activities

Activity 11.1   Keeping a Reflective Journal (All chapter learning targets)

Activity 11.2   Connecting Your Own Experience to Grading Beliefs (Learning Target 1)

Activity 11.3   Reflecting on the Purpose for Grades (Learning Target 1)

Activity 11.4   Developing Alternative Solutions to Behavior Problems (Learning Target 2)

Activity 11.5   Reflecting on the Five Steps for Summarizing Achievement Information (Learning Target 3)

Activity 11.6   Reflecting on Recommendations for Incorporating Rubric Scores into the Grade (Learning Target 4)

Activity 11.7   Comparing Your Experiences with Information from the Chapter (All chapter learning targets)

Activity 11.8   Answering an Interview Question (All chapter learning targets)

Activity 11.9   Reflecting on Your Learning from Chapter 11 (All chapter learning targets)

Activity 11.10   Adding to Your Growth Portfolio (All chapter learning targets)

Activity 11.1: Keeping a Reflective Journal

Keep a record of your thoughts, questions, and insights as you read Chapter 11.

Activity 11.2: Connecting Your Own Experiences to Grading Beliefs

After reading the section "What Is the Purpose for Grades?" identify a grading practice you have encountered as a student that may have derived in part from one of the two underlying beliefs described. Explain its effects, if any, on your motivation and/or your subsequent learning.

Activity 11.3: Reflecting on the Purpose for Grades

After reading the section "What Is the Purpose for Grades?" write a short explanation of each of the three purposes described. Then explain in your own words why grades should only be used to communicate.

Activity 11.4: Developing Alternative Solutions to Behavior Problems

After reading the section "Communicate about What?" turn back to Chapter 9 and read the section "Guideline 3: Keep Track of Work Habits and Social Skills Separately from Achievement Information." Then complete the following activity individually, with a partner, or with a small group.

1. Select one problem to focus on: missing work, late work, academic dishonesty (cheating), or attendance.
2. List the interventions and consequences currently in place in a local school for the problem.
3. Identify which consequences, if any, involve lowering the grade.
4. If you were to remove the "lowered-grade" consequence for the problem, what interventions might you plan to help the student improve? What consequence might you institute to deter students from engaging in the problem behavior? Discuss with a partner or your group and write an explanation of what you believe will be an effective intervention and an appropriate consequence.

Activity 11.5: Reflecting on the Five Steps for Summarizing Achievement Information

After reading the section "Summarizing Assessment Information," reflect on the information given for each step. What new ideas did you encounter? What questions, if any, do you have about the step? How does the step contribute to the accuracy of the final grade?

Step	New Ideas	Questions	Contribution to Accuracy
1. Use most current information.			
2. Verify accuracy of data.			
3. Convert entries to a common scale.			
4. Weight information as needed.			
5. Combine information thoughtfully.			

Activity 11.6: Reflecting on Recommendations for Incorporating Rubric Scores into the Grade

After reading the sections "Converting Rubric Scores to Grades" and "Combining Rubric Ratings with Other Assessment Information," write a short reflection on the processes described: What new ideas did you encounter? What questions do you have? How will you use this information when you begin teaching?

Activity 11.7: Comparing Your Experiences with Information from the Chapter

Read one of the "From the Classroom" entries in Chapter 11 and compare it to your experience as a student.

How is it similar?
What differences do you notice?
What conclusions about the benefits of formative assessment might you draw?

Activity 11.8: Answering an Interview Question

Imagine that you are about to interview for a teaching position. The interview team (often a combination of administrators and teachers) is interested in understanding your level of classroom assessment literacy. Review Chapter 11's learning targets and think about what concepts and procedures were most significant to you from the chapter. Then think about what type of question an interview team might ask related to this significant learning. Write the question and draft a short response—one that you could give in one to two minutes orally.

Activity 11.9: Reflecting on Your Learning from Chapter 11

Review the Chapter 11 learning targets and select one that struck you as most significant from this chapter. Write a short reflection that captures your current understanding. If you are working with a group, discuss what you have written.

Activity 11.10: Adding to Your Growth Portfolio

Any of the activities from this chapter can be used as portfolio entries. Select any activity you have completed or artifact you have created that will demonstrate your mastery of the Chapter 11 learning targets:

1. Understand the purpose for report card grades
2. Select information about a student's current level of academic achievement for inclusion in the report card grade
3. Summarize assessment information accurately
4. Combine rubric ratings with other assessment information to arrive at an accurate, fair, and defensible end-of-term grade

Effective Communication with Conferences

Chapter 12 Learning Targets

As a result of your study of Chapter 12, you will be able to do the following:

1. Select conference options best suited to your students' and their parents' needs
2. Prepare for, conduct, and debrief feedback and goal-setting conferences
3. Prepare for, conduct, and debrief achievement conferences
4. Prepare for, conduct, and debrief intervention conferences

Scene: A classroom in the late afternoon at the end of the term
Players: Sixth-grade student Anna, her teacher Mr. Doe, and Anna's father and mother

> Anna: *Hi Mom and Dad. This is my teacher, Mr. Doe. We're going to talk about my work. Here's my math folder and here is my work.* (She slowly flips through pages of assignments, quizzes, and tests with grades and comments sprinkled throughout.)
>
> Dad: *Looks good, Anna.*
>
> Mom: *What does your work tell you?*
>
> Anna: *That I'm doing okay? This is my social studies folder. . . .*

This vignette, a true story, illustrates the reason that conferencing is the subject of the last chapter in this book. Conferences, especially those involving the student, can be used to communicate about all important aspects of a student's education. And they can do so in a far richer manner than that afforded by report cards and grades. The intention in Anna's conference was good. However, the outcome in this instance was less than satisfying for all participants. The purpose for the conference wasn't clear. In fact, Anna thought the purpose was to "share my folders." The learning targets at the heart of her work samples were not clear to Anna or to her parents. And so the evidence she shared lacked sufficient context to communicate in any meaningful way about her learning.

To engage successfully in any conference, you must be prepared—prepared with a purpose, with a learning focus, and with appropriate evidence to be shared in a manner that promotes understanding. If students are a part of the conference, they

figure 12.1 ■ Keys to Quality Assessment

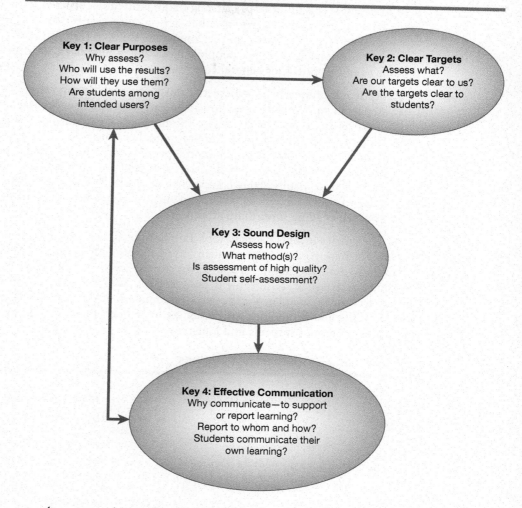

must be prepared as well and in these same terms. In Chapter 12, we conclude our examination of Key 4: Effective Communication (Figure 12.1) by explaining the different conference options available to us and how to prepare for and conduct each successfully to meet the information needs of all participants.

■ Conference Options

All conferences involve sharing information—they can be a communication tool in both formative and summative contexts. Conferences are formative in nature when the purpose is to give or receive feedback, to set goals for further learning, or to note progress toward mastery. They are summative when the purpose is to share the student's current status in terms of learning that has already occurred. If the conference leads to a course correction or further action with respect to learning that has already taken place, the nature of the conference shifts to formative. While there are as many variations as there are people conducting conferences, we can think of the options as falling into four general categories:

1. Feedback conferences, where the purpose is to identify strengths and next steps in a student's progress toward mastery of one or more learning targets
2. Goal-setting conferences, where the purpose is to consider current learning status and set short-term or long-term goals for learning
3. Achievement conferences, where the purpose is to share details about student growth over time, share details about a student's level of achievement at a point in time, or to demonstrate competence or mastery of selected learning targets
4. Intervention conferences, where the purpose is to address one or more areas of concern needing immediate attention

The entries on this list may look familiar. Feedback, self-assessment, and goal setting are major parts of student-involved assessment practices, as described in Chapter 2. And in Chapter 10, we described how to set up portfolios that will become the basis of achievement conferences. While all successful conferences adhere to basic principles of effective communication, the range of purposes represented on the list will require a different set of artifacts (summarized in Figure 12.2) as well as differing protocols and logistics.

figure 12.2 ■ Conference Options

Type	Purpose	Materials Needed
Feedback	■ To identify strengths and areas for continued learning	■ Learning target(s) and rubrics/other tools describing levels of quality, if applicable ■ One or more work samples
Goal Setting	■ To set short- or long-term goals for learning mastery	■ Learning target(s) and rubrics/other tools describing levels of quality, if applicable ■ One or more work samples/growth, project, or achievement portfolio ■ Student self-assessment
Achievement	■ To share growth over time ■ To share level of achievement at a point in time ■ To demonstrate competence or mastery of selected learning targets	■ Learning target(s) and rubrics/other tools describing levels of quality, if applicable ■ Work samples/growth, project, achievement, or celebration portfolio ■ Student self-reflections ■ Other student- or teacher-maintained records of student learning status
Intervention	■ To address one or more areas of concern	■ Learning target(s) or description of expectations ■ Evidence illustrating current status and issue(s) of concern

MyEdLab **Application Exercise 12.1** Selecting conference options

■ Feedback Conferences

As you recall from Chapter 2, offering descriptive feedback is Strategy 3 of the seven strategies of assessment for learning. Remember also from Chapter 2, feedback is most effective when it does the following: directs attention to the learning, occurs during the learning, addresses at least partial understanding, requires students to think, and limits corrective guidance to what the student can act on in a given amount of time (Figure 12.3). In subsequent chapters you read suggestions for offering written feedback with selected response assessment results (Chapter 5), written response assessment results (Chapter 6), and performance assessment results (Chapter 7). Sometimes, however, offering feedback in person is preferable to providing it in writing. And students can be taught to offer each other face-to-face feedback as well.

The Purpose for a Feedback Conference

In a feedback conference, students receive someone else's opinion about strengths and areas for improvement in their work. The primary purpose, whether it is the teacher or another student who is offering the feedback, is to offer information that will provide students insight so they can increase their learning, as demonstrated by improving their work. When the teacher is the feedback provider, a secondary purpose is to model the kind of thinking students will engage in when they begin to self-assess and set goals ("What did I do well? What still needs work?").

Prerequisites   There are prerequisites that must be in place for feedback to cause further learning. First, students must understand the learning target(s) at the focus of the discussion (Strategy 1 of the seven strategies). Second, they must have had

figure 12.3 ■ Characteristics of Effective Feedback

1. Directs attention to the intended learning, pointing out strengths and offering specific information to guide improvement

2. Occurs during learning, while there is still time to act on it

3. Addresses partial understanding

4. Does not do the thinking for the student

5. Limits corrective information to the amount of advice the student can act on

practice assessing samples representing a range of performance levels (Strategy 2). And, although we generally think of the teacher as the source of feedback, when students have a clear vision of the intended learning (Strategy 1) and have had sufficient practice discussing the quality of a range of work samples (Strategy 2), they can be quite effective in providing feedback to one another.

Materials Needed

Because the focus of a feedback conference is generally to examine current evidence of progress toward a learning target (or a small number of learning targets), you will need one or a few work samples that provide evidence of what the student's strengths and needs are with respect to the learning target. It is helpful for the student and you to have the learning target and any rubrics or explanations of desired quality to refer to during the conference.

The Protocol for a Feedback Conference

We encourage you to ask students to prepare for a feedback conference by thinking first about what their strengths and areas of need are. This serves several important purposes. First, it develops the habit of thinking about the quality of the work itself, not just assignment requirements or deadlines, as they do their work. Second, it activates prior knowledge. When students have thought first, they are far more likely to be prepared to understand your comments when you give them—they aren't coming out of the blue. Third, when students think first, your response to their comments about their own work may affirm their evaluation in the form of "I agree," or "in addition . . . ," or redirect them as in "On the contrary . . .". Fourth, it causes the conference to take considerably less time. Fifth, it gives you insight into who understands the vision of quality they are working toward and who doesn't. Those who don't yet have it are candidates for further instruction before moving on to independent work with your feedback. What additional benefits come to mind? The form shown in Figure 12.4 is an example of what students might complete prior to meeting with you or another student for feedback.

First, in the blank next to "Feedback Focus," students write the exact learning target (e.g., "summarize a passage"), the portion of the learning target you will be focusing on, or an aspect of quality from a rubric. For example, if you are offering feedback on their writing, you may only be commenting on their word choice for this draft. So they write "Word choice" as shorthand for the rubric for word choice, which, at its highest level, defines the learning target.

Second, students identify what they believe to be their strengths with respect to the learning target. What parts do they think they have accomplished or done well? Then they examine their work samples to determine what still needs improvement. The "stair step" graphic is intended to help them see that this is not just "what's wrong" but "what's next"—what still needs some work?

Then students meet with you or with a peer to share their judgments. The student talks first. While the student is talking, the teacher listens without interrupting.

figure 12.4 ■ For Example: Feedback Conference Form

Name: _____ Date: _____

Assignment: _____ Feedback Focus: _____

My Judgment:

★ What I did well: _____

_____

_____

⌐ What I need to work on: _____

_____

_____

Feedback:

★ What I did well: _____

_____

_____

⌐ What I need to work on: _____

_____

_____

My Plan

What I will do to improve my learning: _____

_____

_____

_____

If the student has difficulty coming up with reasons for the judgment, you can ask questions such as "Can you show me where in your work you see this?" When the student has finished explaining his or her judgments and reasons, you can share any additional thoughts about strengths and areas for further work. When you have finished (or while you are talking), the student writes a summary of what you said on the form. The teacher doesn't write on the form—only the student. (For younger students who are not yet reading or writing connected text, the conference can be conducted completely orally without writing.)

Last, either with you or after the conclusion of the conference, students think about their comments and your feedback to determine what action they will take. These feedback conferences can often be successfully completed in three minutes or less. For a more in-depth explanation of the characteristics of effective feedback and for more feedback options, see Chappuis (2015).

Logistics   While some of the other conference options can take place at home, we usually conduct feedback conferences at school. You can schedule feedback conferences so that everyone is offering or receiving feedback from a partner at the same time or so that some are working with a partner while others are with you. You may allow students to schedule a conference with a partner whenever they want feedback, or you may give them a date range (e.g., when they are working on a long-term project) within which they need to schedule a feedback conference with you or with a partner. Or you may work with individual students each day until you have touched base with everyone.

■ Goal-Setting Conferences

As noted in Chapter 2, setting goals for improvement is a logical next step after receiving feedback and after self-assessing. As you may remember, it is the second half of Strategy 4 in the seven strategies of assessment for learning. In Chapters 5, 6, and 7 you have read about ways to engage students in self-assessment and goal setting with selected response assessment tasks, written response assessment tasks, and performance assessment tasks. Sometimes students will need individual assistance in setting appropriate goals for further learning and that is where a goal-setting conference becomes useful.

The Purpose for a Goal-Setting Conference

In a goal-setting conference, student and teacher work together to frame a tangible plan based on current evidence. Its purpose is to guide next steps toward mastery with reference to one or more learning targets. The goals set can be short or long term in nature. Not all students will need one-on-one attention in setting specific and appropriately challenging goals in the short term. Once they are clear about the intended learning (Strategies 1 and 2), have received actionable feedback (Strategy 3), and perhaps have had experience with self-assessment (Strategy 4), goal setting may be a fairly straightforward next step, such as the final activity in the feedback conference. However, there are times when working with them individually can help students master the protocols of goal setting, especially if the goal is a longer-term one.

Prerequisites   Prior to planning a goal-setting conference, it is important to have a grasp of the characteristics of goals likely to increase achievement (Sadler, 1989; Hattie, 2009; Wood & Locke, 1997; Locke & Latham, 2002; Halvorson, 2012):

- They are specific rather than vague "do-my-best" statements of the aim of an action
- They are challenging, requiring students to face and deal with difficulty to move beyond their current level of achievement

Locke and Latham (2002, pp. 706–707) explain the mechanisms that their research suggests cause specific and challenging goals to result in increased achievement (Chappuis, 2015):

1. They focus attention on activities that will lead to accomplishment of the goal and divert attention from irrelevant activities.
2. They have an "energizing" function, triggering greater effort than low-challenge goals.
3. They prolong effort. People with challenging goals demonstrate greater levels of persistence.
4. They cause people to tap into knowledge and strategies they already have and also to look for ways to increase their knowledge and strategy repertoire to accomplish the goal.

The elements of effective goals align directly with the three questions that frame the seven strategies of assessment for learning: "Where am I going? Where am I now? How can I close the gap?" The key elements of an effective goal are the following (Chappuis, 2015):

- A clear statement of the intended learning: What do I need to learn or master?
- A description of current status: Where am I now with respect to my desired end point?
- An action plan:
  - What steps will I take?
  - When will I do this?
  - Where will I work?
  - With whom can I work? What materials will I need?
  - What will I use as evidence that I have accomplished my goal? What will my "before" and "after" pictures be?

Materials Needed

Prior to the conference, students (or the teacher, if needed) should select one or more work samples that provide evidence of current status with respect to the learning target. It is helpful for the student and you to have the learning target(s) and any rubrics or explanations of desired quality to refer to during the conference. If students are keeping a growth, project, or achievement portfolio addressing the target(s), these will be useful here. If students have already completed a self-assessment prior to the conference, include that in the materials. Then select a frame that students will complete to capture the elements of their goals. Examples are shown in Figures 12.5, 12.6, and 12.7.

figure 12.5 ▪ For Example: Self-Assessment and Goal-Setting Frame

Where Am I Going?	
My goal:	
Where Am I Now?	
What I can already do:	What I need to work on:
How Will I Close the Gap?	
What I will do:	
When I will do it:	
Where I will do it:	
With help from:	
Using these materials:	

figure 12.6 ■ For Example: Status, Target, Plan

Status: Right now I can _do 2 pushups_

Target: My goal is to _do 10 pushups_   by   _2 weeks_

Plan: To reach my goal I will _do 2 pushups morning & night for 2 days._
Then 2 sets of 3 pushups morning & night for 2 days. Then 2 sets of 4 pushups morning & night for 2
days. Then 2 sets of 6 pushups morning & night for 2 days. Last 2 sets of 8 pushups morning & night for
2 days.

I will get help from _me myself and I_

Source: Chappuis, Jan, *Seven Strategies Of Assessment For Learning,* 2nd Ed., ©2015. Reprinted and Electronically reproduced by permission of Pearson Education, Inc., New York, New York.

figure 12.7 ■ For Example: High School Health Goal and Plan

Name: _John Jurjevich_   Date: _Feb. 20_

Learning target: _Explain how the immune system works_
Current level of achievement: _don't understand how a neutrophil works to fight infection_ **Evidence:** _quiz on communicable diseases 2/19_
What I need to learn: _to explain what a neutrophil does at three stages: chemotaxis, phagocytosis, and apoptosis_
What I will do: _study the pages on pathogens and the immune system in the book and practice drawing the life cycle of a neutrophil, with all stages explained_
When & where: _Mon + Tues night starting at 8 in my room_
Help needed—what and who: _book + me_
Evidence of achieving my goal: _Test 2/26_

Source: Chappuis, Jan, *Seven Strategies Of Assessment For Learning,* 2nd Ed., ©2015. Reprinted and Electronically reproduced by permission of Pearson Education, Inc., New York, New York.

The Protocol for a Goal-Setting Conference

Begin by checking for understanding of the intended learning. The student can open up the conference with a statement of the learning to be achieved, or you can discuss this together. (This will not have been the first time the student has thought about the learning target.) Frame the learning target as a destination—this is the goal statement. It may be helpful to use the analogy of a GPS system with students here. Our learning target is where we want to end up. That is our goal.

Next, examine the work sample(s) and any feedback or self-assessment available for them. Help the students articulate what strengths the work shows. Then guide them (as needed) in framing a statement of what they need to learn or master at this point. Continuing the GPS analogy, this is our current location.

Then ask them to think about how they might go about accomplishing moving from where they are to their destination. In GPS terms, this is where the student or you and the student together plot the route with checkpoints along the way to the destination. Ask these questions to help them craft their plan: What actions will you take? When will you take them? Where will you do the work? Will you need or want assistance? If so, who or what will be most helpful? What materials (if any) will you need? Work with the student to set a time frame for completion. Build a check point in partway through the timeframe where they can discuss their progress toward the goal and you can help them adjust effort or strategies as needed.

Last, help them identify what artifacts they will collect as evidence they have attained their goal. What will they use to establish their starting point? (That may come from the materials you are using to conduct the conference.) What will they use as evidence of having reached their destination? In Figure 12.8 you will see an example of a first-grade student's reflection on his goal accomplishment describing his "before" and "after" pictures.

figure 12.8 ■ For Example: "Before" and "After"

I have become better at	writing on the lines.
My "before" picture:	My letters jumped around.
My "after" picture:	They all sit on the line.

Source: Chappuis, Jan, *Seven Strategies Of Assessment For Learning,* 2nd Ed., ©2015. Reprinted and Electronically reproduced by permission of Pearson Education, Inc., New York, New York.

Logistics   The conference itself can be formal or informal. You can schedule goal-setting conferences so that everyone is engaged in the protocol with a partner at the same time or so that some are working with a partner while others are with you. Or you may work with individual students each day until you have touched base with everyone. If students have experienced sufficient feedback, they can take their work home and conduct a goal-setting conference with a parent or other significant adult.

Goal setting using this protocol can also be one component of a feedback, achievement, or intervention conference. For a more in-depth discussion of the components of effective goals, see Chappuis (2015).

MyEdLab **Self-Check 12.1**

MyEdLab **Application Exercise 12.2** Goal-setting conferences

---

■ Achievement Conferences

If you are familiar with any conference option, you will probably be familiar with this one from your own K–12 education. Traditionally achievement conferences have occurred at the end of a grading period—usually the first one—and involve parents signing up for a 20-minute time slot to visit with the teacher about your progress or lack of it as summarized on your report card. Indeed, the report card may have been the only artifact discussed. Your parents returned home pleased or determined to make some changes. You may have waited anxiously for your parents, greeting them at the door with "What did my teacher say!? What did my teacher say!?" Or you may have studiously attended to homework in your room that evening in the hopes of fending off a lecture.

The Purpose of an Achievement Conference

The primary purpose of an achievement conference is to share information about a student's level of achievement of predetermined content standards. It may also involve discussion of behaviors and work habits that contribute to learning well, but the primary concern is the student's learning. And while much of importance has been successfully communicated in traditional conferences of years past, we have many more options available to us now, all of which can involve the student as the leader or at least as a participant. While there is still a place for the end-of-term conference, there is no need to exclude the student from the communication. (When you or a parent wishes to discuss issues of concern without the student present, we call that an *intervention conference* and conduct it differently, as described later in the chapter.)

Involving Students in Conferences with Parents   When students have kept a record of their achievement and have reflected on it, they are prepared to share their knowledge about their learning with an audience— their parents, another significant adult, other students, or teachers (see Figure 12.9). One powerful benefit of students talking with parents about their achievement is

Students' discussions with parents about their achievement strengthen parents' beliefs about students' capabilities.

figure 12.9 ■ From the Classroom: Harriet Arnold and Pat Stricklin

---

With a combined 35 years of teaching experience, we have rarely found a more valuable educational process than student-led conferences. During preparation the students experienced goal setting, reflected upon their own learning, and created a showcase portfolio.

Once underway, the conferences seem to have a life of their own. We, the teachers, gave up control and became observers, an experience that was gratifying and revealing. It validated our growing belief that students have the ability to direct their own learning and are able to take responsibility for self-evaluation. For many of our students, we gained insights into individual qualities previously hidden from us in the day-to-day classroom routine.

Students blossomed under the direct and focused attention of their parents. In this intimate spotlight, where there was no competition except that which they placed on themselves, they stepped for a moment into the adult world where they took command of explaining their learning. Parents were surprised and pleased at the level of sophistication and competence their children revealed while sharing personal accomplishments.

In order to refine and improve this process, we surveyed both students and parents. Parents were emphatic in their positive response to student-led conferences, with most requesting that we provide this type of conference more often. Students, even those at risk and with behavior problems, overwhelmingly responded with, "We needed more time; a half an hour was not enough."

Source: Used with permission from Harriet Arnold and Patricia Stricklin, elementary teachers, Central Kitsap School District, Silverdale, Washington, 1993.

MyEdLab
Video Example 12.1
Students Sharing Their Learning Progress: Elementary

the impact it can have on parents' expectations. Having analyzed research on home-related factors that contribute to achievement, Hattie (2009) concluded that parents' hopes and expectations for their child's level of achievement were the strongest contributing factor to high achievement across all home variables. Well-planned student-led conferences can significantly influence those hopes and expectations. The teacher's task is to prepare students to engage in these discussions productively so that students and parents do not experience a conference like the one that Anna led in the opening vignette, which unfortunately raised concerns rather than expectations. Watch Video Example 12.1 to hear elementary students and teachers discuss the value of student participation in conferences.

Student-Involved Achievement Conference Options   Think back to Chapter 10 and the types of portfolios we can create: the celebration, growth, project, and achievement status portfolios all tell a story about learning, each in different contexts. Similarly, achievement conferences can be tailored to highlight learning in one of those contexts.

Celebration Conference   In this conference, the purpose is to allow students to share the highlights of their learning achievements in your classroom. It does not need to happen at the end of a reporting period—it can be totally separated from the grading and reporting functions of assessment. Materials required are the celebration portfolio as described in Chapter 10.

Progress Conference   The purpose of this conference is to describe growth over time. It also does not need to occur at the end of the grading period, although that is a logical time to conduct it. In a progress conference the conversation revolves around changes and accomplishments in a student's academic performance over a period of time from a few weeks to a year. The growth portfolio is designed specifically for this conference, but the project and achievement portfolios may also be appropriate, depending on whether their contents also paint a picture of a continued increase in learning.

Achievement Status Conferences   A conference focused on achievement status generally does take place at the end of a grading period. Its purpose is to share evidence that supports a judgment of level of achievement at a point in time. The achievement status portfolio provides the evidence to be discussed. When the purpose is to support a claim of mastery of content standards, the celebration portfolio may also be used, provided it has been assembled to showcase best work, and that best work demonstrates excellence with respect to the learning targets. And sometimes, as is the case with a culminating project, the project portfolio may serve as the evidence for the assertion of mastery.

Preparing Students   To prepare students for a celebration conference, help them create a celebration portfolio (Chapter 10). Let them select the artifacts they want to talk about and help them make notes about each artifact explaining why it is a "celebration" for them. Then you, in collaboration with students, create a conference agenda indicating what will occur and how long it will take.

To prepare students for a progress conference, help them create a growth portfolio (or a project portfolio) (Chapter 10). Students should be prepared to share the learning target(s) to talk about what they did to improve and summarize what they can do or what they know now that they couldn't do or didn't know before. Then you, in collaboration with students, create a conference agenda indicating what will occur and how long it will take. Figure 12.10 shows an example of a form that students can use to organize their thoughts prior to the conference.

To prepare students for an achievement status conference, help them create the appropriate portfolio—achievement status, celebration, or project—as described in Chapter 10. With the achievement status portfolio, make sure students can describe what each artifact they will share illustrates about their learning. With the celebration and project portfolios, guide students in formulating explanations of how their work samples support the claim of mastery: What does each show they have mastered? Then create a conference agenda, indicating what will occur and how long it will take.

figure 12.10 ■ For Example: Preparing for a Progress Conference

---

Learning target(s):

My "before" picture:

My "after" picture:

What I did to improve:

What I can do now that I couldn't do before:

Important things to notice in my work:

Preparing the Parents   First, set the conference agenda with students. Second (if they are able to), have students write an invitation to their parents to attend the conference. Accompany this invitation with a note from you informing parents of the purpose for a student-led conference, what to expect including the agenda and their suggested role—to listen to their child first, and then to offer observations and ask questions. Some teachers find it helpful to send work samples home in advance for parents to review in preparation for the conference.

The Protocol for an Achievement Conference

Achievement conferences can be conducted between students and parents or with students, their parents, and you. The first is known as a two-way conference and the second is known as a three-way conference. Any time one of these formats replaces the traditional parent–teacher conference, as a part of the invitation to parents you can offer them the option of scheduling an additional meeting, without the student present, to address issues or concerns they may not want to discuss in the presence of their child.

The Two-Way Conference   One of the advantages of a two-way conference is that you can schedule several at the same time. The student leads the conference and you circulate to clarify information as needed. It helps to stagger the start times by five minutes or so. At the beginning of the conference, the student introduces his or her parents to you. Then the student and parents go to a designated conference area, for example, the student's desk or tables set up for that purpose. Students begin by sharing the conference agenda. Second, they explain the learning targets that are the focus of the conference. Third, they share the artifacts and the explanation they have prepared for what the artifacts say about their achievement. Parents listen carefully, ask clarifying questions, and offer comments about the student's work and learning. If students have already set goals for future work, they can share them with parents or students and parents may do this together as a part of the conference, depending on the nature of the goals (work at home versus work at school). You make sure to touch base with each group to answer any questions they may have. If conferences are scheduled to begin every five minutes, this allows you to be part of the closure for each.

The Three-Way Conference   Three-way conferences need to be scheduled individually because you will be a full participant in each conference. As with the two-way conference, students begin by introducing their parents to you and then sharing the agenda. The student explains the learning targets and proceeds as in the two-way conference. The parents' role is also the same. Your role is to help students clarify their comments, as needed. If students have already set goals for future work, they can share them with parents, and you may do this together as a part of the conference. We recommend that you conclude the conference with a summary of any decisions made and a comment on the student's positive contributions to the class.

Follow-Up

Offering each participant the opportunity to reflect on the conference experience is one of the keys to successful communication. We recommend that students and parents complete a conference evaluation form, such as the one shown in Figure 12.11. The information helps you identify what worked well and what didn't, what additional information might be needed, and what revisions you might make to the process for next time. It also helps you to reflect on the power of the experience for your students and their parents. In rare instances you may have to address a negative outcome for a student or a parent, in which case you will want to schedule a follow-up conference.

figure 12.11 ■ For Example: Conference Debrief Form

What I learned from this conference:

What I appreciated about it:

What I would like to see changed:

Questions I have:

Other comments:

MyEdLab **Self-Check 12.2**

MyEdLab **Application Exercise 12.3** Achievement conferences

---

■ Intervention Conferences

Upon occasion it is necessary to schedule a conference to address specific difficulties a student is encountering with behaviors, work habits, interactions with peers, or academic achievement. This conference option differs somewhat from the achievement conference, although in an achievement conference you can certainly address issues that need further attention. We schedule an intervention conference when we want to focus on a problem that has not responded to day-to-day modifications by establishing a more targeted plan. Although it can feel difficult to hold these conferences, especially in your first years of teaching, the outcome can be extremely rewarding, both in terms of increased insights into how to help children overcome difficulties and in terms of the gains students make as a result of your thoughtful observation and persistence in caring about them.

The Purpose of an Intervention Conference

In an intervention conference, you meet with one or both parents to discuss a problem that in-class remedies have not successfully addressed. Sometimes the student is also present, depending on the nature of the information to be shared. And sometimes the participants of the intervention conference are you and the student. In all instances, the primary purpose is to identify the problem and make a plan for improvement. Elements of the goal-setting conference can come into play here as appropriate.

Prerequisites Central to the success of the conferences is the quality of the records you keep. When you are working collaboratively with parents and/or students to craft a plan to address a concern, it is very helpful for them to be able to examine credible evidence that supports your explanation of the problem. Additionally, all involved are better able to use the evidence to identify patterns or contributing factors and devise a course of action best suited to addressing the underlying cause(s).

Materials Needed for an Intervention Conference

What type of records you use is determined by the type of problem. For a behavior problem, you will want to assemble the following information:

- Dated anecdotal records describing the behavior
- A copy of classroom, school, or district rules that the behavior violates, if appropriate
- Dated notes about interventions attempted and observed results

For a problem involving work habits, you will want to assemble the following information:

- Dated evidence of the problem (e.g., for late work, what work was late and how late it was)
- A copy of your classroom policy or stated expectations regarding the work habit
- A record of the interventions and consequences that have already been put into place and anecdotal notes of observed results

For academic achievement difficulties, you will want to assemble the following information:

- Student work samples illustrating achievement status
- Explanation of interventions you have conducted

- Any pertinent test results, either from classroom tests or from large-scale tests, along with a draft of a parent-friendly explanation of what the results mean for this student (not for reading from necessarily, but for reference as you are sharing test information)
- A draft of potential next steps to address the difficulties

Intervention conferences can have an emotional component, so also have tissues discreetly available.

The Protocol for an Intervention Conference

This protocol is designed to be used in a conference with parents, with parents and student together, or with the student alone. Because the goal of an intervention conference is to identify and address a problem before it grows further, begin the conference with a statement of its goal. This is a solution-oriented conference. Then share your assessment of the problem along with the evidence of it, explaining what the evidence indicates in parent-friendly (student-friendly) terms. Check with the parents (student) for clarification and ask for their input. Parents often have insight into students' academic difficulties, especially when this is not the first time they have encountered them. Students may also have insights into their academic difficulties. Next share the interventions you and the students have used, along with your assessment of what worked and what didn't. If students are involved, ask for their assessment of what worked and what didn't before sharing your own. Discuss with the parent (and/or student) other interventions that you believe are advisable. Also invite the parents (and/or student) to weigh in on what interventions they believe might work. Let the parents (and/or student) know you will keep them in touch with how the plan is working and identify a time line for progress updates. Either at the close of the conference or immediately afterward, create a written summary of the problem, the agreed-upon next steps (who will do what and when), and the time line for progress updates. Include the summary as part of a thank-you follow-up email to the parents and/or student.

Logistics of Intervention Conferences   These conferences almost always occur at school. Sometimes they are scheduled as phone conferences, in which case it is a good idea to make an appointment for a call rather than just calling and sharing the concern (unless it is an immediate concern requiring immediate action). Intervention conferences are best conducted in a private area so that the concerns may be discussed frankly and confidentially. Even when it is a phone conference, make sure you are in a place that ensures confidentiality of your remarks.

MyEdLab **Application Exercise 12.4** Intervention conferences

■ Summary: Conferences as Effective Communication

Like portfolios, conferences offer ways to communicate about student achievement in greater detail than is permitted by report cards. In these cases, the communication arises from and focuses on actual examples of student work. Unlike report cards, conferences can afford students the opportunity to tell their own rich, complete story to people who are meaningful in their lives. In the majority of the time, conferences about students can include students. They can participate in and even lead them if we prepare them adequately: involve students all along in their learning and in assessing, make sure they can talk about their work in terms of its strengths and needs in terms of the learning it demonstrates, and help them set goals for what they might do next.

In this chapter we have examined four types of conferences: the feedback conference, the goal-setting conference, the achievement status conference, and the intervention conference. We have identified the purpose for each type of conference and then described how to prepare for each meeting. We have also explained how to prepare students and parents for conferences that involve students. In addition we have explained how to conduct each type of conference and what type of follow-up is recommended.

As you begin teaching, we encourage you to prepare to use each of these conference options and most especially to think about how you can involve students as partners in telling the story of their learning journey.

■ Suggested Activities

End-of-chapter activities are intended to help you master the chapter's learning targets. They are designed to deepen your understanding of the chapter content, provide opportunities for personal reflection on ideas presented, and serve as a basis for discussion among peers. You may wish to do all of them or select those that you believe will be most useful to your learning. Each activity is correlated to one or more chapter learning targets to help with your selection.

Chapter 12 Learning Targets

As a result of your study of Chapter 12, you will be able to do the following:

1. Select conference options best suited to your students' and their parents' needs
2. Prepare for, conduct, and debrief feedback and goal-setting conferences
3. Prepare for, conduct, and debrief achievement conferences
4. Prepare for, conduct, and debrief intervention conferences

Chapter 12 Activities

Activity 12.1   Keeping a Reflective Journal (All chapter learning targets)

Activity 12.2   Engaging in a Student-Led Conference (All chapter learning targets)

Activity 12.3   Comparing Your Experiences with Information from the Chapter (All chapter learning targets)

Activity 12.4   Answering an Interview Question (All chapter learning targets)

Activity 12.5   Reflecting on Your Learning from Chapter 12 (All chapter learning targets)

Activity 12.6   Adding to Your Growth Portfolio (All chapter learning targets)

Activity 12.1: Keeping a Reflective Journal

Keep a record of your thoughts, questions, and insights as you read Chapter 12.

Activity 12.2: Engaging in a Student-Led Conference

Select one of the achievement conference options from this chapter (celebration, progress, or achievement status) and prepare to engage in the conference with yourself as the student and your learning from this course as the subject of the discussion.

1. Identify the learning targets from this course that will be the focus of your conference.
2. Assemble the materials needed for the conference option you have selected as described in this chapter. If you have been keeping a portfolio as a part of your learning, you may find appropriate artifacts in it.
3. Determine with whom you will conduct the conference. Who will be your audience and responder(s)— peers, your own parents, an instructor, others? Prepare them by writing a short explanation of their role in the conference and then sharing it with them as a part of a written invitation.
4. Write out your conference agenda.
5. Conduct the conference.
6. Debrief the conference with the participant(s) using the form shown in Figure 12.10 (modified if you wish).
7. Write up your own thoughts about the conference. What did you learn about yourself as a learner? What worked well for you? What didn't work well? If you were to have your students lead a conference, what (if anything) would you do differently?

Activity 12.3: Comparing Your Experiences with Information from the Chapter

Read the "From the Classroom" entry in Chapter 12 and compare it to your experience in grades K through 12.

How is it similar?

What differences do you notice?

What conclusions about the benefits of student participation in conferences might you draw?

Activity 12.4: Answering an Interview Question

Imagine that you are about to interview for a teaching position. The interview team (often a combination of administrators and teachers) is interested in understanding your level of classroom assessment literacy. Review Chapter 12's learning targets and think about what concepts and procedures were most significant to you from the chapter. Then think about what type of question an interview team might ask related to this significant learning. Write the question and draft a short response—one that you could give in one to two minutes orally.

Activity 12.5: Reflecting on Your Learning from Chapter 12

Review the Chapter 12 learning targets and select one that struck you as most significant from this chapter. Write a short reflection that captures your current understanding. If you are working with a group, discuss what you have written.

Activity 12.6: Adding to Your Growth Portfolio

Any of the activities from this chapter can be used as portfolio entries. Select any activity you have completed or artifact you have created that will demonstrate your mastery of the Chapter 12 learning targets:

1. Select conference options best suited to your students' and their parents' needs
2. Prepare for, conduct, and debrief feedback and goal-setting conferences
3. Prepare for, conduct, and debrief achievement conferences
4. Prepare for, conduct, and debrief intervention conferences

APPENDIX A

Assessing Dispositions

Desire and motivation to succeed in school are not academic achievement characteristics. They are affective characteristics. Feelings. Emotions. We have established that we can assess achievement. But can we assess these feelings or dispositions as well? Yes. And, from time to time, it may be helpful to your students to assess them and use the results to support their learning.

When we assess dispositions, we tap into student feelings about school—the inner motivations or desires that influence their thoughts and their actions. In this case, we center not on what students know and can do, but on the attitudes, motivations, and interests that predispose students to behave in academically productive ways. Our assessment challenge in this case is easy to understand. Students' feelings about school vary in their focus (feelings about what, exactly), in their direction (from positive through neutral to negative), and in their intensity (from very strong to moderate to very weak emotions). Our assessment task is to specify the focus and ask about direction and intensity.

With these features in mind, we can share why we have adopted the label *dispositions* in this appendix. Our goals for developing student feelings are not value neutral. Often we hope for strong, either positive or negative, feelings in our students when it comes to learning. We strive to develop learners predisposed to behave in certain academically productive ways in school. Often we seek a strong positive work ethic, positive motivation, intense interests, positive attitudes, and a positive academic self-concept. We want them to have a strong sense of internal control over their own academic success, that is, a strong sense of academic self-efficacy. Indeed, assessment *for* learning is entirely about helping students develop these very feelings.

We have advocated student involvement in classroom assessment throughout this book because research tells us it can lead to greater student learning. It is imperative that you understand how this works. When applied effectively, the principles of assessment *for* learning help students feel like capable learners and feel in control of their own success. They enhance students' confidence and desire to learn.

Our point is that we cannot ignore dispositions in our quest for academic achievement. As teachers, we must know how to help students develop academically empowering dispositions and must be ready to teach them how to use those dispositions to promote their own success. Very often students fail, not because they cannot achieve, but because they choose not to attempt to achieve. Often they have given up and are not motivated to learn. Why? There can be many reasons: they don't understand the work, find it too hard to do, lack prerequisite achievement, and so on. And so they fail, which in turn robs them of (1) the prerequisites for the next learning and (2) a sense that they could succeed if they tried. This can become a vicious cycle, a self-fulfilling prophecy. They feel academically powerless and thus become so. This negative sense of themselves as learners drives out of students any motivation to try. This downward spiral can result from the complex interaction between achievement and dispositions. These students become predisposed to fail.

But this spiral also can take a very positive direction. Right from the time students arrive at school, they look to us, their teachers, for evidence of the extent to which they are succeeding. If that early evidence (from our classroom assessments) shows areas in which they are succeeding, what can begin to grow in them is a sense of hope for the future and expectation of further success down the road. This, in turn, fuels their motivation to strive for excellence, which spawns more success and results in the upward spiral of positive dispositions and academic achievement that every parent and teacher dream of for their children. These students become predisposed to succeed.

Clearly, many forces in a student's life exert great influence on attitudes, values, interests, self-concept, and indeed on dispositions to try to achieve excellence. Chief among these are family, peer group, religious affiliation, and community. But schools are prominent on this list of contributors, too, especially when it comes to dispositions to invest the energy required to learn. To the extent that we wish to help students to take advantage of dispositions as driving forces toward greater achievement, it will be important for us to understand and apply the principles of assessment *for* learning. In these ways, student-involved assessment can fuel a strong sense of hope for success on the part of all students, predisposing them to pursue academic excellence.

■ A Crucial Difference between Achievement and Affect

There is one very important difference between student achievement and student affect that bears directly on differences in the manner in which we use assessment. It has to do with the reasons for assessing. It is perfectly acceptable to hold students accountable for mastery of knowledge, reasoning, performance skill, and/or product targets. In assessment *of* learning contexts, where students are responsible for learning, we assess to verify that students have met our academic achievement standards.

However, it is rarely acceptable to hold students accountable in the same sense for their dispositions. It is never acceptable, for example, to lower a student's grade in response to a negative attitude about the subject. Evidence of learning or the lack of it must speak for itself at grading time, regardless of attitudes expressed in class. Nor, conversely, is it acceptable to raise a student's grade just because of a positive attitude or other disposition, regardless of achievement.

Rather, we assess dispositions in the hope of finding positive, productive attitudes, values, sense of academic self, or interest in particular topics so we can take advantage of these—build on them—to promote greater achievement gains. We can also use the information to identify and address barriers to success.

We believe responsibility for school-related student dispositions should rest with us, their teachers. We hold ourselves accountable for your dispositions regarding assessment. If we don't help you feel strongly about the critical importance of quality assessment, if you don't leave our classes or complete this book feeling a strong sense of responsibility to create accurate assessments and if you don't feel a strong desire to use them to benefit your students, then we regard that as our fault. We must strive to find better ways to motivate you, our students, to act responsibly with respect to the quality of your classroom assessments. We believe you have that same responsibility with your students.

Important Ground Rules

Know your limits when dealing with student feelings. There are two important interrelated limits you should be aware of. First, as you come to understand and assess student dispositions, you will occasionally encounter students who are troubled, personally and/or socially. Be caring but careful in these instances. These are not occasions for you to become an amateur psychologist. If you find yourself in a situation where you feel uneasy with what you are learning about a student or about your ability to help that student deal productively with feelings or circumstances, get help. The most caring and responsible teachers are those who know when it is time to contact the principal, a counselor, or a school psychologist to find competent counseling services for students. Do not venture into personal territory for which you are not trained.

Second, we urge you to focus your attention on those classroom-level dispositions over which you are likely to (and in fact should) have some influence. When assessing and evaluating student dispositions, stick with those feelings as they relate to specific school-related objects: dispositions toward particular subjects or classroom activities, academic interests students would like to pursue in school, personal dispositions as learners in an academic setting, and so on. These have a decidedly school-oriented bent, and they represent values families and school communities are likely to agree are important as parts of the schooling experience. You need not go too far over those classroom-related limits before members of your community may begin to see your actions on behalf of positive, productive affect as invading their turf. Many families and communities are protective of their responsibility to promote the development of certain strongly held values and will not countenance interference from schools. This is their right.

■ Defining Affect as It Relates to Dispositions

School-related attitudes, school-related values, academic self-efficacy, academic interests, academic aspirations, and assessment anxiety represent significant dimensions of classroom affect that bear directly on students' motivation to learn (Anderson & Bourke, 2000). They represent students' attributes that predispose them to behave in academically and socially productive ways. In addition, each has been clearly defined in the professional literature, is relatively easy to understand, and can be assessed in the classroom using relatively straightforward procedures.

School-Related Attitudes

An attitude is a feeling about someone or something. Attitudes vary in direction (favorable to unfavorable) and intensity (strong to weak). The stronger the feelings (attitudes), the greater is the likelihood that they will influence behavior.

Obviously, the range of attitudes within any individual is as broad as the array of experiences or objects to which that person reacts emotionally. In schools, students might have favorable or unfavorable attitudes about each other, teachers, administrators, math, science, reading, writing, instructional activities, and so on. It is our hope as educators that increments of success breed positive attitudes, which then fuel the desire for greater achievement, which in turn breeds more positive attitudes. Thus, certain attitudes predispose students to academic success.

School-Related Values

Our values are our "beliefs about what should be desired, what is important or cherished, and what standards of conduct are . . . acceptable. Second, values influence or guide behavior, interests, attitudes, and satisfactions. Third, values are enduring. That is, they tend to remain stable over fairly long periods of time" (Anderson & Bourke, 2000, p. 32). Values also are learned, tend to be of high intensity, and tend to focus on enduring ideas.

A belief in the value of education as a foundation for a productive life, in the benefits of strong effort in school, a strong sense of the need for ethical behavior at testing time (no cheating), and belief that a healthy lifestyle (for example, no drugs) underpins academic success represent school-related values that influence behavior and predispose students to succeed in school.

Academic Self-Efficacy

No affective characteristic is more school related than the judgment one makes about one's possibility of success and/or productivity in an academic context. In essence, it is an attitude (favorable or unfavorable) about one's self when viewed in a classroom setting. Academic self-concept, Anderson and Bourke (2000) instruct us, is a learned vision that results largely from evaluations of self by others over time. Quite simply, those who see themselves as capable learners are predisposed to be capable learners.

In this case, the characteristic of interest is students' attributions or beliefs about the reasons for academic success or failure (this is referred to in the literature as locus of control). One kind of attribution is defined as internal: "I succeeded because I tried hard." Another possible attribution is external, where chance rules: "I sure was lucky to receive that A!" Yet another external attribution assigns cause to some other person or factor: "I performed well because I had a good teacher." At issue here are students' perceptions of the underlying reasons for the results they are experiencing. These, too, are learned self-perceptions arising from their sense of the connection of effort to academic success. As with other affective characteristics, self-efficacy varies in direction (can succeed, cannot succeed) and intensity (weak to strong) and is learned.

Academic Interests

Let's define an interest as a learned preference for some activity, skill, idea, or understanding. This preference influences students' behavior in that it causes us to pursue its object. Feelings range from a high level of excitement to no excitement about the prospect of engaging in a particular activity.

Assessment Anxiety

Hall and Lindsay define anxiety as "the experience of [emotional] tension that results from real or imagined threats to one's security" (1970, p. 145). This feeling varies from a sense of relaxed safety on one end to extreme tension on the other. When faced with the prospect of having their achievement evaluated, students will experience varying levels of this kind of anxiety, depending on their record of success or the lack thereof, their knowledge of what they are being held accountable for having learned, and the extent and nature of their preparation to succeed on the assessment.

■ Variations in Dispositions

As mentioned earlier, dispositions vary along three important dimensions: focus, direction, and intensity. They focus on our feelings about specific aspects of the world around us. Some, such as attitudes and values, can focus outside of ourselves. Others, such as academic self-concept and locus of control, focus on our inner views.

Affect also can vary in direction, stretching from a neutral point outward in both directions along a continuum to differing anchor points. Figure A.1 lists those end points.

And finally, feelings vary in their intensity, from strong to moderate to weak. As you visualize the continuum for each type of affect and move further and further away from neutral, think of feelings as increasing in intensity. In the extremes, feelings become strong.

Bear in mind also that some feelings can be volatile, especially among the young. Such student dispositions as attitudes, interests, and anxiety can quickly change both in direction and intensity for a large number of reasons, only some of which are rational or understandable to adults. On the other hand, values, self-concept dimensions, and aspirations may be more enduring. We mention this to point out that it may be important to sample volatile dispositions repeatedly over time to keep track of them. The results of any one assessment may have a very short shelf life.

figure A.1 ■ The Range of Dispositions

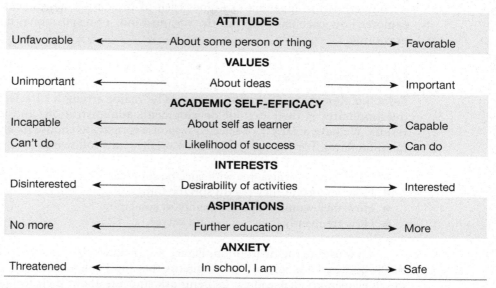

Source: From *Assessing Affective Characteristics in Schools*, 2nd ed. (p. 38) by L. W. Anderson, & S. F. Bourke, 2000, Mahwah, NJ: Lawrence Erlbaum & Associates. Copyright © 2000 by Lawrence Erlbaum & Associates. Adapted by permission.

■ Matching Method to Targets

How do we assess the focus, direction, and intensity of feelings about school? Just as with achievement, we can rely on three forms of assessment: selected response, open-ended written response, and personal communication with students.

In this case, let's group selected response and essay into a single paper-and-pencil assessment form because the two options represent different ways that questions can appear on a basic affective assessment tool: the questionnaire. We can ask students questions about their feelings on a questionnaire and either offer them a few response options to select from, or we can ask them open-ended questions and request brief or extended written responses. If we focus the questions on affect, we can interpret responses in terms of both the direction and intensity of feelings. Examples are coming right up. But, first, let's see the other options.

Assessments of dispositions via personal communication typically take the form of interviews, either with students alone or in groups. In addition, we can interview others who know the students. These can be highly structured or very casual, as in discussions or conversations with students. The questions we ask and the things we talk about reveal the direction and intensity of feelings.

We will now consider procedural guidelines that can enhance the quality of questionnaires, performance assessment, and interview planning and design. The remainder of this appendix examines each of these basic assessment options and explores how each can help tap the various kinds of dispositional targets defined previously.

Questionnaires

Selected Response Questionnaires The major strength of selected response questionnaires is their ease of development, administration, and processing of results. We have a variety of selected response formats to choose from as we design questionnaires. For example, we can ask students the following:

- If they agree or disagree with specific statements
- How important they regard specific things
- How they would judge the quality of something
- How frequently they feel certain ways

To illustrate the first option, Figure A.2 includes the eight items that make up the "The Way I See School" questionnaire that Jim Popham and Rick developed for use in elementary classrooms. Its items ask students about their feelings about two aspects of their classroom experience that relate directly to assessment *for* learning processes: academic self-efficacy and eagerness to learn, as well as two classroom practices that might influence those feelings: their sense of the clarity of the learning targets and availability of information to allow them to self-monitor their progress. The form includes two items for each of these four foci.

Using these kinds of scales, students can easily reveal their attitudes, interests, school-related values, academic self-concept, and the like. Further, it is usually easy to summarize results across respondents. The pattern of responses and, therefore, the feelings of a group of students are easily seen by tallying the number and percent of students who select each response option. This can lead to a straightforward summary of results.

Open-Ended Written Response Another way to assess affect is to offer open-ended questions to which respondents are free to write their responses. If we ask specific questions eliciting direction and intensity of dispositions about specific school-related issues, we may readily interpret responses:

> *Write a brief paragraph describing your reaction to our guest speaker today. Please comment on your level of interest in the presentation, how well informed you thought the speaker was, and how provocative you found the message to be. As you write, be sure to tell me how strong your positive or negative feelings are. I will use your reactions to plan our future guest speakers.*

Or here's an interesting option—consider combining assessment of affect with practice in evaluative reasoning:

figure A.2 ■ Assessment FOR Learning Affect Questionnaire

Directions: Please indicate how you feel about each statement as follows:

SA = Strongly Agree   A = Agree   U = Undecided   D = Disagree   SD = Strongly Disagree

1. I usually understand what I am supposed to learn.

   SA   A   U   D   SD

2. If I'm asked to learn new things, even if it's difficult, I know I can learn them.

   SA   A   U   D   SD

3. Typically, I don't know if I'm making progress as fast as I should.

   SA   A   U   D   SD

4. I'm excited about learning new things in school.

   SA   A   U   D   SD

5. Very often, I'm not certain what I'm supposed to be learning.

   SA   A   U   D   SD

6. Lots of the time, I don't look forward to learning new things in school.

   SA   A   U   D   SD

7. Even if I get lots of help and plenty of time, it is hard for me to learn new things.

   SA   A   U   D   SD

8. I get plenty of information to help me keep track of my own learning growth.

   SA   A   U   D   SD

Thank you for completing this form.

Source: From *Assessing Student Affect Related to Assessment For Learning*, by R. J. Stiggins and W. J. Popham. Washington DC: Council of Chief State School Officers FAST SCASS.

As you think about the readings we did this month, which three did you find most worthwhile? For each choice, specify why you found it worthwhile.

A thoughtful reading of the responses to these kinds of questions will reveal similarities or differences in students' opinions and can help you plan future instruction.

Personal Communication as a Window to Student Feelings

Direct communication is an excellent path to understanding student feelings about school-related topics. We can interview students individually or in groups, conduct discussions with them, or even rely on casual discussions to gain insight about their attitudes, values, and aspirations. In addition, if we establish a trusting relationship with students that permits them to be honest with us, we can understand their sense of self-efficacy and even the levels of anxiety that they are feeling.

This method offers much. Unlike questionnaires, we can establish personal contact with respondents and can ask follow-up questions. This allows us to more completely understand students' feelings. Unlike performance assessment, we can gather our information directly, avoiding the danger of drawing incorrect inferences. This assures a higher level of accuracy and confidence in our assessment results.

■ Keys to Success

Three keys are worthy of your attention. One key to success in tapping true student dispositions is trust. We cannot overemphasize its critical importance. Respondents must be comfortable honestly expressing the direction and intensity of their feelings. Another key is the limits mentioned above. Stick with school-related dispositions and only school-related. And the final key is good intentions. Only ask for information about student dispositions if you have a concrete and specific reason for doing so. Know in advance what action(s) you might take depending on the results you receive. Why are you asking and what do you plan to do with the results to help students succeed academically?

APPENDIX B

Understanding Standardized Tests

Education in the United States has included a strong standardized test tradition for nearly a century. The idea is to have large numbers of students respond to the same or similar sets of test items under approximately the same conditions. Thus, the test itself, the conditions under which it is administered, scoring procedures, and test score interpretation are the same, or "standardized," across all examinees. As a result, users can interpret the scores to mean the same thing for all examinees. The benefit is that scores can be compared across students and compiled over students to compare classrooms, schools, districts, states, and even nations, depending on the context.

Such comparable scores can help identify relatively strong or weak students, so as to channel limited resources to those most in need. Scores on some standardized tests, averaged across students within schools or districts, can help evaluate and identify strong and weak programs.

Although standardized tests are developed and published to assess students' achievement and their aptitude or intelligence, this appendix is limited to the consideration of achievement tests only.

Often school districts participate in several layers of standardized achievement testing, from districtwide testing to statewide to national and sometimes even to international programs. Some districts may administer a dozen or more different standardized testing programs in a given year for different purposes involving different students.

Some standardized tests produce scores that are norm referenced; they communicate in a manner that permits us to compare a student's achievement to that of other students who took the same test under like conditions. Scores on these tests can communicate information about how students rank in achievement. Other standardized tests yield criterion-referenced results; they communicate how each student's test score compares, not to other students, but to a preset standard of acceptable performance. These kinds of scores permit us to detect which specific achievement standards students have and have not met, that is, to determine individual strengths and weaknesses in achievement. Clearly, these kinds of results are of greatest value to classroom teachers.

Professional test publishers develop standardized tests, either to sell directly to schools or under contract for a local, state, or national educational agency. Tests are available to cover virtually all school subjects across all grade levels. Further, they can involve the use of any of our four basic forms of assessment, although historically most have relied on selected response formats because they can be automatically scanned and scored in great numbers with great efficiency.

■ The Various Layers of Annual Testing

From the beginning of our testing traditions in the United States in the first part of the twentieth century, we have evolved into a school culture that has increasingly relied on centralized assessment of student achievement, resulting in the layers of annual testing programs that we see in place today.

College Admissions Testing

This level of testing began modestly early in the twentieth century with a few local scholarship testing programs, which relied on essay tests to select winners. Thus, right from the outset, quality tests were those that could differentiate among levels of student achievement. These differences would serve to rank examinees for the award of scholarships.

These local applications were so effective that they gave rise to our first national college admissions testing programs, the College Boards (also known as the SATs). While the earliest tests relied on essay assessment, in the 1930s the huge volume of national testing soon forced a change as the College Board turned to multiple-choice testing technology as a more efficient format. With this change dawned the era of selected response testing for college selection purposes. Then in the 1940s, the second college admissions test appeared on the scene, the ACT Assessment Program. Some selective postsecondary institutions continue to include scores on these tests in their admissions selection processes.

The College Board recently launched a major revision in its testing programs to offer great support for teachers striving to prepare students for college and workplace training. The tests focus on lifelong learner proficiencies, provide diagnostic information on student strengths and weaknesses, and link results directly to supplementary instructional programs.

Districtwide Testing

The most commonly used form of assessment in districtwide programs is the commercially published, norm-referenced, standardized achievement test battery. However, most tests try to provide information on student strengths and weaknesses. Test publishers design, develop, and distribute these tests for purchase by local users. Each battery covers a variety of school subjects, offering several test forms tailored for use at different grade levels. Users purchase test booklets, answer sheets, and test administration materials, as well as scoring and reporting services. Some tests are administered and scored online.

The unique feature of these tests is the fact that they are nationally "normed" to facilitate test score interpretation. This simply means that the designers administered the tests to large numbers of students before making them available for general purchase. Test results from this preliminary administration provide the basis for comparing each subsequent examinee's score, as we later explain.

Statewide Testing

In the 1960s in response to the challenge that schools might not be "working" (i.e., to evaluate their programs) administrators turned to their only source of objective, "third-party"—and thus believable—student achievement data: scores from commercially available standardized objective paper-and-pencil achievement tests. The accountability movement was born.

This change represented a profoundly important shift in society's perceptions of these tests. They would no longer be seen as just one more piece of information for teachers. Now they would be seen as standards of educational excellence. Understand that the underlying testing technology did not change. These were still tests designed to sort students based on assessments of very broad domains of content. All that changed was our sense of how the tests should be used. They came to be seen as the guardians of our highest academic expectations, a use their original developers had never intended. Educational policy makers began to believe that standardized tests could drive major improvements in school effectiveness. We moved rapidly from districtwide testing to statewide testing applications and beyond.

We began the decade of the 1970s with just a handful of such tests and ended with a majority of states conducting their own testing programs. Now virtually every state conducts its own program. Significantly, many states opted to develop their own tests to be sure they focused on important academic standards in that state. They tended to move from tests designed to sort to tests reflecting student attainment of specific achievement targets (i.e., from norm-referenced to criterion-referenced tests).

National Assessment

Beginning in the late 1970s, we added the National Assessment of Educational Progress (NAEP) in the hope that testing achievement at ever more centralized levels would somehow lead to school improvement in ways that other tests had not. NAEP is a federally funded testing program that periodically samples student achievement across the nation to track the pulse of changing achievement patterns. These biannual assessments gauge the performance of national samples of 9-, 13-, and 17-year-olds, as well as young adults, reporting results by geographic region, gender, and ethnic background. Results are intended for use by policy makers to inform decisions. Since its first test administration in 1969, NAEP has conducted criterion-referenced assessments of valued outcomes in reading, writing, math, science, citizenship, literature, social studies, career development, art, music, history, geography, computers, life skills, health, and economics.

International Assessment

Periodically, the United States, Canada, and other nations around the world collaborate in competitive assessments specifically designed to determine the relative standing of nations with respect to student achievement. Content and assessment experts from around the world meet for the following purposes:

- Define achievement targets common to the participating nations' collective curricula.
- Design exercises that pose problems that make sense in all particular cultures.
- Translate those exercises into a range of languages.
- Devise scoring criteria reflecting differing levels of proficiency.

Given the cultural and linguistic diversity of the world, you can anticipate the challenges in conducting such an assessment.

State Consortium Assessment of Common Core Standards

Recently steps have been taken by the U.S. Department of Education in collaboration with the Council of Chief State School Officers and the National Governor's Board to create standardized tests for the Common Core State Standards in English language arts and mathematics. Those standards have been adopted by many states to guide development of their curricula and instructional programs. Many of these states have entered into collaborative consortiums to develop a common assessment of student mastery of the Common Core standards.

■ Standardized Test Development

While standardized tests may differ in coverage from context to context, they all are developed in roughly the same way regardless of context. Some are developed by test publishers for their own proprietary use—to sell to schools. Others are developed under contract for clients, such as state departments of education for state assessments. We explore the typical test development process here, so you may understand the work developers must do.

Step 1: Clarify Targets

Typically, standardized test developers begin with the thoughtful study of the valued achievement targets they wish to assess—the academic achievement standards that students are to master. In terms of our five attributes of sound assessment, therefore, these tests typically arise from very clear targets.

Step 2: Translate Targets into Assessments

Developers of large-scale standardized tests know how to match their target with a proper assessment method. In the past, they have relied on selected response formats; of late, very brief essay responses have become more common.

The most popular mode of assessment in this context by far is and always has been selected response because it is relatively easy to develop, administer, and score in large numbers. When the achievement targets are content mastery and/or certain kinds of reasoning and problem solving, its great efficiency makes this the method of choice for large-scale test developers. Its major drawback, as you know, is the limited range of targets test developers can translate into these formats.

Historically, written response assessment has been infrequently used in standardized testing in the United States. Recently, however, this has begun to change. Short-answer essays have begun to appear in the content-area exams, such as science and social studies, of state assessments. This popularity arises directly from the fact that, these days, state proficiency standards typically include reasoning and problem-solving targets. Document scanning technology and computer-driven paper management systems have permitted test scoring services to evaluate written work with great dependability and efficiency. These services can now have students respond on their computers or may scan student essays so trained raters can read and score them electronically.

The assessment research and development community is exploring performance assessment applications in writing, mathematics problem solving, science, reading, foreign languages, the arts, interdisciplinary programs, and other performance areas. The great strength of this methodology is its ability to capture useful information about student performance on complex targets. Its limitations are the cost of sampling and scoring. This is a labor-intensive option (i.e., expensive) when large numbers of examinees are involved.

Personal communication is almost never used in large-scale standardized testing due to cost. One-on-one standardized testing is simply too expensive.

Step 3: Develop Test Items

When assessment plans are ready, test construction begins. Some developers use their own in-house staff of item writers; others recruit qualified practicing teachers to create exercises. In either case, item writers are trained in the basic principles of sound item construction. Further, once trained, item writers must demonstrate an appropriate level of proficiency on a screening test before being asked to contribute to test development.

Step 4: Assemble Test and Evaluate for Appropriateness

Once items have been assembled into tests that sample the content in a representative manner, that test is reviewed by qualified test development experts and content-area experts. Members of minority groups review the exercises for accuracy, appropriateness, and bias. Poor-quality or biased exercises are replaced. This review and evaluation process removes possible extraneous sources of bias and distortion.

To uncover and eliminate other potential problems, the next step in test development is to pretest or pilot test the items. Developers recruit classrooms, schools, or districts to administer the exercises under conditions as similar as possible to those in which the final test will be used. Their objectives are to find out if respondents interpret exercises as the authors intended and to see how well the exercises "function." Test developers also want to know how difficult the items are and how well they differentiate between those who know and do not know the material. All of this information helps them retain only the most appropriate exercises for the final test.

Step 5: Administer Test to Establish Norms (Norm-Referenced Tests)

When a test is created for national sale and distribution by a test publisher (not under contract to a client), the next step typically calls for administering the final test as a whole for further quality control analysis and, in the case of norm-referenced tests, to establish norms for score interpretation. As soon as a test is ready, the publisher launches a national campaign to recruit school districts to be part of the "norming sample." The aim is to involve large and small, urban and rural districts in all geographic regions, striving to balance gender and ethnicity, in short, to generate a cross section of the student population in the United States.

Even though thousands of students may be involved, these norm districts are volunteers. For this reason, they cannot be regarded as systematically representative of the national student population. Thus, when we compare a student's score to national norms, we are not comparing them with the actual national student population but rather to the norm group recruited by that test publisher for that particular test.

Norm-referenced standardized tests are revised and re-normed regularly to keep them up to date in terms of content priorities and to adjust the score scale. This is necessary because, as the test remains on the market, districts align their curricula to the material covered. This is how they meet the accountability challenge of producing high scores. Over time, more and more students will score higher on the test. To adjust for this effect and to accommodate changes in the student populations, test publishers re-norm their tests to adjust the score scale downward.

Setting Standards of Acceptable Performance

As states have established statewide achievement standards and transformed them into state assessments, an important issue has come to the fore: How do we decide if a student's score is "high enough" to be judged competent? This is a critically important issue when decisions such as grade-level promotion, high school graduation, and the award of certificates of mastery hang in the balance.

Typically, these "cutoff scores" are established by pooling the collective opinions of teachers, administrators, parents, and representatives of the business community—a cross section of society within that state. The processes employed to accomplish this are too complex to describe here. But suffice it to say that this test scoring technology is very well developed and is very precise when carried out by experts.

Once those cutoff scores are established, then each new test developed for use in subsequent years can be "equated" to the original to ensure comparability of score meaning, even though it might use different test items. This is important to ensure equity of opportunity for students regardless of the year when they happen to be tested. Again, for our purposes, it's not important that you know how this is done. We just want you to know that it is done.

■ Interpretation of Commonly Used Test Scores

Standardized tests that rely on selected response items can report any of a variety of kinds of scores. It is imperative that users understand what these different kinds of scores mean and do not mean because it will be your responsibility to interpret them to the parents of your students or to your students themselves. It is your responsibility to promote clear understanding.

Scores Reported on State Assessments

State assessments typically are designed to reflect student mastery of specific academic achievement standards. State departments of education hire professional test developers to translate their standards into test items that yield evidence of student mastery of those standards. This process can yield either of two kinds of scores showing mastery of each standard or a composite mastery score.

Mastery of Each Standard   When the evidence is to take this form, the test developer will include enough items on the test for each standard to permit a determination of each student's mastery of it. The number of items will vary as a function of the scope of the standard. Simple, focused standards will require a smaller sample of performance to yield a dependable result. The student must answer a certain number or percentage right to be judged to have mastered that standard. In any event, interpretation is straightforward and criterion referenced: Did each student provide evidence of having met each standard? We prefer this kind of score to the one we discuss next because it is more precise.

Composite Mastery Score   Our standardized testing traditions have focused on assessing student mastery of material in broad domains. You will see in the next subsection, for example, commercial tests report scores labeled "reading," "mathematics," and so on. Each test includes a set of items that samples these domains broadly.

This kind of thinking also has carried over into many state assessments. Test developers will pool all of the individual academic achievement standards into a broad set and build the test to lead to a conclusion about student mastery of that "domain"—reading, math, and so on. Then a cutoff score is established, identifying the number of items the student must answer correctly to be judged to have mastered this domain of standards. In fact, often multiple cut scores are calculated: mastered, nearly mastered, and clearly did not master or words to that effect. The contention is that, because standards drove test development, this represents a standards-referenced examination.

Scores Reported on Norm-Referenced Tests

In this case, you can encounter five different kinds of scores: raw score, percent correct, percentile score, stanine score, and grade-equivalent score. Each provides a different perspective on student achievement.

Raw Score This is the easiest score to explain and understand. When students take a test, the number of items they answer right is called their raw score. In the standardized test context, this score forms the basis of all the other scores. In other words, all other scores are derived from it, as you will see. It is the foundation of any communication arising from a standardized test.

Percent Correct This score is as familiar and easy to understand as the raw score. Percent correct reflects the percent of test items the examinee answered correctly: raw score divided by total test items. This is the kind of score we use in the classroom to promote a common understanding and interpretation of performance on classroom tests. As the total number of items changes from test to test, we can always convert raw scores to percent correct and obtain a relatively standard index of performance.

Percentile Score The percentile score (sometimes called percentile rank) represents the essence of a norm-referenced test score. This score tells us what percent of the norm group a student with any given raw score outscored. A student with a percentile rank of 85 outscored (scored higher than) 85 percent of the examinees in that test's original norm group. They allow us to see how each student's score ranked among others who have taken the same test under the same conditions. Did the student score higher or lower than most or somewhere in the middle?

It also should be clear how percent correct and percentile differ. The former refers scores back to the number of items on the test for interpretation, while the latter compares the score to those of other examinees for interpretation. Their points of reference are fundamentally different.

Stanine A student may also be assigned a stanine score based on percentile rank. Stanine simply represents a less precise score scale, each point of which can be interpreted quite easily (Table B.1). In this case, the percentile scale is divided into nine segments, each of which represents a "standard nine" or, abbreviated, *stanine*. When interpreted in terms of the general descriptors listed in the right-hand column

table B.1 ■ Understanding Stanines

Stanine	Percent of scores	Percentile range	Descriptor
9	4	96–99	well above average
8	7	89–95	
7	12	77–88	above average
6	17	60–76	
5	20	40–59	average
4	17	23–39	
3	12	11–22	below average
2	7	4–10	
1	4	1–3	well below average

on Table B.1, this score is easy to understand. A student who attains a stanine of 3 on a test is interpreted to have scored below average in terms of the performance of the norm group.

Grade-Equivalent Scores   This score scale represents yet another way to describe the performance of a student in relation to that of other students. The basis of the comparison in this case is students in the norm group at specified grade levels. A student with a grade equivalent of 3.5 in reading is said to have scored about the same as students in the norm group who were in the fifth month of third grade. Those whose grade-equivalent score is below their current assigned grade are said to have scored below grade level. Those whose grade-equivalent score is higher are said to be performing above grade level.

The strength of this kind of score is its apparent ease of interpretation. But this very strength also turns out to be its major weakness. Grade-equivalent scores are easily misinterpreted. They don't mean what most people think they mean. Following is an example of what can go wrong.

Let's say a very capable fifth-grade student attains a grade-equivalent score of 8.5 in math. An uninformed parent might see that and say, "We must start this fifth grader using the eighth-grade math book at once!"

This is an incorrect conclusion for two reasons. First of all, no information whatever was gathered about this student's ability to do seventh- or eighth-grade math content. All that was tested was fifth- and sixth-grade math content. No inference can be made about the student's proficiency at higher-level work. Second, eighth graders have probably never taken the test. The score represents an extrapolation on the part of the test score analyst as to how eighth graders would be likely to score if they had taken the test of fifth- and sixth-grade math. Thus, again no reliable conclusion can be drawn about any connections to eighth-grade math.

■ Implications for Teachers

Your primary responsibility is to keep your students free from harm. First, make sure they have the opportunity to learn to hit the achievement targets reflected in whatever standardized tests they take. Second, ensure that the scores reported for your students are accurate—that they reflect each student's real level of achievement. Third, you must do everything you can to be sure all students come out of large-scale assessment experiences with their academic self-concepts intact. Let's consider several specific things you can do to fulfill these professional obligations.

Prepare Your Students by Providing Opportunities to Learn

Do all in your power to gather information about and to understand the achievement targets to be assessed in upcoming standardized tests. If a state assessment is pending that reflects state standards, it is your job to know what those standards are and how they apply to your students. Remember the very important lesson you learned in Chapter 3 on achievement targets. Deconstruct each state standard into the enabling knowledge, reasoning, performance skill, or product development targets that form the scaffolding leading up to that standard. Plan instruction and assessment for learning to bring students up that scaffolding in ways that let you and them know they are progressing appropriately over time.

If a published test is to be administered, consult the teacher's guide or the user's materials for that test to know precisely what knowledge, reasoning, performance skill, or product targets it will be assessing. Again, make these targets the focus of instruction.

Another lesson from Chapter 3 needs reaffirming here: Be sure you yourself are a master of the achievement targets your students will be expected to master. Be sure you have the vision of success and then share that vision with your students in terms they can understand.

Strive for Accurate Results   When asked to administer standardized tests, take the responsibility seriously and follow the prescribed instructions. This contributes to the quality of the results. You must follow accepted standards of ethical practice. Anything you may do to cause students to misrepresent their real levels of achievement has the potential of doing harm to them, to you as a professional, and to the integrity of the educational community as a whole. If you are opposed to a particular set of standardized testing practices, bring all of your assessment literacy tools to bear during the debate. That is your right and your responsibility. But when assessment begins, adhere to prescribed procedures so users can accurately interpret the results.

Sometimes to ensure accuracy demands more than merely following prescribed test administration procedures. Some students bring physical or intellectual disabilities to the testing environment that require you to adjust test administration procedures to obtain accurate scores for them. Most often these days, test publishers or state testing agencies will issue guidelines for such accommodations.

Encourage Student Self-Confidence   Prepare your students to participate productively and as comfortably as possible in large-scale testing programs. Take time to be sure they understand why they are taking these tests and how the results will be used. Our next suggestion may startle you, but take it seriously. If the scores are complex or technical in nature, such as percentiles or state assessment mastery scores, and students are likely to have difficulty understanding, do not report them to students. If the scores can't help students in any purposeful way to make productive decisions about their own learning, then do not give them the scores. Under these circumstances, the scores will do more harm than good. But if you do report them, be sure students know what the scores mean and do not mean—how they will and will not be used. Provide practice with the kinds of test item formats they will confront, so they know how to deal with and feel confident with those formats. This includes practice with accommodations in place for special education students.

Communicate with parents about the importance of keeping these tests in perspective. Be sure they know the meaning of the scores. And, above all, be positive and encouraging to all before, during, and after these assessments and encourage parents to do the same. All of these steps help students become "test wise." Positive talk can send students into uncomfortable testing circumstances knowing that you are on their side—and that helps.

REFERENCES

Akron Global Polymer Academy (2011). "Wait Time." *K-12 Science Education at the Akron Global Polymer Academy.* http://www.agpa.uakron.edu/p16/btp.php?id=wait-time

Allen, K., & Hancock, T. (2008). Reading comprehension improvement with individualized cognitive profile and metacognition. *Literacy Research and Instruction, 47*, 124–139.

Ames, C. (1992). Classrooms: Goals, structures, and student motivation. *Journal of Educational Psychology, 84*(3), 261–271.

Anderson, L. W., & Bourke, S. F. (2000). *Assessing affective characteristics in schools,* 2nd ed. Mahwah, NJ: Lawrence Erlbaum & Associates.

Andrade, H. (2013). In J. H. McMillan (Ed.), *The SAGE handbook of research on classroom assessment* (pp. 17–34). Los Angeles, CA: SAGE Publications, Inc.

Bartlett, L. (1987). Academic evaluation and student discipline don't mix: A critical review. *Journal of Law and Education, 16*(2), 155–165.

Black, P. (2013). Formative and summative aspects of assessment: Theoretical and research foundations in the context of pedagogy. In J.H. McMillan (Ed.), *The SAGE handbook of research on classroom assessment* (pp. 167–178). Los Angeles, CA: SAGE Publications, Inc.

Black, P., & Wiliam, D. (1998a). Assessment and classroom learning. *Assessment in Education, (5)*1, 7–74.

Black, P., & Wiliam, D. (1998b). Inside the black box: Raising standards through classroom assessment. *Phi Delta Kappan, 80*(2), 139–148.

Bloom, B. S., Englehard, M. D., Furst, E. J., Hill, W. H., & Krathwohl, D. R. (1956). *Taxonomy of educational objectives, handbook 1: The cognitive domain.* New York: Longman.

Butler, R. (1988). Enhancing and undermining intrinsic motivation: The effects of task-involving and ego-involving evaluation on interest and performance. *British Journal of Educational Psychology, 58*, 1–14.

Chappuis, J. (2015). *Seven strategies of assessment for learning* (2nd ed.). Upper Saddle River, NJ: Pearson Education.

Chappuis, J., Stiggins, R., Chappuis, S., & Arter, J. (2012). *Classroom assessment for student learning: Doing it right—Using it well* (2nd ed.). Upper Saddle River, NJ: Pearson Education.

Council for Economic Education. (2010). *Voluntary national content standards in economics,* 2nd ed. New York: Author. Retrieved January 2011 from http://www.councilforeconed.org/ea/standards/standards.pdf

Covington, M. (1992). *Making the grade: A self-worth perspective on motivation and school reform.* New York: Cambridge.

Fried, R.L. (2001). *The passionate learner: How teachers and parents can help children reclaim the joy of discovery.* Boston: Beacon Press, p. 191.

Gardner, H. (1993). *Frames of mind: The theory of multiple intelligences.* New York: Basic Books.

Hall, C. S., & Lindsay, G. (1970). *Theories of personality* (2nd ed.). New York: John Wiley & Sons.

Halvorson, H. G. (2012). *Succeed: How we can reach our goals.* New York: Penguin.

Harlen, W. (2007). Formative classroom assessment in science and mathematics. In J. H. McMillan (Ed.), *Formative classroom assessment: Theory into Practice* (pp. 116–135). New York: Teachers College Press.

Hattie, J. (2009). *Visible learning: A synthesis of over 800 meta-analyses relating to achievement.* New York: Routledge.

Hattie, J., & Timperley, H. (2007). The power of feedback. *Review of Educational Research, 77*(1), 81–112.

Johnston, P. J. (2004). *Choice words.* Portland, ME: Stenhouse.

Kendall, J., & Marzano, R. (1997). *Content knowledge: A compendium of standards and benchmarks for K-12 education* (2nd ed.). Aurora, CO: Mid-Continent Regional Educational Laboratory.

Klauer, K. J., & Phye, G. D. (2008). Inductive reasoning: A training approach. *Review of Educational Research, 78*(1), 85–123.

Locke, E. A., & Latham, G. P. (2002). Building a practically useful theory of goal setting and task motivation. *American Psychologist, 55*(9), 705–717.

Marzano, R., Pickering, D., & McTighe, J. (1993). *Assessing student outcomes: Performance assessment using the dimensions of learning model*. Aurora, CO: Mid-Continent Regional Educational Laboratory.

McMillan, J. H. (Ed.). (2013). *The SAGE handbook of research on classroom assessment*. Los Angeles, CA: SAGE Publications, Inc.

National Governors Association Center for Best Practices, Council of Chief State School Officers. (2010a). *Common Core State Standards for English language arts and literacy in history/social studies, science, and technical subjects*. Washington, DC: Author. Retrieved January 2011 from http://www.corestandards.org/assets/CCSSI_ELA%20Standards.pdf

National Governors Association Center for Best Practices, Council of Chief State School Officers. (2010b). *Common Core State Standards for mathematics*. Washington, DC: Author. Retrieved January 2011 from http://www.corestandards.org/assets/CCSSI_Math %20Standards.pdf

NGSS Lead States. (2013). Next Generation Science Standards: For states, by states. Washington, DC: The National Academies Press.

O'Connor, K. (2011). *A repair kit for grading: 15 fixes for broken grades* (2nd ed.). Upper Saddle River, NJ: Pearson Education.

Popham, W.J. (2009.) Instruction that measures up: Successful teaching in the age of accountability. Alexandria, VA: Association for Supervision and Curriculum Development.

Rowe, M. B. (1978). Specific ways to develop better communication. In R. Sund and A. Carin (Eds.), *Creative questioning and sensitivity: Listening techniques* (2nd ed.). Upper Saddle River, NJ: Merrill/Prentice Hall.

Rowe, M. B. (1972). Wait-time and rewards as instructional variables: Their influence on language, logic, and fate control. Paper presented at the annual meeting of the National Association for Research in Science Teaching, Chicago, April. ERIC-ED061103.

Sadler, D. R. (1989). Formative assessment and the design of instructional systems. *Instructional Science, 18*, 119–144.

Schunk, D. H. (1996). Goal and self-evaluative influences during children's cognitive skill learning. *American Educational Research Journal, 33*(2), 359–382.

Shepard, L. A. (1997). *Measuring achievement: What does it mean to test for robust understanding?* Princeton, NJ: Educational Testing Service.

Spandel, V., & Culham, R. (1995). *Putting portfolio stories to work*. Portland, OR: Northwest Regional Educational Laboratory.

Sternberg, R. J. (1996). Myths, countermyths and truths about intelligences. *Educational Researcher, 25*(2), 11–16.

Stiggins, R. J., & Conklin, N. F. (1992). *In teachers' hands: Investigating the practice of classroom assessment*. Albany, NY: SUNY Press.

Walsh, J.A., & Sattes, B.D. (2005.) *Quality questioning: Research-based practice to engage every learner*. Thousand Oaks, CA: Corwin Press.

White, B.Y., & Frederiksen, J.R. (1998.) Inquiry, modeling, and metacognition: Making science accessible to all students. *Cognition and Instruction, 16*(1), 3–118.

Wiliam, D. (2013). Feedback and instructional correctives. In J. H. McMillan (Ed.), *The SAGE handbook of research on classroom assessment* (pp. 197–214). Los Angeles, CA: SAGE Publications, Inc.

Wiliam, D., & Lee, C. (2001, September). Teachers developing assessment for learning: Impact on student learning. Paper presented at the 27th annual conference of the British Educational Research Association, University of Leeds, England.

Wood, R. E., & Locke, E. A. (1987). The relation of self-efficacy and grade goals to academic performance. *Educational and Psychological Measurement, 47*, 1013–1024.

CREDITS

INDEX